Communications in Computer and Information Science 1184

Commenced Publication in 2007
Founding and Former Series Editors:
Simone Diniz Junqueira Barbosa, Phoebe Chen, Alfredo Cuzzocrea,
Xiaoyong Du, Orhun Kara, Ting Liu, Krishna M. Sivalingam,
Dominik Ślęzak, Takashi Washio, Xiaokang Yang, and Junsong Yuan

More information about this series at http://www.springer.com/series/7899

Patricia Pesado · Marcelo Arroyo (Eds.)

Computer Science – CACIC 2019

25th Argentine Congress of Computer Science, CACIC 2019
Río Cuarto, Argentina, October 14–18, 2019
Revised Selected Papers

 Springer

Editors
Patricia Pesado 🆔
RedUNCI Chair
National University of La Plata
La Plata, Argentina

Marcelo Arroyo
National University of Río Cuarto
Río Cuarto, Argentina

ISSN 1865-0929   ISSN 1865-0937 (electronic)
Communications in Computer and Information Science
ISBN 978-3-030-48324-1   ISBN 978-3-030-48325-8 (eBook)
https://doi.org/10.1007/978-3-030-48325-8

This Springer imprint is published by the registered company Springer Nature Switzerland AG
The registered company address is: Gewerbestrasse 11, 6330 Cham, Switzerland

Preface

Welcome to the proceedings of the 25th Argentina Congress of Computer Science (CACIC 2019), held in Río Cuarto, Córdoba, Argentina, during October 14–18, 2019. CACIC 2019 was organized by the National University of Rio Cuarto (UNRC) on behalf of the Network of National Universities with Computer Science Degrees (RedUNCI).

CACIC is an annual congress dedicated to the promotion and advancement of all aspects of computer science. It aims to provide a forum within which the development of computer science as an academic discipline with industrial applications is promoted, trying to extend the frontier of both the state of the art and the state of the practice. The main audience for and participants of CACIC are researchers in academic departments, laboratories, and industrial software organizations.

CACIC 2019 covered the following topics: intelligent agents and systems; distributed and parallel processing; software engineering; hardware architecture; networks and operating systems; graphic computation, visualization, and image processing; computer technology applied to education; databases and data mining; innovation in software systems; computer security; innovation in computer science education; signal processing and real-time system; and digital governance and smart cities.

This year, the congress received 185 submissions. Each submission was reviewed by at least two, and on average 3.1, Program Committee members and/or external reviewers. A total of 135 full papers, involving 265 different authors from 48 universities, were accepted. According to the recommendations of the reviewers, 27 of them were selected for this book.

During CACIC 2019, special activities were also carried out, including a plenary lecture, a discussion panel, an invited keynote address, a special track titled "Digital Governance and Smart Cities", and an International School with four courses.

Special thanks to the members of the different committees for their support and collaboration. Also, we would like to thank the Local Organizing Committee, reviewers, lecturers, speakers, authors, and all conference attendees. Finally, we want to thank Springer for their support of this publication.

April 2020   Patricia Pesado

Organization

The 25th Argentine Congress of Computer Science (CACIC 2019) was organized by National University of Rio Cuarto (UNRC) on behalf of the Network of National Universities with Computer Science Degrees (RedUNCI).

Editors

Patricia Pesado (RedUNCI Chair)	National University of La Plata, Argentina
Marcelo Arroyo	National University of Rio Cuarto, Argentina

Editorial Assistant

Pablo Thomas	National University of La Plata, Argentina

General Chair

Marcelo Arroyo	National University of Rio Cuarto, Argentina

Program Committee

Maria Jose Abásolo	National University of La Plata, Argentina
Claudio Aciti	National University of Buenos Aires Center, Argentina
Hugo Alfonso	National University of La Pampa, Argentina
Jorge Ardenghi	National University of South, Argentina
Marcelo Arroyo	National University of Río Cuarto, Argentina
Hernan Astudillo	Technical University Federico Santa María, Chile
Sandra Baldasarri	University of Zaragoza, Spain
Javier Balladini	National University of Comahue, Argentina
Luis Soares Barbosa	University of Minho, Portugal
Rodolfo Bertone	National University of La Plata, Argentina
Oscar Bria	National University of La Plata, Argentina
Nieves R. Brisaboa	University of La Coruña, Spain
Carlos Buckle	National University of Patagonia San Juan Bosco, Argentina
Alberto Cañas	University of West Florida, USA
Ana Casali	National University of Rosario, Argentina
Alejandra Cechich	National University of Comahue, Argentina
Edgar Chávez	Michoacana University of San Nicolás de Hidalgo, Mexico
Carlos Coello Coello	CINVESTAV, Mexico

Sponsors

RedUNCI

Network of Universities
with Degrees in
Computer Science

Facultad de Ciencias Exactas,
Físico-Químicas y Naturales

National University
of Río Cuarto

Secretaría de Políticas
Universitarias

Secretary of University
Policies

Ministry of Science and
Technology, Córdoba

Chamber of Business of
Software and Information
Services

Sadosky Foundation

Contents

Digital Governance and Smart Cities

Intelligent Agents and Systems

Predicting Information Quality Flaws in Wikipedia by Using Classical and Deep Learning Approaches

Gerónimo Bazán Pereyra[1], Carolina Cuello[1], Gianfranco Capodici[1],
Vanessa Jofré[1], Edgardo Ferretti[1,2]([⊠]) [iD], Rodolfo Bonnin[1] [iD],
and Marcelo Errecalde[1,2] [iD]

[1] Universidad Nacional de San Luis (UNSL), San Luis, Argentina
{ferretti,merreca}@unsl.edu.ar
[2] Laboratorio de Investigación y Desarrollo en Inteligencia Computacional, UNSL,
San Luis, Argentina

Abstract. Quality flaws prediction in Wikipedia is an ongoing research trend. In particular, in this work we tackle the problem of automatically predicting five out of the ten most frequent quality flaws; namely: *No footnotes*, *Notability*, *Primary Sources*, *Refimprove* and *Wikify*. Different classical and deep learning state-of-the-art approaches were studied. From among the evaluated approaches, some of them always reach or improve the existing benchmarks on the test corpus from the 1st *International Competition on Quality Flaw Prediction in Wikipedia*; a well-known uniform evaluation corpus from this research field. Particularly, the results showed that under-bagged decision trees with different aggregation rules perform best improving the existing benchmarks for four out the five flaws.

Keywords: Wikipedia · Information Quality · Quality Flaws Prediction · Deep Learning

1 Introduction

The automatic assessment of text quality using machine-learning techniques has become a topic of enormous interest. This particularly applies to user-generated Web content, which can be attributable to two main factors: first, the rapidly evolving data volumes that render manual quality assurance activities infeasible, and second, the increasing diversity of produced content quality (see e.g. [7]). A specific example is the online encyclopedia Wikipedia, which is one of the largest and most popular user-generated knowledge sources on the Web.

Considering its size and dynamic nature, (e.g., authors are heterogeneous and contributions are not reviewed by experts before their publication), a comprehensive manual quality assurance of information is infeasible. Information Quality (IQ) is a multi-dimensional concept and combines criteria such as accuracy, reliability and relevance. A widely accepted interpretation of IQ is the "fitness for use in a practical application" [34], i.e. the assessment of IQ requires

© Springer Nature Switzerland AG 2020
P. Pesado and M. Arroyo (Eds.): CACIC 2019, CCIS 1184, pp. 3–18, 2020.
https://doi.org/10.1007/978-3-030-48325-8_1

the consideration of context and use case. In Wikipedia the context is well-defined by the encyclopedic genre, that forms the ground for Wikipedia's IQ ideal, within the so-called *featured article criteria*.[1] A featured article exemplifies Wikipedia's very best work and is distinguished by professional standards of writing, presentation and sourcing. Indeed, a good deal of the existing research targets the classification of articles into this quality schemes viz. "featured" or "non-featured" (see e.g. [15,25–27]).

In fact, as pointed out by Anderka et al. [5], this kind of research provides only limited support for Wikipedia's quality assurance process as the rationale why a non-featured article violates Wikipedia's quality standards is not revealed. That is why, they made a first step towards an automatic quality assurance in Wikipedia by proposing the *detection of quality flaws* in Wikipedia articles. This approach provides concrete hints for human editors about what has to be fixed in order to improve article quality. The detection of quality flaws is based on user-defined cleanup tags, which are commonly used in the Wikipedia community to tag content that has some shortcomings. Thus, the tagged articles serve as human-labeled data that is exploited by a machine learning approach to predict flaws in untagged articles. Particularly, Anderka et al. [4,5] stated quality flaws prediction as a one-class classification problem and in 2012 the 1st *International Competition on Quality Flaw Prediction in Wikipedia* (overviewed in [3]) was organized.

As detailed in Sect. 2, from this competition, different classification approaches to tackle quality flaw prediction have been studied [1,9,12,13,17]. In particular, our work extends the study from [9], where the so-called *Refimprove (Refimp)* flaw was evaluated by means of classical classification methods based on alternative formulations of SVM and bagging of decision trees as well. We extend it by evaluating the same flaw with new deep-learning approaches, and also by incorporating to our comparative study four more flaws belonging to the ten most frequent one from Wikipedia [3]. These flaws are: *No footnotes (No-foot)*, *Notability (Notab)*, *Primary Sources (PS)* and *Wikify (Wiki)*.

The remaining five flaws, from among these ten, were not included in our study given that three of them, viz. *Unreferenced, Orphan* and *Empty Section* can be detected in a very efficient way by means of the so-called intentional modeling paradigm [6], where no training data is required since it is based on a rule-based pattern matching approach which relies on few basic features of the document model; or put it in another way only a few specific features need to be computed to check whether an article suffers the flaw. The other two flaws, namely: *Advert* and *Original Research*, where not tackled given that in our view, the document model used in our experiments (detailed in Sect. 3.3) does not contain specific features to address these flaws (cf. [32], for a discussion on the need of using factual external information from Wikipedia, in order to capture the gist of a flaw like *Original Research* in its assessment).

The rest of the article is organized as follows. Section 2 introduces related work with the aim of providing a well-specified context of the problem faced

---

[1] http://en.wikipedia.org/wiki/Wikipedia:Featured_article_criteria.

in this work. Then, in Sect. 3, we present the formal problem statement and the different prediction approaches evaluated are briefly described. Also, the document model used to represent the articles is discussed. Section 4 reports on the experimental setting carried out and the obtained results. Finally, Sect. 5 offers the conclusions.

2   Related Work

As mentioned above in the introductory section, as far as we know, the first exploratory analysis targeting the existence of IQ flaws in Wikipedia articles was reported in [5]; where the flaw detection task was evaluated as a one-class classification problem presuming that only information about one class, the so-called target class, is available. Then, [4] extends [5] by formally stating quality flaw prediction as a one-class classification problem for the ten most frequent quality flaws compiled by Anderka et al. [3]. Moreover, in [2] it was pushed further the exploratory analysis reported in [5] by presenting the first complete breakdown of Wikipedia IQ flaws for the snapshot from January 15, 2011.

These studies gave rise to the 1st *International Competition on Quality Flaw Prediction in Wikipedia*. Despite the fact that the evaluation task was proposed as a one-class classification problem, the two best approaches of the competition belong to the semi-supervised and supervised learning domains. In this respect, a tailored PU-learning algorithm (see [14]) achieved the best average F_1 score of 0.815 over the ten flaws evaluated. In the second place, with an average F_1 score of 0.798, Ferschke et al. [16] tackled the problem as a binary classification problem. Later, in [17], they stated the quality flaw prediction problem as a binary classification problem for another subset of quality flaws, and they also argued practically and theoretically in favor of casting quality flaw prediction in Wikipedia as a binary classification problem.

Since then, several classification approaches to tackle quality flaw prediction and IQ assessment in Wikipedia have been proposed [1, 8, 9, 11–13, 24, 30, 33, 35]. The approaches mainly differ in the IQ problem faced and hence in the type of classification algorithm that is applied (e.g., semi-supervised or supervised) as well as in the underlying document model (e.g., the number of features, features complexity, the rationale to quantify flaws and whether the features were learned or built). Moreover, the approaches are not directly comparable in terms of their prediction effectiveness that is reported in the individual experimental evaluation studies. This is mainly because the experimental settings differ in the task (e.g., the number of flaws to be detected and their types or the quality grading schemes to be predicted) and the data set (e.g., the employed Wikipedia snapshot, the applied sampling strategy, and the ratio between positive and negative articles in the test set). This diversity makes a conceptual comparison of the existing IQ assessment methods difficult.

For example, [1, 9, 12, 13] have followed working methodologies close to the original one proposed by Anderka et al. [4, 5]. In [1], the quality flaw prediction task was faced as a one-class classification problem and the used classification approach combines density estimation with class probability estimation [21]. The idea is to apply a density estimator to build a reference density for the target class, then use this reference density to generate artificial negative data suitable for a class probability estimator, and finally combine the predictions of the reference density and the class probability model to form predictions for new test objects. This approach was applied to a more recent Wikipedia snapshot than the one used for the competition [3]. Besides, it was used a document model composed of 95 features capturing aspects of documents related to their content, structure, edit history, and how they are embedded into Wikipedia's network. Given the so-called optimistic test set of [4] and a balanced class distribution, eight out of ten most important flaws can be detected with a precision close to 1.

In [13], the same document model used by Anderka [1] was evaluated on the corpus from the "1st International Competition on Quality Flaw Prediction in Wikipedia", where a modified version of the PU-learning winning approach [14] was proposed. A key issue of this new proposed approach consists of using a balanced setting for training the first-stage classifier. The obtained results showed an improvement of 18.31%, averaged over the ten flaws. From among the ten flaws of the competition, the so-called *Refimprove* flaw –which alerts that the tagged article needs additional citations for verification–, has been particularly studied in [9,12]. It is worth mentioning that this information quality flaw, ranks among the five most frequent flaws and represents 12.4% of the flawed articles in the English Wikipedia [1].

In particular, Bazán et al. [9] used the same document model proposed by Anderka [1] and it was also evaluated on the corpus from the 1st international competition mentioned above. With respect to the classification algorithms, three different state-of-the-art binary approaches were used with the aim of handling the existing imbalances between the number of articles tagged as flawed content, and the remaining untagged documents that exist in Wikipedia. These approaches were under-bagged decision trees, biased-SVM and centroid-based balanced SVM. The results showed that under-bagged decision trees with the *min* rule as aggregation method, perform best achieving an F_1 score of 0.96. Likewise, biased-SVM and centroid-based balanced SVM, also achieved F_1 scores that outperform previously published results [13].

These three classification approaches had not been used before to assess quality flaw prediction in the English Wikipedia, but in the Spanish version they were evaluated for the first time in [12]; where seven classification methods were experimentally compared, including PU-learning and the one-class classifier v-SVM [31]. The obtained results showed that the binary approaches like under-bagged decision trees (with sum or majority voting rules), biased-SVM, and centroid-based balanced SVM, perform best. The document model used was composed of 42 features; 41 already present in Anderka's document model [1] and a new one specifically engineered to assess the *Refimp* flaw—so-called *reference ratio*.

To the best of our knowledge, Anderka's document model [1] and the one proposed in [8], are the most comprehensive document models built so far based on a features engineering approach. In particular, Bassani and Viviani document model [8] is composed of 264 features and in principle it seems to contain the 95 features from Anderka's document model. They evaluated their model with the aim of building a suitable ground truth for a (single-label) multi-class classification task, where each article is assigned exactly to one of the seven classes from the quality grading scheme that Wikipedia employs nowadays.[2] They evaluated eight state-of-the-art classifiers and Gradient Boosting performed best achieving and accuracy of 90% in some experiments.

A similar classification problem to that reported in [8] was evaluated by Zhang et al. [35], since that a 6-class classification task was performed – considering the Wikipedia quality grading scheme mentioned above–, but where AC was skipped on the grounds that is not a real quality class and it overlaps with FA and GA classes. The proposed history-based article quality assessment model combines feature engineering with learned features by a Recurrent Neural Network (RNN); and it only contains 16 features. Zhang et al. argue that this can be one of the reasons why the best-achieved accuracy value rounds 69%.

In [30], the same 6-class classification task performed by Zhang et al. [35] was tackled but with a different document model that relies on explicitly defined features. Moreover, as classification method it was used gradient boosted trees (XGBoost); a powerful state-of-the-art approach that allows computing the relative importance of each feature, ultimately enabling to derive the most decisive features. Furthermore, a deep learning-based baseline was used for assessing the performance of XGBoost given the same feature set. In this respect, the accuracy achieved by XGBoost was 73% against 67% of the deep learning-based baseline. Additionally, XGBoost was also compared against the RNN-LSTM evaluated by Dang and Ignat in [11], where the classification of Wikipedia articles in English, French, and Russian languages in different quality grading schemes was promising without the need of a feature extraction phase. In particular, for the English dataset, XGBoost outperformed the RNN-LSTM by 5%; i.e. RNN-LSTM achieved an accuracy of 68%.

Finally, in [33], following a feature engineering approach to build articles' documents models –composed of 68 features–, Wang and Li present a comparative study of state-of-the-art deep-learning approaches by distinguishing high quality articles from low quality. With this aim, a 6-class classification problem on the Wikipedia quality grading scheme mentioned above, was reduced to a binary classification problem where the high-quality class includes FA, AC and GA; and the low-quality class includes BC, SC and SB. Stacked-LSTM networks achieved the best performance reporting an F_1 measure of 0.8. Also, the influence of different features and feature sets on the proposed models were extensively investigated.

---

[2] https://en.wikipedia.org/wiki/Template:Grading_scheme.

3   Problem Statement and Flaw Prediction Approaches

We start with a formal definition of the problem faced in this paper, namely the algorithmic prediction of quality flaws in Wikipedia (Sect. 3.1). We then provide the theoretical background of the flaw prediction approaches used in our work (Sect. 3.2) and finally, we introduce the document model used to represent articles (Sect. 3.3).

3.1   Problem Statement

Following [1], quality flaw prediction is treated here as a classification problem. Let D be the set of English Wikipedia articles and let f_i be the specific quality flaw that may occur in an article $d \in D$. Let $\mathbf{d}$ be the feature vector representing article d, called document model, and let $\mathbf{D}$ denote the set of document models for D. Hence, for flaw f_i, a specific classifier c_i is learned to decide whether an article d suffers from f_i or not; that is, $c_i : \mathbf{D} \to \{1, 0\}$. For flaw f_i a set $D_i^+ \subset D$ is available, which contains articles that have been tagged to contain f_i (so-called *labeled* articles). However, no information is available about the remaining articles in $D \setminus D_i^+$—these articles are either flawless or have not yet been evaluated with respect to f_i (so-called *unlabeled* articles).

In recent studies, c_i is modeled as a one-class classifier, which is trained solely on the set D_i^+ of labeled articles (see e.g. [1]). However, in the Wikipedia setting, the large number of available unlabeled articles may provide additional knowledge that can be used to improve classifiers training. Thus, addressing the problem of exploiting unlabeled articles to improve the performance of c_i lead us to cast the problem as a binary classification task.

3.2   Flaw Prediction Approaches

Despite its theoretical one-class nature, quality flaw prediction has been tackled in prior studies as a binary classification task –which relates to the realm of supervised learning– and the results achieved in practice have been quite competitive [9,12,16,17]. Supervised learning deals with the situation where training examples are available for all classes that can occur at prediction time. In *binary classification*, the classification $c_i(\mathbf{d})$ of an article $d \in D$ with respect to a quality flaw f_i is defined as follows: given a sample $P \subseteq D_i^+$ of articles containing f_i and a sample $N \subseteq (D \setminus D_i^+)$ of articles not containing f_i, decide whether d belongs to P or to N. The binary classification approach tries to learn a class-separating decision boundary to discriminate between P and a particular N. In order to obtain a sound flaw predictor, the choice of N is essential. N should be a representative sample of Wikipedia articles that are flawless regarding f_i.

ANN. An Artificial Neural Network (ANN) is just a collection of units (mathematical model that it simply "fires" when a linear combination of its inputs exceeds some hard or soft threshold; that is, it implements a linear classifier) connected together; the properties of the network are determined by its topology and the properties of the "neurons" [29]. In this work, we will refer as an ANN, a feed-forward network; that is, every unit receives inputs from "upstream" units and delivers output to "downstream" units, i.e. there are no loops—like in the case of Recurrent Neural Networks [28]. A feed-forward network represents a non-linear function of its current input; thus, it has no other internal state than the weights themselves.

DNN. As stated in [18], the quintessential example of a deep learning model is the feedforward deep network (DNN), or multilayer perceptron; that is an ANN with more than one hidden layer. The input of the model is presented to the so-called "input layer", because it contains the variables that we are able to observe. Then a series of hidden layers extracts increasingly abstract features from the input. These layers are called "hidden" because their values are not given in the data; instead the model must determine which concepts are useful for explaining the relationships in the observed data.

Stacked-LSTM. Long short-term memory (LSTM) [22] are a modification of the original Recurrent Neural Networks, which includes three types of gates: the forget gate, the input gate, and the output gate. The original LSTM model is comprised of a single hidden LSTM layer followed by a standard feedforward output layer. Stacked-LSTM model [19] extends the reach of this type of network, to the realm of deep neural architecture, in that it has multiple hidden LSTM layers where each layer contains multiple memory cells. Every LSTM in the stack obtains all the information from the preceding layer only.

Biased SVM. Since the ratio between the unlabeled data and the positive samples is unbalanced, a more principled approach to solve the problem allows having independent penalty terms for both classes, in opposition to the standard formulation of SVM, where the penalty factor C is applied to elements of both classes in the same way. Hence, we will have a penalty term C_+ for elements belonging to the positive class P and a penalty term C_- for elements belonging to the so-called negative class N (unlabeled data). It is expected that these penalty terms reflect the underlying imbalance proportion of the classes in the dataset.

Under-Bagged Decision Trees. In this ensemble learning approach, many different decision trees are bagged by under-sampling the majority class, in order to train each decision tree with a balanced dataset. Let us suppose that we split the positive set P in k chunks. We will refer them as $P_1, \ldots, P_k$, respectively. Then, from the unlabeled data N, we under-sample the set by uniformly selecting k subsets $N_1, \ldots, N_k$, such that $|P_i| = |N_i|, \forall i = 1, \ldots, k$. Therefore, k different training sets $(T_{i=1,\ldots,k})$ can be built by combining P_1 with N_1, P_2 with N_2, and so on. When there are no enough positive samples, like in [12], set P can be matched with each subset N_i. In turn, each sampled dataset $T_{i=1,\ldots,k}$ is used to train a C4.5 decision tree that will be referred as $C_{i=1,\ldots,k}$. Then, for each document j from the test set, the prediction of each classifier $C_{i=1,\ldots,k}$ has to be aggregated in a final prediction to decide if article j is found flawed or not.

3.3   Document Model

To model the articles, we used Anderka's document model [1], that is one of the most comprehensive document model proposed so far for quality flaw prediction in Wikipedia. It comprises 95 article features, including all of the features that have been used in [5,14] and many of the features that have been used in [16]. Formally, given a set $D = \{d_1, d_2, \ldots, d_n\}$ of n articles, each article is represented by 95 features $F = \{f_1, f_2, \ldots, f_{95}\}$. A vector representation for each article d_i in D is defined as $d_i = (v_1, v_2, \ldots, v_{95})$, where v_j is the value of feature f_j. A feature generally describes some quality indicator associated with an article.

In [1] four such subsets were identified by organizing the features along the dimensions *content, structure, network* and *edit history*. Content features are computed based on the plain text representation of an article and mainly address aspects like writing style and readability. Structure features rely on an article's wiki markup and are intended to quantify the usage of structural elements like sections, templates, tables, among others. Network features quantify an article's connectivity by means of internal and external links. Edit history features rely on an article's revision history and model article evolution based on the frequency and the timing of edits as well as on the community of editors. Table 1 details the specific features included in the document model.

4   Experiments and Results

To perform our experiments, we have used the corpus available in the above-mentioned Competition on Quality Flaw Prediction in Wikipedia [3], which has been released as a part of PAN-WQF-12,[3] a more comprehensive corpus related to the ten most important article flaws in the English Wikipedia, as pointed out in [2]. The training corpus of the competition contains 154 116 tagged articles (not equally distributed) for the ten quality flaws, plus additional 50 000 untagged articles. The test corpus (19 010 articles) contains a balanced number of tagged articles and untagged articles for each of the ten quality flaws, and it is ensured that 10% of the untagged articles are featured articles. Table 2 introduces a brief description for each flaw evaluated in our work. Moreover, for each flaw, the numbers of tagged and untagged articles in the training and test corpus of the 2012-competition is specified. The training corpus does not contain untagged articles for the individual flaws, but it comprises 50 000 additional randomly selected untagged articles.

4.1   Experimental Setting

For the biased-SVM classifier, as usual, their parameters were experimentally derived by a ten-fold cross-validated grid-search with different kernels. For the linear kernel, C was set to values in the range $C \in \{2^{-1}, \ldots, 2^{11}\}$. For the RBF kernel, in addition to the values evaluated for C, $\gamma \in \{0.125, 0.5, 1, 2\}$.

---

[3] The corpus is available at https://webis.de/data/pan-wqf-12.html.

Different configurations of polynomial kernels were also evaluated with $d \in \{2, 3, 4\}$ and $r \in \{0, 1\}$. It is well known that increasing γ and d parameters from the RBF and polynomial kernels allows for a more flexible decision boundary, but if they are increased too much, this might yield in principle an over-fitting of the model and hence obtaining a poor capability of generalization of the classifier.

Moreover, the penalty terms C_+ and C_- mentioned above, in LIBSVM [10] are obtained by multiplying the C value by parameters w_+ and w_-, respectively. Thus, w_- was set to 1 and w_+ was experimentally set to different proportions so as to reflect different penalization values close to the existing imbalances between the classes. As estimated by Anderka's study [1], the flaw ratios for the five flaws we are evaluating are: 1:8 for *Refimp*, 1:34 for *No-foot*, 1:30 for *Notab*, 1:44 for *PS* and 1:79 for *Wiki*. These flaw ratios are interpreted as follows: for example, for the *Refimp* flaw this means that approximately about every nine English Wikipedia articles, one is expected to contain the flaw. For all the flaws except for *Wikify* the maximum amount values were evaluated; that is, w_+ was set to 8, 34, 30 and 44, respectively. As expected the maximum ratio was not evaluated for *Wikify* flaw given that only 50 000 untagged articles are available.

The achieved results with this setting were not promising for *No-foot*, *Notab* and *PS* flaws. That is why, we decided to evaluate lower ratios like half of the maximum amount, a quarter of it, etc. For example, for *Notability* flaw $w_+ \in \{7.5, 15\}$, and consequently $|P| = 1000$ and $|N| \in \{7500, 15000\}$, respectively. We proceeded in the same way for the remaining flaws, including *Wikify*. Besides, we decided to set up $|P| = 1000$, given that this was the amount of positive samples used in [9,13,14], and more importantly in [9,13] where it was also used the document model proposed in [1] to represent the articles. Fourth row of Table 4, presents the best performance values achieved with this method during validation stage. The kernel used and its particular parameters setting are reported as table notes.

In our implementation of the under-bagged decision trees, we performed different experimental settings varying the number of decision trees to be bagged. In particular, for the *Refimp* flaw up to 23 decision trees were bagged, given that it is the flaw containing more positive samples. For the remaining flaws experiments with 3, 5, 7 and 9 trees were carried out. For the *PS* flaw, the bagging of 5 decision trees reported the best F_1 values in the validation stage; which are reported in Table 4. For *No-foot*, *Notab* and *Wiki* flaws, the best values presented in Table 4 correspond to the case where 7 decision trees were bagged. It is worth mentioning that to perform the experiments with decision trees, we have used the WEKA Data Mining Software [20]. Moreover, the five ensemble rules presented in Table 3 were programmed in AWK language.

For the case of the *Refimp* flaw, in order to train each decision tree with a balanced dataset, the 23 decision trees were bagged with under-sampling of the untagged documents. Hence, 23 different training sets were built by combining chunks of 1000 articles. From the 23 144 positive samples, 23 chunks of 1000 articles were selected. We will refer them as $P_1, \ldots, P_{23}$, respectively. The remaining 144 articles were discarded. Similarly, from among the 50 000 untagged articles, 23

Table 1. The 95 features used in our document model organized along the four dimensions: content, structure, network, and edit history. (For a detailed feature description, refer to [1].)

Dimension	Features
Content	*Text statistics*: character count, complex word rate, information-to-noise ratio, long sentence rate, long word rate, longest sentence length, one-syllable word count, one-syllable word rate, paragraph count, paragraph length, question count, question rate, sentence count, sentence length, short sentence rate, shortest sentence length, syllable count, word count, word length, word syllables
	Part of speech: article sentence rate, auxiliary verb rate, conjunction rate, conjunction sentence rate, interrogative pronoun sentence rate, nominalization rate, passive sentence rate, preposition rate, preposition sentence rate, pronoun sentence rate, pronoun rate, subordinate conjunction sentence rate, "to be" verb rate
	Readability formulas: automated readability index, Bormuth index, Coleman-Liau index, FORCAST readability, Flesch Reading Ease, Flesch-Kincaid, Gunning Fog index, LIX, Miyazaki EFL readability index, new Dale-Chall, SMOG grading
	Closed-class word sets: common word rate, difficult word rate, peacock word rate, stop word rate, weasel word rate
Structure	Category count, file count, heading count, image count, images per section, list ratio, reference count, reference sections count, references per section, references per text length, section count, section length, section nesting, shortest section length, shortest subsection length, shortest subsubsection length, subsection count, subsection length, subsection nesting, subsubsection count, subsubsection length, longest section length, longest subsection length, longest subsubsection length, table count, template count, trivia sections count
Network	Broken internal link count, external link count, external links per section, incoming internal link count, internal link count, internal links per text length, inter-language link count, PageRank, reciprocity
Edit history	Age, age per edit, anonymous editor rate, currency, discussion edit count, edit count, edits per editor, editor count, editor rate, registered editor rate

chunks of 1000 articles were randomly selected following a uniform distribution. We will refer them as $N_1, \ldots, N_{23}$, respectively. The remaining 27 000 articles were kept aside. Therefore, 23 different training sets ($T_{i=1,\ldots,23}$) were built by combining P_1 with N_1, P_2 with N_2, and so on. That is: $T_1 = P_1 \cup N_1$, $T_2 = P_2 \cup N_2, \ldots, T_{23} = P_{23} \cup N_{23}$. In turn, each sampled dataset $T_{i=1,\ldots,23}$ was used to train a C4.5 decision tree (with default parameters) that will be referred as $C_{i=1,\ldots,23}$. The performance of each decision tree C_i was evaluated by a tenfold cross-validation. For the other

Table 2. Five out of the ten quality flaws of English Wikipedia articles that are comprised in the PAN-WQF-12 corpus.

Flaw name	Flaw description	Training corpus		Test corpus	
		Tagged articles	Untagged articles	Tagged articles	Untagged articles
No footnotes	The article's sources are unclear because of its inline citations	6 068	–	1 000	1 000
Notability	The article does not meet the general notability guideline	3 150	–	1 000	1 000
Primary sources	The article relies on references to primary sources	3 682	–	1 000	1 000
Refimprove	The article needs additional citations for verification	23 144	–	999	999
Wikify	The article needs to be wikified (internal links and layout)	1 771	–	999	999
Additional random (untagged) articles		–	50 000	–	–

four remaining flaws, we followed a working methodology analogous to that mentioned above for the *Refimp* flaw, evenly splitting the maximum number of positive samples available for each flaw (cf. tagged articles column of Table 2) and then discarding the remaining files.

Finally, for each document j belonging to the test set (cf. test corpus column of Table 2), the prediction stated by each classifier $C_{i=1,...,|N_t|}$ ($|N_t| \in \{5, 7, 23\}$) has to be aggregated in a final prediction to decide if article j is found flawed or not. Table 3 presents the five ensemble rules evaluated in our experiments. Whatever the rule used, when it holds that $R_1 \geq R_2$ then the evaluated article is deemed positive; otherwise negative.

For the neural-based approaches, due to resource and time-execution constraints, in the validation stage cross validation was not used and a split of 80%–20% was used instead. All the networks (ANN, DNN and Stacked-LSTM) consist of an input layer of 95 units and a sigmoid layer output. All the neurons in the hidden layers use ReLU activation functions and Adam optimization strategy. The loss function used was *sparse categorical crossentropy*. In order to obtain the best possible model, we carried out a random search over the different variables that influence each model. Besides, each model on the random search was trained during 10 epochs, using the whole training set.

Table 3. Strategies and descriptions for ensemble rules as proposed by [23].

Rule	Strategy	Description
Max	$R_1 = \arg\max_{1 \leq i \leq K} P_{i1}$,	Use the maximum classification probability of these K classifiers
	$R_2 = \arg\max_{1 \leq i \leq K} P_{i2}$	For each class label
Min	$R_1 = \arg\min_{1 \leq i \leq K} P_{i1}$,	Use the minimum classification probability of these K classifiers
	$R_2 = \arg\min_{1 \leq i \leq K} P_{i2}$	For each class label
Product	$R_1 = \prod_{i=1}^{K} P_{i1}$,	Use the product of classification probability of these K classifiers
	$R_2 = \prod_{i=1}^{K} P_{i2}$	For each class label
Majority vote[a]	$R_1 = \sum_{i=1}^{K} f(P_{i1}, P_{i2})$,	For the ith classifier, if $P_{i1} \geq P_{i2}$, class C_1 gets a vote, if $P_{i2} \geq P_{i1}$,
	$R_2 = \sum_{i=1}^{K} f(P_{i2}, P_{i1})$	Class C_2 gets a vote
Sum	$R_1 = \sum_{i=1}^{K} P_{i1}$,	Use the summation of classification probability of these K classifiers
	$R_2 = \sum_{i=1}^{K} P_{i2}$	For each class label

[a]Function $f(x,y)$ is defined as 1 if $x \geq y$; 0 otherwise.

For the case of the ANN, different hidden layer widths were tried (from 512 to 2018, in 512 units steps) and values 0.001 and 0.005 were evaluated as Adam's learning rate. In the first row of Table 4, we can observe the performance values achieved for each flaw, where the reported values correspond to a learning rate of 0.001 and for four out of the five flaws 1024 units were used in the hidden layer, except for the *Wiki* flaw where the hidden layer width was of 512 units. For the DNN, a variable number of hidden layer (up to three) was evaluated with optional dropout layers. Similarly, for the Stacked-LSTM, a variable number of LSTM layers (up to four) was tried. The width of each hidden/LSTM layer was set from 128 units up to 2048, in 128 units steps and the learning rate was varied from 0.0001 to 0.005. First and second rows of Table 4, show the obtained results for these approaches in the validation stage. The particular settings of number of layer and units per layer are described as table notes, indicating in brackets and separated by commas the amount of layers, and in each position, the number of units per layer. Also, the learning rate (α) used is specified. All the experiments with the above-mentioned neural-based approaches were implemented in Keras 2.2.4-tf and TensorFlow 2.0.0.

Table 4. F_1 comparative performance measures for the validation set.

Algorithm	No-foot	Notab	PS	Refimp	Wiki
ANN	0.96	0.87	0.89	0.99	0.68
DNN	0.97[a]	0.86[b]	0.89[c]	0.99[d]	0.68[e]
Stacked-LSTM	0.94[f]	0.97[g]	0.97[h]	0.97[i]	0.94[j]
Biased-SVM	0.98[k]	0.98[l]	0.96[m]	0.95[n]	0.98[o]
Under-bagged DT (Max rule)	0.98	0.99	0.99	0.98	0.99
Under-bagged DT (Min rule)	0.98	0.99	0.99	0.99	0.99
Under-bagged DT (Product rule)	0.98	0.99	0.99	0.98	0.99
Under-bagged DT (Majority rule)	0.98	0.99	0.99	0.99	0.99
Under-bagged DT (Sum rule)	0.98	0.99	0.99	0.99	0.99

[a] $(1024, 1536, 2048), \alpha = 0.001$ [b] $(512, 1536, 512), \alpha = 0.002$
[c] $(512, 1536, 1536), \alpha = 0.001$ [d] $(1536, 1024), \alpha = 0.001$
[e] $(1024, 1536, 1024), \alpha = 0.001$ [f] $(384, 128, 128, 128), \alpha = 0.0001$
[g] $(384, 384), \alpha = 0.001$ [h] $(256, 256, 256, 384), \alpha = 0.001$
[i] $(384, 512, 384, 256), \alpha = 0.0001$ [j] $(256, 256, 384, 384), \alpha = 0.0001$
[k] $w_+ = 5, C = 2^5$ [l] $w_+ = 15, C = 2^9, \gamma = 0.125$
[m] $w_+ = 7.5, C = 2^5$ [n] $w_+ = 8, C = 2^3, \gamma = 0.5, d = 3, r = 1$
[o] $w_+ = 7.5, C = 2^5, \gamma = 0.125, d = 2, r = 0$

4.2   Results

The state-of-the-art F_1 scores for the assessed flaws on the test set of the
1st *International Competition on Quality Flaw Prediction in Wikipedia* are
reported in brackets in the first row of Table 5. As we can see in this table,
ANN and DNN did not reach any of the existing benchmarks and their performances were below our expectations. Stacked-LSTM performed well and reach
the existing benchmark for the *Refimp* flaw. Biased-SVM also reach the benchmark for *No-foot*, *Notab* and *PS* flaws, it was close to the benchmark of the
Refimp flaw and performed a little worse for the *Wiki* flaw. Finally, as reported
in [9] for the *Refimp* flaw, under-bagged decision trees was the approach with
best performance in general improving the benchmarks for four out the five flaws.
In particular, majority vote and the sum rules were the two aggregation methods which achieved the best performance values (for three out of the five flaws).
Notab and *PS* flaws are those with the highest benchmarks ($F_1 = 0.99$), the
former was the easiest one to assess for most of the evaluated methods while the
latter was the most difficult one; only biased-SVM achieved an F_1 score of 0.99
for this flaw. Nonetheless, it is worth mentioning that the existing benchmarks
are quite competitive and the new results presented push the classification performance to an almost perfect level; being in our view the *Refimp* flaw the only
one which leaves in principle room for improvement.

Table 5. F_1 comparative performance measures for the test set.

Algorithm	No-foot	Notab	PS	Refimp	Wiki
(Benchmark from [13])	(0.98)	(0.99)	(0.99)	(0.94)	(0.98)
(Benchmark from [9])	–	–	–	(0.96)	–
ANN	0.72	0.97	0.88	0.64	0.71
DNN	0.78	0.98	0.90	0.64	0.69
Stacked-LSTM	0.96	0.97	0.96	**0.96**	0.96
Biased-SVM	**0.98**	**0.99**	**0.99**	0.95	0.91
Under-bagged DT (Max rule)	0.94	**0.99**	0.98	0.94	0.94
Under-bagged DT (Min rule)	0.94	**0.99**	0.94	**0.96**	0.95
Under-bagged DT (Product rule)	0.94	**0.99**	0.98	0.94	0.94
Under-bagged DT (Majority rule)	**0.99**	**0.99**	0.98	0.94	**0.99**
Under-bagged DT (Sum rule)	**0.99**	**0.99**	0.98	0.94	**0.99**

5   Conclusions

In this work, we carried out a comparative study of different state-of-the-art approaches to automatically assess information quality of Wikipedia articles; in particular, to identify five quality flaws of the ten proposed in 1st *International Competition on Quality Flaw Prediction in Wikipedia*. The obtained results showed that a classical approach like under-bagged decision trees is robust and improved the existing benchmarks for two out the five flaws; thus yielding new state-of-the-art benchmarks for *No footnotes* and *Wikify* flaws. Moreover, our results are directly comparable to the values found in [13], since we used the same data set and document model for representing the articles. As stated in [33] (for other information quality assessment problem), Stacked-LSTM performed well and reach the existing benchmark for the *Refimprove* flaw. To the best of our knowledge, this is the first time that this approach is used for quality flaws prediction and in our view, the presented results can be improved exploring in a more intensive way the search space of the variables that influences the model.

Acknowledgments. This work has been partially founded by PROICO P-31816, Universidad Nacional de San Luis, Argentina. Likewise, we gratefully acknowledge the support of NVIDIA Corporation for the donation of the Titan Xp GPU used in different experiments of this research.

References

1. Anderka, M.: Analyzing and predicting quality flaws in user-generated content: the case of Wikipedia. Ph.D. thesis, Bauhaus-Universität Weimar, June 2013
2. Anderka, M., Stein, B.: A Breakdown of quality flaws in Wikipedia. In: 2nd Joint WICOW/AIRWeb workshop on Web quality (WebQuality 2012). ACM (2012)
3. Anderka, M., Stein, B.: Overview of the 1st international competition on quality flaw prediction in Wikipedia. In: Forner, P., Karlgren, J., Womser-Hacker, C. (eds.) Working Notes Papers of the CLEF 2012 Evaluation Labs (2012)

4. Anderka, M., Stein, B., Lipka, N.: Detection of text quality flaws as a one-class classification problem. In: Proceedings of the 20th ACM International Conference on Information and Knowledge Management (CIKM 2011). ACM (2011)
5. Anderka, M., Stein, B., Lipka, N.: Towards automatic quality assurance in Wikipedia. In: 20th International Conference on World Wide Web, pp. 5–6. ACM (2011)
6. Anderka, M., Stein, B., Lipka, N.: Predicting quality flaws in user-generated content: the case of Wikipedia. In: 35rd Annual International ACM SIGIR Conference on Research and Development in Information Retrieval. ACM (2012)
7. Baeza-Yates, R.: User generated content: how good is it? In: 3rd workshop on Information Credibility on the Web (WICOW 2009), pp. 1–2. ACM (2009)
8. Bassani, E., Viviani, M.: Quality of Wikipedia articles: analyzing features and building a ground truth for supervised classification. In: Proceedings of the 11th International Joint Conference on Knowledge Discovery, Knowledge Engineering and Knowledge Management, pp. 338–346. ScitePress (2019)
9. Bazán-Pereyra, G., Cuello, C., Capodici, G., Jofré, V., Ferretti, E., Errecalde, M.: Automatically assessing the need of additional citations for information quality verification in Wikipedia articles. In: Actas del XXV Congreso Argentino de Ciencias de la Computación (CACIC), pp. 42–51 (2019). ISBN 978-987-688-377-1
10. Chang, C.C., Lin, C.J.: LIBSVM: a library for support vector machines. ACM Trans. Intell. Syst. Technol. **2**, 27:1–27:27 (2011)
11. Dang, Q.V., Ignat, C.L.: An end-to-end learning solution for assessing the quality of Wikipedia articles. In: 13th International Symposium on Open Collaboration (2017)
12. Ferretti, E., Cagnina, L., Paiz, V., Donne, S.D., Zacagnini, R., Errecalde, M.: Quality flaw prediction in Spanish Wikipedia: a case of study with verifiability flaws. Inf. Process. Manag. **54**(6), 1169–1181 (2018)
13. Ferretti, E., Errecalde, M., Anderka, M., Stein, B.: On the use of reliable-negatives selection strategies in the PU learning approach for quality flaws prediction in Wikipedia. In: 11th International Workshop on Text-Based Information Retrieval (2014)
14. Ferretti, E., Fusilier, D.H., Guzmán-Cabrera, R., Gómez, M.M., Errecalde, M., Rosso, P.: On the use of PU learning for quality flaw prediction in Wikipedia. In: CLEF (Online Working Notes/Labs/Workshop) (2012)
15. Ferretti, E., Soria, M., Casseignau, S.P., Pohn, L., Urquiza, G., Gómez, S.A., Errecalde, M.: Towards information quality assurance in Spanish Wikipedia. J. Comput. Sci. Technol. **17**(1), 29–36 (2017)
16. Ferschke, O., Gurevych, I., Rittberger., M.: FlawFinder: a modular system for predicting quality flaws in Wikipedia. In: CLEF (Online Working Notes/Labs/Workshop) (2012)
17. Ferschke, O., Gurevych, I., Rittberger, M.: The impact of topic bias on quality flaw prediction in Wikipedia. In: 51st Annual Meeting of the Association for Computational Linguistics, pp. 721–730. ACL (2013)
18. Goodfellow, I., Bengio, Y., Courville, A.: Deep Learning. MIT Press, Cambridge (2016)
19. Graves, A., Mohamed, A., Hinton, G.E.: Speech recognition with deep recurrent neural networks. CoRR abs/1303.5778 (2013)
20. Hall, M., Frank, E., Holmes, G., Pfahringer, B., Reutemann, P., Witten, I.H.: The WEKA data mining software: an update. SIGKDD Explor. **11**(1), 10–18 (2009)

21. Hempstalk, K., Frank, E., Witten, I.H.: One-class classification by combining density and class probability estimation. In: Daelemans, W., Goethals, B., Morik, K. (eds.) ECML PKDD 2008, Part I. LNCS (LNAI), vol. 5211, pp. 505–519. Springer, Heidelberg (2008). https://doi.org/10.1007/978-3-540-87479-9_51
22. Hochreiter, S., Schmidhuber, J.: Long short-term memory. Neural Comput. **9**(8), 1735–1780 (1997)
23. Kittler, J., Hatef, M., Duin, R.P.W., Matas, J.: On combining classifiers. IEEE Trans. Pattern Anal. Mach. Intell. **20**(3), 226–239 (1998)
24. Lewoniewski, W., Wecel, K., Abramowicz, W.: Multilingual ranking of Wikipedia articles with quality and popularity assessment in different topics. Computers **8**, 60 (2019)
25. Lex, E., et al.: Measuring the quality of web content using factual information. In: 2nd Joint WICOW/AIRWeb Workshop on Web Quality (WebQuality). ACM (2012)
26. Lipka, N., Stein, B.: Identifying featured articles in Wikipedia: writing style matters. In: 19th International Conference on World Wide Web. ACM (2010)
27. Pohn, L., Ferretti, E., Errecalde, M.: Computer Science & Technology Series: XX Argentine Congress of Computer Science - selected papers, chap. Identifying featured articles in Spanish Wikipedia, pp. 171–182. EDULP (2015)
28. Rumelhart, D., Hinton, G., Williams, R.: Learning representations by back-propagating errors. Nature **323**, 533–536 (1986)
29. Russell, S., Norvig, P.: Artificial Intelligence: A Modern Approach, 3rd edn. Prentice Hall, Upper Saddle River (2010)
30. Schmidt, M., Zangerle, E.: Article quality classification on Wikipedia: introducing document embeddings and content features. In: 15th International Symposium on Open Collaboration (OpenSym) (2019)
31. Schölkopf, B., Williamson, R., Smola, A., Shawe-Taylor, J., Platt, J.: Support vector method for novelty detection. In: Proceedings of the 12th International Conference on Neural Information Processing Systems (NIPS). MIT Press (1999)
32. Velázquez, C.G., Cagnina, L.C., Errecalde, M.L.: On the feasibility of external factual support as Wikipedia's quality metric. Procesamiento del Lenguaje Natural **58**, 93–100 (2017)
33. Wang, P., Li, X.: Assessing the quality of information on Wikipedia: a deep-learning approach. J. Assoc. Inf. Sci. Technol. **71**(1), 16–28 (2020)
34. Wang, R., Strong, D.: Beyond accuracy: what data quality means to data consumers. J. Manag. Inf. Syst. **12**(4), 5–33 (1996)
35. Zhang, S., Hu, Z., Zhang, C., Yu, K.: History-based article quality assessment on Wikipedia. In: IEEE 5th International Conference on Big Data and Smart Computing (BigComp), pp. 1–8 (2018)

Dynamic Tuning of a Forest Fire Prediction Parallel Method

Paola Caymes-Scutari[1,2](✉) [ID], María Laura Tardivo[1,3] [ID],
Germán Bianchini[1] [ID], and Miguel Méndez-Garabetti[1] [ID]

[1] LICPAD, UTN-FRM, Mendoza, Argentina
pcaymesscutari@frm.utn.edu.ar
[2] CONICET, Consejo Nacional de Investigaciones Científicas y Técnicas,
Buenos Aires, Argentina
[3] Departamento de Computación, Universidad Nacional de Río Cuarto,
Río Cuarto, Argentina
http://www.frm.utn.edu.ar/licpad/

Abstract. Different parameters feed mathematical and/or empirical models. However, the uncertainty (or lack of precision) present in such parameters usually impacts in the quality of the output/recommendation of prediction models. Fortunately, there exist uncertainty reduction methods which enable the obtention of more accurate solutions. One of such methods is ESSIM-DE (Evolutionary Statistical System with Island Model and Differential Evolution), a general purpose method for prediction and uncertainty reduction. ESSIM-DE has been used for the forest fireline prediction, and it is based on statistical analysis, parallel computing, and differential evolution. In this work, we enrich ESSIM-DE with an automatic and dynamic tuning strategy, to adapt the generational parameter of the evolutionary process in order to avoid premature convergence and/or stagnation, and to improve the general performance of the predictive tool. We describe the metrics, the tuning points and actions, and we show the results for different controlled fires.

Keywords: Dynamic tuning · Differential Evolution · Fire prediction · Parallel computing

1 Introduction

Year after year, forest fires constitute a great threat in different regions of the world, especially in summer, where high temperatures and prolonged drought provide an environment favorable to the development of these phenomena. In 2019, several serious fires occurred worldwide, including the case of the Amazon area with a loss of 2.5 million hectares of rainforest, and the case of Australia with a loss of 6 million hectares, as shown in Fig. 1. Due to the serious consequences they produce, it is important to have tools that allow predicting the behavior of fire to collaborate in fire fighting and fire prevention plans.

© Springer Nature Switzerland AG 2020
P. Pesado and M. Arroyo (Eds.): CACIC 2019, CCIS 1184, pp. 19–34, 2020.
https://doi.org/10.1007/978-3-030-48325-8_2

Fig. 1. Left: Forest fire in the Amazon area [14]. Right: Forest fire in Australia [15].

The prediction of a forest fire consists in determining how the fire will spread on the terrain in an instant of future time. Figure 2 illustrates both the general view of the simulation process and the particular case of the forest fire simulation for prediction. Generally, the prediction methods implement models that describe the behavior of the fire, and use as input data a set of variables representing those factors that condition the propagation. Some of the variables that are worth mentioning are: the wind speed and direction, the slope of the terrain, the type of combustible material, the humidity of the material, etc.

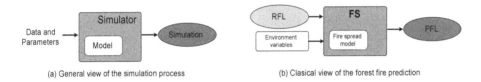

(a) General view of the simulation process   (b) Clasical view of the forest fire prediction

Fig. 2. General view of simulation and prediction process. **RFL**: Real Fire Line. **PFL**: Predicted Fire Line. **FS**: Fire Simulator.

Unfortunately, in general it is not possible to have the exact values for these factors, due to two main reasons: on the one hand, it is not feasible to provide all forest land with sensors and measuring instruments. On the other hand, the value of some of the parameters can vary dynamically throughout the development of the fire itself. This lack of information and/or precision regarding the values of the parameters is called **uncertainty**. There are also other sources of uncertainty, such as the limitations for mathematically modeling all the details of the system under consideration, the computer representation of the information (which for example causes truncation), the implementation of the simulator, etc. Every uncertainty source could cause drastic consequences if the output of the model provides a solution certainly different from reality. All of them are detrimental to the accuracy of the simulator and the quality of the prediction. In [11] we introduced a series of methods belonging to the class of so-called Data

Driven Methods with Multiple Overlapped Solutions (DDM-MOS [1]). In this article, we provide some details about them, as can be appreciated in Fig. 3.

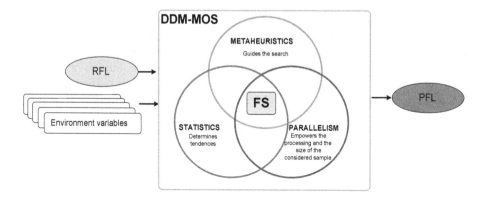

Fig. 3. Subjects involved by Data Driven Methods with Multiple Overlapped Solutions (DDM-MOS). **RFL**: Real Fire Line. **PFL**: Predicted Fire Line. **FS**: Fire Simulator.

On the one hand, the DDM-MOS take the initial state of the phenomenon as input parameter, in this case the real fire line (RFL). On the other hand, unlike what is observed in Fig. 2(b) in which the simulator takes as input a single combination of input parameters, the DDM-MOS take into account a certain number of combinations of values for the input parameters, valid within the possible search space. Each combination is called a *scenario* or *individual*, and is considered a possible solution to the problem. Since several individuals are considered at the same time, DDM-MOS are considered multiple solution methods. The set of individuals is called a *population*. As can be seen in Fig. 3, the operation of the simulator is enriched by the interrelation of Metaheuristics, Statistics and Parallelism. The metaheuristic allows to orientate the search within the extensive search space. Statistics allow to determine the tendency of the behavior of the individuals under consideration, by aggregating the results obtained for each of them; and this is why the DDM-MOS are considered as multiple overlapping solutions methods. Finally, the parallelism provides the necessary power to face the large amount of computation required by so many simulations in parallel and the consequent treatment of the results to yield a single prediction (PFL). The level of parallelism of DDM-MOS is also determined by the amount of populations considered: some DDM-MOS manage a unique population, whilst other operate on several populations in parallel, obeying to the Island Model [9]. In summary, these methods obtain predictions of the fireline based on the aggregation of multiple solutions, and focus on reducing the negative impact caused by uncertainty.

In particular, we have developed the ESSIM-DE method (Evolutionary Statistical System with Islands Model and Differential Evolution), a DDM-MOS which involves Differential Evolution as metaheuristic [8], and increases the level of parallelism by considering the Master/Worker pattern [5] and the Island Model [9] with several islands each responsible for the evolution of an independent population. In order to improve the performance of ESSIM-DE, we have defined and incorporated into the method a dynamic and automatic tuning strategy, which was presented in [11] and is extended in this work. Given that dynamic tuning is the core of this work, in the following we provide the general background necessary to understand this new version of the method: **ESSIM-DE(ldr)**. In general, the Tuning process [2,6] allows to calibrate, improve, adjust, or modify any critical aspect, bottleneck or factor that limits application performance. It consists of incorporating the phases of instrumentation, monitoring, analysis and tuning, during the execution of the program, as Fig. 4 illustrates.

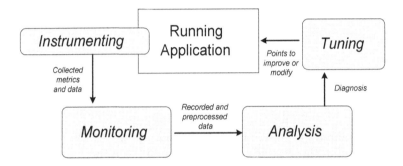

Fig. 4. The tuning process and its phases operating on the improvement of the application

In the Instrumentation phase, the code of the application is augmented or annotated with sentences or record certain metrics of interest. These metrics, in general, correspond to some model of the behavior of the application, and define specific knowledge about the behavior of it. This knowledge can respond to mathematical performance models, fuzzy logic, ad hoc heuristics, among others. Along the Monitoring phase the metrics are detected and recorded, for later analysis and tuning. The Analysis phase is focused on the processing and analysis of the recorded metrics. The type of expert knowledge considered (mathematical performance models, fuzzy logic, ad hoc heuristics, etc.) defines how the analysis process is carried out to determine the tuning actions necessary to improve the performance of the application. Subsequently, in the Tuning phase the defined actions are applied in order to improve the critical aspects. In this work, all these phases are performed with no user intervention, at runtime. This is why the proposed tuning strategy is classified as automatic and dynamic. In particular, in this paper we present a performance model to dynamically and automatically tune one of the key stages of ESSIM-DE: the Optimization stage, which involves the Differential Evolution algorithm (more details are provided in the next section). This metaheuristic is a population optimizer (based on multiple solutions) and consists of an iterative process in which a population of individuals evolves. Each individual represents a possible solution to the problem.

Stagnation and/or premature convergence towards a local optimum constitute possible performance problems associated with Differential Evolution [4]. This paper establishes a criterion by which it is possible to tune the number of generations by which populations have to evolve in order to detect in advance a tendency to stagnation and/or premature convergence. The performance model uses statistical information from the trend of population dispersion, monitored in a distributed manner. The objective is to prevent the performance of the ESSIM-DE method from being affected by stagnation or premature convergence, both in the quality of the predictions and in the response time. Another objective is that the tuning can be carried out independently of the case of burning considered and the particular characteristics of the execution. We call ESSIM-DE(ldr) this version of the method, given that it is capable of tuning the **limit** of evolutionary generations for a given prediction step, according to the analysis of the tendency of the **distributions**; what is more, it is capable of **restart** the populations along the successive prediction steps. In [11], we presented a general view of ESSIM-DE(ldr) and all the related basis of it. In this article, we are extending some key concepts (such as uncertainty, DDM-MOS, differential evolution, architecture and operation of ESSIM-DE), we provide some complementary graphics, and we include two new experimental cases of study that allow for confirming the effectiveness of ESSIM-DE(ldr). Section 2 provides more details about the architecture and operation of ESSIM-DE. In Sect. 3 we explain the performance problem addressed by ESSIM-DE(ldr). In Sect. 4 we show the results obtained for five study cases. Finally, in Sect. 5 we present the main conclusions of this work.

2   Forest Fires Prediction with ESSIM-DE

To make the prediction of the fire front, ESSIM-DE divides the total development of the fire into different discrete time slots, called *simulation steps*. For the simulation step i, ESSIM-DE operates in the manner explained in Fig. 3. It takes as input the real fire line at instant $i - 1$, and also takes a sample of candidate individuals which manages in several parallel populations. After processing them through Differential Evolution, parallelism and statistics, ESSIM-DE yields the corresponding prediction for instant i. The *Differential Evolution* (or DE) algorithm [8,13] is a population-based optimizer that uses multi-dimensional vectors to represent candidate solutions, also called population of individuals. Each dimension encodes a variable of the problem to be optimized and is represented with a value belonging to real numbers. The population evolves in different generations or iterations, in which the mutation, crossing and selection operators are applied to all of the individuals in the population. The mutation operator disturbs each individual in the current population, and for each one generates a new individual, called a "mutated vector". To do this, vector differences are applied between each individual considered and other randomly selected individuals. Subsequently, each mutated vector is submitted together with the original individual to the crossing operator, generating a new vector, called "trial vector". Finally, the selection stage determines the best candidate between the original individual and the trial vector. The one that has the best value regarding the function to be optimized will be the one that will survive the next generation. Below we present more details about the architecture and operation of ESSIM-DE. We also explain how the quality of an individual and a prediction is evaluated. In the next section we focus on the tuning component that allows to improve the performance of ESSIM-DE, constituting ESSIM-DE(ldr).

Architecturally, ESSIM-DE has a double hierarchy of processes that are organized in parallel islands and collaborate through migration, under the supervision of a Monitor process. Figure 5 presents how ESSIM-DE organizes its processes in a double hierarchy model, basing on the Master/Worker pattern [5] and the Island Model [9]. At a lower hierarchy level, each island manages a population of individuals, that is, different scenarios that constitute subsets of the total search space. On each island operates a main process called Master (green box), which is responsible for generating the initial population and applying the evolutionary operators of DE to improve the scenarios. In turn, each island has a group of Workers processes (light-blue "W" boxes) that are responsible for accelerating the prediction process, thanks to the parallel simulation of the different individuals or burning scenarios. In a higher hierarchy, a Monitor process (yellow box) coordinates the interaction between the Master processes of each island. These communicate with each other to exchange individuals from their islands through the Migration operator [9], a particular operator related to the evolutionary island models. The migration process promotes the global exploration of the search space represented by the populations of the different islands.

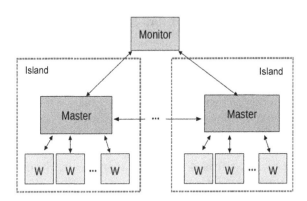

Fig. 5. Architecture of ESSIM-DE: double hierarchy of processes. **W**: Worker. (Color figure online)

Taking into account the ESSIM-DE architecture and the operation of the DE algorithm, we can now concentrate on the mode of operation of ESSIM-DE. The general operational scheme of ESSIM-DE is described in Fig. 6. For each prediction step four main stages operate: Optimization stage (OS), Statistical stage (SS), Calibration stage (CS) and Prediction stage (PS). Because ESSIM-DE uses a hierarchical process scheme, these four stages are subdivided to be cooperatively performed by the different entities of the process hierarchy: Master (M), Workers (W) and Monitor (Mon).

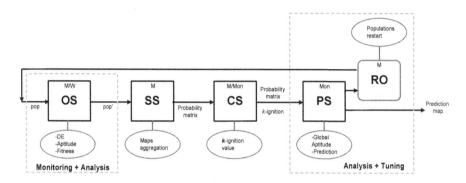

Fig. 6. General operation of ESSIM-DE. **OS**: Optimization stage. **SS**: Statistical stage. **CS**: Calibration stage. **PS**: Prediction stage. **RO**: Restart Operator. **DE**: Differential Evolution. **M**: Master. **W**: Worker. **Mon**: Monitor. Dotted line: tuning process in ESSIM-DE(ldr). (Color figure online)

In Fig. 6 can be seen the four stages involved in the method, of which we will focus on the **Optimization Stage (OS)**, which is carried out between the Workers (W) and the Master (M) processes of each island. This stage allows a population of individuals to evolve based on the Differential Evolution algorithm. Each individual represents a combination of values for variables that determine the progress of the fire (the wind speed, direction and slope of the land, type of combustible material, humidity of the living combustible material, etc.). The Master process initializes the population (*pop*), applies the DE mutation and crossing operators to generate new candidate individuals, and distributes the individuals among the Workers. These use the current state of the fire, together with an individual to perform the simulation. Subsequently, each Worker evaluates the aptitude of the prediction obtained, weighing the accuracy of the simulation by comparing the cells burned in the real fire and the cells reached by the fire on the simulated map. The evaluation of the prediction quality is quantified based on a **fitness function**, which obeys to the Jaccard index [7], where the division between A and B is performed, being A the set of cells on the real map without the subset of cells burned before starting the predictive process, and being B the set of cells on the simulated map, without the subset of cells burned before starting the prediction (the subset of cells burned before starting the predictive process are not considered to avoid biased results). Therefore, the fitness value can be considered the percentage of coincidence between the map obtained from the simulation and the real map, and will be in the range $[0, 1]$: a value equal to 1 will represent a perfect prediction, and a value equal to zero would indicate the maximum error. Therefore, aptitude represents the percentage of coincidence between both maps. Subsequently, the following stages are carried out: Statistics (**SS**), Calibration (**CS**) and Prediction (**PS**), which collect the information and results obtained by all the islands in the **OS** stage, and based on this, they allow to obtain the global prediction of the state of the fire. As the Prediction stage finishes and the following fire step is going to start, ESSIM-DE also involves the Restart Operator (RO). This operator generates a new population (new search space). For more detail on the operation of the ESSIM-DE stages it is possible to consult [10].

3   Dynamic Tuning: Performance Model

In this section we concentrate on the performance model defined to enhance ESSIM-DE, constituting ESSIM-DE(ldr). For each prediction step, the Master process of each island determines when the evolution of its population finishes to continue with the next stages of the prediction process. In the OS stage of ESSIM-DE, the termination condition of the evolutionary cycle consists in determining a certain maximum level or limit of iterations. This condition has a double influence on the optimization process, since it limits the amount of evolutionary generations through which each population will evolve, and consequently determines the execution time of the evolutionary process. In part, these were the reasons why it was proposed to define the dynamic tuning process applied to the limit of evolutionary iterations.

In the definition of the tuning process we have considered two possible problems associated with the evolution process carried out by DE: premature convergence and stagnation. *Premature convergence* is the situation in which the population converges to a local optimum, due to the loss of diversity; for its part, *stagnation* is the situation in which the optimizer is not able to generate new solutions better than its predecessors, even when the population has a certain diversity [4]. The problem of population stagnation depends on the effective movements of the DE optimizer. When a new individual is generated, there is a movement in the search space. This movement is considered effective if the new generated individual has a better aptitude compared to his predecessor [13]. Among all the possible movements that are made in the population, some are effective, while others are not, and therefore the latter involve a computational effort in vain. To address the treatment of these problems, it was proposed to quantify two different metrics for the population:

- **Effective movements (EM metric):** quantifies the number of individuals that have been improved after an evolutionary cycle (better fitness value than that of their predecessor).
- **Population diversity (IQR metric):** quantifies the dispersion of the population (variability of the population distribution). It is computed based on the Interquartile Range [3] of the fitness values of individuals.

These metrics are proposed after an experimental analysis in which they were monitored, recorded and studied for different cases of controlled burning. In a first approximation, a fixed threshold value was used for each metric. However, analyzing the results presented in Fig. 7, it was possible to note that the graphic of the IQR metric is variable from case to case, throughout the iterations, even when the same seeds are involved in the different fire cases. This is because the distribution of the values of fitness is influenced by multiple factors (method convergence speed, mutation factor, crossing probability, migration rate, map dimensions, among others). For this reason, the proposed performance model uses the information of the dispersion of the population, considering the successive IQR values obtained throughout the evolutionary generations. The purpose is –according to the current burning case considered– to detect states with some tendency to stagnation and/or premature convergence, making use of recent information about fitness distributions.

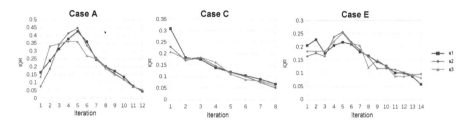

Fig. 7. The distribution of IQR is dependent of the study case. The same three seeds were used for the three illustrated cases: *s1*, *s2* and *s3*.

To achieve this, it was proposed: (*i*) to record the minimum IQR value obtained; (*ii*) to update such minimum IQR value throughout the iterations; and (*iii*) to compare it with respect to the IQR value obtained in the current iteration. This idea is exemplified in Fig. 8.

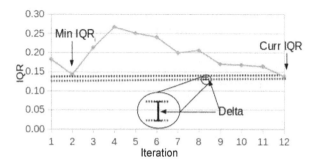

Fig. 8. Example: how is *Delta* determined.

The x axis represents the evolutionary generation (iteration) whilst the y axis represents the registered IQR value. The graph shows the minimum IQR recorded ($MinIQR$) and the IQR of the current iteration ($CurrIQR$). If the difference between both of them –called $Delta$– is very small, it means that the population has achieved a very similar distribution (in terms of fitness values) to that achieved in any of the previous iterations. Defining $Delta = (MinIQR - CurrIQR)$, the tuning criterion is defined by the Eq. 1 in which it is verified that the tendency of IQR is decreasing ($Delta >= 0$) and Delta is bounded by a certain small $thresholdDELTA$ value.

$$Delta \leq thresholdDELTA \quad \wedge \quad Delta \geq 0 \quad \wedge ME \leq thresholdME \quad (1)$$

For its part, the value of the ME metric is also considered, required to analyze whether the optimizer still has effective movements to be made on the search space, bounded to a certain threshold value $thresholdME$. In ESSIM-DE, the Eq. 1 is computed in each iteration throughout the OS, according to the current population distribution, for each burning map and particular conditions of execution. The proposal aims to improve response times with respect to the method without tuning, since the new condition used as a cut-off criterion is a specific property of each population, which avoids unnecessary cycles. The tuning process is included in Fig. 6 (see the boxes in red dotted lines). The aptitude values are recorded along the Monitoring phase and the metrics are computed in the Master Analysis phase. When analyzing each iteration, each Master sends the metrics of its island to the Monitor (Mon) process, who makes an aggregation of the values received in its Analysis phase, and determines if there is any island with a tendency to stagnation and/or premature convergence. If some island evaluated as true the Eq. 1, the Monitor decides: (a) to stop the evolution of all the islands; (b) to make the prediction by aggregating the information of all of them; and (c) to resume the next prediction step.

4   Experiments

In [11] the proposal was validated based on experimentation with three cases of controlled burning belonging to the SPREAD project [12] (see Table 1, cases A, B and C). In this article we extend such experimentation, including two additional cases also from SPREAD project (see Table 1, cases D and E). For each case of burning, the experiment was performed to compare two different scenarios:

– Fire prediction with ESSIM-DE (with no tuning process).
– Prediction of the fire with ESSIM-DE(ldr) (ESSIM-DE empowered by dynamic tuning).

It should be remembered that **ldr** is the acronym with which we call the method with the process of dynamic tuning of the iteration limit and with the population restart operator. Each experiment was executed 10 times with different seeds. We present the average of the results obtained along the ten executions. The island model was configured with 5 islands, of 7 Workers each. The migration process involves 20% of the individuals in the population, and it is carried out in each iteration. The size of each population was defined as 200 individuals. For ESSIM-DE and ESSIM-DE(ldr) the same configuration of the evolutionary parameters was used: crossover probability 0.3, mutation factor 0.9, and binomial crossover. The value used as the *thresholdME* was set at 20%. The value established for the *thresholdDELTA* parameter was 10^{-3}.

Table 1. Study cases: dimension, slope, start time, end time, and increase.

Case	Width (m)	High (m)	Slope (degrees)	St. T. (min)	Incr. (min)	End T. (min)
A	89	109	21	2	2	14
B	60	90	6	2	2	10
C	89	91	21	2.5	2.5	12.5
D	95	123	21	2	2	12
E	75	126	19	3	1	9

The results obtained are presented in Fig. 9, 10, 11, 12 and 13. Two graphics are included in each figure. The graph (a) represents the fitness averages for each prediction step, obtained by ESSIM-DE(ldr), and compared with respect to the ESSIM-DE with no tuning. Graph (b) shows the distribution of fitness values obtained for each prediction step and method, which allows analyzing the dispersion of the results and the robustness of the method in terms of obtaining different solutions under different executions. Table 2 shows the average runtime values obtained.

Figure 9 shows the results obtained for the case of burning A of Table 1. The fire starts in minute 2 and lasts for 14 min, constituting a calibration step and five prediction steps (calibration: minute 2 to 4; prediction steps: minutes 4 to 6 first step, minutes 6 to 8 second step, minutes 8 to 10 third step, minutes 10 to 12 fourth step, and minutes 12 to 14 fifth step). In general, it can be seen from graph (a) that ESSIM-DE obtains low quality of prediction, especially in the prediction step 3. Figure 9(b) shows how step 1 and step 5 present a wide variability of the results obtained with ESSIM-DE, whilst for ESSIM-DE(ldr) there is less distribution in all prediction steps, which indicates robustness in terms of obtaining solutions under different executions. In general, ESSIM-DE(ldr) gets better performance, with average of fitness greater than 0.7 in all the prediction steps, and with a reduction of the execution time of approximately 38%. This reduction in time is associated with the ability of ESSIM-DE(ldr) to prematurely detect the tendency to stagnation and/or premature convergence, avoiding unnecessary cycles, and therefore, achieving less response time. Execution time reductions are very relevant in the context of prediction methods, allowing decisions to be made in advance of the fire. It is important to note that the reduction of time not only depends on the speed with which the stagnation and premature convergence is detected, but also depends on the characteristics of the burning case and the

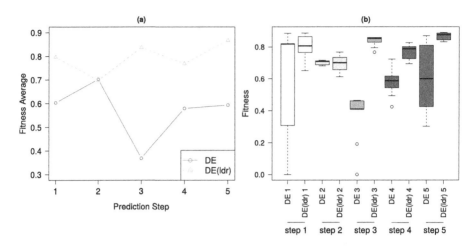

Fig. 9. Case A. (a) *fitness* average for ESSIM-DE and ESSIM-DE(ldr). (b) Distribution of the fitness values obtained in the successive prediction steps.

size of the considered map, which influences the overall behavior of the system in the different stages.

Table 2. Average execution times and percentage reduction.

Case	ESSIM-DE	ESSIM-DE(ldr)	Time reduction
A	3540	1292	63.5%
B	1696	446	73.7%
C	2332	1438	38.3%
D	3582	1265	64.7%
E	2406	702	70.8%

Figure 10 shows the results obtained for the case of burning B of Table 1. The fire consists of three prediction steps (minutes 4–6, 6–8, 8–10). It can be seen from the Fig. 10(a) that ESSIM-DE has a decreasing trend in the quality of the predictions, with a low percentage of coincidence in the third prediction step, less than 60%. Although in the first prediction step can be observed good quality (higher than 0.8) and low distribution (see the results obtained in Fig. 10(b), step 1 for ESSIM-DE), ESSIM-DE(ldr) improves all prediction steps, with fitness averages greater than 0.85 in all steps. In addition, in this case ESSIM-DE(ldr) obtains a gain in runtime, with a significant reduction of approximately 73%.

Figure 11 shows the results obtained for the case of burning C of Table 1. The fire consists of three prediction steps. It can be seen from the Fig. 11(a) that ESSIM-DE(ldr) obtains a better fitness average in the first and third prediction step, while ESSIM-DE obtains a quality close to 0.9 in the second prediction step.

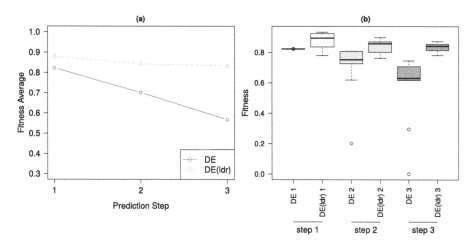

Fig. 10. Case B. (a) *fitness* average for ESSIM-DE and ESSIM-DE(ldr). (b) Distribution of the fitness values obtained in the successive prediction steps.

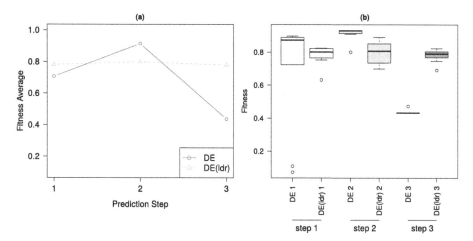

Fig. 11. Case C. (a) *fitness* average for ESSIM-DE and ESSIM-DE(ldr). (b) Distribution of the fitness values obtained in the successive prediction steps.

It is important to highlight in this experiment that ESSIM-DE(ldr) significantly improves the quality of the prediction obtained in the third prediction step with respect to ESSIM-DE, achieving a percentage of coincidence with the real fire close to 80% of coincidence (fitness close to 0.8). In addition, it can be seen from the results in Table 2 that ESSIM-DE(ldr) reduces the execution times approximately by 63% compared to ESSIM-DE.

Figure 12 shows the results obtained for the case of burning D of Table 1. The fire consists of four prediction steps (minutes 4–6, 6–8, 8–10, 10–12). It can be seen from the Fig. 12(a) that ESSIM-DE present good results. However,

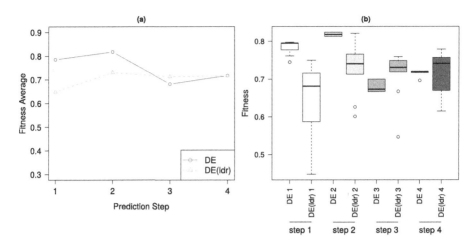

Fig. 12. Case D. (a) *fitness* average for ESSIM-DE and ESSIM-DE(ldr). (b) Distribution of the fitness values obtained in the successive prediction steps.

it has a decreasing trend in the quality of the predictions, showing a loss in the percentage of coincidence in the third prediction step, less than 70%. Even when ESSIM-DE(ldr) overtakes ESSIM-DE only in the third prediction step, it is possible to note that the quality of ESSIM-DE(ldr) is maintained around a 70% of coincidence with the real fire situation along the four prediction steps, and from Table 2 it is possible observe that ESSIM-DE(ldr) obtains a gain in runtime, with a significant reduction of approximately 65%.

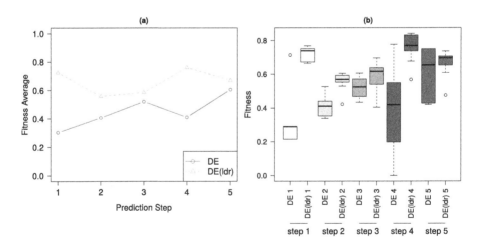

Fig. 13. Case E. (a) *fitness* average for ESSIM-DE and ESSIM-DE(ldr). (b) Distribution of the fitness values obtained in the successive prediction steps.

Figure 13 shows the results obtained for the case of burning E of Table 1. The fire consists of five prediction steps. It can be seen from the Fig. 12(a) that ESSIM-DE(ldr) improves the average fitness in every prediction step, whilst ESSIM-DE obtains a quality at most close to 0.6 in the last prediction step. It is important to highlight in this experiment that ESSIM-DE(ldr) significantly improves the quality of the prediction obtained in the first and fourth prediction steps with respect to ESSIM-DE, achieving a percentage of coincidence with the real fire over 70% of coincidence, in contrast to the 30% or 40% reached by ESSIM-DE without tuning. Figure 13(b) shows that in this case, the fitness distributions for ESSIM-DE(ldr) do not present major variability, confirming the robustness of the method. In addition, it is important to note that ESSIM-DE(ldr) reduces the execution times approximately by 70% compared to ESSIM-DE, as shows Table 2.

In general, considering all studied cases, the quality of the predictions obtained by ESSIM-DE(ldr) was improved regarding ESSIM-DE (the method without tuning). With respect to response times, ESSIM-DE(ldr) obtained the results with a significant reduction in the execution time: between 38% and 73% savings with respect to ESSIM-DE. Both improvements are associated with the early detection of stagnation and premature convergence, avoiding unnecessary cycles to the Evolution Differential optimizer, and obtaining better individuals that contribute to the overall solution. It is important to highlight that the use of a mathematical/statistical model as the basis of expert knowledge for the dynamic tuning process allows for the reduction of the time taken in decision making, unlike other strategies with higher computational cost, such as search, iterative processes, logic diffuse, neural networks, approximations, among others. This is because the analysis and tuning decisions are based only on the evaluation of mathematical expressions. In the context of prediction methods such as ESSIM-DE, these time reductions are essential to obtain short-term predictions.

5 Conclusions

In this paper, we proposed a performance model to dynamically tune the ESSIM-DE method, a general method for the uncertainty reduction in the prediction of spread phenomena. We proposed to incorporate the tuning process in order to improve the ESSIM-DE performance both in terms of quality of the obtained predictions, and the response time. The defined performance model uses the information of the dispersion of the population in the succession of values obtained throughout the evolutionary generations, in order to detect tendency to stagnation and/or premature convergence of the population. The state and distribution of the search space (populations) is computed at two different levels: (i) in a distributed manner, given that each island analyzes the current distribution of its own population, for each burning map and particular conditions of execution, and (ii) in a centralized manner as the Monitor process analyzes the search space in a global view. The results obtained have shown that the proposal improves both the quality and the response times with respect to the method without tuning, since the new condition used as a cut-off criterion is a specific property of each population, which avoids unnecessary cycles once certain level of convergence has been detected. As future work, we propose to tune the threshold values of the metrics defined in the performance model, and consider other parameters of the method that may be potentially tunable, such as the population size, or the parameters related to the parallel/distributed model.

References

1. Bianchini, G., et al.: Wildland fire growth prediction method based on multiple overlapping solution. J. Comput. Sci. **1**(4), 229–237 (2010)
2. Caymes-Scutari, P., Bianchini, G., Sikora, A., Margalef, T.: Environment for automatic development and tuning of parallel applications. In: International Conference on High Performance Computing & Simulation (HPCS), Innsbruck, pp. 743–750 (2016)
3. Healey, J.: The Essentials of Statistics: A Tool for Social Research. Thomson/Wadswort, Belmont (2007). ISBN 9780495009757
4. Lampinen, J., Zelinka, I.: On stagnation of the differential evolution algorithm, In: Ošmera, P. (ed.) Proceedings of MENDEL 2000, 6th International Mendel Conference on Soft Computing, pp. 76–83. Brno, Czech Republic (2000). http://www.lut.fi/jlampine/MEND2000.ps
5. Mattson, T., et al.: Patterns for Parallel Programming. Addison-Wesley, Boston (2004)
6. Naono, K., Teranishi, K., Cavazos, J., Suda, R. (eds.): Software Automatic Tuning: From Concepts to State-of-the-Art Results. Springer, New York (2010). https://doi.org/10.1007/978-1-4419-6935-4
7. Real, R., Vargas, J.M.: The probabilistic basis of Jacard's index of similarity. Syst. Biol. **45**(3), 380–385 (1996)
8. Price, K.V., Storn, R.M., Lampinen, J.A.: Differential Evolution: A Practical Approach to Global Optimization. NCS. Springer, Heidelberg (2005). https://doi.org/10.1007/3-540-31306-0
9. Talbi, E.: Metaheuristics: From Design to Implementation. Wiley, Reading (2009)
10. Tardivo, M.L., Caymes-Scutari, P., Méndez-Garabetti, M., Bianchini, G.: Optimization for an uncertainty reduction method applied to forest fires spread prediction. In: De Giusti, A.E. (ed.) CACIC 2017. CCIS, vol. 790, pp. 13–23. Springer, Cham (2018). https://doi.org/10.1007/978-3-319-75214-3_2
11. Tardivo, L., Caymes-Scutari, P., Bianchini, G., Mendez-Garabetti, M.: Sintonización Dinámica del Método Paralelo de Predicción de Incendios Forestales ESSIM-DE. In: Proceedings XXV Congreso Argentino de Ciencias de la Computación (CACIC 2019), pp. 115–124. UniRio Editora, Río Cuarto (2019). ISBN 978-987-688-377-1
12. Viegas, D.X.: Project Spread Forest Fire Spread Prevention and Mitigation (2004). https://cordis.europa.eu/project/rcn/60354/factsheet/fr. Accessed Sept 2019
13. Yang, M., Li, C., Cai, Z., Guan, J.: Differential evolution with auto-enhanced population diversity. IEEE Trans. Cybern. **45**, 302–315 (2015)
14. El País. https://elpais.com/elpais/2019/09/11/album/1568221457_486259.html#foto_gal_1
15. Radio Gráfica. https://radiografica.org.ar/2020/01/08/australia-la-ciencia-predijo-los-incendios-y-la-politica-lo-ignoro/

Distributed and Parallel Processing

Optimization of the N-Body Simulation on Intel's Architectures Based on AVX-512 Instruction Set

Enzo Rucci[1]($\boxtimes$)(iD), Ezequiel Moreno[2], Adrián Pousa[1], and Franco Chichizola[1](iD)

[1] III-LIDI, Facultad de Informática, UNLP – CEA CICPBA,
1900 La Plata, Bs As, Argentina
{erucci,apousa,francoch}@lidi.info.unlp.edu.ar
[2] Facultad de Informática, UNLP, 1900 La Plata, Bs As, Argentina
morenoezequiel8@gmail.com

Abstract. The N-body simulations have become a powerful tool to test the gravitational interaction among particles, ranging from a few bodies to complete galaxies. Even though N-body has already been optimized on many parallel platforms, there are hardly any studies which take advantage of the latest Intel architectures based on AVX-512 instruction set. This SIMD set was initially supported by Intel's Xeon Phi Knights Landing (KNL) manycore processors launched at 2016. Recently, it has been included in Intel's general-purpose processors too, starting at the Skylake (SKL) server microarchitecture and now in its successor Cascade Lake (CKL). This paper optimizes the all-pairs N-body simulation on both current Intel platforms supporting AVX-512 extensions: a Xeon Phi KNL node and a server equipped with a dual CKL processor. On the basis of a naive implementation, it is shown how the parallel implementation (can) reach, through different optimization techniques, 2355 and 2449 GFLOPS on the Xeon Phi KNL and the Xeon CKL platforms, respectively.

Keywords: N-body · AVX-512 · Xeon Phi · Knights Landing · Xeon Platinum · Skylake · Cascade Lake

1 Introduction

Nowadays, the scientific community is experimenting with a new revolution on parallel processor technologies in the road to the Exascale. The novelties and enhancements not only involve hardware technologies but also changes in parallel programming models [6]. Beyond that, one of the most important challenges that still remains is how to perform large-scale simulations in a reasonable time using affordable computer systems. In that sense, a deep knowledge of hardware and software optimization is required in these cases to fulfill that purpose.

Physics is one of the areas affected by the above-mentioned challenges due to an increasing number of simulation-based applications demanding High-Performance Computing (HPC) to meet time requirements. One of these applications is the N-body simulation, which approximates a in numeric manner

© Springer Nature Switzerland AG 2020
P. Pesado and M. Arroyo (Eds.): CACIC 2019, CCIS 1184, pp. 37–52, 2020.
https://doi.org/10.1007/978-3-030-48325-8_3

the evolution of a system of bodies where each body interacts with the rest of them [1].

The best-known use of this simulation corresponds to Astrophysics, where each body represents a galaxy or a single star that experiment attraction due to the gravitational force. The N-body simulations have become a powerful tool to test the gravitational interaction among particles, ranging from a few bodies to complete galaxies. However, they are also used in other areas. For example, for protein folding in computational biology [3] or for global illumination in computer graphics [4].

There are different methods to compute the N-body simulation [12]. The simplest way is known as *all-pairs* (or *direct*) and involves evaluating all interactions among all pairs of bodies. It is a brute force method with high computational cost $(O(n^2))$. Due to its complexity, the direct version is only used when the number of bodies is small or moderate at most. When the number of bodies is large, this version is still employed to calculate the interactions between near bodies but combined with a distinct strategy to distant bodies. This is the approach used by advanced methods, like the Barnes-Hut ($O(n\ log\ n)$) or the Fast Multipole Method ($O(n)$). Therefore, optimizing the direct version also benefits the other alternatives that makes use of it.

This paper optimizes the all-pairs N-body simulation on Intel's architectures based on the latest AVX-512 instruction set, which allows the exploitation of 512-bit vectorial instructions. This SIMD set was initially supported by Intel's Xeon Phi Knights Landing (KNL) manycore processors but has been recently included in Intel's general-purpose processors too (starting at the Skylake server microarchitecture). The contributions of this work can be seen as an extension of [8], where the optimization process only considered the Xeon Phi KNL architecture. By incorporating Intel's general-purpose processors to the study, this work is able to offer insights regarding both Intel's architectures based on the AVX-512 instructions. Additionally, the power-performance perspective is also addressed.

The rest of the paper is organized as follows. Section 2 introduces the basic concepts of the N-body simulation. Section 3 briefly introduces Intel's architectures based on AVX-512 instruction set. The optimized implementation is described in Sect. 4. In Sect. 5, performance results are presented and finally, in Sect. 6, conclusions and some ideas for future research are summarized.

2   N-Body Simulation

The problem consists in simulating the evolution of a system composed by N bodies during a time-lapse. Given the mass and the initial state (speed and position) for each body, the motion of the system is simulated through discrete instants of time. In each of them, every body experiences an acceleration that arises from the gravitational attraction of the rest, which affects its state.

The simulation basis is supported by Newtonian mechanics [9]. The simulation is performed in 3 spatial dimensions and the gravitational attraction between two bodies C_1 and C_2 is computed using Newton's law of universal gravitation:

$$F = \frac{G \times m_1 \times m_2}{r^2} \tag{1}$$

where F corresponds to the *magnitude* of the gravitational force between bodies, G corresponds to the gravitational constant[1], m_1 corresponds to the body mass of C_1, m_2 corresponds to the body mass of C_2, and r corresponds to the Euclidean distance[2] between C_1 and C_2.

When N is greater than 2, the gravitational force on a body corresponds to the sum of all gravitational forces exerted by the remaining $N-1$ bodies. The force of attraction leads each body to accelerate and move, according to the Newton's second law, which is given by the following equation:

$$F = m \times a \tag{2}$$

where F is the force vector, calculated using the magnitude obtained from the equation of gravitation and the direction and sense of the vector going from the affected body to the body exerting the attraction.

Regarding the above equation, it is clear that the acceleration of a body can be calculated by dividing the total force by its mass. During a small time interval dt, the acceleration a_i of the body C_i is approximately constant, so the change in velocity is approximately:

$$dv_i = a_i dt \tag{3}$$

The change in body position is the integral of its speed and acceleration over the dt time interval, which is approximately:

$$dp_i = v_i dt + \frac{a_i}{2} dt^2 = (v_i + \frac{dv_i}{2}) dt \tag{4}$$

This formula uses an integration scheme called Leapfrog [13], in which one half of the position change is because of the old speed while the other half is because of the new speed.

3 Intel's Architectures Based on AVX-512 Instruction Set

AVX-512 is a set of new 512-bit SIMD x86 instructions presented by Intel in 2013. It was initially supported by Xeon Phi KNL manycore processors but has been

---

[1] Equivalent to 6.674×10^{11}.

[2] The Euclidean distance is given by $\sqrt{((x_2 - x_1)^2 + (y_2 - y_1)^2 + (z_2 - z_1)^2)}$, where (x_1, y_1, z_1) is the position of $C1$ and (x_2, y_2, z_2) is the position of C_2.

recently included in the general-purpose sector too (starting at the Skylake-X microarchitecture). A single AVX-512 instruction can pack eight double-precision multiply-add operations (16 FLOPS) or 16 single-precision multiply-add operations (32 FLOPS).

3.1 Intel Knights Landing

KNL is the second generation of the Intel Xeon Phi family and the first one capable of operating as a standalone processor. The KNL architecture features up to 72 cores based on the Intel's Atom microarchitecture, which are organized in *Tiles*. A Tile includes 2 cores and is interconnected with the rest of them by a 2D mesh. Additionally, each Tile features 2 Vector Processing Units (VPUs) and a shared L2 cache of 1 MB. Besides supporting the AVX-512 SIMD set, these VPUs are also compatible with prior vector sets such as SSE*x* and AVX*x* [7].

The 2D mesh can be configured in three different cluster operating modes: 1) *All-to-All*; 2) *Quadrant/Hemisphere*; and 3) *SNC-4/SNC-2*. The main difference between these modes is whether the cores will access in UMA or NUMA manner to a particular memory.

The KNL architecture also features a 3D-stacked DRAM known as Multi-Channel DRAM (MCDRAM). This special memory offers 3 operating modes: 1) *Cache*, where the MCDRAM works as an L3 cache; 2) *Flat*, where the MCDRAM has a physical addressable space offering the highest bandwidth and lowest latency; and 3) *Hybrid*, where this memory is divided in two parts: one part in, *Cache mode* and one in *Flat mode*. From a performance point of view, Flat mode can achieve better results. However, programmer intervention may be required, as opposed to the Cache mode [2].

3.2 Intel Cascade Lake

Cascade Lake (CKL) is the latest microarchitecture presented by Intel for general-purpose processors. This microarchitecture is an optimization of the previous Skylake (SKL), which was the first to support the AVX-512 SIMD set in the general-purpose segment. As the SKL case, Intel distinguishes between two CKL processor versions: *client* and *server*, being the latter considerably larger than the former.

CKL server processors present up to 56 cores, which share a last level cache of (up to) 80 Mb. In a similar way to the KNL case, CKL server cores are organized in Tiles that are interconnected by a 2D mesh. Additionally, these cores also feature AVX-512 extensions and support previous vector instructions such as SSE*x* and AVX*x*.

4   Optimization of the N-Body Simulation

This section describes the optimization techniques that were applied to the parallel implementation for both target architectures.

4.1 *Naive* Implementation

Initially, a naive implementation was developed, which served as a baseline in order to assess the improvements introduced by the subsequent optimization techniques. The pseudo-code of the naive implementation is shown in Fig. 1.

4.2 Multi-threading

The first optimization consists in introducing thread-level parallelism through OpenMP directives. The loops on lines 4 and 25 are parallelized by inserting *parallel for* directives. In this way, the dependencies of the problem are guaranteed since one body cannot move until the rest have finished calculating their interactions. And they cannot advance either to the next step until the others have completed the current step. Finally, the *static* option for the *schedule* clause permits an equal distribution of bodies among the threads, achieving a minimum cost load balance.

4.3 Vectorization

The ICC optimization report makes possible to identify loops that are automatically vectorized. Given its feedback, it was possible to know that the compiler detects false dependencies in some operations, disabling the generation of SIMD instructions. Consequently, in order to guarantee the vectorization of operations, a guided approach was implemented through the use of the OpenMP 4.0 *simd* directive. In particular, the vectorized loops are those of lines 8 and 25, the latter being combined with the *parallel for* directive (as mentioned in the previous

```
1  // For each discrete instant time
2  for (t = 1; t <= D; t += DT){
3      // For each body that experiences a force
4      for (i = 0; i < N; i++){
5          // Force of body i
6          forcesx[i] = forcesy[i] = forcesz[i] = 0.0;
7          // For each body that exerts a force
8          for (j = 0; j < N; j++){
9              // Newton's gravitational force law
10             dx = xpos[j] - xpos[i]; dy = ypos[j] - ypos[i]; dz = zpos[j] - zpos[i];
11             dsquared = (dx*dx) + (dy*dy) + (dz*dz) + SOFT;
12             F = G * masses[i] * masses[j]; d32 = 1/POW(dsquared,1.5);
13             // Calculate the total force
14             forcesx[i] += F*dx*d32; forcesy[i] += F*dy*d32; forcesz[i] += F*dz*d32;
15         }
16         // Calculate the acceleration
17         ax = forcesx[i] / masses[i]; ay = forcesy[i] / masses[i]; az = forcesz[i] / masses[i];
18         // Calculate the speed
19         dvx = (xvi[i] + (ax*DT*0.5)); dvy = (yvi[i] + (ay*DT*0.5)); dvz = (zvi[i] + (az*DT*0.5));
20         // Calculate the position
21         dpx[i] = dvx * DT; dpy[i] = dvy * DT; dpz[i] = dvz * DT;
22         // Update the velocity
23         xvi[i] = dvx; yvi[i] = dvy; zvi[i] = dvz;
24     }
25     // Update the positions
26     for(i = 0; i < N; i++){
27         xpos[i] += dpx[i]; ypos[i] += dpy[i]; zpos[i] += dpz[i];
28     }
}
```

Fig. 1. Pseudo-code of the naive implementation.

section). Finally, to avoid the overhead of potential misaligned memory accesses, the data was aligned to 64-bytes and the *aligned* clause was added to the *simd* directives.

4.4 Block Processing

Block processing is implemented to exploit data locality. The pseudo-code of the parallel block implementation is shown in Fig. 2. Regarding the naive implementation, the *i*-loop (line 4) is divided and placed inside the *j*-loop (line 8). Consequently, one loop is replaced by two others: a loop that iterates over all blocks (line 5) and an inner loop that iterates over the bodies of each block (line 12). This minimizes the traffic between cache and main memory by increasing the number of times that each data is used in the innermost loop.

4.5 Loop Unrolling

Loop unrolling is another optimization technique that can improve the performance of a program. In particular, it was found beneficial to completely unroll the innermost loop of the implementation presented in Fig. 2 (line 9), in addition to the one that will update the body positions later (line 35).

```
1  // For each discrete instant time
2  for (t = 1; t <= D; t += DT){
3      // For each block of bodies (size = BS)
4      #pragma omp parallel for schedule(static) private(i,j)
5      for(ii = 0; ii < N; ii+=BS){
6          // Force of body i
7          forcesx[BS] = forcesy[BS] = forcesz[BS] = {0.0};
8          // For each body that exerts a force
9          #pragma unroll
10         for(j = 0; j < N; j++){
11             // For each body that experiences a force
12             #pragma omp simd aligned
13             for (i = ii; i < ii+BS; i++){
14                 // Newton's gravitational force law
15                 dx = xpos[j] - xpos[i]; dy = ypos[j] - ypos[i]; dz = zpos[j] - zpos[i];
16                 dsquared = (dx*dx) + (dy*dy) + (dz*dz) + SOFT;
17                 F = G * masses[j]; d32 = 1/POW(dsquared,1.5);
18                 // Calculate the total force
19                 forcesx[i-ii] += F*dx*d32; forcesy[i-ii] += F*dy*d32; forcesz[i-ii] += F*dz*d32;
20             }
21         }
22         #pragma omp simd aligned
23         for (i = ii; i < ii+BS; i++){
24             // Calculate the acceleration
25             ax = forcesx[i-ii] / masses[i]; ay = forcesy[i-ii] / masses[i]; az = forcesz[i-ii] / masses[i];
26             // Calculate the speed
27             dvx = (xvi[i] + (ax*DT*0.5)); dvy = (yvi[i] + (ay*DT*0.5)); dvz = (zvi[i] + (az*DT*0.5));
28             // Calculate the position
29             dpx[i] = dvx * DT; dpy[i] = dvy * DT; dpz[i] = dvz * DT;
30             // Update the velocity
31             xvi[i] = dvx; yvi[i] = dvy; zvi[i] = dvz;
32         }
33     }
34     // Update the positions
35     #pragma unroll
36     #pragma omp parallel for simd aligned
37     for(int i = 0; i < N; i++){
38         xpos[i] += dpx[i]; ypos[i] += dpy[i]; zpos[i] += dpz[i];
39     }
40 }
```

Fig. 2. Pseudo-code of the optimized parallel implementation.

5   Experimental Results

All tests were carried out using the platforms described in Table 1[3]. To generate explicit AVX2 instructions, the flag -xAVX2 was used in both servers. In similar manner, the flags -xMIC-AVX512 and -xCORE-AVX512 -qopt-zmm-usage=high were employed to exploit AVX-512 extensions in the Xeon Phi and in the Xeon Platinum platforms, respectively. Also, the flag -fp-model fast=2 was enabled to accelerate floating-point operations. Regarding the Xeon Phi server, the *numactl* utility was used to take advantage of its MCDRAM memory (no source code modification is required). Finally, different workloads were tested in both platforms: $N = \{65536, 131072, 262144, 524288\}$[4].

Table 1. Experimental platforms used in the tests.

Platform	Processor	Memory	OS + Compiler
Xeon Phi KNL	Intel Xeon Phi 7250 64-core 1.30 GHz (4 hw threads per core)	16 GB HBW + 192 GB DDR4	Ubuntu 16.04.3 LTS + ICC (v19.0.0.117)
Xeon Platinum CKL	2×Intel Xeon Platinum 8276 28-core 2.20 GHz (2 hw threads per core)	256 GB DDR4	Ubuntu 18.04.3 LTS + ICC (v19.1.0.166)

5.1   Performance Results on the Intel Xeon Phi 7230

The metric GFLOPS (billion floating-point operations per second) was selected as performance metric and is calculated by using the formula $GFLOPS = \frac{20 \times N^2 \times I}{t \times 10^9}$, where N is the number of bodies, I is the number of simulation steps, t is the runtime in seconds, and 20 represents the amount of floating-point operations required for each interaction[5].

Figure 3 shows the performance for the different affinity types when $N = 65536$ and the number of threads varies. It can be observed that enabling multi-threading significantly improves the performance, especially when all hardware threads are active (except with *scatter* affinity). Regarding affinity, it can be seen that it is advisable to select one of the available strategies instead of delegating the distribution to the operating system (*none*). Unlike *scatter*, *balanced* and *compact* guarantee the proximity among OpenMP threads with consecutive

---

[3] The Xeon Phi server was used in All-to-all cluster mode and the MCDRAM memory was set to Flat mode. Because DDR memory modules present different sizes, it was impossible to configure the processor in a different mode.

[4] The number of simulation steps was set to $I = 100$.

[5] A widely accepted convention in the available literature for this problem.

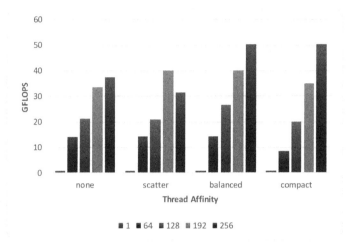

Fig. 3. Performance for the different affinity types when $N = 65536$ and the number of threads varies on the Xeon Phi 7230.

identifiers, minimizing in this way the data communication that each thread requires[6].

As it was mentioned in Sect. 4.3, the compiler detects false dependencies in that loop and it is not able to generate SIMD binary code by itself. Figure 4 presents the performance for the different SIMD sets used varying the number

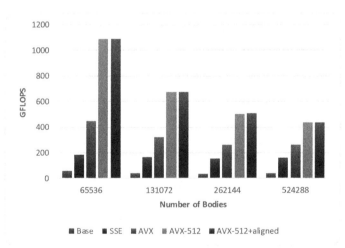

Fig. 4. Performance for the different SIMD sets used when the number of bodies varies on the Xeon Phi 7230.

---

[6] Since all processor cores are in the same package, *balanced* and *compact* produce the same distribution when using all hardware threads.

of bodies. By adding the corresponding *simd* constructs, the compiler generates SSE4.1 instructions, reaching a 3.9× speedup. Re-compiling the code including the `-xAVX2` and `-xMIC-AVX512` flags force the compiler to generate AVX2 and AVX-512 SIMD instructions, respectively. AVX2 extensions accelerated the previous version by a factor of 7.4× while AVX-512 instructions achieved a speedup of 15.1×. Therefore, it is clear that this application benefits from wider vectorial instructions. Additionally, no performance improvement was noted from memory alignment.

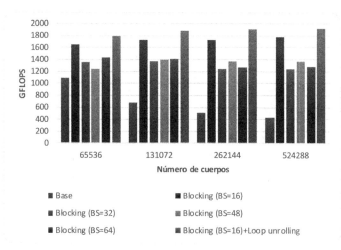

Fig. 5. Performance for the block processing and loop unrolling techniques when the number of bodies varies on the Xeon Phi 7230.

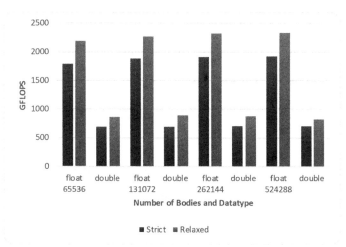

Fig. 6. Performance for precision relaxation when both the dataytpe and the number of bodies varies on the Xeon Phi 7230.

As it can be seen in Fig. 5, the block processing technique significantly improves performance and its benefit enlarges as the number of bodies increases. In particular, this technique yields an average speedup of 2.9× and a peak of 4.1× (BS = 16). Besides, if the loop unrolling is applied, this technique leads to a 9% performance improvement.

Figure 6 presents the performance for precision relaxation when both the datatype and the number of bodies varies. Performance increases 22% when using the compiler optimization to relax precision. On the contrary, performance drops by approximately 60% when doubling numeric precision (double datatype).

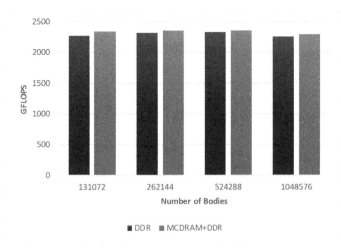

Fig. 7. Performance for MCDRAM exploitation when the number of bodies varies on the Xeon Phi 7230.

Finally, from Fig. 7 it can be seen that the performance remains (almost) constant as the number of bodies increases, obtaining a maximum of 2355 GFLOPS. Also, the MCDRAM exploitation produces a free, small performance improvement (2%). This behavior is similar to the one observed in [10] and is related to the fact that memory latency is more influential than bandwidth in this application[7].

5.2   Performance Results on the Intel Xeon Platinum 8276

As in the previous subsection, the performance metric selected is GFLOPS. Figure 8 shows the performance for the different affinity types used when $N = 65536$ and the number of threads varies. A similar behavior was observed in the

---

[7] The latencies of DDR4 and MCDRAM memories are similar.

Xeon Phi case: multi-threading improves performance and the best results are obtained when all hardware threads are active. However, two small differences can be mentioned. The first one is that the naive implementation reaches higher GFLOPS in this platform. As the Xeon Platinum CKL processor is designed as a general-purpose device, serial codes perform better than in Xeon Phi architecture. The second difference is that thread affinity does not play an influential role in this platform when hyper-threading is enabled.

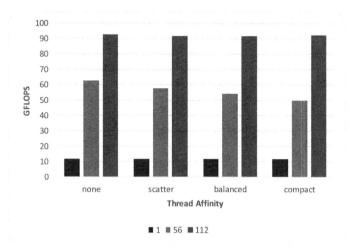

Fig. 8. Performance for the different affinity types used when $N = 65536$ and the number of threads varies on the Xeon Platinum 8276.

Figure 9 presents the performance for the different SIMD sets used when the number of bodies varies. As in the Xeon Phi architecture, higher GFLOPS are obtained when using wider vectorial instructions. Average speedups of $3.7\times$, $7.2\times$ and $10.5\times$ are achieved when using SSE, AVX and AVX-512 instructions, respectively. In addition, memory alignment does not affect performance.

The performance for the block processing and loop unrolling techniques when the number of bodies varies is illustrated in Fig. 10. The blocking version (BS = 16) runs $2.1\times$ faster than the non-blocking one. The improvement factor is smaller than in the Xeon Phi case due to the larger cache subsystem of the CKL microarchitecture. Still, it represents a key factor to improve performance in this implementation. Moreover, 2% of additional GFLOPS are obtained through loop unrolling.

Lastly, Fig. 11 shows the performance for precision relaxation when both the dataytpe and the number of bodies varies. As opposed to the Xeon Phi case, no performance improvement is obtained in relaxed mode. By analyzing the assembly code, it was observed that the compiler generated the same binary

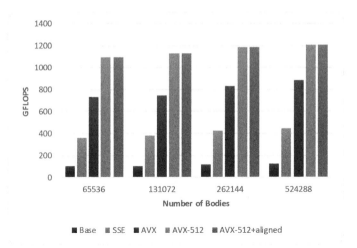

Fig. 9. Performance for the different SIMD sets used when the number of bodies varies on the Xeon Platinum 8276.

code for both versions in this architecture (with or without floating-point optimization). Furthermore, doubling the numerical precision reduces performance by approximately 78%, a larger penalty compared to the Xeon Phi architecture. Considering the increase in the number of bodies, the performance remains (almost) constant, obtaining a peak of 2449 GFLOPS.

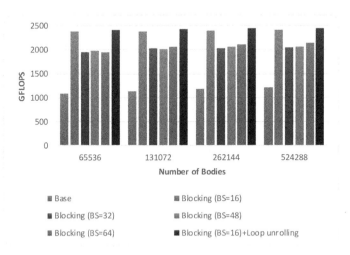

Fig. 10. Performance for the block processing and loop unrolling techniques when the number of bodies varies on the Xeon Platinum 8276.

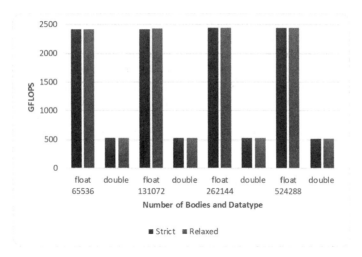

Fig. 11. Performance for precision relaxation when both the dataytpe and the number of bodies varies on the Xeon Platinum 8276.

5.3 Performance and Power Efficiency Comparison Between Platforms

Currently, in the HPC community not only performance matters but also energy efficiency does. Table 2 presents power efficiency ratios considering the GFLOPS peak performance and the Thermal Design Power (TDP) of each platform. Considering the single-precision case (SP), while Xeon Platinum CKL server reaches more GFLOPS than the Xeon Phi platform, the associated high power consumption results in lower GFLOPS/Watt quotient. On the contrary, the Xeon Phi platform becomes the best option in both aspects in the double-precision scenario (DP).

Table 2. Performance and power efficiency comparison between platforms.

Platform	GFLOPS (peak)		TDP (Watt)	GFLOPS/Watt	
	SP	DP		SP	DP
Xeon Phi KNL	2355	883	215	10.95	4.1
Xeon Platinum CKL	2449	532	2×165	7.42	1.61

6   Related Works

The acceleration of the N-body simulation has been widely studied in the literature. However, few works considered the Xeon Phi architecture, using mostly the first generation of this family (KNC) [5,11,12]. Regarding KNL, the work of Vladimirov and Asai [10] can be mentioned, which has some similarities and differences with the present investigation. As in this paper, the authors study the parallelization of the all-pairs version of the simulation. They show how it is possible to improve the performance through different optimizations, although the final implementation reaches a higher peak performance (2875 GFLOPS). Unlike this study, the work prioritizes the optimizations for KNL, simplifying some calculations of the simulation, such as employing a simpler integration scheme (requiring fewer operations) and just computing a single simulation step. By using the same performance metric[8], they overestimate the FLOPS obtained. In relation to the performance analysis, several additional aspects were considered in this paper, such as the number of threads and their affinity, the different SIMD instruction sets, the tuning of the block size, the impact of doubling numerical precision, and the variation in the number of bodies.

With respect to Intel's general-purpose processors based on AVX-512 instructions, to the best of the authors' knowledge, this is the first work studying the all-pairs N-body optimization on these processors.

Finally, from the energy efficiency point of view, Zecena et al. [14] evaluated the performance and energy efficiency of different N-body codes on CPUs and GPUs. In this work, they showed that GPU-based implementations can boost the performance and energy efficiency by orders of magnitude compared to CPUs. No power-performance study considering Intel's architectures based on AVX-512 instructions was found.

7 Conclusions and Future Work

This paper focused on the optimization of the all-pairs N-body simulation on Intel's architectures based on the AVX-512 instruction set. On the basis of a naive implementation, it was shown how the parallel implementation reached, through different optimization techniques, 2355 and 2449 GFLOPS on the Xeon Phi and the Xeon Platinum platforms, respectively. Among the main conclusions of this research, it can be mentioned that:

- In general, a higher number of threads bettered performance. Regarding affinity, significant differences were found among the different options in the Xeon Phi platform, so this is a factor that should not be omitted when running a parallel application.
- Vectorization represented a fundamental factor to improve performance. In that sense, it was possible to achieve almost linear speedups with regard to the number of simultaneous operations of each SIMD set, at a low programming cost.
- The exploitation of the data locality through block processing was another key aspect to obtain high-performance. The impact of this optimization was larger in the Xeon Phi platform due to its smaller cache subsystem.

---

[8] They also assume that 20 floating point operations are performed per interaction but the real number is lower because of the simpler integration scheme (fewer operations are computed).

– Accuracy is usually an important aspect of N-body simulations. Double precision reduces performance to less than the half, so it must be used only when required.
– The MCDRAM memory usage did not provide large performance improvements in this application. However, no source code modification was required to reach it.
– From a power efficiency perspective, the Xeon Phi platform resulted as the best option in both single and double precision computations.

As future work, two possible research lines can be mentioned:

– Implementing advanced methods for this simulation considering the results obtained with all-pairs version.
– Extending the power-performance comparison in order to include GPUs since they are the dominant accelerators today.

References

1. Andrews, G.R.: Foundations of Multithreaded, Parallel, and Distributed Programming. Addison-Wesley, Boston (2000)
2. Codreanu, V., Rodríguez, J., Saastad, O.W.: Best Practice Guide - Knights Landing (2017). http://www.prace-ri.eu/IMG/pdf/Best-Practice-Guide-Knights-Landing.pdf
3. Freddolino, P.L., Harrison, C.B., Liu, Y., Schulten, K.: Challenges in protein-folding simulations. Nat. Phys. **6**(10), 751–758 (2010). https://doi.org/10.1038/nphys1713
4. Goradia, R.: Global illumination for point models. In: Fourth Annual Progress Seminar, 2008 (2008). https://tinyurl.com/y5nqel39
5. Lange, B., Fortin, P.: Parallel dual tree traversal on multi-core and many-core architectures for astrophysical N-body simulations. In: Silva, F., Dutra, I., Santos Costa, V. (eds.) Euro-Par 2014. LNCS, vol. 8632, pp. 716–727. Springer, Cham (2014). https://doi.org/10.1007/978-3-319-09873-9_60
6. Prat, R., Colombet, L., Namyst, R.: Combining task-based parallelism and adaptive mesh refinement techniques in molecular dynamics simulations. In: Proceedings of the 47th International Conference on Parallel Processing. ICPP 2018, Association for Computing Machinery, New York (2018). https://doi.org/10.1145/3225058.3225085
7. Reinders, J., Jeffers, J., Sodani, A.: Intel Xeon Phi Processor High Performance Programming Knights Landing Edition. Morgan Kaufmann Publishers Inc., Boston (2016)
8. Rucci, E., Moreno, E., Camilo, M., Pousa, A., Chichizola, F.: Simulación de N Cuerpos Computacionales sobre Intel Xeon Phi KNL. In: Actas del XXV Congreso Argentino de Ciencias de la Computación (CACIC 2019), pp. 194–204 (2019)
9. Tipler, P.: Physics for Scientists and Engineers: Mechanics, Oscillations and Waves, Thermodynamics. Freeman and Co, New York (2004)
10. Vladimirov, A., Asai, R.: N-body simulation. In: Intel Xeon Phi Processor High Performance Programming Knights Landing Edition. Morgan-Kaufmann, Burlington (2016)

11. Vladimirov, A., Karpusenko, V.: Test-driving intel xeon phi coprocessors with a basic n-body simulation. Technical report, Stanford University and Colfax International, March 2013. https://tinyurl.com/y5vtj34a

12. Yokota, R., Abduljabbar, M.: N-body methods. In: High Performance Parallelism Pearls - Multicore and Many-core Programming Approaches, chap. 10, pp. 175–183, 1 edn. Morgan-Kaufmann (2015)

13. Young, P.: The leapfrog method and other "symplectic" algorithms for integrating newton's laws of motion. Technical report, Physics Department, University of California, USA, April 2014. https://young.physics.ucsc.edu/115/leapfrog.pdf

14. Zecena, I., Burtscher, M., Jin, T., Zong, Z.: Evaluating the performance and energy efficiency of n-body codes on multi-core CPUS and GPUS. In: 2013 IEEE 32nd International Performance Computing and Communications Conference (IPCCC), pp. 1–8, December 2013. https://doi.org/10.1109/PCCC.2013.6742789

Unified Power Modeling Design for Various Raspberry Pi Generations Analyzing Different Statistical Methods

Juan Manuel Paniego[1] , Leandro Libutti[1(✉)] , Martin Pi Puig[1] ,
Franco Chichizola[1] , Laura De Giusti[1,2] , Marcelo Naiouf[1] ,
and Armando De Giusti[1,3]

[1] Computer Science Research Institute LIDI (III-LIDI) (CEA-CIC),
National University of La Plata, 1900 La Plata, Argentina
{jmpaniego,llibutti,mpipuig,francoch,ldgiusti,
mnaiouf,degiusti}@lidi.info.unlp.edu.ar
[2] Scientific Research Agency of the Province of Buenos Aires (CICPBA),
La Plata, Argentina
[3] National Council of Scientific and Technical Research (CONICET),
Buenos Aires, Argentina

Abstract. Monitoring processor power is important to define strategies that allow reducing energy costs in computer systems. Today, processors have a large number of counters that allow monitoring system events such as CPU usage, memory, cache, and so forth. In previous works, it has been shown that parallel application consumption can be predicted through these events, but only for a given SBC board architecture. In this article, we analyze the portability of a power prediction statistical model on a new generation of Raspberry boards. Our experiments focus on the optimizations using different statistical methods so as to systematically reduce the final estimation error in the architectures analyzed. The final models yield an average error between 2.24% and 4.45%, increasing computational cost as the prediction error decreases.

Keywords: Power · Raspberry Pi · Hardware counters · Modeling · Statistical models

1 Introduction

One of the main challenges in system design is the need for fast and accurate energy consumption prediction. In recent years, various innovations have helped meet this requirement.

The underlying idea is that power consumption depends not only on hardware, but also on the use of the software and its internal characteristics. For example, more complex software will require more CPU cycles, or a single huge disk write operation can require less power than multiple small write operations. In general, if a person is aware of how much power they are using, they can find their own suitable solution to save energy when using their device [1, 2].

© Springer Nature Switzerland AG 2020
P. Pesado and M. Arroyo (Eds.): CACIC 2019, CCIS 1184, pp. 53–65, 2020.
https://doi.org/10.1007/978-3-030-48325-8_4

While it is possible to perform hardware measurements on the system to implement fine-grained power control, such instrumentation is expensive and not frequently available.

However, with information about application execution, power consumption can be estimated. These data are collected through hardware counters that can be used to monitor a wide variety of events related to system performance with high precision. Since each event is associated with a certain level of energy consumption, any one of them can be used as a parameter in a performance model. While some events represent activities with little impact on energy, correlation is high in others. Even though the number of counters is usually limited, they can be used to count a wide variety of events.

One way to estimate energy consumption is by generating a statistical model based on these counters. To obtain a real-time prediction, a limited set of events must be selected that describes most of the variation in power.

In [3], a power estimation model was developed using hardware counters which did not contemplate the variation in the number of threads of the parallel application. Similarly, the statistical linear regression model was used, which is intrinsically simple to apply, but may result in greater estimation error. This model was implemented using the Raspberry Pi 3 model B (RPI3B) development board.

In [4], the error obtained using the aforementioned model on the successor board Raspberry Pi 3 model B+ (RPI3B+) is analyzed. Then, to improve predictions, the power model developed for multi-thread applications supported by both boards is optimized.

This work is an extension of [4]; here, different statistical methods are analyzed that allow obtaining better accuracy in the prediction.

The article is organized as follows: Sect. 2 presents an overview of related works in the energy consumption prediction field using different CPU and GPU architectures. Section 3 presents the process for obtaining a statistical model that is compatible with RPI3B and RPI3B+ boards and validates the model generated using linear regression. Section 4 analyzes other statistical methods present in the development tool and compares them to the one discussed in Sect. 3. Finally, in Sect. 5, conclusions and future works are presented.

2 Related Work

This section presents some related previous research works. Lee et al. [5] proposed regression modeling as an efficient approach to accurately predict performance and power for various applications that use any microprocessor configuration considering various microarchitecture designs, addressing cost simulation as a fundamental challenge to obtain correct values in the prediction. With the appearance of hardware counters, Weaver et al. [6] analyzed the values obtained with them to check if there is a good correlation with what was happening inside the processor architecture. From their results indicated that it is reasonable to expect that counters reflect processor behavior. This allowed many researchers to use tools to extract performance values.

Singh et al. [7] developed a model to measure processor power consumption in real time by compiling the information provided by the counters.

On the other hand, Bircher et al. [8–10] explored the use of performance counters to predict the energy consumption of various subsystems such as CPU, memory, chipset, I/O, disk, and GPU. It was developed and validated on two different platforms. Likewise, Rodrigues et al. [11] studied the use of applied performance counters for estimating energy consumption in real time on two different architectures – one oriented to high performance, and the other based on low consumption.

On the other hand, Lively et al. [12] developed a set of hybrid application-centric performance and consumption estimation models. They analyze a set of scientific codes in their MPI/OpenMP implementation, and generate an appropriate procedure to carry out modeling and validation.

Asymmetric core architectures have recently emerged as a promising alternative in an environment with power and thermal limitations. They typically integrate cores with different power and performance characteristics, which makes assigning workloads to the appropriate cores a challenging task. Pricopi et al. [13] presented a model for asymmetric multi-cores in which the performance and power consumption of the workloads assigned to each core can be obtained using the hardware counters.

More recently, with the use of FPGAs, O'Neal et al. [14] developed predictive performance and power consumption models for CPUs, GPUs, and FPGAs, saving simulation costs.

With the appearance of low consumption Single Board Computers (SBCs) boards, the authors of [3] designed a statistical model to predict the energy consumption of applications run on the RPI3B board. However, this model is limited in that it only allows consumption to be predicted for sequential execution and with four cores, added to the disadvantage that different prediction coefficients are used based on the number of threads. This article is an evolution of that previous work, and focuses on developing a model that allows evaluating parallel applications taking into account the variation in the number of cores used. Likewise, the need to build a multi-architecture model that considers the technological changes of new generations of SBC boards is highlighted.

3 Generating a Single Power Model for Various Raspberry Pi Generations

Because this work is based on statistical models, information extracted from applications with different computational behaviors should be used, so as to obtain data related to performance and energy consumption for the analyzed architectures.

In particular, the methodology used in our previous work [3] is applied: use of NAS [15] and RODINIA [16] benchmarks, which have different computational behaviors; instrumentation and parallel applications source code compilation; collection of performance counters and instantaneous power sampling; counter-power correlation and mutual correlation between counters; linear regression model training and model validation through the technique of leaving one out.

Taking into account the model obtained in [3] (which we will call the "Original Model"), the necessary modifications are applied to include the new Raspberry generation, generating a new statistical model that allows reducing the final estimation error; we will call this updated version the "Unified Model".

Since RPI3B and RPI3B+ are compatible SBC boards, the instrumented source code is reused for the different applications.

The model is based on linear regression, a statistical engine that presents a regressand, an offset constant and predictor or independent variables. Based on the architecture used, five independent variables are used, which correspond to the performance counters L2_DCM, L2_DCA, SR_INS, BR_INS and TOT_INS. In addition, the TOT_CYC counter is included in order to normalize previous events, obtaining five performance ratios.

First, the predictions obtained using the Original Model on the new generation of Raspberry boards are studied. All necessary optimizations are then carried out to reduce the error and thus obtain an accurate estimate [4].

3.1 Prediction with the Original Model

The model presents a constant that is added to the normalized values of the five counters, which have an associated weight. Equation 1 shows how to obtain the estimated power for the parallel applications.

$$Y_i = 1.595 + 14.696L2_{DCM} + 2.308L2_{DCA} + 0.108SR_{INS} + 0.093BR_{INS} + 0.058TOT_{INS}$$

$$(1)$$

To estimate the power required by the RPI3B+ board, we started by compiling all applications. Then, we proceeded to record used power and performance counters in each application running with 1, 2 and 4 threads.

Once the information is generated, the values obtained for each parallel application from the six counters used in the model are used to estimate power for the new board.

This prediction has an average percentage error of 30% in the RPI3B+ , as opposed to the 6.8% recorded for RPI3B [3]. This increase in error for the new boards is explained by the architectural difference between generations, since the new version has a higher clock rate.

3.2 Generating the Unified Model

Figure 1 shows the actual power used by the different parallel applications on each board. The increase in power as more threads are used is similar in both architectures. The 23 sequentially run applications (1 thread), found in the first third in the figure, represent the lowest power consumption on both boards. On the other hand, with 2-thread and 4-thread parallel execution (second and third thirds in the figure, respectively) devices are better exploited and, therefore, power consumption is greater.

For the RPI3B board, consumption ranges between 2–3 watts, while for the RPI3B+ model, this range is between 3–4 watts approximately. The first step in finding a unified consumption prediction model for both boards is to study the cause of this difference.

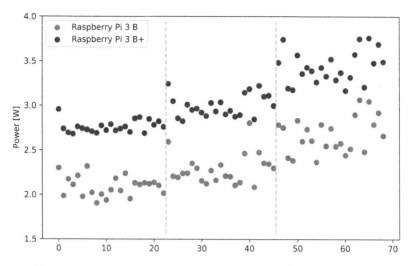

Fig. 1. Actual power for each application, considering number of threads.

First, the values recorded by performance counters feeding the model for each application are analyzed. In this case, the CFD application is chosen as an example; however, the other algorithms show the same behavior in their counters. Figure 2 shows that all events have the same trend in both development boards. Since these boards have several architectural similarities (cache levels and sizes, volatile memory, execution pipeline, etc.), running the same applications yields similar behavior results. Therefore, since there is no variation in performance counter values between the boards, the model cannot be used to differentiate application execution between them.

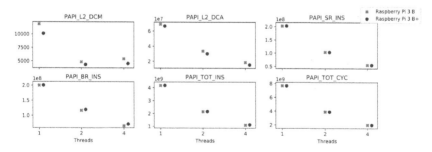

Fig. 2. Performance counter values on each development board considering number of threads running on the CFD application.

Subsequently, the generational changes between the two boards are analyzed to assess their effect on the prediction. The most significant change between both boards is the increase in clock rate from 1.2 GHz to 1.4 GHz. As a result, applications require more power to run, which can cause the increase analyzed in Fig. 1. To verify this, a predictor corresponding to maximum frequency value at runtime is added to the statistical model. This change decreased the error in the estimate, reaching 14% on average.

When training the original model, only the execution of 1- and 4-threaded applications was taken into account, since the goal in [3] was to evaluate the power for sequential and parallel executions with the maximum number of cores available in the processor. Therefore, to consider the impact of the level of parallelization used in the application, a predictor that considers the number of threads (cores) necessary for execution is added, since the applications are developed with the OpenMP shared memory multi-thread programming interface [17].

These optimizations allow estimating used power in both versions of the development board. Thus, the final statistical model based on linear regression (Unified Model) is described in Eq. 2.

$$Y_i = \beta_0 + \beta_1 L2_{DCM} + \beta_2 L2_{DCA} + \beta_3 SR_{INS} + \beta_4 BR_{INS} + \beta_5 TOT_{INS} + \beta_6 THREADS + \beta_7 MAX_{FREQUENCY}$$

$$(2)$$

To build the statistical model, the RapidMiner development tool was replaced by Python. This allows optimizing data cleaning time and the creation process of the prediction model with the inclusion of embedded libraries within the tool. It also provides different statistical models with efficient training. In addition, it allows to easily customize parameters to train each model. Table 1 shows weight β_i values after the model has been trained.

Table 1. Weights obtained for each predictor.

Predictor	Counter	Coefficient	Value
–	INTERCEPT	β_0	−2.656
X_1	L2_DCM	β_1	18.437
X_2	L2_DCA	β_2	4.381
X_3	SR_INS	β_3	0.037
X_4	BR_INS	β_4	−0.032
X_5	TOT_INS	β_5	0.169
X_6	THREADS	β_6	0.221
X_7	MAX_FREQUENCY	β_7	3.546

3.3 Evaluating the Unified Model

After training the model, which results in a set of weights that are applied to the aforementioned predictors, the result is evaluated against the actual power values measured. The predictions obtained for both Raspberry generations can be seen in Fig. 3, together with actual power used. Two types of samples are observed – circles represent the applications run on RPI3B, while triangles correspond to applications run on RPI3B+ .

Finally, prediction errors for each model can be seen in Fig. 4. The X axis lists each application analyzed, the Y axis represents the model used to run the applications, and the Z axis corresponds to the percentage error in the prediction. Model 0 corresponds to the Original Model developed in [3]. In model 1 (Model Opt. 1) clock rate is added as a predictor. As a last improvement, model 2 (Unified Model) adds the independent variable that corresponds to the number of threads that the application uses for its parallel execution.

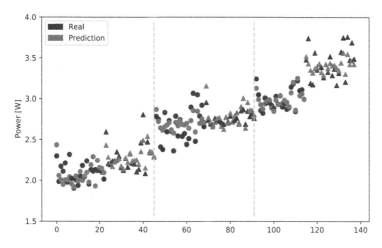

Fig. 3. Used power prediction for both boards.

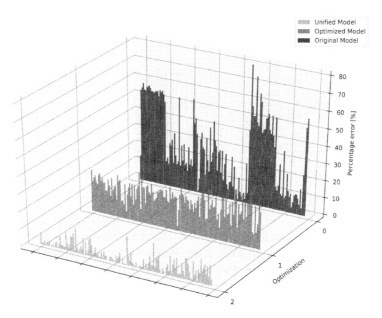

Fig. 4. Application prediction error comparison for the improvements proposed in the statistical model.

In the Unified Model, the average prediction error taking into account all tests carried out is 4.45%, the maximum prediction error is 16.95%, and error dispersion or standard deviation for the sample set is 3.85%.

3.4 Validating the Unified Model

To estimate model accuracy, the leave-one-out cross-validation (LOOCV) technique is used. This evaluation method is better than residual ones. The main problem with residual methods is that they do not generate an indicator of how the model behaves with predictions for applications not included in the training phase.

One possible solution is not using the entire set of applications for training. After obtaining the model, the set of applications that was removed for training is used to make the prediction. This type of evaluation methods is known as cross-validation.

Among the different cross-validation variants, the leave-one-out technique is used in our model, which allows separating the information in such a way that, for each iteration, a single sample is destined for the test data while the remaining set makes up the model's training data. Then, the average of the errors in each iteration is calculated to obtain the final error for the validation.

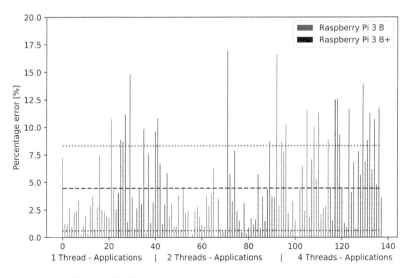

Fig. 5. Prediction error percentage for each application.

Figure 5 shows the error for each iteration with the validation technique used. The maximum prediction error is 18.46%. Error dispersion or standard deviation for the sample set is 4.14%. The average error for all iterations is 4.76%, which is considered acceptable and does not result in great differences between actual and estimated power to run a parallel application.

4 Analysis of Other Statistical Models

In an attempt to minimize the estimation error of the linear regression statistical method, various models from the Python's *Sklearn* library [18] were studied.

4.1 Support Vector Regression (SVR)

This algorithm is a modified version of SVM (Support Vector Machine) used for classification in machine learning. SVM generates a hyperplane that separates data maximizing margin. To create the margin, two lines including all data are defined. Each predictor used generates one dimension, resulting in a hyperplane with D (number of predictors) dimensions. Kernels allow decreasing the number of input dimensions. Finally, Support Vectors refers to all the data enclosed by margin lines [19].

The model generated with this statistical method is evaluated for each application, obtaining the percentage error relative to actual power consumption. Figure 6 shows the application errors for each generation of RPI3 for different number of execution threads (1, 2 and 4 threads). SVR generates an average prediction error of 2.24% and a maximum error of 17.66%.

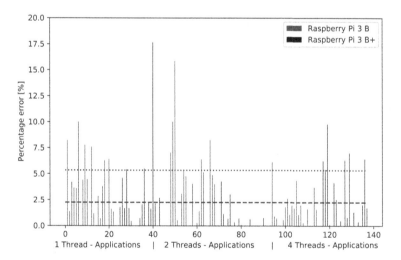

Fig. 6. Prediction error for each application evaluated with the SVR model.

4.2 Gaussian Regression (GR)

The regression of the Gaussian process is not parametric (that is, it is not limited by a functional form) so, instead of calculating the probability distribution of the parameters of a specific function, GPR calculates the probability distribution over all allowable functions that fit the data. GPR has several benefits, including good performance in small data sets and the ability to provide uncertainty measurements on predictions [20]. For this model, the procedure used in the previous method is repeated. Figure 7 shows an average error of 2.58% and a maximum error of 11.21%.

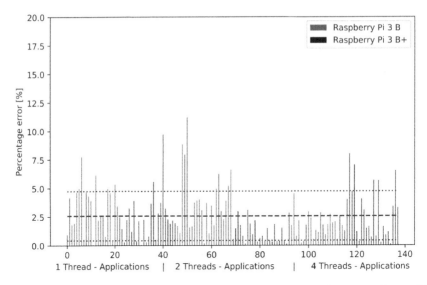

Fig. 7. Prediction error for each application evaluated with the Gaussian Regression model.

4.3 Kernel Ridge Regression (KRR)

Kernel ridge regression is a non-parametric form of *ridge regression* [21, 22]. The aim is to learn a function in the space induced by the respective kernel k by minimizing a squared loss with a squared norm regularization term. The form of the model learned by *KernelRidge* is identical to SVR. However, different loss functions are used: KRR uses squared error loss while support vector regression uses e-insensitive loss.

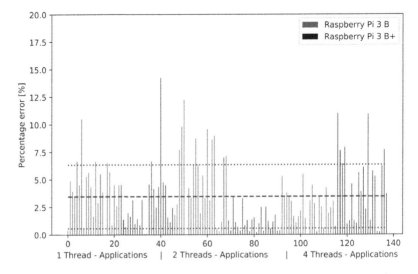

Fig. 8. Prediction error for each application evaluated with the Kernel Ridge Regression model.

Figure 8 shows that the average prediction error is 3.45%, and the maximum error is 12.23%.

4.4 Statistical Models Comparison

After generating the prediction models based on the different statistical methods, each behavior should be analyzed to choose the one with the best performance and the lowest cost at runtime.

Table 2 shows, for each statistical method, prediction average and maximum error, as well as the increase in training time compared to the Linear Regression model.

To achieve a training process with lower execution time but higher error percentage, the Linear Regression method should be used. On the other hand, if a higher prediction accuracy is desired, regardless of how long training takes, then the SVR model is better.

Table 2. Average prediction error for supplementary models.

Model	Mean error [%]	Max error [%]	Increase training time
SVR	2.24	17.66	55.9X
Gaussian Regression	2.58	11.21	1.56X
Kernel Ridge Regression	3.45	14.22	1.25X
Linear Regression	4.45	16.95	1X

5 Conclusions and Future Work

In this article, power consumption prediction for various parallel applications based on readings from performance counters present on the RPI3B and RPI3B+ development boards was discussed.

We considered the possibility of adding to a previously built power model (compatible only with RPI3B), new predictors that allow integrating new board generations, as well as considering the level of parallelism applied to each algorithm.

A statistical power model based on linear regression was designed for multi-thread applications, and it was validated using samples obtained from the analyzed boards. The previously created model was optimized by adding the number of threads used by the application and maximum board frequency as predictors.

Model validation (using LOOCV) yielded an average prediction error of 4.76%, meaning that power consumption was estimated with a high degree of accuracy for both boards.

Different statistical techniques were analyzed in an attempt to reduce the estimation error: SVR, KRR, and GR. These achieved estimation average error reductions between 22.48% and 49.67%, compared to the Linear Regression method, which help achieve significant improvements in the prediction. As a disadvantage, there is an increase in training time as prediction accuracy increases.

Based on the target error margin for the prediction, one of the different models can be chosen:

- Linear Regression is simple and requires less training time. Its disadvantage is that it has a high average prediction error.
- SVR yields the lowest average error, but it is the most expensive method in terms of training time. Additionally, it does not minimize maximum prediction error.
- On the other hand, GR has a low average error (close to that achieved by SVR), but with the advantage that it minimizes maximum prediction error.

As a future line of work, we are planning to apply the methodology developed to the new *Raspberry Pi 4* development board. Similarly, we are planning on implementing a tool that collects all required information in real time, applies the proposed statistical model and generates a report on power consumption for a given parallel application.

References

1. Bekaroo, G., Santokhee, A.: Power consumption of the Raspberry Pi: a comparative analysis. In: 2016 IEEE International Conference on Emerging Technologies and Innovative Business Practices for the Transformation of Societies, EmergiTech, pp. 361–366. IEEE (2016)
2. Procaccianti, G., Ardito, L., Vetro, A., Morisio, M., Eissa, M.: Energy efficiency in the ict-profiling power consumption in desktop computer systems. In: Eissa, M., (ed.) Energy Efficiency-The Innovative Ways for Smart Energy, the Future Towards Modern Utilities/InTech, pp. 353–372 (2012)
3. Paniego, J.M., et al.: Modelado estadístico de potencia usando contadores de rendimiento sobre Raspberry Pi. In: XXIV Congreso Argentino de Ciencias de la Computación. (2018)
4. Paniego, J.M., et al.:Armando De Giusti Modelado de potencia en placas SBC: integración de diferentes generaciones Raspberry Pi. In: Libro de actas XXV Congreso Argentino de Ciencias de la Computación, CACIC 2019, pp. 159–169 (2019). ISBN 978-987-688-377-1
5. Lee, B.C., Brooks, D.M.: Accurate and efficient regression modeling for microarchitectural performance and power prediction. ACM SIGOPS Oper. Syst. Rev. **40**(5), 185–194 (2006)
6. Weaver, V.M., McKee, S.A.: Can hardware performance counters be trusted?. In: 2008 IEEE International Symposium on Workload Characterization, pp. 141–150. IEEE (2008)
7. Singh, K., Bhadauria, M., McKee, S.A.: Real time power estimation and thread scheduling via performance counters. ACM SIGARCH Comput. Archit. News **37**(2), 46–55 (2009)
8. Bircher, W.L., John, L.K.: Complete system power estimation using processor performance events. IEEE Trans. Comput. **61**(4), 563–577 (2011)
9. Bircher, W.L., John, L.K.: Complete system power estimation: a trickle-down approach based on performance events. In: 2007 IEEE International Symposium on Performance Analysis of Systems & Software, pp. 158–168. IEEE (2007)
10. Bircher, W., Law, J., Valluri, M., John, L.K.: Effective use of performance monitoring counters for run-time prediction of power. University of Texas at Austin Technical report TR-041104, 1 (2004)
11. Rodrigues, R., Annamalai, A., Koren, I., Kundu, S.: A study on the use of performance counters to estimate power in microprocessors. IEEE Trans. Circuits Syst. II Express Briefs **60**(12), 882–886 (2013)

12. Lively, C., et al.: Power-aware predictive models of hybrid (MPI/OpenMP) scientific applications on multicore systems. Comput. Sci. Res. Dev. **27**(4), 245–253 (2012)
13. Pricopi, M., Muthukaruppan, T.S., Venkataramani, V., Mitra, T., Vishin, S.: Power-performance modeling on asymmetric multi-cores. In: Proceedings of the 2013 International Conference on Compilers, Architectures and Synthesis for Embedded Systems, p. 15. IEEE Press (2013)
14. O'Neal, K., Brisk, P.: Predictive modeling for CPU, GPU, and FPGA performance and power consumption: a survey. In: 2018 IEEE Computer Society Annual Symposium on VLSI, ISVLSI, pp. 763–768. IEEE (2018)
15. Bailey, D.H., et al.: The NAS parallel benchmarks. Int. J. Supercomput. Appl. **5**, 63–73 (1991)
16. Che, S., et al.: Rodinia: a benchmark suite for heterogeneous computing. In: IEEE International Symposium on Workload Characterization, IISWC, pp. 44–54 (2009)
17. OpenMP. https://www.openmp.org/
18. Scikit-learn. https://scikit-learn.org/stable/
19. Epsilon-Support Vector Regression. https://scikit-learn.org/stable/modules/generated/sklearn.svm.SVR.html
20. Quick Start to Gaussian Process Regression. https://towardsdatascience.com/quick-start-to-gaussian-process-regression-36d838810319
21. Kernel Ridge Regression. https://scikit-learn.org/stable/modules/generated/sklearnkernel_ridge.KernelRidge.html
22. Ridge Regression. https://scikit-learn.org/stable/modules/linear_model.html#ridge-regression

Computer Technology Applied to Education

A Flexible Web Authoring Tool for Building Mobile Learning Experiences

Alejandra B. Lliteras[1,2(✉)] iD, Julián Grigera[1,2,3] iD,
Federico R. Mozzon Corporaal[1] iD, Federico Di Claudio[1] iD,
and Silvia E. Gordillo[1,2] iD

[1] Fac. de Informática, LIFIA, Univ. Nac. La Plata,
Calle 50 &, Av. 120, CP 1900 La Plata, Buenos Aires, Argentina
{lliteras, jgrigera, fmozzon, fdiclaudio,
gordillo}@lifia.info.unlp.edu.ar
[2] CICPBA, Buenos Aires, Argentina
[3] CONICET, Buenos Aires, Argentina

Abstract. This paper presents a flexible web authoring tool called MoLE for teachers to build their own mobile learning experiences. MoLE allows teachers to define learning activities (set of learning tasks within a workflow) that can be accessed from a mobile learning application. Through MoLE, the reuse of learning tasks and learning activities is favored so that a community of teachers can co-create activities and share them. Additionally we present an evaluation of it in order to assess the usability of the tool for users with different backgrounds.

Keywords: Mobile learning · Authoring tool · Mobile learning application · Web tool · Workflow · Human interaction · Learning activity · Learning task · Data collection

1 Introduction

New opportunities are presented in different fields from the mass use of mobile devices. Moreover, these devices have been widely adopted by users from a wide range of ages, and for different activities (entertainment, games, social networks, messaging, etc.). Particularly in education, these devices represent an opportunity for teachers to add them in their educational proposals as another tool to add to the motivation of their students. Within this context teachers are called to act not only as creators of educational materials, but also as creators of mobile-mediated learning experiences for their students [1]. Such creation and adoption can promote a safe and appropriate use of mobile devices in educational contexts and serves to carry out what is known as M-learning [2].

Mobile learning however is more than the use of mobile devices, since it allows, on the one hand, to learn at any time and in any place and on the other, to take advantage of the place where the student is to study about the real world that surrounds him at a given time [1]. The above allows educational experiences to be different according to the objective of the teacher. On the other hand, this type of learning has been analyzed from different perspectives: technological, mobility and proper education [1].

© Springer Nature Switzerland AG 2020
P. Pesado and M. Arroyo (Eds.): CACIC 2019, CCIS 1184, pp. 69–83, 2020.
https://doi.org/10.1007/978-3-030-48325-8_5

Different proposals for the creation of this type of experiences have been presented [3–5], however, in many of them it is necessary for the teacher (creator) to know some technical aspects such as block programming.

In a previous work, we have presented MoLE [6], an authoring tool for designing mobile learning experiences. MoLE is a web authoring tool that allows teachers to design, implement and carry out mobile learning experiences in an intuitive and independent way. These experiences are meant to be used by their students through mobile devices.

In this work, we present a more advanced version of the web authoring tool where visual aspects of the user interface were developed, in particular, for the creation of task sequencing (creation of workflows for human interaction). Additionally, refactoring was carried out in the proposed API code and its standardized documentation was generated. Finally, a first test with end users has been carried out to evaluate aspects of usability of the authoring tool, including the access phase of the activity created using MoLE from a mobile device.

This paper is structured as follows: Sect. 2 presents related works, Sect. 3 the implementation of MoLE, Sect. 4 a Validation of the web authoring tool and finally, Sect. 5 present Conclusions and Futures Works.

2   Related Work

Different approaches for creating mobile applications that can be used in education have been presented in the literature. In this section we analyze some authoring tools for this purpose.

App Inventor [3], allows users to generate their own mobile applications using block programming and allows them to use features such as GPS, camera, storage and other functionalities provided by the mobile devices. Many users of App Inventor cannot exploit all of its functionalities since they are not familiar with programming. As mentioned in [7], users do not use something that is not intuitive.

Vedils [4], is based on App Inventor. This tool incorporates augmented reality and learning analytics features and it maintains most of the features of the App Inventor [3]. In [8] Vedils tool is studied by a case of use where it is presented for teachers to develop their own educational activities, but for this, teachers first had to carry out workshops about programming in blocks assisted by technological experts. In [9] there is another case of use of Vedils tools to support teaching a mathematics course. Again in [10] Vedils tool is used to generate an application, this time is added support for internet of things such as hand gesture sensors or electroencephalography (EEG) headsets, among other features.

The above suggests that Vedils requires its users advanced knowledge or even more knowledge about block programming to design and implement learning activities with mobile devices on their own. Moreover, in the particular case of [9] an extra difficulty is added since whoever uses the authoring tool must have knowledge of the internet of things and of connection with peripherals.

In [11] authors present a proposal to unify the creation of games based on geolocation (given the different amount of methods that exist for this). This article presents, on the one hand, different patterns that occur in this type of application and on the other, an implementation in its own language, called LEGaL, which is based on NCL (Nested Context Language) and XML. The use of LEGaL requires prior knowledge of the languages on which it is based, in addition to the study of the wide range of options available to create the application. Its syntax can be confusing for users unfamiliar with it. In general, because of the above, this tool is not defined for end users.

In [5] authors propose a framework that provides the necessary tools to the developer to implement mobile applications based on outdoor geopositioning. Its focus is on microservices that work with Google Cloud, which makes it essential that the developer has the necessary knowledge about these technologies. Although it is a tool to generate mobile applications, it is not an authoring tool designed for end users and its use is through GPS positioning, which limits its use for indoor spaces.

In [12] authors propose a web tool to generate games for mobile devices that can support virtual reality and geopositioning. Its focus is general purpose games based on missions (for example, touring a physical space looking for the pieces needed to build a bomb). Every time you want to make a new game it is necessary to create a new application without allowing to share missions between games and thus facilitate reuse. Additionally, this means that different games cannot be accessed from the same app.

In the work done in [13] the focus is on educational experiences, being a platform that allows the creation of games based on positioning, mainly oriented to closed spaces. Within the enclosed space, positioning is considered through the use of sensors, QR codes and Bluetooth beacons. The games are based on a narrative that consists of different positioned missions. An example of a mission is for the student to collect "lines of code" on a campus. In a mission, the user receives informative multimedia content or digital elements (for example, a "line of code"). In this work, the user does not generate content as part of the missions, but only receives it.

Another work is described in [14], where a web authoring tool is developed so that mathematics teachers can design learning activities based on positioning, in which students must go through a series of locations on a map, guided by mobile devices. Although no specific programming knowledge is required to design an educational activity with this tool, it is aimed exclusively at the area of mathematics, and the locations on the map are only used to build a route, so the student does not receive specific content in each of them.

The tools discussed above do not yet have the necessary flexibility so that end users without advanced knowledge or programming can design and generate their own mobile educational applications, even more so that they can be used in both indoor and outdoor spaces. As a result, in [6], the authors present a preliminary version of a web authoring tool called MoLE.

3   MoLE Authoring Tool

Based on the need to have a flexible authoring tool that allows the teacher to create mobile learning activities, in [6] we propose a work in progress named "MoLE". MoLE is a web authoring tool that allows teachers without knowledge about mobile development or programming to create their own learning activities to be used mediated by mobile technology.

The construction of mobile learning activities using MoLE follows the stages proposed in [15] (a conceptual framework). This implies that the learning activity is defined in terms of the following aspects: tasks (educational content), the physical space where it will take place, the identification of relevant places within that space (these last two characteristics are optional since sometimes the learning activity means a free movement around a non pre defined space, for example a town), the structuring of the task (linear, sequential or free) and finally indicating in which place of the physical space each component of the chosen structure will be carried out (optional). Defining the activity in this way favors the possibility of reusing the aspects involved [15].

MoLE authoring tool allows creating different types of tasks (learning content):

- **Multiple choice tasks**, where the student who performs the activity must choose the correct option (could be more than one) from a set of options created by the teacher (creator of the task).
- **Open question tasks**, where a text should be written in answer to a question defined by the teacher (creator of the task).
- **Collection tasks**, where students collect real-world objects based on a criterion defined by the teacher (creator of the task).
- **Deposit tasks**, where students drop the elements recollected in the previous tasks (or assigned while the learning activity) in an appropriate deposit.
- **Tasks for multimedia content**, either through capturing images, recording audio or video that respond to a given statement.

In addition to describe above, it is possible to extend the different types of tasks in the future and is contemplated in a simple way in order to provide more flexibility to the teacher when it comes to diagramming the tasks. For example composing different types of tasks among themselves.

The educational content (represented by task) is structured by a workflow. Each step indicates the task and the place (optional) within the physical space where it will be provided (or indicates the order in which tasks should be performed regardless of location). Finally, the teacher (creator) sets the order. For this, they can choose between three workflow structures: Sequential, Free (without pre-established order) or Custom. Figure 1 shows an example of a customized workflow edited from MoLE. In addition, each learning activity created by a teacher can be reused on any mobile device that has installed the educational application for mobile devices.

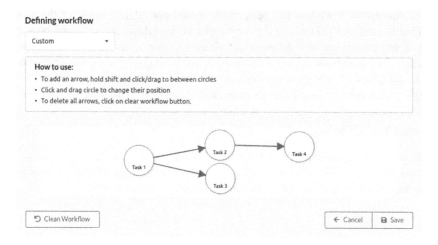

Fig. 1. Workflow creation using MoLE authoring tool.

The type of each task can be single-choice question, multiple choice question, open question, or multimedia tasks (image captures, video or sounds) according to a statement, collection or deposit of pre-established elements as part of the task.

Figure 2 shows how to create a multiple choice task in particular; in the example shown in the above figure all the options are correct.

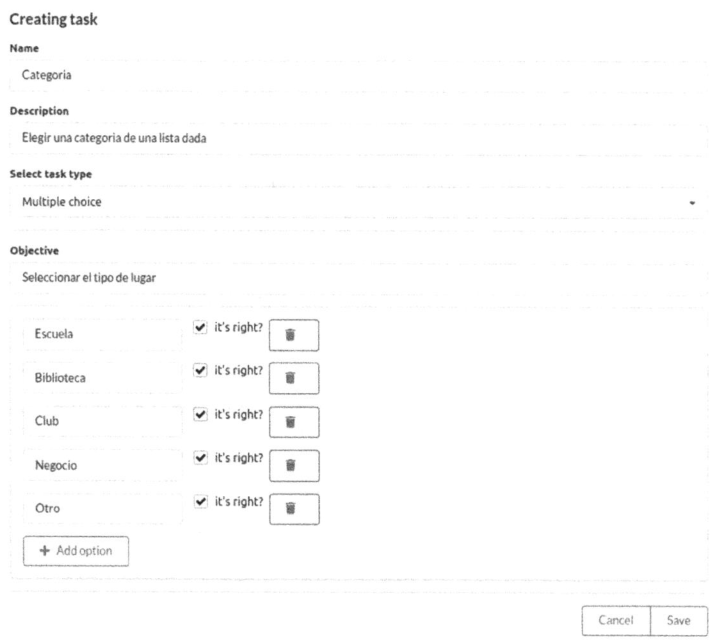

Fig. 2. Multiple choice task

The concept of workflow has been implemented considering some of the aspects described in [16] and [17] where different types of workflows are seen and how each one can be convenient for different activities and for different user experiences. According to the authors, an important aspect when designing a workflow is that the user, in this cases the teachers, get constant feedback of what they are doing.

Figure 2 shows the visual tool to create a customizable workflow.

3.1 MoLE Architecture

MoLE architecture consists of three components that interact with each other: a web authoring tool, a REST API and a mobile learning application. Figure 3 shows the architecture of the implementation. Below is a brief description of each one.

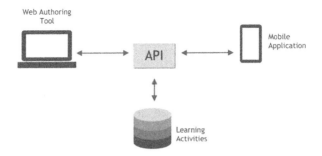

Fig. 3. Architecture of the proposed implementation

3.2 Web Authoring Tool

The web authoring tool guides teachers in the creation of learning activities. Each learning activity can be composed by tasks of different types. Each task can be done in a relevant place in the physical space. The authoring tool guides stages of creation following the conceptual framework proposed in [15] and implements the activities approach presented in [18]. The front-end of this tool was developed using the libraries ReactJS[1] and Redux[2], and for the backend it connects with an API (see Sect. 3.3). The tool's source code is public and can be found in GitHub[3]

Figure 4 shows the home page of the authoring tool. From which it is possible to select the language, download the mobile learning application (see Sect. 3.4), view the learning activities already created and create new learning activities.

---

[1] https://reactjs.org.

[2] https://redux.js.org.

[3] https://github.com/cientopolis/MOLE-Authoring-Tool:AuthoringTool-MoLE-.

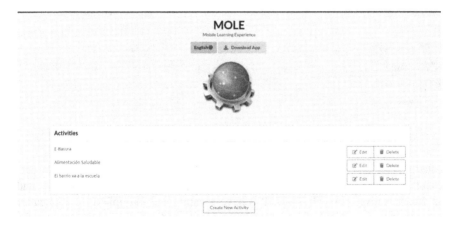

Fig. 4. Mole home page

3.3   REST API

The REST API component provides an interface to a MongoDB[4] database. The API provides methods to save the generated learning activities and then retrieve them and be able to consult information about them. This mechanism offers the possibility of retrieving information from both the web tool (described in Sect. 3.2) and the mobile learning application (described in Sect. 3.4) and if a new type of device is added eventually, do so through these same methods.

The API has been designed and developed following methodological guidelines[5]. This API was implemented using Loopback[6], which uses NodeJS[7] and Express[8] library and respect the standards. It is also public and accessible in GitHub[9].

Part of the REST API documentation[10] generated by Loopback can be visualized in Fig. 5.

3.4   Mobile Learning Application

With the mobile learning application (available also at GitHub[11]), students can download the learning activities (defined with the web authoring tool) from the API described in Sect. 3.3, allowing in one hand to have multiple learning activities in the mobile application and in other hand, to execute each one, independently of each other,

---

[4] https://www.mongodb.com.

[5] https://github.com/argob/estandares/blob/master/estandares-apis.md.

[6] https://loopback.io/.

[7] https://nodejs.org.

[8] https://expressjs.com.

[9] https://github.com/cientopolis/MoLE-API.

[10] https://api-mole.lifia.info.unlp.edu.ar/explorer/#/.

[11] https://github.com/cientopolis/MOLE-mobile-app.

Activity		Show/Hide List Operations Expand Operations
PATCH	/Activities	Patch an existing model instance or insert a new one into the data source.
GET	/Activities	Find all instances of the model matched by filter from the data source.
PUT	/Activities	Replace an existing model instance or insert a new one into the data source.
POST	/Activities	Create a new instance of the model and persist it into the data source.
PATCH	/Activities/{id}	Patch attributes for a model instance and persist it into the data source.

Fig. 5. API REST documentation

repeatedly. This mobile learning application was implemented considering the aspects of usability and the lessons learned introduced in [19]. The development was made using React Native[12], which allowed to have a native and multiplatform application. This application is available for mobile devices with Android version greater than 5.0, or a version of IOs greater than 10.0.

Particularly when a user (student) wants to access an educational activity for the first time from the mobile learning application, they must read a QR code of access that the teacher (creator) gave him. The Fig. 6.a shows the home screen of the mobile learning application ("*Resuelvo Explorando*") that allows the student to read the code of the educational activity created from MoLE. Figure 6.b shows an educational activity, called "*El barrio va a la escuela*" already loaded in the mobile educational application ("*Resuelvo Explorando*") and available to start being used.

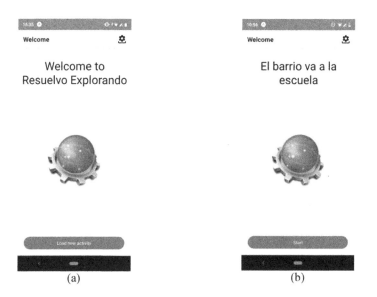

Fig. 6. Mobile learning application interface

---

[12] http://www.reactnative.com.

4   Validation

In order to validate the authoring tool we ran a validation with a group of participants acting as end users. We asked them to use the tool to generate a learning activity with provided information, and then load the activity on the mobile device. We captured different data such as completion rate and times, satisfaction, and direct observations about any issue preventing the participants to complete the assigned tasks efficiently.

The learning experience we selected was based on a document published by "*Dirección General de Cultura y Educación de la Provincia de Buenos Aires, Argentina*" [20], that promotes the use of ITCs as an aspect that cuts through different curricular areas. This way, a set of potential learning sequences are proposed to the teachers for them to adapt and enrich. Considering the former, we took a sequence from this document as a basis for a representative sample learning experience, which consisted in having the students go out and roam the school's neighborhood, taking pictures and writing down observations for different points of interest. This activity had as a goal the creation of a collaborative map of the school's surrounding.

4.1   Participants and Preparation

We recruited a total 18 volunteer participants with different backgrounds (10 female, 8 male, age $\hat{x} = 34.3$, $S = 13,5$. The average time of web use per day was 8,40 h, and average use of mobile devices per day was 6,20 h. None of the participants had previous knowledge about the web authoring tool or the mobile learning application.

Before running the validation, we prepared a desktop computer (mouse & keyboard) with a browser for participants to use the web authoring tool. We preloaded the tool with 2 sample activities to emulate a context where the tool is in being periodically used. The tool was served from a local server, which resulted in an overall fast response.

A mobile device with Android OS 8.0 (Android Oreo) was also provided, with the mobile application already installed. This was the device in which we requested participants to load the learning activity they created. This allowed us to evaluate non-obvious aspects of the final stage of the configuration process.

4.2   Design and Execution

All participants were asked to follow through a series of given steps for the creation of a mobile learning activity, using the web authoring tool. For each session, we measured time spent for each task separately, success rate for both the creation of the learning activity and loading in the mobile device, and overall satisfaction. We also captured demographic data that was informed in the previous subsection.

The detailed set of steps each participant went through was the following:

1. **Read an overall introduction.** This handout briefly explained the full session, and the rationale behind the tool, i.e. what it was intended for, and why.

2. **Use the web authoring tool to create a learning activity.** The activity contents, step by step were provided in a handout. Participants had to make sure they enter the right data in the different fields for each step.
3. **Edit the activity's workflow.** Editing the way that the different steps in the learning activity should be carried is considered as a distinctive part of the creation process. Participants were required to set a sequential workflow for the 4 steps.
4. **Load the activity in the App.** After creating the complete learning activity, the participants had to load it in the mobile application (App) using the provided device. This consisted in using the device's camera to read a QR code generated for the activity within the web authoring tool.
5. **Complete Forms.** Before ending the session, we asked each participant to complete their demographic data and a standard SUS questionnaire-

Appendix A includes the complete text for the provided instructions handout, in original Spanish.

We ran each test with a single participant at a time, using printed instructions and no (or little) additional assistance. Only when participants were noticeably unable to complete a step, we intervened with assistance to help them continue, but in those cases we marked the task as not completed. Besides the total 18 participants, we ran a first trial session with a first volunteer, which we used to adjust some aspects of the protocol, and whose results were discarded.

During each session we recorded all the interaction with the web authoring tool via a screencast capture. This allowed us to measure the completion times and success with precision after having run the tests.

4.3   Results

The completion times per task are listed in Table 1, along with the completion percentages. The completion time for the full activity was between 6:31 and 15:01 ($\tilde{x} = 10:31$ S = 0.11). This time was shared between the learning activity creation (10.84% of the total time in average), the creation of the 4 steps (61.91% in average), the adjustment of the workflow (9.42%), and the loading & selection of the learning activity within the mobile app (17.81%). The complete breakdown is shown in the table.

Regarding the completion percentages, all tasks were completed by 100% of the participants, except for 3, namely: creation of step 4, workflow edition and the activity selection within the mobile app. In the case of the former 2, i.e. the creation of step 4 of the activity and the workflow edition, only one of the participants wasn't able to finish (a different participant on each task). It's worth noting that in both cases the participants were able to continue, as these tasks were not required for the following ones. In the case of the activity selection, which was the last task, 2 participants were unable to finish it. Percentages different than 100% in the table actually reflect these 3 cases.

Table 1. Validation results

# Task	Task description	Time (mean)	SD (seconds)	AVG % of full activity
1	Activity creation	1:08	26,89	10,84%
2	Activity step 1	1:08	36,91	16,53%
3	Activity step 2	2:13	44,17	21,11%
4	Activity step 3	1:23	27,37	13,29%
5	Activity step 4	1:09	33,26	10,98%
6	Workflow edition	0:59	33,92	9,43%
7	Activity loading	0:41	23,72	6,62%
8	Activity selection	1:10	68,60	11,20%
	Total	10:31	172,80	100,00%

With respect to the satisfaction level using the authoring tool, we obtained the scores for the standard SUS questionnaires, which range between 0 and 100. The average for all 18 participants was 82.5 (S = 18.51)

4.4   Discussion

The validation's main objective was to assess the degree to which end users are able to create learning activities using the proposed web authoring tool. In this regard, the results are positive, since only 4 times users were unable to complete a given step of the full activity creation. Being 18 participants following through 8 tasks each, this represents a 97.22% effectiveness for the overall tasks set, or a 83.3% of users with perfect effectiveness score (i.e. who completed all tasks). Even if participants had mixed backgrounds and not necessarily representative of the expected audience, this is not considered as an critical bias in early tests, given that users with different profiles usually encounter similar usability problems [21].

Even if there is no reference for comparing completion times, we believe the results in this aspect were also positive in the sense that most users were able to complete a given set of tasks in a web application unknown to them with very little hesitation time in most cases, even more considering that most of the time was spent in typing the descriptions for the given activities. In fact, after the first trial run, we shortened the original texts so we could spend more time evaluating the web application's interaction.

Satisfaction scores were high, all above 70, except for one outlier of 17.5. This could mean that participants didn't consider the tool to be exceptionally worse than the applications they're used to operate with, usually more mature than the evaluated prototype.

Another useful outcome of the validation was the detection of different issues, either with interaction or conceptual. The main conceptual issue we found was the use of terminology: not all participants had a clear idea of what the different fields meant (e.g. *description* vs. *assignment*), especially the meaning of *workflow* which some participants knew beforehand, but others had to make out from the context, or ask the facilitators. Interaction also presented issues in aspects like navigation, especially in the short task on the mobile device - it was not clear for all participants how to tell whether the activity had been correctly loaded.

5 Conclusions and Future Work

This article presented a web authoring tool for the construction of mobile learning experiences that optionally consider the position of the student to provide tasks consistent with it. This work includes access to the code repositories of each of the components of the proposed architecture, and presents a preliminary evaluation of the web authoring tool from the perspective of the teacher (creator) which carries out a particular case study used for the evaluation of the tool.

The evaluation we ran showed that end users were able to create a complete learning activity using the web authoring tool, with 83.3% of them having perfect completion, and the remaining only finding 1 or 2 problems that didn't prevent them to reach the end of the test. Completion times were satisfactory since there we found little idle times during the evaluations. Having established a baseline, these times can now be improved in future iteration. We also found interaction problems that need to be addressed, but they are not critical to the success of the main purpose of the tool that is enabling end users to create mobile learning activities by themselves.

As future work we plan to improve the development of the authoring tool presented considering the present evaluation and to propose new evaluations by end users, considering aspects of learnability and usability of both the authoring tool and the resulting mobile learning application. We also plan to work in the management of a community of teachers (creators) who use this tool to design their own learning activities, in order to get real feedback regarding the tool's functionality and usefulness. Another proposal consists in using the modeling approach that implements our tool and the lessons learned to perform activities that involve data or samples collection (e.g. images, audio, video, guided observations) to be used in Citizen Science projects.

Appendix

In this appendix we show the original instructions handout (original Spanish).

Prueba de la herramienta MoLE

¡Gracias por participar!

Queremos crear una actividad educativa para alumnos de nivel primario, en la que se utilizan dispositivos móviles. En esta actividad se le propone a los alumnos salir a recorrer el barrio de su escuela, tomando fotos y realizando ciertas anotaciones.

Tenemos una herramienta web para crear este tipo de actividades, necesitamos que la utilices para crear una actividad ya planificada que te mostraremos a continuación.

1. **Ingresar a la herramienta web: <url>**
2. **Crear la actividad con la siguiente información:**

Título: El barrio de la escuela
Descripción: Desarrollar producciones utilizando recursos TI.

3. **Crear las tareas de la actividad**

   3.1. Crear la primera tarea, que consiste en tomar una foto con la siguiente información:

   Nombre: Foto
   Descripción: Tomar una foto del frente de una lugar que le resulta de su interés
   Tipo de Tarea: Tarea multimedia
   Una vez creada, completar con la siguiente información:
   Consigna: Tomar una foto del lugar que considere de interés
   Tipo de contenido: Foto

3.2. Crear la segunda tarea, que es una tarea de clasificación, con la siguiente información:

   Nombre: Categoría
   Descripción: Elegir una categoría de una lista dada
   Tipo de Tarea: Opción Múltiple
   Una vez creada, completar con la siguiente información. Al momento de crearla es necesario tildar, una por una, para indicar que cada opción es correcta.:
   Consigna: Seleccionar el tipo de lugar

- Escuela
- Biblioteca
- Club
- Negocio
- OTRO

   3.3. Crear la tercera tarea, que consiste en una pregunta de respuesta libre, con la siguiente información:

   Nombre: Opinión
   Descripción: Indicar el motivo por el cual considera de interés el lugar
   Tipo de Tarea: Respuesta libre
   Una vez creada, completar con la siguiente información:
   Consigna: Contanos por qué te resulta de interés este lugar
   Respuesta esperada: Me gusta visitarlo.

3.4. Crear la última tarea, que consiste en una pregunta de respuesta libre, con la siguiente información:

   Nombre: Datos generales
   Descripción: Cargar datos del lugar de interés
   Tipo de Tarea: Respuesta libre
   Una vez creada, completar con la siguiente información:
   Consigna: Contanos a qué se dedica el lugar
   Respuesta esperada: *<en blanco>*

4. **Organizar el workflow.** Editar la actividad para definir la secuencia en la que el alumno deberá realizar las tareas. Organizar el workflow de manera secuencial para que las tareas se sigan en orden, de la 1ra a la 4ta. Guardar.
5. **Cargar la actividad en la aplicación móvil.** Tomar el dispositivo móvil provisto y cargar la actividad recién creada.

References

1. Pegrum, M.: The what and why of mobile learning design. Mobile Lenses on Learning, pp. 45–96. Springer, Singapore (2019). https://doi.org/10.1007/978-981-15-1240-7_2
2. Sharples, M., Arnedillo-Sánchez, I., Milrad, M., Vavoula, G.: Mobile learning. In: Balacheff, N., Ludvigsen, S., de Jong, T., Lazonder, A., Barnes, S. (eds.) Technology-Enhanced Learning, pp. 233–249. Springer, Dordrecht (2009). https://doi.org/10.1007/978-1-4020-9827-7_14
3. App Inventor. http://appinventor.mit.edu
4. Vedils. http://vedils.uca.es
5. Forte, J.L.B., Gázquez, D.P., Arango-López, J., Vela, F.L.G., Moreira, F.: Geolympus - cloud platform for supporting location-based applications: a pervasive game experience. In: Rocha, Á., Adeli, H., Reis, L.P., Costanzo, S. (eds.) WorldCIST'19 2019. AISC, vol. 932, pp. 256–266. Springer, Cham (2019). https://doi.org/10.1007/978-3-030-16187-3_25
6. Dal Bianco, P.A., Mozzon Corporaal., F.R., Lliteras, A.B., Grigera, J., Gordillo, S.E.: MoLE: a web authoring tool for building mobile learning experiences. In: XXV Congreso Argentino de Ciencias de la Computación, pp. 325–334 (2019). ISBN 978-987-688-377-1
7. Xie, B., Shabir, I., Abelson, H.: Measuring the usability and capability of App inventor to create mobile Applications. In: 3rd International Workshop on Programming for Mobile and Touch (PROMOTO 2015), pp. 1–8. ACM, New York (2015). http://dx.doi.org/10.1145/2824823.2824824
8. Augmented reality mobile app development for all: Mota., J.M., Ruiz-Rube, J., Dodero, J.M., Arnedillo-Sánchez. J. Comput. Electr. Eng. **65**, 250–260 (2018). https://doi.org/10.1016/j.compeleceng.2017.08.025
9. Person, T., et al.: Authoring of educational mobile apps for the mathematics-learning analysis. In: García-Peñalvo, F.J. (ed.) Sixth International Conference on Technological Ecosystems for Enhancing Multiculturality (TEEM 2018), pp. 299–305. ACM, New York (2018). https://doi.org/10.1145/3284179.3284234
10. Ruiz-Rube, I., Mota, J.M., Person, T., Corral, J.M.R., Dodero, J.M.: Block-based development of mobile learning experiences for the Internet of Things. Sensors **19**(24), 5467 (2019). https://doi.org/10.3390/s19245467
11. Ferreira, C., Maia, L. F., Salles, C., Trinta, F., Viana, W.: A model-based approach for designing location-based games. In 2017 16th Brazilian Symposium on Computer Games and Digital Entertainment (SBGames), pp. 29–38. IEEE, November 2017. https://doi.org/10.1109/sbgames.2017.00012
12. Maia, L.F., Nolêto, C., Lima, M., Ferreira, C., Marinho, C., Viana, W., Trinta, F.: LAGARTO: A LocAtion based Games AuthoRing TOol enhanced with augmented reality features. Entertain. Comput. **22**, 3–13 (2017). https://doi.org/10.1016/j.entcom.2017.05.001

13. Arango-López, J., Valdivieso, C.C.C., Collazos, C.A., Vela, F.L.G., Moreira, F.: CREANDO: tool for creating pervasive games to increase the learning motivation in higher education students. Telematics Inform. **38**, 62–73 (2019). https://doi.org/10.1016/j.tele.2018.08.005

14. Sollervall, H., Gil de la Iglesia, D., Zbick, J.: Supporting teachers' orchestration of mobile learning activities. In: Calder, N., Larkin, K., Sinclair, N. (eds.) Using Mobile Technologies in the Teaching and Learning of Mathematics. MEDE, vol. 12, pp. 91–111. Springer, Cham (2018). https://doi.org/10.1007/978-3-319-90179-4_6

15. Lliteras, A.B., Challiol, C., Gordillo, S.E.: Location-based mobile learning applications: a conceptual framework for co-design. In: Twelfth Latin American Conference on Learning Technologies (LACLO), La Plata, pp. 1–8. (2017) https://doi.org/10.1109/laclo.2017.8120946

16. Sprinks, J., Wardlaw, J., Houghton, R., Bamford, S., Morley, J.: Task Workflow Design and its impact on performance and volunteers' subjective preference in Virtual Citizen Science. Int. J. Hum Comput Stud. **104**, 50–63 (2017). https://doi.org/10.1016/j.ijhcs.2017.03.003

17. Crowston, K., Kitchell, E.M., Østerlund, C.: Coordinating advanced crowd work: extending citizen science. In: 51st Hawaii International Conference on System Sciences, vol. 4, no. 1, pp. 1681–1690 (2018). https://doi.org/10.24251/hicss.2018.212

18. Lliteras, A.B., Gordillo, S.E., Dal Bianco, P.A., Corporaal, F.R.M.: A customizable location-based Mobile Learning Prototype: a case of study. In: 2018 XIII Latin American Conference on Learning Technologies (LACLO), pp. 149–156. IEEE, October 2018. https://doi.org/10.1109/laclo.2018.00040

19. Lliteras, A.B., Grigera, J., dal Bianco, P.A., Corporaal, F.M., Gordillo, S.E.: Challenges in the design of a customized location-based mobile learning application. In: 2018 XIII Latin American Conference on Learning Technologies (LACLO), pp. 315–321. IEEE, October 2018. https://doi.org/10.1109/laclo.2018.00062

20. Secuencias Didácticas para primer ciclo. Planificar con TIC. Material complementario 2. Dirección General de Cultura y Educación, Subsecretaría de Educación, Dirección de Educación Primaria, Dirección de Formación Continua. Provincia de Buenos Aires, Argentina (2018)

21. Why You Only Need to Test with 5 Users. https://www.nngroup.com/articles/why-you-only-need-to-test-with-5-users/. Accessed 9 Mar 2020

Training Job Interview Online Simulator for Hearing-Impaired People

Nelba Quintana[1] (iD), Alcira Vallejo[2] (iD),
Alejandro Héctor González[3(✉)] (iD), and José María Pereyra[3] (iD)

[1] Facultad de Humanidades y Cs. de la Educación de la Universidad
Nacional de la Plata, La Plata, Argentina
[2] Comisión de Investigaciones Científicas, Pcia. Buenos Aires, Argentina
[3] Instituto de Investigación en Informática III-LIDI, Facultad de Informática
de la Universidad Nacional de la Plata, La Plata, Argentina
agonzalez@lidi.info.unlp.edu.ar

Abstract. This article describes an online training course for adult hearing-impaired individuals who use hearing aids or cochlear implants. This training course developed in HTML5 and JavaScript consists of a set of training activities to be solved online. The originality of this development is the recreation of a virtual scenario where a hearing-impaired person faces a job interview situation. This simulation strategy with multimedia features is based on a series of videos that recreate an office scenario where an interviewer asks questions that the interviewee must answer by choosing one of the options presented after every interviewer's question. The simulator prototype and the other activities make up a website developed in HTML5 and the PHP programming language. The user requires identification to have access to the site which has the ability to store in a MySQL relational base, the data of each registered person including the educational activities that he is carrying out each time he enters the training. The design of the proposal includes a pilot experience for the evaluation of the tool by a group of users by means of online surveys and personal interviews. According to the results, the optimization of the tool is foreseen for its subsequent implementation.

Keywords: Hearing impaired · Educational simulators · Technology applied in education

1 Introduction

1.1 Hearing-Impaired People and Their Limitations

One of the ways in which the existence of limitations for the full development of disabled people can be addressed is the approach to learning and participation barriers, based on the social model of disability, which states that the limitations or restrictions disabled people face are mainly social [1].

In the case of people with hearing impairment, communication and discrimination were identified as the two major obstacles for their development, their independent

P. Pesado and M. Arroyo (Eds.): CACIC 2019, CCIS 1184, pp. 84–95, 2020.
https://doi.org/10.1007/978-3-030-48325-8_6

evolution and their active participation in the construction of their rights and satisfaction of their needs.

A person with severe hearing loss faces significant consequences on his general development and thus his educational and work alternatives can be limited.

Current technology can provide a variety of appropriate tools to diminish the social environment and communication limitations people with hearing disabilities usually face. These information and communication technologies (ICT) already have been used as tools for educational purposes in general, whereas multimedia has been used for dynamic interaction, simulation and communication processes for special educational needs [2].

1.2 New and Advanced Hearing Aid Technology

Hearing aid technology has improved considerably in the past decades providing efficient therapeutic benefits to people with severe or profound hearing impairment (deafness). Technological development thus contributed to the creation of various devices, systems and resources to help communicative interaction in difficult listening situations.

In the case of hearing-impaired individuals, there are already technological instruments that are being constantly developed to optimize the quality of life of people with hearing loss, providing them better accessibility and, therefore, enhancing their personal autonomy. This is the case of hearing aids and cochlear implants (CI). These devices allow people with hearing impairment to understand the oral information they receive from their environment more accurately.

On the one hand, modern hearing aids based on digital technology can be adapted to individuals quite precisely and effectively. These devices have a processor which allows speech therapists to program their sound software very precisely and adjust it to the characteristics of the individual's hearing loss. This fact makes the performance of modern hearing aids significantly superior to the previous analog headphones.

During the past 30 years, the cochlear implant has become the routine treatment for severe to profound hearing loss. The cochlear implant consists of a prosthesis that transforms acoustic signals into electrical ones. A cochlear implant consists of an external part, generally worn behind the ear, and an internal one. The latter is introduced into the cochlea by surgical intervention. In this way the acoustic sound waves captured by the external part of the device reach the internal part through the receiver. These acoustic sound waves are then transformed into electrical signals which are passed on to the brain through the auditory nerve [3].

Another instrument that begins to be used is the Modulated Frequency system, which consists of an accessory used by people either with hearing aids or cochlear implants to improve their oral understanding of speech-in-noise (SIN) such as in classes, meetings or conferences. This device consists of a microphone that is located close to the sound source and that transmits the signal to a receiver that is placed in the hearing aid or implant, thus making oral messages sound and clear.

1.3   Technology as Basis of the Educational Project

The project presented in this work was developed with a multidisciplinary approach, with the intervention of specialists in virtual education, a computer programmer, a graphic designer, and the central idea and fundamental participation of a teacher with a typology of postlocutive hearing loss.

The high visual character of the project, accompanied by written text, confirms that computer technology is capable of providing highly effective tools for the design of educational strategies for hearing impaired people.

The use of technology to increase, maintain or improve the functional capacities of these individuals has become an essential resource, which includes training and training actions, such as those described in this paper.

This research and development project were proposed as the basis for a Master's Thesis in Applied Information Technology in Education of the Faculty of Informatics of the National University of La Plata. The proposal is intended for the training of hearing-impaired adults who use hearing aids, assuming that the majority of educational proposals are intended for children, so that hearing-impaired adults are a rarely considered age group in learning situations.

The training is aimed at supporting the insertion of these individuals in working life, for which an admission interview situation is reproduced, using a simulator based on video sequences articulated with JavaScript, included in a website specifically developed in HTML5, which also provides content with text and multimedia format, as well as the proposal of interactive activities prior to the use of the simulator itself.

This article enlarges with greater precision the description previously made in the work presented in October, 2019 at the XXV Argentine Congress of Computer Science (CACIC 2019) [4]. The conceptual framework of multimedia learning, the detail of the simulator structure and the planning of the training evaluation stage as a whole are depicted here.

Although these instruments reduce the communication barriers suffered by the hearing impaired people, the limiting factor is their availability, due to their high costs and the small number of countries in which they are manufactured.

2   Conceptual Approaches

2.1   The Emotional Influence on the Learning of Hearing-Impaired Individuals

Unlike other types of disabilities, such as visual or motor impairment, hearing loss is not noticed at first sight by a normal hearing person. A priori ignorance of the situation of the hearing impaired obliges him to permanently report his hearing loss situation. This reiteration of their limiting condition negatively affects their emotional state and their self-esteem, so it eventually causes their social isolation. It is important, then, to use different means to facilitate their incorporation into their socio-cultural environment, in which orality predominates. In this sense, we understand that education and training are fundamental factors to achieve this goal. The educational proposal that we develop through a simulation strategy seeks to provide the apprentice with a previous experience, which by its own emulation characteristic of a real situation trains the individual not only to choose suitable answers, but also confronts them with a situation which involves the management of emotional skills, in order to facilitate their subsequent performance and improve their autonomy in a situation of an admission job interview in real life.

2.2 Design as a Contribution to Communication

Communication design acquires a fundamental cognitive role in learning and knowledge; which is increasing along with nowadays technological development. The presentation of knowledge and communication fundamentally need the intervention of the design to be mediated by an interface that can be perceived and assimilated [5]. For an effective communication, the design must consider elements of different hierarchy based on a defined structure, taking into account the sensory management, that is, the appropriate choice of stimuli which will guide users keeping their attention, thus reducing the complexity of knowledge and contributing to clarity and understanding.

The way in which information is structured in digital media determines the user interaction. This can take for example a non-linear form, such as hypertext or have an interlaced structure where the user can choose how to move within a network of semantic nodes [6].

Current multichannel media require high competence to successfully manage the most appropriate way to present information to the user: sound, music, voice, typography, images, movies, movement. The cognitive load, defined as the demand for information processing that each task implies, varies according to the contents or activities of a multimedia educational material. As the information processing capacity of individuals is limited, the challenge to design these materials is to avoid the demand on information processing or cognitive load. According to Mayer [7], to achieve this we can:

- Reduce the superficial processing of information caused by design errors which does not contribute to the appropriation of information.
- Optimize the essential processing of information, required to organize and represent it in working memory.
- Promote the generative processing of information, aimed at understanding information and relating it to previous knowledge.

According to Mayer, cognitive theories argue that the process of acquiring knowledge taught through intentional instruction begins in sensory memory. There, the stimuli of the environment are perceived, and the learning process begins. In a second moment, working memory, through the attention process, selects some stimuli and processes them to construct cognitive schemes, which vary in degree of complexity, based on their integration with knowledge recovered from long-term memory and returns to be stored in this latter memory.

Sensory memory uses an independent channel to capture the stimuli that each sense perceives, that is, the sounds perceived by the ear are received in the auditory or echoic channel, while the graphics and texts that visualize the view, in the visual channel. Like sensory memory, working memory also includes two channels: one for processing visual information and one for auditory.

Due to the complexity of the steps in the processing of a multimedia message, an adequate analysis is necessary to design effective messages. This complexity, which is present in normal hearing individuals, is accentuated in hearing impaired individuals, who may have deficiencies in auditory sensory memory and working memory, attention and processing speed [8].

From a more general point of view, it is essential to consider the most frequent possible accessibility barriers in the design. The development phase involves the written text, the video material, the web pages and multimedia resources. It also includes the student's activities and the evaluation instance. Due to the diversity of tasks, this phase is more likely to unintentionally introduce accessibility obstacles, mainly in web development [9].

To avoid these barriers, at least the following recommendations should be considered for all content and activities: 1. Transcription of texts for audios or podcasts. 2. Subtitling of videos with sound content. 3. The use of written language appropriate to the competencies of the recipients. These recommendations are limited to materials intended for individuals with postlocutive hearing loss, who can interpret written language. In materials intended for hearing impaired people who do not access this language, translation into sign language should be considered, although this option exceeds the scope of this work.

2.3 Simulators as a Pedagogical Strategy

The use of simulation for training purposes began in the field of military training several decades ago. It was then disseminated to other disciplines, mainly in the economic sciences and is currently a fundamental strategy in the teaching of medicine, engineering and other areas of knowledge. At present, modern and sophisticated simulators, many of them based on artificial intelligence, which can reproduce real scenarios, have been developed [10].

In the present article we will refer to the process in which a model is created to replace real situations with artificially created ones, but where the model reproduces the appearance, structure and dynamics of the system [11]. The simulation consists of a simplified and artificial experimental environment, but with enough plausibility to provoke authentic reactions on the participants, since the aim is to instruct them about some real-world situations. The basic idea is to create experiential situations which participants can then transfer to real life.

One of the classic educational theories that sustains the use of simulators is the concept "learning by doing" developed by Dewey [12], which is now widely naturalized in the educational fields. By generating a direct link between theory and practice, new knowledge can be applied and obtained from discovery, as well as the validity of theoretical concepts. For this purpose, the student must have a direct experience generated by an authentic problem that motivates their interest, thus being able to build the necessary knowledge to solve it [13]. The problem to be solved should resemble "real" problems, regardless of the "academic" type of problems, without direct connection with real life. This approach to learning by doing leads students to be personally involved with a problem that is significant to them.

Within this framework, current simulators developed based on technology are fundamental in the construction of meaningful knowledge; that is, they can be the solution to the decontextualization of learning.

From the emergence of the concept of situated learning, Brown, J. and his collaborators suggest that educational activities and the acquisition of concepts must take place in the environments in which learning takes place. The construction of knowledge is generated dynamically, through interaction with the situation. The authors declare that "knowledge is located, being partly a product of the activity, context and culture in which it is developed and used" [14].

Simulators can represent an alternative that resembles the context of reality, promoting situated learning, if they present to the learner an environment credible enough to resemble a real system.

Another theoretical support for the use of simulators in learning is the constructivist learning environment model stated by Jonassen [15], which emphasizes the involvement and commitment of the learner in the construction of his own knowledge. When considering a problem through a simulation, there are three components of Jonassen's model that are present: the context of the problem, the simulation itself and a manipulation space that allows the learner to appropriate the problem and interact with it. This interaction allows the learner to influence and modify the environment, thus achieving significant learning [16].

In the educational proposal, the simulator, the teaching materials and the proposed activities must be designed in such a way that they allow the apprentice experience a learning process through the anchoring of new knowledge in those already available: that is, he can use his preexisting knowledge as an ideational and organizational matrix that will facilitate the incorporation, understanding, retention and organization of new ideas.

3   Educational Proposal

3.1   Recipients

This proposal under development is primarily intended for people with different degrees of hearing loss who use hearing devices (hearing aids or cochlear implants), who have secondary or tertiary level of education and aspire to obtain a job.

3.2   Aims

It was determined as a general aim to guide and prepare the target individuals of the proposal to successfully resolve the instances of a possible job interview. Specific objectives are to familiarize the student with the use of a simulator as a learning resource, develop experience in decision-making that promotes successful responses in a job interview and train him to acquire effective communication techniques.

3.3   Design and Characteristics of Materials and Activities

The training proposal consists of several instances, which are presented to the apprentice through the website developed for this purpose. The first action required is enrollment, where the apprentice must complete minimum personal data that allows identification, which will be necessary in individual activities and assessments. The teaching materials are presented in text, images and video format, as learning instances of different aspects related to the skills necessary to face the interview situation, represented in the last instance by means of the multimedia simulator.

The resources in text format were included because they are considered essential to train people with hearing loss [17]. Since people with hearing loss develop predominantly visual memory [18], materials based on images, infographics, presentations and subtitled videos were included.

Formative evaluations were prepared on the different contents. These evaluations are presented in a multiple-choice question type with automatic and immediate qualification, including a specific feedback on each item. The training includes collaborative activities in the form of group tasks, to promote interaction and communication between participants.

The simulator prototype has included the recreation of scenarios and the interaction with them, considering different behavior patterns, also stimulating the development of competences linked to the teaching and learning process [19, 20].

The cognitive functions that this simulator aims to stimulate are:

Attention and concentration, which facilitates the understanding of oral language.
Memory, to remember appropriate attitudes and language for an interview
Executive, to plan activities
Language, for more effective communication.
Perception and recognition or emotional intelligence, understood as the cognitive ability of a person to understand the emotional universe of another. The orientation in this sense is considered necessary due to the fact that the emotional experience of hearing impaired people can affect or distort the identification of emotions that are perceived in others.

3.4   Technical Development

The educational resource is presented as a website developed in HTML5 and the PHP programming language.

For the design, the Materialize framework, based on Material Design was used on the client side. Materialize has a grid system that generates a responsive design, adaptable to different formats and devices.

During development, we chose to follow the MVC architecture pattern (Model-View-Controller) together with the Twig template engine to improve the maintenance and scalability of the software.

Among its features, Twig allows to define the framework of a site, making all pages fit to it. With this engine the content of the structure has become independent, as well as able to eliminate repetitive code.

The site works with a MySQL relational database, managed through the PhpMyAdmin tool to store the required information to each user in the access instance, as well as the educational activities that it is carrying out.

The interactions with the user are managed by JavaScript using JQuery as a framework to facilitate this work. This allows communication to be more enjoyable, responding to the actions taken by the user through the graphical interface. AJAX was also used for asynchronous communication, obtaining results without the need to reload or switch to other page of the website.

The mail system, used to validate user registration and recovery, was implemented under an SMTP server configured with the PHPMailer library.

The simulator prototype was initially developed using the online tool called "Decision Scenario", which is part of the 40 free educational instruments based on multimedia technology offered on the H5P portal (http://h5p.org). This tool was selected for its user-friendliness, thanks to its intuitive interface, which does not require knowledge of programming languages to design the decision tree architecture. It is a new tool of the H5P set, developed in HTML5 and JavaScript. The H5P portal, it should be noted that it is completely free and open source, community development [21], designed under license from the MIT (Massachusetts Institute of Technology).

For the selection of this open source tool, its ease of use and its wide potential were considered.

Several stages were followed in the construction of the simulation system [13]:

- *The definition of the problem* to be solved and the delimitation of the limits of the system that was to be simulated. In this case, the training of hearing-impaired individuals was raised in a job admission interview situation. As mentioned, the system was delimited for cases of postlocutive hearing loss compensated with technological devices, such as headphones, hearing aids or cochlear transplantation. This delimitation of the recipient implies certain characteristics of the simulator, such as the absence of a sign language translation, since the recipients, in principle, understand written language.
- *The design of the model*, starting from flow charts or blocks to the preliminary experimental design. The prototype flowchart was made directly with the H5P tool itself, which offers the possibility of generating the diagram, relating the flows and editing the steps for the necessary changes or corrections (see Fig. 1). This tool supports text, images and video in its content, and offers two interchangeable interface types, which facilitate the design of the material: a preview interface that shows the author the results of its production, and a specific interface that allows the construction of the Navigation scheme in the form of a diagram.
- *The translation of the model into computational language*. Although in a first approach the prototype was developed with H5P, it was decided in a second stage the direct inclusion in the website by programming it, so that all user interactions can be stored to evaluate the correct and incorrect paths followed by each one.
- *The verification of the operation and verification of the validity of the model*. The development of the prototype made in H5P is currently under verification.
- *Experimentation and implementation*. The simulator will soon be implemented with a group of volunteers.

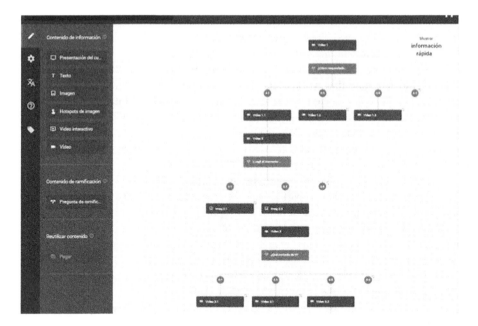

Fig. 1. Partial view of the flow chart built in H5P (https://h5p.org/node/723193)

This type of simulator does not require artificial intelligence. It is based on branched options, so it has low processing requirements. The user has three or more choice options in a sequence of events that represent the different steps of the interview.

The decision scenario consists of a branched series of job interview situations represented by videos filmed with real actors, where the interviewer character asks questions that will require the interviewed user to make decisions regarding the different response alternatives, obtaining a score that will be added in accordance with the assessment previously assigned to each response. If the user chooses an inappropriate response, he must go back to reflect on the choice made and try again for a better option based on the knowledge acquired during the previous training. The participant moves forward in the simulator path only if he takes the most appropriate option as seen in the study material.

During the simulation, participants must go through the 8 (eight) steps that make up the proposal, making decisions about 23 (twenty-three) options.

In this way, it seeks to train the hearing impaired people to face a job interview successfully related to aspects such as communication skills, control of emotional aspects and appropriate information they must provide to the interviewer regarding their disability.

4 Planning a Future Evaluation of the Project

4.1 Methodology

The didactic usefulness of the simulator will be evaluated through an opinion survey conducted on the participants in order to collect information about the learning process results on certain aspects such as: the application of theoretical concepts, attention, memory, communication strategy and emotional intelligence are improved at the time of the job application interview. The aspects to be evaluated are: the potential of the tool to decide on the most appropriate communication strategies, the participant's attention to his body language and the interviewer's one, the application of what has been learned, self-control under stressing situations.

4.2 Sample

The sample will consist of an initial group of recipients with the characteristics already explained, who wish to apply for a job. His previous experience in the use of digital technology in general and simulators in particular will be considered, which will be obtained through an online questionnaire made at the time of registration.

4.3 Information Collecting Tools

Online Survey. The instrument will be a survey with an online form format based on a Likert-type scale, which will gather the opinion and perception of the participants regarding the following aspects:

a) advantages related to the use of the simulator
b) functions enhanced with the interaction promoted by the simulator
c) skills they consider having developed
d) acquired communication skills

On the other hand, the collected pieces of information will be about how the training has contributed to the assimilation and retention of information, the application of searching strategies and the treatment of information, organizational skills, interest in applying for a job, motivation to adopt or maintain a competitive job position, development of emotional intelligence, decision-making skills under pressure levels, problem-solving skills and abilities to move in the normal world.

Personal Interviews. Personal interviews will be conducted to a group of participants to enlarge the answers obtained from the simulator data analysis and the survey responses.

5 Conclusions

The work has presented the foundation, design and functionalities of a simulator aimed at job interviews with hearing impaired people, although it is adaptable to other educational functionalities for people with hearing disabilities.

The design has placed emphasis on communication, interactivity, simplicity for the user and collaborative activities.

An evaluation of the tool by a group of users that will constitute a pilot experience is in the elaboration stage. The evaluation will be carried out through online surveys and personal interviews. According to the results, the optimization of the tool is foreseen for its subsequent implementation.

6 Future Work

Once the simulator currently under development on a conventional PC platform has been tested and validated, work will be done to optimize a multiplatform version with the purpose to offer the possibility of its use on mobile devices. The project will be open to modifications according to the results of the online survey and personal interviews obtained through the pilot experience. The improvements can be implemented both pedagogically and technologically with the participation of the multidisciplinary team of specialists.

For the next stage, the diversification of the educational aim delimited to the use of simulation for a job interview is presented with the purpose of offering new possibilities with the same basic platform and other content oriented to the specific problem of hearing loss.

References

1. Palacios, A.: El modelo social de discapacidad: orígenes, caracterización y plasmación en la Convención Internacional sobre los Derechos de las Personas con Discapacidad. CERMI, Madrid (2008)
2. Roig Vila, R.: Las tecnologías de la información y la comunicación (TIC) como recurso en la atención a las necesidades educativas especiales. En A. Lledó Carreres, La discapacidad auditiva, pp. 183–189. Barcelona, Edebé (2008)
3. Bell Rodríguez, R.: Algunos puntos para una reflexión integral en torno a la discapacidad auditiva, el uso de audífonos y los implantes cocleares. Revista de Investigación, Formación y Desarrollo 5(2), 11–20 (2017)
4. Quintana, N., Vallejo A., Pereyra, J.M., González, A.H.: Simulador en línea para capacitación de individuos hipoacúsicos adultos. Congreso Argentino de Ciencias de la Computación, CACIC 2019, Universidad Nacional de Río Cuarto, Córdoba. http://entornosvirtuales.unlp.edu.ar/assets/files/cacic2019.pdf. Accessed 21 Feb 2020
5. Bonsiepe, G.: Una Tecnología Cognoscitiva. 2000–2008 (2009). http://guibonsiepe.com.ar/guiblog/text/. Accessed 21 Feb 2020
6. Sangrà, A., Wheeler, S.: Nuevas formas informales de aprendizaje: ¿O estamos formalizando lo informal? RUSC. Universities and Knowledge Society Journal 10(1), 107–115 (2013)

7. Mayer, R.E.: Cognitive theory of multimedia learning. In: Mayer, R.E. (ed.) The Cambridge Handbook of Multimedia Learning. Cambridge University Press, New York (2015)
8. Calderón-Leyva, I., Díaz-Leines, S., Arch-Tirado, E., Lino-González, A.L.: Análisis de la relación entre las habilidades cognitivas y la pérdida auditiva sensorial unilateral. Neurología **33**(5), 283–289 (2018)
9. Ferreiro-Lago, E.: Accesibilidad para personas sordas y con discapacidad auditiva en el diseño instruccional e-learning basado en ADDIE. https://www.researchgate.net/publication/ 322276350_Accesibilidad_para_personas_sordas_y_con_discapacidad_auditiva_en_el_ diseno_instruccional_e-learning_basado_en_ADDIE. Accessed 29 Jan 2020
10. García-Carbonelli, A., Watts, F.: Perspectiva histórica de simulación y juego como estrategia docente: de la guerra al aula de lenguas para fines específicos. Ibérica, 13, pp. 65–84 (2007)
11. Amaya Franky, G.: La simulación computarizada como instrumento del método en el proceso de enseñanza y aprendizaje de la física, desde la cognición situada: ley de Ohm. Revista Electrónica "Actualidades Investigativas en Educación", vol. 8, no. 1 (2008)
12. Cabero-Almenara, J., Costas, J.: La utilización de simuladores para la formación de los alumnos. Prisma Social, núm. **17**, 343–372 (2016)
13. Cataldi, Z.; Lage, F., Dominighini, C.: Fundamentos para el uso de simulaciones en la enseñanza, Revista de Informática Educativa y Medios Audiovisuales **10**(17), 8–16 (2013)
14. Brown, J., Collins, A., Duguid, P.: Situated Cognition and the culture of learning. Educ. Res. **18**(1), 33–42 (1989)
15. Jonassen, D.H.: El diseño de entornos constructivistas de aprendizaje. In: Reigeluth, Ch., Diseño de la instrucción. Teoría y modelos. Madrid, Aula XXI Santillana, pp. 225–249. (2000)
16. Casanovas, I.: La utilización de indicadores didácticos en el diseño de simuladores para la formación universitaria en la toma de decisiones, TE&ET, Revista Iberoamericana de Tecnología en Educación y Educación en Tecnología, No. 2 (2007)
17. ONU: "Convención sobre los Derechos de las Personas con Discapacidad y Protocolo facultativo"; Fundación AEquitas y Colegio de Escribanos de la Provincia de Buenos Aires; FEN Editora Notarial (2008)
18. Sacco, A.: Estrategias para la utilización de tecnología en educación especial. Análisis de la implementación de las TICs en la atención a la diversidad. Propuestas para su eficaz aprovechamiento (2009). http://sedici.unlp.edu.ar/handle/10915/4165
19. Fernández, C.A.: Diseño pedagógico del simulador SIPAD Trabajo fin de grado. Facultad de ciencias de la educación. Curso 2013/2014 (2013) http://www.terras.edu.ar/biblioteca/31/ 31DE-LA-TORRE-saturnino-Cap3-Parte1-exito-error.pdf
20. Ainciburu, M.C.: Simulación en la Web2 y los lenguajes específicos, la comunicación profesional a través de la red Universidad de Siena (2009). Recuperado de: http://cvc. cervantes.es/ensenanza/biblioteca_ele/asele/pdf/20/20_0103.pdf
21. Buhu, A., Buhu, L.: Developing interactive elearning courses based on HTML5 for students in textile engineering. In: 9th International Conference on Education and New Learning Technologies, Barcelona (2017)

Profiles of Thesis Students in the Field of Computer Science and Their Link with UM Research Projects

Iris Sattolo$^{(\boxtimes)}$ ⑩, Marisa Panizzi ⑩, Javier Lafont ⑩,
and Nicolás Armilla ⑩

School of Computer and Communication Sciences, and Special Techniques,
University of Morón, Cabildo 134, Morón, Buenos Aires, Argentina
iris.sattolo@gmail.com, marisapanizzi@outlook.com,
lafontjavier@hotmail.com, nicolasarmilla@hotmail.com

Abstract. Participation of undergraduate students in research projects allows to detect their vocations so they can develop their career as researchers in the academic field and/or recognize the importance of research in an industrial context. The objective of this study is to find the relationship between characteristics of undergraduate thesis students and their link with research projects implemented in the University of Morón (UM), as well as to identify the thesis students who have experience in other activities linked to research. To meet this goal, a set of experiments was performed using the Kmeans, Expectation Maximization, J4.8, Naïve Bayes and BayesNet algorithms; along with WEKA and Elvira environments. The experiments results showed that the reason for thesis topic choice is the attribute of greater incidence in research projects participation, as well as in other research activities proposed in the Thesis Seminar.

Keywords: Computer science undergraduate thesis students · Profiles · Research projects · Data mining

1 Introduction

The application of data mining to solve different types of problems in the field of Education has experienced a great boom in the last decade. Educational Data Mining (EDM) is a discipline that is concerned with developing methods for extracting useful information from data generated in educational environments and using the data to improve such environments. The information thus obtained becomes an indispensable input for decision making [1].

In the international context, previous publications have shown that data mining can be used to detect students at risk of abandoning their studies. Luan [2] successfully applied data mining techniques to predict which groups of students might drop out; Lin [3] used data mining techniques to optimize efforts to retain students. Researchers at Bowie State University developed a system based on data mining that allows the institution to identify and assist students at risk of abandoning their studies [4].

© Springer Nature Switzerland AG 2020
P. Pesado and M. Arroyo (Eds.): CACIC 2019, CCIS 1184, pp. 96–109, 2020.
https://doi.org/10.1007/978-3-030-48325-8_7

In recent years, the University of Morón, through the Secretariat of Science and Technology (SeCyT-UM) has prioritized research within its strategic plan. The presentation and the development of research projects is aimed at stimulating and strengthening systematic activities in the UM that are closely related to the generation, improvement and application of knowledge in Science and Technology. It is expected that this effort will promote - within the science and technology fields - research and innovation, human resources training, dissemination activities, technological services (databases, specialized library, etc.) development and knowledge transfer to the community [5].

This study aims at defining the profiles of students who have participated in research projects for their bachelor's or undergraduate degree. Additionally, it intends to characterize students who have experience in writing scholarly articles and have given presentations at scientific events, even if they have not taken part in a UM research project. We intent to complement our previous work [6].

Section 2 describes Related Work, Sect. 3 describes each of the steps performed in the Development of the data mining process; finally, Sect. 4 presents the Conclusions and Future Work.

2 Related Work

In previous works [7], the authors conducted a Systematic Mapping Study (SMS) following the process proposed in [8]. In this section, some of the SMS elements are synthetized: Objective, Research Questions, Search String, the Data-Extraction Form used, Classification Scheme for primary studies and Distribution of Studies according to the proposed classification. A list of primary studies used for the SMS can be found in the Appendix: https://doi.org/10.6084/m9.figshare.11852637.v1.

The aim of the SMS was to analyze the state of the art of educational data mining in higher education, in order to answer the following research question (RQ): *What is the state of art of educational data mining in higher education?*

To answer the proposed research question (RQ), it was broken down into 5 questions (RQ1–5) (see Table 1).

Table 1. Research questions.

	Question	Motivation
RQ1:	What is EDM (Educational Data Mining) intended for?	To find out what is solved with data mining in the educational context
RQ2:	What methodologies are used to apply data mining in higher education academic institutions?	To identify the mostly used methodologies in higher education academic institutions
RQ3:	Which tools and programming languages are used to perform data mining?	To find the mostly used tools and programming languages
RQ4:	Which algorithms are applied?	To determine which data mining algorithms are the mostly used to solve problems in higher education
RQ5:	What types of research are presented in the articles?	To classify the primary studies according to Wieringa [9]

Table 2 shows the search strings used.

Table 2. Search strings.

S1: Data Mining AND Higher Education
S2: Educational AND Data Mining
S3: Educational AND Data Mining AND Higher Education
S4: Data Mining AND Higher Education

Table 3 shows the data extraction form, which is composed of two parts: 1) metadata of the primary studies, 2) research questions dimensions and categories.

Table 3. Data extraction form.

Metadata	ID: article registration identifier, search string, Year, Title, Author(s), Source (Name of Congress or Journal), Type of Publication (R = Journal, C = Congress), Search source, Country, Keywords, Citations (APA), Number of Citations, Problem, Proposal, Results.
RQ/Dimension	Categories
RQ1/Contribution:	Academic performance, student behavior, student dropout, profiles analysis/classification, educational quality, student procrastination, gender differences in university applicants, student employability, cooperative education, does not mention
RQ2/Methodologies:	KDD[a], CRISP-DM[b], SEMMA[c], does not mention
RQ3/Tools and Languages:	WEKA, Rapid Miner, Knime, Orange, Python, other, does not mention
RQ4/Algorithms:	Naïve Bayes, Clustering in general, J4.8, Decision trees (unspecified), K-means, Neural Networks, Prediction in general (unspecified), ID3, other
RQ5/Types of research:	Evaluation, validation, solution proposal, experience report, comparison, opinion

[a]KDD: Knowledge Discovery in Databases.
[b]Cross Industry Standard Process for Data Mining.
[c]SEMMA methodology is defined by SAS Institute Inc.

Table 4 shows the classification scheme.

Table 4. Classification scheme.

Contribution:	Academic performance, student behavior, student dropout, profiles analysis/classification, educational quality, student procrastination, gender differences in university applicants, student employability, cooperative education, does not mention	RQ1
Methodologies:	KDD, CRISP-DM, SEMMA, does not mention	RQ2
Tools and programming languages:	This dimension considers the tools and programming languages used for data mining processes: WEKA, Rapid Miner, Knime, Orange, Python, other, does not mention	RQ3
Algorithms:	This dimension considers data mining algorithms: Naïve Bayes, Clustering in general, Decision trees (unspecified), J4.8, Decision trees (unspecified), K-means, Neural Networks, Prediction in general (unspecified), ID3, other	RQ4
Types of research:	Evaluation, validation, solution proposal, personal experience, comparison, opinion	RQ5

The search chain was applied, and 160 articles were found. Then, the selection process was applied, and 110 primary scientific articles were found, which were selected for analysis and for answering the research questions (RQ) (see Table 5).

Table 5. Synthesis of primary articles.

Research questions/(RQ)	Distribution of primary studies by research questions
What is solved?/ (RQ1):	Academic performance: [EP4], [EP6], [EP9], [EP11–EP12], [EP16–EP18], [EP20–EP29], [EP31], [EP33], [EP36], [EP40–EP41], [EP43], [EP45], [EP47–EP50], [EP54], [EP57–EP59], [EP61–EP62], [EP65], [EP67–EP68], [EP73], [EP79], [EP81], [EP83–EP84], [EP86], [EP88–EP90], [EP92], [EP94], [EP97–EP98], [EP100], [EP102–EP104], [EP107–EP110]
	Student Behavior: [EP74], [EP96], [EP98], [EP100], [EP103–EP104], [EP106]
	Student dropout: [EP2], [EP-21], [EP27], [EP37–EP38], [EP44], [EP60], [EP62], [EP82], [EP84–EP86], [EP90], [EP92], [EP106–EP108]
	Profiles analysis/classification: [EP1] [EP6–EP13], [EP17–EP19], [EP23], [EP27], [EP46], [EP51], [EP53–EP54], [EP57], [EP59], [EP65], [EP67–EP68], [EP74–EP75], [EP79], [EP90], [EP94–EP96], [EP101-EP102] [EP1], [EP6–EP13], [EP17–EP19], [EP23], [EP27], [EP46], [EP51], [EP53–EP54], [EP57], [EP59], [EP65], [EP67–EP68], [EP74–EP75], [EP79], [EP90] [EP94–EP96], [EP101–EP102]
	Student Procrastination: [EP30], [EP42], [EP51], [EP55], [EP58–EP59], [EP63–EP64], [EP69–EP70], [EP76], [EP78], [EP80], [EP86], [EP88–EP89], [EP91–EP93], [EP95–EP96], [EP99], [EP100–EP102], [EP105]
	Gender Differences in University Applicants: [EP34]
	Student Employability: [EP52]
	Cooperative Education: [EP35]
	Does not mention: [EP3], [EP4], [EP5], [EP14], [EP32], [EP39], [EP66], [EP71], [EP77], [EP87]

(continued)

Table 5. (*continued*)

Research questions/(RQ)	Distribution of primary studies by research questions
Methodologies/ (RQ2):	KDD: [EP2–EP3], [EP26], [EP29], [EP47], [EP54–EP55], [EP57], [EP62], [EP67–EP68], [EP77], [EP79], [EP84], [EP90], [EP94], [EP100–EP101]
	CRISP-DM: [EP1], [EP27], [EP30], [EP44], [EP82], [EP86], [EP109].
	SEMMA: No study performed
	Does not mention: [EP4–EP25], [EP28], [EP31–EP43], [EP45–EP46], [EP48–EP53], [EP56], [EP58–EP61], [EP63–EP66], [EP69–EP76], [EP78], [EP80–EP81], [EP83], [EP85], [EP87–EP89], [EP90–EP93], [EP95–EP99], [EP102–EP108], [EP110]
Tools and Languages/ (RQ3):	WEKA: [EP2–EP3], [EP21], [EP24], [EP31], [EP39], [EP41], [EP46], [EP48–EP49], [EP60–EP62], [EP66–EP68], [EP73], [EP76], [EP79], [EP83–EP84], [EP90–EP91], [EP94], [EP96–EP97], [EP99–EP100], [EP103], [EP106–EP110]
	Rapid Miner: [EP3], [EP23], [EP30], [EP38–EP40], [EP64], [ÈP85]
	Knime: [EP3]
	Orange: [EP3]
	Python: [EP52], [EP75], [EP82], [EP91]
	Other: [EP3], [EP17], [EP18], [EP25], [EP39], [EP44], [EP46], [EP54–EP55], [EP69], [EP72], [EP78], [EP81–EP82], [EP91], [EP98], [EP104].
	Does not mention: [ÈP1], [EP4–EP16], [EP19–20], [EP22], [EP26–EP29], [EP32–EP37], [EP39], [EP42–EP43], [EP45], [EP47], [EP50–EP51], [EP53], [EP70–EP71], [EP74], [EP77], [EP80], [EP86], [EP88–EP89], [EP92–EP93], [EP95], [EP101–EP102], [EP105]
Algorithms (RQ4):	Naïve Bayes: [EP2–EP4], [EP6–7], [EP12], [EP17], [EP24], [EP31] [EP41], [EP45], [EP48–EP49], [EP52],[EP55], [EP59–EP60], [EP62], [EP65–EP66], [EP73], [EP78–EP79], [EP81–EP82], [EP87–EP88], [EP94], [EP96] [EP99–EP100], [EP104], [EP106–EP107], [EP109–EP110]
	Clustering in general: [EP1], [EP8], [EP15–EP18], [EP23], [EP27–EP28], [EP42–EP43], [EP51], [EP54], [EP67], [EP77], [EP83], [EP86], [EP89–EP91], [EP97], [EP101], [EP110]
	J4.8: [EP21], [EP23–EP24], [EP31], [EP38], [EP40], [EP45–EP46], [EP48], [EP55], [EP58–EP59], [EP61–EP62], [EP73], [EP76], [EP83], [EP90], [EP94], [EP100], [EP107], [EP109]
	Decision Trees (unspecified): [EP10], [EP19], [EP57], [EP72], [EP78], [EP102], [EP108]
	K-means: [EP17–EP18], [EP23], [EP30], [EP34], [EP37], [EP39], [EP40], [EP59], [EP63], [EP65], [EP80], [EP83], [EP101], [EP110]
	Neural Networks: [EP2–EP3], [EP6], [EP13–EP14], [EP19], [EP25], [EP28], [EP45], [EP59], [EP75], [EP79], [EP86], [EP88], [EP92]
	Prediction in general (unspecified): [EP4], [EP6], [EP9], [EP11], [EP42], [EP77], [EP91], [EP97]
	ID3: [EP46], [EP68], [EP79], [EP90], [EP100], [EP103], [EP108]
	Other: [EP1], [EP14], [EP15], [EP17], [EP19–EP23], [EP27–EP28], [EP29], [EP31–32], [EP35], [EP37], [EP40], [EP42], [EP44–EP45], [EP48], [EP52], [EP55–EP57], [EP59–EP67], [EP69], [EP72–EP73], [EP75–EP82], [EP85], [EP88], [EP90-EP91], [EP94], [EP97], [EP101–EP109]

(*continued*)

Table 5. (*continued*)

Research questions/(RQ)	Distribution of primary studies by research questions
Types of Research (RQ5):	Evaluation: [EP2], [EP4], [EP7–EP9], [EP12–EP20], [EP22–EP25], [EP27–EP32], [EP37–EP38], [EP43], [EP46], [EP49–EP50], [EP54], [EP57], [EP63], [EP66–EP67], [EP72–EP76], [EP79], [EP81], [EP84–EP85], [EP87–EP100], [EP102], [EP104–EP110]
	Validation: [EP2], [EP9], [EP27], [EP61], [EP86–EP88], [EP90], [EP96–EP97], [EP102], [EP104–EP108], [EP110], [EP2], [EP9], [EP27], [EP61], [EP86–EP88], [EP90], [EP96–EP97], [EP102], [EP104–EP108], [EP110]
	Solution Proposal: [EP5], [EP6], [EP9–EP11], [EP14], [EP19], [EP44], [EP50], [EP54–EP55], [EP58–EP65], [EP67–EP69], [EP78], [EP80–EP87], [EP92], [EP95], [EP99]
	Experience Report: [EP1], [EP2], [EP10–EP11], [EP19], [EP21], [EP53], [EP58–EP59], [EP61], [EP64], [EP66–EP69], [EP74], [EP82–EP83], [EP85–EP90], [EP92–EP94], [EP96–EP100], [EP102], [EP104–EP110]
	Comparison:[EP2], [EP4], [EP6], [EP7], [EP9], [EP12], [EP16–EP18], [EP24], [EP31–EP35], [EP38], [EP39–EP40], [EP45], [EP48], [EP51–EP52], [EP55], [EP56], [EP57], [EP60–EP62], [EP72–EP73], [EP75–EP76], [EP78], [EP80], [EP91], [EP94], [EP109]
	Opinion: [EP2], [EP3], [EP26], [EP30], [EP35–EP37], [EP39], [EP47], [EP53], [EP56], [EP70–EP71], [EP77], [EP85]–[EP89–EP93], [EP96], [EP99], [EP102], [EP104], [EP106–EP110]

From a total of 110 primary studies analyzed, some studies define student profiles; nevertheless, the relationship with research projects of their university is not addressed in the profiles characterization. These studies do not discuss whether the students wrote scholarly articles and/or participated in scientific events. We acknowledge that our SMS is not absolute; however, it has allowed us to find the characteristics considered in other research studies in order to define student profiles.

3   Development

In order to find the information, the steps of the KDD process (Knowledge Discovery in Databases) [10] were applied, in correspondence with previous studies [11] and [12]. The steps, along with the tasks carried out for each of them, are described below.

3.1   Data Integration and Collection

In the present study, surveys of students who got their degrees during the last 10 years were used. A record of research projects implemented in the UM has been kept for such period, which resulted in a sample of 97 records composed of 47 graduates with a Bachelor's Degree in Computer Systems and 50 graduates with a Bachelor's Degree in Computer Engineering.

3.2   Data Selection, Cleaning and Transformation

In this phase, the appropriate characteristics that take part in model building are identified. The objective of this study was to determine whether there is a relationship between the profiles obtained from thesis students of Computer Science degree programs of the University of Morón and their participation in research, both in projects and assignments proposed by the chair. For this reason, we used profiles derived from our previous works [11] and [12], in which the attributes are: degree, age, family group, field of work (labor), subject area of thesis work (academic). The following attributes were incorporated: reason for thesis topic choice and whether any publication resulted from the thesis work (both recovered from the survey).

For the class attribute, the survey question used was, *"Was any publication derived from your thesis work?"*; all answers were verified against the research projects records.

Table 6 shows the attributes used in the data mining step with their associated values, after data cleaning and transformation.

Table 6. Significant attributes for the data mining step.

Attributes	Values
Thesis subject area	Agents and Intelligent Systems/Software Engineering/Database and Data Mining/Innovation in Software Systems/Architecture, Networks and Operating Systems/Computer Security/Technology and Education/Real-time Signal Processing and Systems
Degree	Bachelor in Computer Systems/Bachelor in Computer Engineering
Field of work (Work-in)	Functional Analysis and Requirements/Databases and Data Mining/Development/Infrastructure/Business Processes/Computer Security/Testing/Various/Does not Work
Age	Under 25 years/Between 25 and 30 years/Over 30 years
Family group	Engaged/Not engaged
Reason for thesis topic choice	Related to your job/Personal interest/Assignments proposed by the department/Lines of research/Other
	"Proposed in the Thesis Seminar": means that the student can select the subject area of thesis work offered by the chair in the first class. For the definition of subject areas of work, those proposed in the Argentine Congress of Computer Science (CACIC), a scientific event organized by the RedUNCI (Network of Universities Offering Computer Science Programs) [13], were considered. "Lines of Research": are the research lines of the projects which are being implemented at the beginning of the academic year; students are offered to participate in order to develop their undergraduate dissertation within the framework of the project
It has been published	No, Yes-with research project, Yes-without research project

Table 7 shows the computer science projects implemented at the UM during the last 10 years and their corresponding research areas.

Table 7. Computer science research projects of the UM.

Area of research	Name of the research project
Software engineering	Software engineering in the development of context-sensitive applications
	Validation of the tools developed for the implementation of automated information systems
	Approach to a methodology for the implementation of computer-based information systems
	Analysis and strengthening of the software process implementation stage
Agents and intelligent systems	Robotic reinforcement learning with biosignal monitoring and control
	Brain computer interfaces applied to domotics and robotics
	Emotion-oriented control of artifacts and robots
	Exploratory research for the development of a framework in the context of cyber defense and cybersecurity
	Influence on the biometric-emotional state of people
	Exploitation of EEG data and physiological parameters of users interacting in virtual environments
Technology for education	Immersive virtual learning environments oriented to training and development of simulations in risk situations
	Immersive virtual environments - interactive elements
Data mining	Applying intelligent technologies for information exploitation to the analysis of profiles of undergraduate thesis students of computer science programs at the UM

3.3   Data Mining

Selecting features or attributes is a fundamental pre-processing technique for performing data mining tasks. Feature selection algorithms have two main objectives:

- Reduce the computational cost associated with both learning and the generated knowledge model (by eliminating irrelevant or redundant attributes).
- Increase the precision of such model (by eliminating attributes that are harmful for learning) [14].

In general, feature selection techniques can be classified into two large groups:

- Filter Methods: Evaluate attributes according to heuristics, based on the data general characteristics that are independent of the learning algorithm.
- Wrapper Methods: Work together with the algorithm used for learning to determine which attributes are the most relevant.

In this instance, different evaluators were applied to determine what attributes the new experiments would work on. Table 8 shows the results obtained with each evaluator used [14].

Of the proposed evaluators, all select as relevant attribute: Reason for Thesis Topic Choice, with 100% correspondence. It is observed that Family Group is the least relevant attribute. For this reason, it was decided to eliminate the family group attribute for the following phases.

Table 8. Results for the selected evaluators.

Evaluators	Evaluation mode	Method	Attribute evaluation	
cfsSubSet Eval (filter)	Cross-validation	Best first	**Reason for topic choice 100%**	
ChiSquareAttribute Evalue (filter)	Cross-validation	Ranker:	Rank	attribute
			1 ± 0	**6 reason-choice**
			2 ± 0	5 thesis-area
			3.1 ± 0.3	4 works
			3.9 ± 0.3	2 age
			5.1 ± 0.3	1 degree
			5.9 ± 0.3	3 fam.-group
ReliefAttributeEval (filter)	Cross validation	Ranker	Rank	attribute
			1 ± 0	**6 reason-choice**
			2.3 ± 0.64	5 thesis-area
			3.1 ± 0.54	2 age
			3.6 ± 0.66	4 works
			5.4 ± 0.49	1 degree
			5.6 ± 0.49	3 fam.-group
WrapperSubsetEval-B weka.classifiers.bayes BayesNet 5 parents wrapper	Cross-validation	Greedy-Stepwise	**Reason for topic choice 100%**	
WrapperSubsetEval-B weka.classifiers.bayes BayesNet 5 parents wrapper	Cross validation	Best-first	1 degree 20% 2 age 10% 3 family-group 0% 4 works-in 10% 5 thesis-area 0% **6 reason-choice 100%**	

Experiment 1. In the first instance, the following research question arose:

Is there any correlation between the Computer Science thesis students' profiles obtained and the proposed class attribute: has been -published?

The software used was WEKA [15], from which a classification model was obtained with clustering techniques. These techniques try to find groups within a set of individuals; the main objective lies in grouping subjects with similar characteristics, that are, in turn, different from those characteristics of individuals belonging to the rest of the groups [10]. Clusters were observed in the SMS very frequently during data mining.

Clustering algorithms used for this study were: K-means or k-media, partition-based, and probability-based EM (Expectation–Maximization). K-means needs the input of the number of groups into which the population will be segmented. From this number k of clusters, the algorithm first places k random points (centroids). Then, it allocates all samples with the shortest distances to any of those points. Later, the point moves towards the average of the nearest samples. This will generate a new sample allocation, since some samples are now closer to other centroids. This process is repeated iteratively, and the groups are adjusted until the allocation no longer changes by moving the points. The EM algorithm begins to randomly predict the distributions parameters and uses them to calculate the probabilities for each instance to belong to a cluster and uses those probabilities to estimate the probabilities parameters again [15].

The number k (number of clusters) was initialized for both algorithms as equal to 3, and these were run using the class for their evaluation. Table 9 shows the results obtained for both algorithms, where cluster 0 = "It has not been published", cluster 1 = "It has been published, (with no research project)", and Cluster 2 = "It has been published (with research project)".

Table 9. Comparison between K-means and EM algorithms.

Algorithm used	Number of instances obtained in each class			Incorrect regarding class
	Cluster 0 64	Cluster 1 13	Cluster 2 20	
K-means	43	4	8	43,29%
EM	45	3	12	38,14%

The interpretation of these results *is that there is a low correlation between the obtained clusters and the class attribute "has been -published."*

Table 10 shows the distribution of the centroids obtained by K-means, where the number in the first row of each cluster (59, 23,15) represents the number of instances considered for the group.

Table 10. Centroids obtained by K-means.

Attribute	Cluster 0 (59 instances)	Cluster 1 (23 instances)	Cluster 2 (15 instances)
Degree	Bach-S-Eng	Bach-Sys	Bach-Sys
Age	25–30	Over-30	Over-30
Works-in	Various	Fun-An-Req	Various
Thesis-area	Ag.Int-Sys	Soft-Eng	Ag.Int-Sys
Reason-choice	Per-Int	Per-Int	L-of-research

This experiment demonstrates that, when using clustering algorithms, there is no correlation between the profiles obtained by the cluster and whether the thesis student published a scientific article or not.

Experiment 2. The research question was: *How do the classification algorithms react to the data set with the new attributes: "reason for thesis topic choice and has been-published"?*

Among the classification algorithms, the one selected was J4.8 (supervised algorithm), in which there is a dependent variable, or class, and the objective of the classifier is to determine the value of said class for new cases.

The algorithms used were J4.8, Naïves Bayes, and Bayes Net (with 5 parents and 3 parents). In all cases, cross validation was used with 10 folders. The results of comparing these algorithms with WEKA in experimenter mode are shown in Table 11, in percentages of attributes correctly classified.

Table 11. Percentage of attributes correctly classified.

Algorithm	J4.8	Naïve Bayes	Bayes Net (5 parents)	Bayes Net (3 parents)
Percentage of correct attributes	82,52%	78,07	76,30	76,30

It is observed that, when applying probabilistic algorithms such as Naïves Bayes or Bayes Net, in no case does the classification obtained by algorithm J4.8 improve its performance.

The tree obtained by algorithm J4.8, where 82.48% of a total of 97 instances were correctly classified is shown below.

```
reason-thesis-choice = Per-Int: No (50.0/9.0)
reason-thesis-choice = Prop- Thesis Seminar
| Age = 25-30: No (6.0/1.0)
| Age = under-25: Yes-WITHOUT-PUB (2.0)
| Age = over-30: No (6.0/1.0)
reason-thesis-choice = L-of-research: Yes-WITH-PUB (20.0/2.0)
reason-thesis-choice = Rel-job: No (10.0/1.0)
reason-thesis-choice = Other: No (3.0/1.0)
```

It can be interpreted from this experiment that the attribute "reason for thesis topic choice" is the one with the greatest influence in the class.

Experiment 3. The research question was: *Is it possible to obtain a reliable predictive model for our data?*

One of the problems data mining faces is dealing with uncertainty; such problem is solved by working with Bayesian methods and techniques, since one of their main characteristics is the explicit use of probability theory.

The reason for using Bayes' theorem, for any machine learning problem, is that the posterior probability of any hypothesis consistent with the data set can be estimated.

The algorithm used was the one designed by Duda and Hart in 1973 [16], the Naïve Bayes classifier, which assumes that all attributes are independent of each other, when the value is known. Elvira software [14] was used for this purpose. Figure 1 shows the network obtained, where the class variable is: has been-published (publication) and the child nodes are the independent variables: degree, age, family group, field of work (work-in), thesis area and reason for thesis topic choice. The network displays the joint distribution of probabilities obtained by Bayes' theorem.

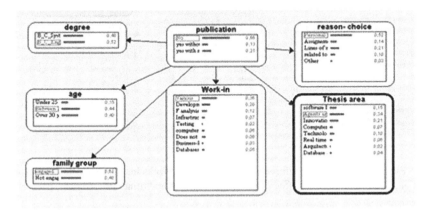

Fig. 1. Network obtained with Elvira software applying Naïves Bayes. Joint distribution of probabilities.

Figure 2 shows a new case, in which the evidence is: Degree = Engineering, Age = over 30, Works in = Various, Thesis work area = Agents and Intelligent Systems, Reason for thesis choice = Personal interest (all nodes in gray) where the node class publication has a 90% probability that the thesis student does not publish an article.

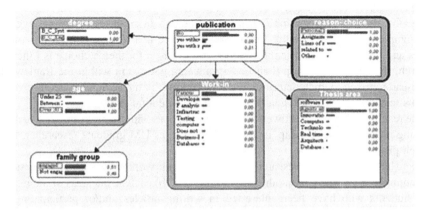

Fig. 2. Evidence 1: Degree: Engineering, Age: Over 30, Works in: Various, Thesis work area: Agents and Intelligent Systems, Reason for thesis topic choice: Personal interest.

If, in this case, only the reason for thesis topic choice is modified for lines of research, the class values change to "yes- publishes with projects 75%" (see Fig. 3).

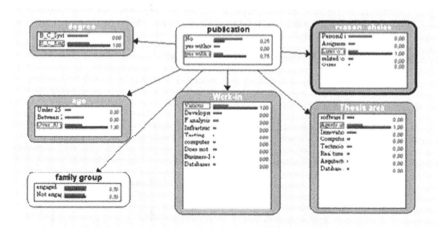

Fig. 3. Evidence 2: Degree: Engineering, Age: Over 30, Works in: Various, Thesis work area: Agents and Intelligent Systems, Reason for thesis topic choice: Lines of research.

4   Conclusions and Future Works

We have presented related papers that were reviewed with the systematic mapping study (SMS) research method. This revision allowed to identify what problems can be solved with educational data mining. We were able to demonstrate that the primary studies focused on the definition of student profiles; however, none of them considers the characteristics of the students approach to research activities.

The thesis students' profiles found by using clusters did not allow to demonstrate the students' participation in a research project.

The thesis students' degree of interest in certain areas of research was found through the attribute "Reason for Thesis Topic Choice". In the case of Personal Interest or Assignments Proposed by the Thesis Seminar there is a tendency towards writing articles and participating in scientific events. If the reason for theme choice is Lines of Research, the students develop their undergraduate dissertation within the framework of a research project; which demonstrates that working for a research project motivates students to write articles and then present them in scientific events.

The results of this study allowed to provide graduates with a series of offers, such as obtaining a doctoral scholarship and/or participating, as UM graduate researcher, in a research project.

There are two lines of research arising from this work which will be pursued: (a) continue to experiment with other algorithms; and (b) analyze the areas of interest of those students who have been interested in writing articles and/or participating in scientific events, with the objective of making the presentation of research projects in these areas viable.

References

1. Romero, C., Ventura, S., Pechenizkiy, M., Baker, R.S.: Handbook of educational data mining. CRC Press, Boca Raton (2010)
2. Luan, J.: Data mining and its applications in higher education. New Dir. Inst. Res. **113**, 17–36 (2002)
3. Lin, S.H.: Data mining for student retention management. J. Comput. Sci. Coll. **27**(4), 92–99 (2012)
4. Chacon, F., Spicer, D., Valbuena, A.: Analytics in support of student retention and success. Res. Bul. **3**, 1–9 (2012)
5. Universidad de Morón. Secretaria de Ciencia y Tecnología (SeCyT-UM). https://www.unimoron.edu.ar/area/cienciaytecnologia
6. Sattolo, I., Panizzi, M., Lafont, J., Armilla, N.: Perfiles de tesistas de la disciplina informática y su vinculación con los proyectos de investigación de la UM. In: XXV Congreso Argentino de Ciencias de la computación (CACIC 2019). Universidad Nacional de Río Cuarto, Río Cuarto, Córdoba. ISBN 978-987-688-377-1
7. Panizzi, M.D.: "Establecimiento del estado del arte sobre la Minería de Datos Educacional en el Nivel Superior: Un Estudio de Mapeo Sistemático" (Establishing the State of the Art of Educational Data Mining in Higher Education: A Systematic Mapping Study). Revista de Investigaciones Científicas del Universidad de Morón. (Univ. Morón J. Sci. Res.), 3(1) (2019)
8. Kitchenham, B., Charters, S.: Guidelines for performing Systematic Literature Reviews in Software Engineering. Versión 2.3 EBSE-2007-01 (2007)
9. Wieringa, R., Maiden, N., Mead, N., Rolland, C.: Requirements engineering paper classification and evaluation criteria: a proposal and a discussion. Requir. Eng. **11**(1), 102–107 (2005)
10. Hernández, O.J., Ramírez, Q.M.J., Ferri, R.C.: Introducción a la Minería de Datos (Introduction to Data Mining). Pearson Education, Madrid (2004)
11. Sattolo, I., et al.: Hacia la caracterización de perfiles de tesistas de Carreras de Informática de la Universidad de Morón (Towards a Characterization of Profiles of Computer Science degree programs thesis students at University of Morón). In: XIII Congreso Nacional de Tecnología en Educación y Educación en Tecnología (TE&ET 2018). Universidad Nacional de Misiones, Posadas, Misiones. Argentina, 14 and 15 June 2018
12. Sattolo, I., et al.: Descubrimiento de las áreas de investigación seleccionadas por los tesistas de las carreras de informática de la UM mediante árboles de decisión (Discovering Research Areas Selected by Thesis Students of Computer Science Degree Programs of The University of Morón Through Decision Tres). In: XXIV Congreso Argentino de Ciencias de la computación (CACIC 2018) Tandil Universidad Nacional del Centro de la Pcia. De Bs.As. ISBN 978-950-658-472-6
13. RedUNCI (Red de Universidades con carreras de Informática). http://redunci.info.unlp.edu.ar/
14. Elvira soft. http://www.ia.uned.es/investig/proyectos/elvira/
15. Weka. University of Waikato. Machine Learning Group. www.cs.waikato.ac.nz/ml/Weka/downloading.html
16. Castillo, Gutiérrez y Hadi. Sistemas Expertos y Modelos de Redes Probabilísticas (Expert Systems and Probabilistic Networks Models). https://personales.unican.es/gutierjm/papers/BookCGH.pdf

Experience Analysis for the Use of Desafiate Serious Game for the Self-assessment of Students

Federico Héctor Archuby[1]($\boxtimes$), Cecilia Sanz[1,2,3], and Patricia Pesado[1]

[1] Instituto de Investigación en Informática LIDI - CIC, Facultad de Informática,
Universidad Nacional de La Plata, La Plata, Argentina
{farchuby,csanz,ppesado}@lidi.info.unlp.edu.ar
[2] Universidad Nacional de Río Negro - Directora del Proyecto PI-UNRN-40-C-486,
Viedma, Argentina
[3] Investigador Asociado de la Comisión de Investigaciones Científicas de la Prov.
de Buenos Aires, La Plata, Argentina

Abstract. In recent years, the development and use of serious games for the educational field has proliferated. One of the aspects linked to this phenomenon is the motivation achieved with the activities offered in them. On the other hand, there is another technology that has been growing for some time now, which are the Virtual Learning and Teaching Environments (VLTEs). These environments allow carrying out various activities and usually include self-assessment. In this article, we analyze the use of the serious mobile game Desafiate, aimed at student self-assessment and integrated into the IDEAS VLTE. The analysis is based on the intrinsic motivation achieved when using this game, compared to other methods used for self-assessment. Three contrasting groups are used for the analysis – one of them uses the serious game, another one uses pen and paper for their self-assessment, and the third one uses the IDEAS VTLE (and its assessment tool). As an instrument to measure intrinsic motivation, the Intrinsic Motivation Inventory (IMI) questionnaire is used. This questionnaire considers utility, perceived usefulness, pressure/tension, and effort during the activity as variables that affect motivation, among other factors that are not contemplated in this work. Results show that students value self-assessment as a useful activity, and they have shown greater interest in this process when working with Desafiate.

Keywords: Using serious games · Education · Self-assessment · Mobile devices · Virtual Learning and Teaching Environments

1 Introduction

Today, information and communication technologies (ICTs) are present in various aspects of daily life and of society in general. The educational field is integrating some tools at a slower pace, even to carry out teaching and learning processes. Such is the case of virtual learning and teaching environments (VLTEs),

P. Pesado and M. Arroyo (Eds.): CACIC 2019, CCIS 1184, pp. 110–123, 2020.
https://doi.org/10.1007/978-3-030-48325-8_8

which today are commonly used in many educational institutions. VLTEs are web-centric systems that allow both students and educators to experience educational processes mediated by digital technologies. This is achieved through the integration of the different tools offered in VLTEs, which also favors monitoring and tracking student activities for better support and customization [1–4]. There are currently a large number of VLTEs, some even widely used in academic environments, and others that have been developed ad-hoc by some universities.

Experiences can be found where these environments are used to complement classroom work, adopting extended classroom-type approaches, or hybrid approaches that combine different mediation and face-to-face strategies. Among the tools included with these environments, there are usually a few aimed at students' self-assessment. These allow creating different types of assignments (multiple choice, two options, relationship, etc.). In this article, the functionalities of these self-assessment tools included in VLTEs are integrated into a game.

On the other hand, serious games have become an alternative for educators when planning educational activities to achieve changes in behaviour and attitude and/or certain learning goals. Games in general have always been used in education, especially at the kinder and primary levels [5]. The concept of serious games was proposed by Clark Abt in 1970 [6]. In his book, serious games are directly linked to education, since they are defined as games with an explicitly, well thought-out educational purpose. Back then, the term was not oriented to digital games. However, as a result of the popularity of video games have gained in recent years, which is paralleled on their use for educational purposes, many authors started using the term to refer only to digital games whose goal goes beyond entertainment [7]. Considering the possibilities offered by serious games and the possibilities of self-assessment offered by VLTEs, the serious mobile game Desafiate was developed. Desafiate's goal is helping students' with their self-assessment.

In this article, we present the analysis and results of a series of sessions in which Desafiate was used as a self-assessment strategy for students. Our study focused on student intrinsic motivation when faced with a self-assessment activity following other strategies (pen and paper and VLTE). Two hypotheses were proposed: 1- Self-assessment using the serious game Desafiate improves student motivation, and 2- Self-assessment using a serious game (Desafiate) reduces the pressure students feel during that process. The results of the sessions carried out are analyzed to corroborate the validity of these hypotheses for the analyzed sample. This article is an extension of the one presented in [8]. It presents the results of a second session that has been carried out. Besides the analysis of the hypothesis was extended regarding all sessions. Also, the background section was modified, with some reviews related to the analysis of methodologies for designing, creating and evaluating serious games. From here, the article is organized as follows: in Sect. 2, relevant background works are analyzed. Section 3 briefly describes Desafiate, the serious game implemented and used in the context of these sessions with students. Section 4 presents the organization and general description of the sessions with the students, as well as the tools used for data measurement and analysis. In Sect. 5, the results obtained during the first and second sessions are analyzed; while in Sect. 6, the hypotheses are discussed together and the results obtained are analyzed. Finally, in Sect. 7, conclusions and future work are presented.

2 Background

Serious games have been linked to education since the term was coined in 1970. Despite this, the term has been changing and its meaning has expanded. For example, [9] use a broader definition of serious games and say that serious games are those that are used to educate, train and inform. This adds a component related to training and giving information to the user. But serious games are not limited to those goals only. In [10], the definition given by [11] is discussed, which considers that a serious game is a digital game created with at least one defining goal in addition to entertaining. With this definition, serious games are given a more general scope, since they are not limited to the educational field only. Despite this, there are numerous investigations and experiences that assess the advantages of using this type of tools and their impact on the educational field, such as [12–15].

Already in [6], it is mentioned that people must learn the rules and dynamics to be able to play. In [5], the authors state that the latest advances in cognitive science generally support the learning principles incorporated by games. For example, they highlight the active and leading role that students have when solving problems in real time and with immediate feedback. In [16], it is explained that video games use design strategies to generate virtual environments that capture user perception abilities, create sensory gratification, and generate a feeling of immersion in which the player feels that he/she can participate. And it is through this interactivity that the fundamental factors of the learning process are achieved – attraction, immersion, emotion and motivation.

Taking into account that serious games can be used for learning, the advantages of this type of tools for the educational field should also be studied. Several research works that have explored this aspect have been reviewed. [12] carry out an experiment to learn about the safety measures required in case of an airplane accident, and they found that the serious game used helped achieve longer-term learning. [17] developed a serious game called PLMAN to carry out artificial intelligence practices. Among their results, they mention that they were able to reduce student dropout rates for that course from 13% to 9% in connection with the use of these tools and the motivation they produce. Some authors also state that a reduced level of anxiety is observed in students, as seen in [18]. In this article, the serious game Semideus is used to evaluate students' knowledge about fractions. Another advantage that has been mentioned by various authors when integrating serious games to their educational proposals, is increased enjoyment and fun for students while they work. An example of this is presented in [13], where the use of the game Gem-Game is described.

There are various advantages related to the use of serious games in educational processes. However, motivation is an advantage that is often mentioned in different research works [14,15,19,20], including some articles already referred to [12,13,17,18]. This is important, since motivation is essential for learning. Thus, serious games are considered as a potentially useful tool for educators' didactic proposals.

Still, it should be noted that most of these works focus on the learning process itself, and only a few consider student evaluation specifically, such as [18] or [17]. If evaluations are considered to be stressful for university students [21], using serious games in this instance could be of interest.

It is based on this that we consider the use of serious games for the evaluation process, under the hypothesis that they can help improve student motivation and reduce the pressure they feel.

As part of the research supporting this proposal, a set of methodologies for designing, creating and evaluating serious games was studied, such as the ones presented in [22–25]. These methodologies usually have a series of stages that guide the decisions to be made in relation to each of the desired goals. One of these stages, as discussed in [26], is assessing the game. [23], for instance, propose using [27] ARCS model to measure motivation increase when using the game. This model analyzes four dimensions – namely, attention, relevance, confidence based on feedback, and satisfaction. [22] designed a table that summarizes various approaches used for evaluating serious games. For each approach, the following is included: what to measure (for example, game influence, satisfaction, motivation, attitudes, skills, learning, etc.), when is it measured (before, during and/or after using the game), and how is it measured (self-reports, tests, etc.). This background information allowed us making decisions about how to set up sessions to use the serious game Desafiate, and what type of evaluation method to use.

3   Introducing Desafiate

Desafiate is a serious game that was developed specifically for mobile devices that use the Android operating system (at the moment). Its purpose is providing self-assessment tools to students. It is a quiz-type game where questions are obtained through integration with the self-assessment tool of a specific VLTE.

In this game, the user plays as a pirate who has found some treasure maps. The game tells the story of a pirate that decides to go out in an adventure and sail through an archipelago of islands. His goal is to collect all the treasures shown on the maps. To achieve this, on each island there is a person who presents a challenge. The pirate will be able to get the corresponding treasure only by correctly solving the challenge.

The adventure ends when the pirate solves all challenges and returns to his starting port, where the results of the adventure are displayed. As previously stated, the questions in Desafiate are obtained through communication with a VLTE. However, communication is not limited to this alone. Several elements in Desafiate are linked to elements in the VLTE, in particular to those in the self-assessment module. First, the player must log into the game from a mobile device with the credentials already obtained for the VLTE. This home screen can be seen in Fig. 1.

Fig. 1. Login screen in Desfiate

After this, the player will be able to see different available adventures, each representing a self-assessment that the student has in the VLTE. The status of the self-assessment indicates whether the player can embark on the adventure or only see its results (if it has already been solved). Each of the questions in a self-assessment task is related to the challenges that make up an adventure in Desafiate and that are presented on the islands. The grade that the student gets in the self-assessment will depend on the results of the challenges. Figure 2 graphically shows these relationships, using the IDEAS VLTE, which is currently integrated into Desafiate. It should be noted that the game has a layered design, where its communication layer with the VLTE allows integration with other environments as well, not just IDEAS, without affecting game logic. More information about these aspects can be found in [28].

4   Methodology Used in Sessions

The objective of this research is establishing if the game Desafiate, used for self-assessment, has an impact on student motivation, as proposed in some of the methodologies mentioned in the previous section. More specifically, two different hypotheses are proposed:

Fig. 2. Link between Desfiate and IDEAS.

H1: Using the serious game Desafiate for self-assessment improves student motivation.

H2: Using a serious game (Desafiate) for self-assessment reduces the pressure that students feel during this process.

To find out if these hypotheses are true, we worked with contrast groups throughout two test sessions, collecting data for comparisons. The goal of the sessions is not only to be able to compare contrast groups, but also the results obtained with each of them.

Sessions were held in the context of the subject Programming I of the Computer Engineering degree. This course of studies belongs to the School of Computer Science of the National University of La Plata. For each of the sessions, a self-assessment task was created in collaboration with the educators. Each of these self-assessments included contents that had been addressed so far in the course. The students who completed the self-assessment were those who attended class on the day of each session.

Since the subject is divided into three different sub-groups, or commissions, as they are referred to, for the first session it was decided to use a different self-assessment strategy for each commission. Thus, one commission used pen and paper to complete the self-assessment, another commission completed it online using the IDEAS VLTE, and the last one did so using Desafiate on mobile devices. Then, in the following test session, self-assessment strategies were rotated among the groups. Thus, the commission that had used pen and paper to complete the self-assessment in the first session, used IDEAS in the second session; the commission that originally used IDEAS now used Desafiate;

and the commission that had used Desafiate switched to pen and paper. This can be seen in Fig. 3.

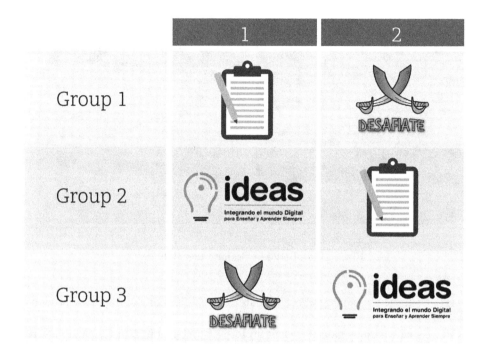

Fig. 3. Methods used in each session by the commissions.

In the case of the commissions that used IDEAS, all necessary arrangements were made to have the computers and tools required to carry out the sessions. To do this, tests were carried out in one of the PC rooms available at the institution. Access to both IDEAS and self-assessment had to be ensured. In the case of the commissions that used Desafiate, a download link was provided to students so that they could install the game on their cell phones. Also, tablets with the Android operating system were prepared to be used by any students who had not been able to install the app.

To measure student motivation, IMI was used, which is an instrument that analyzes and measures various dimensions related to intrinsic motivation. This instrument has been used by [29] and [30]. The instrument consists in answering a questionnaire with statements that give an overall score on different sub-scales or analysis variables, each related to one dimension. Each statement is directly related to a specific analysis variable, and only some of the questions for each variable can be selected. In total, there are seven variables, but only four were used for our test: interest, pressure, effort and usefulness, similar to the dimensions considered by the ARCS model, mentioned above.

The "interest" analysis variable is the most important for our goals, since it is the one that measures intrinsic motivation itself. "Pressure" is considered to be a negative indicator, so a low score is desirable for it. In the case of the "effort" variable, a high score is desirable, since it indicates that activity participants felt motivated to try harder. Finally, "usefulness" indicates how useful participants consider the activity.

To obtain a result for each analysis variable, the score obtained for each answer has to be evaluated. A 7-point Likert scale was used to show different degrees of agreement with a given statement. It allowed obtaining the mean for the results collected for each variable. There are some statements whose score is obtained by subtracting the response value from 8, since they are negative statements (reverse). The goal of using these types of statements and calculating the average score for each variable is minimizing any inconsistencies in responses.

For result analysis, the "interest" and "pressure" variables are considered separately. To validate the hypotheses, the difference between contrast groups should be statistically significant. To this end, an **ANOVA** test is used for all 3 groups, and a **Welch** test is used for group pairs. On the other hand, a general analysis is presented, describing the results for each of the participating commissions. To do this, the mean of each of the variables is used for each of the commissions.

5   Results

In each of the following subsections, the sessions carried out are presented and analyzed. Each subsection describes how the sessions were carried out and discusses the corresponding results.

5.1   Results Obtained in the First Session

A total of 64 students belonging to each of the three commissions that are part of the subject participated in this session. Students were distributed as follows: 23 students completed the self-assessment using pen and paper, 19 completed it using IDEAS, and 22 completed it using Desafiate. After the self-assessment, each student was given the IMI questionnaire, with 24 questions in total. From these questionnaires, only those that were completed correctly were used. Thus, a total of 57 questionnaires were processed. One of the questionnaires completed using pen and paper was discarded due to an ambiguous answer with two possible values. There were six questionnaires completed using IDEAS that were not answered in full, so they were not considered either. The total number of questionnaires processed was, in summary, as follows: 22 questionnaires completed using pen and paper, 13 questionnaires completed using IDEAS, and 22 questionnaires completed using Desafiate.

The results of the means for each of the four analysis variables are shown in Table 1. As it can be seen in that table, the "interest" variable is different for all groups, Desafiate being the assessment strategy with the highest value, and IDEAS with the lowest. If we combine this with the fact that Desafiate was the self-assessment process with which participants felt the least pressure, the serious game is considered to be the most motivating method for students. However, each of these variables will be analyzed separately to check if these differences are significant enough to accept the hypotheses.

Table 1. Means recorded for each commission for the questionnaires completed after the first session.

Method used	Commission	Interest	Pressure	Effort	Usefulness
Pen and paper	1	5.2208	3.2273	4.9818	6.4351
IDEAS	2	4.8132	2.9538	4.6769	6.1209
Desafiate	3	5.7532	2.5364	4.9545	6.2208

When analyzing the following two variables, it can be seen that there are no differences between the three methods used (three contrast groups). If we consider "usefulness", it can be seen that all three methods obtained very high scores. This indicates that students generally see self-assessment as something useful for their learning process. Moving on to "effort", again, all three methods obtained high scores, indicating that students consider self-assessment to be an effort. These two variables are indicative of the importance of self-assessment for students, since they consider it highly useful for their learning process, despite the effort it involves.

5.2   Results Obtained in the Second Session

A total of 52 students participated in the second session: 17 students in the first commission, 19 students in the second commission, and 16 students in the third commission. For this session, the methods used by students to complete the self-assessment were rotated. Thus, students in the first commission used Desafiate, when they had previously used pen and paper. Students in the second commission, who had previously used IDEAS, completed the self-assessment using pen and paper. Finally, the students who had previously worked with Desafiate (third commission), used IDEAS for this second session. After completing the self-evaluations, students completed the same IMI questionnaire again. In this case there was only one student, in the Desafiate commission, who did not complete the questionnaire correctly. Thus, a total of 51 questionnaires were considered for the analysis.

Table 2 shows the means obtained for the four variables for each of the commissions, in addition to the method they used to complete the self-assessment. It can be seen that the interest generated by Desafiate was the highest among the three methods, followed by IDEAS. Compared to the previous session, an increase in the difference between Desafiate and the other methods can be observed. This is because the mean for these other methods decreased, while that of Desafiate remained approximately the same. In the case of "pressure", results were higher compared to the previous session, but the order between the different commissions remained the same. Thus, the first commission recorded the highest mean compared to the other two commissions for both sessions. Similarly, the third commission was the one that recorded the lowest value in both sessions in terms of the variable "pressure". One possible explanation of this increase is that the second test session was carried out closer in time to end-of-course exams.

Table 2. Means recorded for each commission for the questionnaires completed after the second session.

Method used	Commission	Interest	Pressure	Effort	Usefulness
Pen and paper	2	3.9699	4.1789	2.4632	5.9849
IDEAS	3	4.5625	4.6125	2.3	6.0804
Desafiate	1	5.7054	4.55	2.6125	6.1518

As regards "effort" and "usefulness", the values obtained were similar to those recorded in the previous session. In the case of "usefulness", even though lower values were obtained, they were still high, around an average of 6 points. This supports the results obtained in the first session in relation to how useful students perceive self-assessment to be. As regards "effort", lower – but similar – values were recorded. These results support the idea that students consider self-assessment as a useful tool for their learning process, even if it involves an additional effort for them.

6   Results Analysis

In this section, the results obtained in both test sessions with students will be analyzed. To this end, the section is divided into two subsections – one devoted to the analysis of the "interest" variable, and another one dealing with the "pressure" variable.

6.1   Analysis of the "Interest" Variable

To analyze the "interest" variable, groups should be compared to check if the differences between them are statistically significant in each of the sessions. This will allow corroborating whether hypothesis H1 is fulfilled or not (carrying out a self-assessment using the serious game Desafiate improves student motivation).

For the first test session, an **ANOVA** test was performed to evaluate the differences between the three groups. A p-value of **0.05** was set as test threshold. In this case, the test yielded a p-value of **0.054378**, meaning that the hypothesis cannot be corroborated. Pairing up the groups and applying **Welch** test, it can be seen that there is no significant difference between the pen and paper method and the other two methods, since there are no results below **0.05**. The difference between this method and Desafiate yields a p-value of **0.150223**, while the difference with IDEAS yields a p-value of **0.259359**. Even so, the difference between Desafiate and IDEAS does become statistically significant, since the p-value for these populations is **0.00375037**. With these values, hypothesis H1 cannot be corroborated. However, it can be stated that students find Desafiate more interesting than IDEAS for self-assessment.

In the case of the second test session, slightly different results were obtained. When evaluating the difference between the three groups using the **ANOVA** test, a p-value of 0.000466 was obtained. In this case, because the value obtained is below the threshold of 0.05, the result is statistically significant. When analyzing group pairs using **Welch** test, it can be seen that Desafiate obtains significant differences compared to the other methods. When comparing Desafiate with IDEAS, a p-value of **0.0288069** was obtained. These values corroborate hypothesis H1. When comparing with pen and paper, the p-value obtained was even lower – **0.0000251748**.

The results obtained in both tests indicates that using Desafiate generates greater interest in students at a general level. However, when comparing with the other methods, the differences were statistically significant in three of the four cases analyzed using **Welch** test, while this was so only in one of the two cases when applying **ANOVA**. Even though these results are favorable, they are not enough to corroborate the hypothesis. Still, they allow concluding that students find Desafiate to be more interest than IDEAS. As regards the comparison between IDEAS and pen and paper, the differences found were not greater.

Another interesting aspect to analyze is the fact that Desafiate obtained similar results in both sessions. In contrast, the results obtained by the other two methods were reduced by around 1 point on average. In other words, students were less interested in using pen and paper and IDEAS as the course progressed, which does not happen with Desafiate. A possible analysis in relation to this is that the use of serious games allows keeping the level of interest of the students over time. However, further study wold be required in this regard.

6.2   Analysis of the Variable "Pressure"

The procedure used to analyze the results for "pressure" are the same as those used for "interest". In this case, our goal is corroborating whether hypothesis H2 is fulfilled or not (carrying out a self-assessment using the serious game Desafiate reduces the pressure felt by students).

During the first test session, the following results were obtained. When applying the **ANOVA** test, the p-value obtained was **0.139781**. This value is greater than the threshold of **0.05** required to corroborate the hypothesis. When applying the **Welch** test in pairs, the results obtained were in agreement with those of the **ANOVA** test, since there were no statistically significant differences between pairs. Taking into account the pen and paper method, a p-value of **0.471610** was obtained when comparing it to the use of IDEAS, whereas a p-value of **0.0593150** was obtained when comparing it to Desafiate, which is closer to the acceptance criteria for the hypothesis. As for the comparison between IDEAS and Desafiate, a p-value of **0.262056** was obtained. In this case, no result allows corroborating the hypothesis.

The results for the second session maintain the same reading presented so far. The application of the **ANOVA** test for the three groups yielded a p-value of **0.676174**. In the case of **Welch** test, the results corresponding to the pen and paper method yielded a p-value of **0.621546** when compared with IDEAS, and **0.659861** when compared with Desafiate. For the comparison between IDEAS and Desafiate, the result obtained was **0.418569**.

Taking into account the results obtained from each session, it can be seen that hypothesis H2 cannot be corroborated. Even in the second session, the results were even further than those for the first session. It should be noted that both sessions presented the same order. While the first commission felt the most pressure in both cases, the third commission felt the least pressure. Thus, it is likely that the group itself presents characteristics related to this perception regarding pressure in a self-assessment.

7 Conclusions

Serious games are one of the tools that have proliferated thanks to the use of ICTs in Education. Even though they have several advantages, motivation is usually the one most commonly mentioned by reference authors on the subject. In this article, a comparison was made between three different methods to complete a self-assessment activity. The IMI questionnaire was used to measure the level of interest, pressure, effort and perceived usefulness according to students when carrying out this activity. This questionnaire allows measuring activity participants intrinsic motivation.

The results show that students, in general, perceive self-assessment as a useful tool for their learning process, regardless of the effort they perceive it requires. As regards interest and pressure, two different hypotheses were proposed. On the one hand, hypothesis H1 proposed that completing a self-assessment activity using a serious game (in this case, Desafiate) improves students' motivation. The overall result shows that these levels are improved when using a serious game. However, the tests performed showed that not all these improvements are statistically significant to corroborate the hypotheses. When analyzing group pairs, differences were found in most cases (3 out of 4). The only case where no significant differences were found was when comparing Desafiate with pen and paper during the first session. Furthermore, the **ANOVA** tests yielded significant differences in half of the cases (1 out of 2).

Then, hypothesis H2 was analyzed, which proposed that completing a self-assessment activity using the serious game Desafiate reduces the pressure felt by the students. In this case, comparisons between pairs of groups and comparisons between all three groups show that this hypothesis cannot be corroborated. No statistically significant differences were found in any of the cases analyzed.

These results also showed the need for further research around the H1 hypothesis. This opens up the door to continuing research with a larger population and considering the incidence of some input variables, such as group members, gender, previous experience in using VLTEs, etc.

Acknowledgments. This project has been partially funded by the REFORTICCA (Resources for Empowering ICT, Science, and Environment Educators) program of the Scientific Research Agency of the Province of Buenos Aires.

References

1. Cheng, M., Yuen, A.H.K.: Student continuance of learning management system use: a longitudinal exploration. Comput. Educ. **120**, 241–253 (2018)
2. Ramírez-Correa, P.E., Rondan-Cataluña, F.J., Arenas-Gaitán, J., Alfaro-Perez, J.L.: Moderating effect of learning styles on a learning management system's success. Telematics Inform. **34**(1), 272–286 (2017)
3. Sanz, C.V.: Los objetos de aprendizaje, un debate abierto y necesario. Bit Byte **1**(1), 33–35 (2015)
4. Cavus, N., Alhih, M.S.: Learning management systems use in science education. Procedia Soc. Behav. Sci. **143**, 517–520 (2014). 3rd Cyprus International Conference on Educational Research, CY-ICER2014, 30 January – 1 February 2014, Lefkosa, North Cyprus
5. Lárez, B.E.M.: Factores emocionales en el diseño y la ejecución de videojuegos y su valor formativo en la sociedad digital.: El caso de los videojuegos bélicos. Ediciones Universidad de Salamanca, 1 edn. (2014)
6. Abt, C.: Serious Games. Viking Press, New York (1970)
7. Gallego, F.J., Villagrá, C.J., Satorre, R., Compañ, P., Molina, R., Largo, F.L.: Panorámica: serious games, gamification y mucho más. Revisión, 7(2) (2014)
8. Archuby, F.H., Sanz, C.V., Pesado, P.M.: Análisis de la experiencia de utilización del juego serio "desafiate" para la autoevaluación de los alumnos. In: XXV Congreso Argentino de Ciencias de la Computación (CACIC 2019, Universidad Nacional de Río Cuarto) (2019)
9. Michael, D., Chen, S.: Serious Games: Games That Educate, Train, and Inform. Thomson Course Technology (2005)
10. Bione, J., Miceli, P.: AstroCódigo. PhD thesis, Facultad de Informática (2017)
11. Dörner, R., Göbel, S., Effelsberg, W., Wiemeyer, J. (eds.): Serious Games. Springer, Cham (2016). https://doi.org/10.1007/978-3-319-40612-1
12. Chittaro, L., Buttussi, F.: Assessing knowledge retention of an immersive serious game vs. a traditional education method in aviation safety. IEEE Trans. Visual Comput. Graphics **21**(4), 529–538 (2015)
13. Giannakos, M.: Enjoy and learn with educational games: examining factors affecting learning performance. Comput. Educ. **68**, 429–439 (2013)
14. Rutten, N., van Joolingen, W.R., van der Veen, J.T.: The learning effects of computer simulations in science education. Comput. Educ. **58**(1), 136–153 (2012)
15. Vos, N., van der Meijden, H., Denessen, E.: Effects of constructing versus playing an educational game on student motivation and deep learning strategy use. Comput. Educ. **56**(1), 127–137 (2011)
16. Crawford, C.: On Game Design. New Riders, Indianapolis (2003)

17. de Haro, M.J.C., Durán, F.J., Puig, C.P., Pérez, P.S., Villagrá, C., Vaíllo, S.C.: Evaluación en tiempo real (comunicación). Lógica Computacional, July 2009
18. Kiili, K., Devlin, K., Perttula, A., Tuomi, P., Lindstedt, A.: Using video games to combine learning and assessment in mathematics education. Int. J. Serious Games **2**(4), 37–55 (2015)
19. Kiili, K., Ketamo, H.: Evaluating cognitive and affective outcomes of a digital game-based math test. IEEE Trans. Learn. Technol. **11**(2), 255–263 (2018)
20. Boyle, E., Connoly, T.M., Hainey, T.: The role of psychology in understanding the impact of computer games. Entertain. Comput. **2**, 69–74 (2011)
21. Ferrel, G.: A view of the assessment and feedback landscape: baseline analysis of policy and practice from the JISC assessment & feedback programme. JISC (2012)
22. Mayer, I., et al.: The research and evaluation of serious games: toward a comprehensive methodology. Br. J. Educ. Technol. **45**(3), 502–527 (2014)
23. Su, C.-H., Chen, K.T.-K., Fan, K.-K.: Rough set theory based fuzzy TOPSIS on serious game design evaluation framework. Math. Probl. Eng. **2013**, 1–13 (2013)
24. Becker, T.: The character of successful trainings with serious games. Int. J. Emerg. Technol. Learn. (iJET), **5**(SI3) (2010)
25. Nadolski, R.J., et al.: EMERGO: a methodology and toolkit for developing serious games in higher education. Simul. Gaming **39**(3), 338–352 (2008)
26. Cano, S., Arteaga, J.M., Collazos, C.A., Gonzalez, C.S., Zapata, S.: Toward a methodology for serious games design for children with auditory impairments. IEEE Lat. Am. Trans. **14**(5), 2511–2521 (2016)
27. Karoulis, A., Demetriadis, S.: The motivational factor in educational games. interaction between learner's internal and external representations in multimedia environments. Research Report, Kaleidoscope NoE JEIRP (2005)
28. Archuby, F.H., Sanz, C.V., Pesado, P.M.: Desafiate: juego serio para la autoevaluación de los alumnos y su integración con un entorno virtual de enseñanza y aprendizaje. CACIC, 23 (2017)
29. McAuley, E., Duncan, T., Tammen, V.V.: Psychometric properties of the intrinsic motivation inventory in a competitive sport setting: a confirmatory factor analysis. Res. Q. Exerc. Sport **60**(1), 48–58 (1989)
30. Tsigilis, N., Theodosiou, A.: Temporal stability of the intrinsic motivation inventory. Percept. Mot. Skills **97**(1), 271–280 (2003)

Agility in Instructional Design. Strengthening of Digital Skills in Incoming Students at FaCENA-UNNE

Mirta G. Fernandez[(⊠)] [iD], María V. Godoy Guglielmone [iD],
Sonia I. Mariño [iD], and Walter G. Barrios

Facultad de Artes, Diseño y Ciencias de la Cultura (FADyC),
Facultad de Ciencias Exactas y Naturales y Agrimensura (FaCENA),
Universidad Nacional del Nordeste (UNNE), Corrientes, Argentina
mirtagf@hotmail.com

Abstract. In a context of permanent evolution, Higher Education Institutions must plan and develop actions that promote the acquisition of the media, digital and information skills necessary for the insertion of new professionals in a world where Information Technology and Communication (ICT) is increasingly dominant. The article presents an agile educational proposal aimed at facilitating access to ICT and training in its use. The SCRUM-based agile framework that integrates the ADDIE Instructional Design Model is described in the Sprint. The proposal is validated in a course for incoming students of the year 2019. The implementation of the applied innovative strategy is analyzed and evaluated, identifying itself as successful in complex contexts such as education.

Keywords: Agility · SCRUM · ADDIE model · Competency management · Digital competences · Higher education

1 Introduction

Higher education designs different strategies for the development of its substantive activities, such as teaching, extension, research. In all these university functions, ICTs play a fundamental role, providing innovative ways to carry them out, in a knowledge society in which complexity is a constant.

In Educational Technology for Higher Education [1], is conceived that one of the important challenges that prevents the adoption of technology at this educational level has to do with the "improvement of digital competence" [1]. This is not just about providing access to ICTs but about training for proper use [2].

The conceptualization term digital competence varies depending on the organism or organization that formulates it. However, the literature states that it involves the safe and critical use of information society technologies for work, leisure and communication [3].

This article delves into digital competences by proposing an agile framework that takes up the specific roles of SCRUM [4] and integrates them into the ADDIE [5] instructional design model (Analyze-Design-Develop-Implement-Evaluate). To achieve

© Springer Nature Switzerland AG 2020
P. Pesado and M. Arroyo (Eds.): CACIC 2019, CCIS 1184, pp. 124–136, 2020.
https://doi.org/10.1007/978-3-030-48325-8_9

the objectives, various technical, didactic and pedagogical decisions were planned; it was outlined in Congreso Argentino de Ciencias de la Computación [6]. Agile framework providing some preliminary work on planning guidelines was raised. In this case SCRUM is applied integrating the ADDIE instructional design model.

1.1 Digital Skills in Higher Education

Educational institutions agree that basic digital skills have become fundamental tools for human and academic development [7]. Its acquisition of them are today an indispensable condition for individuals to achieve full personal, social and professional development that meets the demands of a globalized world, promotes economic-social development and "... prepare them to function in knowledge societies ..." [8].

At present, children and young people make a profuse use of ICT, especially based on mobile devices and social networks [9, 10]. However, several studies deepen the hypothesis stating that, when used in formal tasks, such as the search for information, comparison, critical thinking, reliable sources of digital information, etc., young people demonstrate ignorance or some difficulty in these aspects [11–14].

In this sense, it coincides with the meta-analysis [14] which indicates that there is no need to make assumptions about the competences and digital knowledge of the apprentices when they enter Higher Education. Generally, no specific time is assigned in the academic calendar to work these knowledges explicitly; rather, they are introduced in the classroom work methodologies and are demanded as competences that should be had previously or that should be acquired during the course of training [15].

The interest in the reform of educational systems, in the search for new ways of conceiving the curriculum and understanding the teaching and learning processes has taken shape through different projects sponsored by international organizations such as UNESCO and OECD [9, 16].

The Consejo Federal de Decanos de Facultades de Ingeniería (CONFEDI) Argentina [17], is one of the organizations that strongly promotes Training by Competences, given that it has developed Second Generation Standards for the accreditation of Engineering careers in the Argentina, based on this educational model.

Meanings and Contributions in Relation to Digital Competences. The conceptualization term digital competition varies depending on the organism or organization that formulates it [2]. However, the literature states that it involves the safe and critical use of information society technologies for work, leisure and communication [3].

UNESCO sustains that digital competences are defined as a spectrum of competences that facilitate the use of digital devices, communication applications and networks to access information and carry out better management of these [16]. Concepts of competence in the educational field are synthesized in [18]. A systematic review of the concept of Digital Competences in Education is provided in [19].

An extended definition that is challenged in this work is that which exposes *"Digital Competence as the combination of knowledge, skills and abilities, in conjunction with values and attitudes, to achieve objectives effectively and efficiently in contexts and with digital tools"* [8, 16, 19]. It is explained in terms of five dimensions to which students must aspire and teachers promote: the *learning dimension* encompasses the transformation of information into knowledge and its acquisition; the *informational dimension* encompasses the collection, evaluation and treatment of information, in digital environments; the *communicative dimension* encompasses interpersonal and social communication; the *dimension of digital culture* encompasses the social and cultural practices of the knowledge society and digital citizenship; the *technological dimension* encompasses technological literacy and the knowledge and mastery of digital environments.

From the aforementioned, it is possible to infer that acquisition of various skills for the management of ICT improve and enrich the preparation of students, promoting their critical thinking skills, independent study and adaptation to the different learning experiences demanded by the today's society.

1.2 Educational Planning to Achieve Expected Results

To planning is about organizing an activity to be carried out to obtain the best results with the minimum of time and resources. It involves the interaction of various dimensions and actors; and to foresee if the goals set aim to achieve the formative action and if it responds to the requirements of the context and of each member of the educational community [20].

Agile Methods in Educational Management Projects. Agile methodologies are described as "a group of project management approaches that are in many ways opposed to traditional cascade project management techniques in which the project is fully defined before you start executing it" [21]. One of the agile methodologies used in different and complex projects is SCRUM. SCRUM as a framework has the "ability to enhance self-organization and cooperation" [22]. Furthermore, it is applied in educational contexts such as the benchmark in [23]. For example, in [21] a systematic review is presented to know how the agile method "is being used to promote key competences of sustainable development" in education. In [24] the roles, phases, artifacts and manifests are mentioned as essential elements. So, in SCRUM there are 3 roles: product owner, team, Scrum master; it consists of 3 phases: planning phase (subdivided into planning and architectural design), development phase and completion phase. The manifests are 4 postulates that refer to a series of associated principles. On the other hand, activities, artifacts and documentation to be produced, tools and notations to be used, order of execution of activities, among other definitions, are defined [25].

Instructional Design for Educational Planning. There are several methodological frameworks that provide prescriptions in educational planning. In [26] seven instructional models mentioned classified according to type of model, the theory of learning that applies the principles on which it is based, the number of phases that comprise the scope. In addition, these authors include their essential characteristics.

About the topic, literature reviews developed around instructional models, such as the two mentioned. In [27] reviews exposed between 1994 and 2017 based on the items available in Scopus, ProQuest, Jstor. In addition, "selected articles describe strategies for incorporating information and communication technologies in teaching or learning". In [28] the review is oriented to identify the evaluation of instructional design models, to know a "theoretical approach in relation to the subject and a discussion of the key aspects currently, given the increasing number of self-evaluation and accreditation processes in educational institutions of higher education".

Schrum describes instructional design as an essential contribution to the creation of virtual education courses. It includes the determination of learning needs and the environment, definition of objectives, the most appropriate resources are chosen, the contents and learning activities are developed and the evaluation is designed.

Wiliams [29] describes the basic model of instructional design, whether based on ICTs or not, valid for any educational context. The author presents models such as ADDIE, "rapid prototyping", and a model based on 4 components (4C/ID).

It is convenient, beyond the select model, to be able to have indicators that determine its quality and improve the possible deficiencies.

Bates proposes ADDIE [5] and to be put into practice, it is helped by the didactic, that is, the set of techniques used in teaching. In turn, it will be influenced by multiple factors: the context of ICT-based education in which it will be applied.

If a virtual learning environment is used, it will be necessary to know its capabilities, potentials and limitations. So, for example, it will be necessary to know if a group work can be developed, if there is the possibility of raising debates, if a certain type of activities and practices can be performed, the types of interaction that can occur, etc.

In relation to the evaluation of the model, Williams presents different levels of evaluation, where he distinguishes 5 of them. In the first one, activities are designed to evaluate the course and how to improve it. At the next level (level 2), the assessment of students' knowledge is carried out. In 3, the process of transfer of training is evaluated and in 4 the economic impact of the course (not applicable in this work) is measured [29].

2   Methodological Framework

Agile framework providing some preliminary work on planning guidelines was raised. In this case SCRUM is applied integrating the ADDIE instructional design model.

Synthetically it was worked in the framework summarized in Fig. 1 in relation to SCRUM.

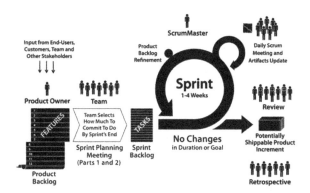

Fig. 1. Key roles, artifacts, and principal events in SCRUM based on [4]

Also, in Fig. 2 the phases linked with Model ADDIE considering coincidences phases with the literature reviewed are schematized.

Analyze	Design	Develop	Implement	Evaluate
to identify all the variables that must be taken into account when designing the course, such as the characteristics and the previous knowledge of the students, the resources, etc.	this stage focuses on the identification of the learning objectives for the course and how the materials will be created and designed, and decide on the choice and use of technology.	it refers to the modality of distribution of the course, which includes any previous training or training of the staff that provides support to the student, and evaluation of the students.	it refers to the modality of distribution of the course, which includes any previous training or training of the staff that provides support to the student, and evaluation of the students.	feedback and data are analyzed to identify areas that require improvements and that will be considered in the design, development and implementation of the next edition of the course.

Fig. 2. ADDIE phases applied for this experience based on [5]

In particular, the roles or profiles of individuals that intervene in the proposal and how they integrate in the phases of the ADDIE model presented in [6] are considered. The meetings were considered for planning and the stages of the ADDIE Model, suitable to be applied in education, are applied in the Sprint.

3   Results

The results are presented based on the agile methodological framework that integrates the roles defined by SCRUM with the ADDIE instructional model. In addition, it is exposed as context validation, an implementation developed with incoming students of FACENA 2019.

As summarized in Fig. 3, the resultant integration, is the applied model.

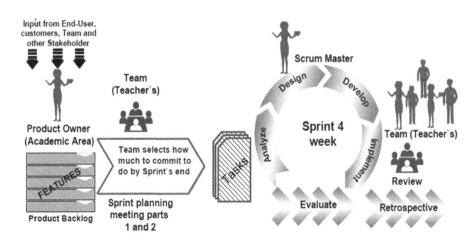

Fig. 3. Key roles, artifacts, and principal events in SCRUM following established phases for this experience based on [5]

The SCRUM roles processes were adopted and the Sprint activities were adapted to those that support the ADDIE model.

3.1 Methodological Application

It should be noted that these phases can be iterated within the framework of a Sprint, another concept supported by the perspective established by SCRUM. This is how roles are defined:

- *Product owner*: Academic area; represents internal and external stakeholders, so you must understand and support the needs of all users and the SCRUM Team.
- *Scrum master*: Coordinator of the module, he is responsible for ensuring the development of the process and works to ensure that the team adheres to the practices, as well as training the team to overcome difficulties.
- *Team*: Team of teachers - Tutors - Content Specialists. It is a directed and self-organized team that has everything they need within the team to carry out the work (or training action).

In this context for the Product Backlog, the following phases defined by the chosen ADDIE instructional design model were considered.

Analyze. Focused on training in digital competences, a review was made around generic competences and specifically on these, the object of this study. The importance of knowing previous training is recognized, as well as access to ICT; for this purpose, surveys and specifications specific to the academic area were consulted. Also, identifying antecedents to delimit possible scenarios.

Linked to the above, the Academic Unit maintains a number of incoming students, sustained over time, as shown in Fig. 4. In its 2019 school year, it had approximately 1300 pre-registered students in first year, almost 90% participated in the project (the remaining percentage, are students who relapse in the first-year course).

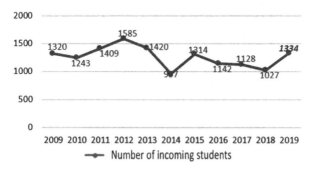

Fig. 4. Evolution of FaCENA's incoming students (https://www.unne.edu.ar/index.php?option=com_joomdoc&task=document.download&path=doc_estadisticas/nvosinscriptos2019.pdf&lang=es).

Roles Involved: Scrum master, Product Owner; who are in charge of providing information about the student's profile, context, among other concrete specifications.

Design. It included the description of the content areas to be incorporated, and the storyboard that defines the presentation of them in different formats (text, audio and video and their order), as well as deciding on the choice and use of technology to support the educational offer; the virtual classroom to be used was outlined. The Moodle platform is used by the University as a teaching environment and virtual activities are developed for students in it. It established:

I. General objective
"To introduce students in digital competitions for their appropriate development at the university". Articulating the activities with the other modules for incoming students, which were developed simultaneously.

II. Specific objectives
To provide general information of the communication channels that the faculty possesses.
To develop basic skills in the proper use of educational interaction tools. In particular, the SIU Guaraní, Virtual Classroom in Moodle and the FaCENA Institutional site platforms.

Roles Involved. The team proposes a design that is discussed with the Scrum master and the Product Owner.

Develop. The production of audiovisual materials was carried out and the virtual classroom was configured as such, projected in the previous phase, as shown in Fig. 5.

Fig. 5. Interface developed for the virtual environment Moodle.

Roles Involved: The Scrum master and the Product Owner, who transmit their decision to the team. Some artifacts can be built by the team and other outsourced items. Including the team ensures the relevance and commitment to shared work.

Implement. It refers to the modality of execution. Training in ICT skills and the way the courses are distributed are taken into account. The training of personnel that provide student support and the evaluation of students are also contemplated.

The implementation was carried out in meetings during the month of February with virtualized activities that extended until April. The work focused on elucidating repeated issues, according to the following themes:

- Main resources to use in the modules on the Moodle platform of the university: users' management, access, forums and tasks.
- In relation to SIU Guaraní management academic information system, the most frequent questions collected from the Student Center and the Studies Management Area were pointed out; they are linked to the users administration, course and exams dates, certificates, consulting academic history, and others.
- The use of the FaCENA's Institutional Web Site was discussed. It was presented as an official communication channel and the medium to obtain information about:
  - the final enrollment requirements of the school year,
  - the scholarships,
  - and procedures guide (application for university book, legalization of approved subject programs, time load of subjects, recognition of approved subjects in other careers or faculties, mandatory annual re-registration, etc.).

Roles Involved: The team that implements the training proposal based on the guidelines previously agreed with the Scrum master and the Product Owner. The implementation can take place in several iterations.

Evaluate. In reference to the evaluation of the contents, the ADDEI model proposes the formative and summative modality. In this case, a questionnaire was applied to generate aimed at reviewing the content addressed.

Feedback and data were analyzed to identify areas that require improvement and that will be considered in future design, development and implementation. These changes will be considered in the next edition of the course. Regarding the evaluation of the model, in the first instance the evaluation of the training transfer process was carried out. Activities were designed to evaluate the course and to define how to improve it. In addition, opinions were collected from the participants of the training action that was part of the Team.

Roles Involved. An evaluation of the project in process is carried out, the 3 defined roles intervene.

Some issues can be improved in this process, which mediates between the implementation and evaluation phases. Other substantial evaluations can be planned for a next stage.

3.2   Validation of the Proposal

The validation of the proposal was developed within the framework of the courses for incoming students. It focused on the roles: team, -represented by the tutors- and end user, characterized by the incoming students in the year 2019.

Inquiring about the overall experience, 87% of the students rated the implementation of the modules as Useful and Very Useful; and only 13% thought otherwise.

Figure 6 illustrates the results of the report extracted about two questions: what do you think about the course for incoming students 2019? Were the modules dictated useful for your incorporation into university life?

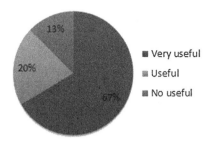

Fig. 6. Student's opinion: usefulness of the modules

In the evaluation of the module on Digital Competences, 80.4% answered Good or Excellent. Only 19.6% considered it Regular; as shown in Fig. 7.

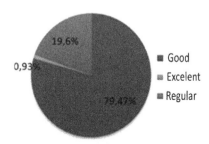

Fig. 7. Students' opinions about the Digital Competences module

Related to the adequacy of the duration of the modules; 20% of the students leaned towards the Digital Competencies module, as shown in Fig. 8.

The question was: Which of the modules do you think should be more extensive?

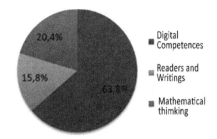

Fig. 8. Students' opinions about the duration of the modules

Another of the matters investigated dealt with the contents (expectations, depth and clarity). The Fig. 9 shows that in general, students responded positively on an average of 80%.

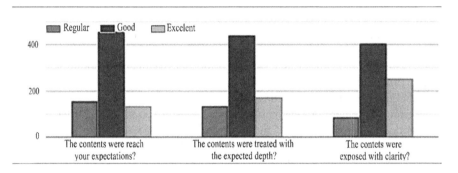

Fig. 9. Students' experience about the content developed in "digital competences".

From a qualitative point of view, the students were asked: What aspects of the modules should be improved? They referred more frequently to the following issues:

4. "Greater depth of content, for example, in the Mathematical Thinking Module".
5. "They should start with more anticipation to the subjects' courses".
6. "They could have been a bit more demanding/more dynamic".
7. "To divide into smaller commissions".
8. "To promote instances of interaction between incoming students".
9. "Increment the time extension of the modules".

4 Conclusions

Education and training systems require more agile strategies, in order to face complexities of the knowledge society.

Agile methodologies allow to make more flexible the design, development and maintenance of complex products. One of these products is the instructional design, a digital formative competence oriented to students using IT. In particular, the article presents an integration of SCRUM's roles, phases, artifacts and manifests in the phases of the ADDIE model.

So, in the validation context, through the proposed dynamics, the realization of the different dimensions of digital competences was evidenced:

– The technological dimension encompasses technological literacy and knowledge and mastery of digital environments. In this particular case, it was specified through the face-to-face meetings. In addition, it was completed through the technological literacy support resources provided in the virtual classroom designed for this proposal. It should be clarified that the design of other actions aimed at strengthening this dimension can be derived from data analysis.
– The communicative dimension encompasses interpersonal and social communication. In this experience it was mediated through the interactions promoted by the specially designed virtual classroom environment, especially reflected in the forums.
– The informational dimension covers the collection, evaluation and treatment of information, in digital environments. In this dimension, in particular, the active participation of the subject as responsible for their significant learning is encouraged. This is an essential tool in a society marked by ICT and where the use of technologies prevails from various media.
– The learning dimension encompasses the transformation of information into knowledge and its acquisition. In the e-society -which requires an individual in constant training and capable of overcoming infotoxication- students are required to acquire strategies addressed for the construction and re-construction of significant knowledge that contribute both in their personal training as in their social and cultural relationships. In addition, learning is marked by the internalization of these knowledges that are incorporated into the collection of each subject of the s. XXI.
– The dimension of digital culture encompasses the social and cultural practices of the knowledge society and digital citizenship. This proposal – in its entirety – contributes to this dimension. It is recognized that previous knowledge about digital competences may vary in university students – incoming or not –. Therefore, it is necessary to provide all students with spaces for interaction that encourage social and cultural practices with a view to achieving informed, responsible citizens who are capable of contributing to society.

Also, it is noted that this preliminary study provides reference information for the design of institutional plans based on agile framework oriented to strengthening the digital competence. This proposal follows the trends defined by CONFEDI, in order to define the curricula based on the competency approach.

Finally, the article proposes and validates a transdisciplinary approach when dealing with models of instructional design and management of agile projects in the context of higher education.

Acknowledgments. The authors are part of the Project accredited by the General Secretariat of Science and Technology by Resol. 1015/19 of the Northeast National University, PI 19F014, whose title is "Computer Systems: models, methods and tools". Director of the same Prof. Mariño, Sonia I. and Co-Director, Prof. Godoy Guglielmone, Maria V. The support of the Secretariat is appreciated.

References

1. Alexander, B., Ashford-Rowe, K., Barajas-Murphy, N., Dobbin, G., Knott, J., McCormack, M., Weber, N.: NMC Horizon Report: 2019 Higher Education Edition. Educause, Louisville (2019)
2. Gros Salvat, B., Contreras, D.: La alfabetización digital y el desarrollo de competencias ciudadanas. Revista Iberoamericana de Educación (OEI), 2006, num. 42, pp. 103–125 (2006)
3. Europeas, C.: Competencias clave para el aprendizaje permanente. Un marco de referencia europeo. Oficina de Publicaciones Oficiales de las Comunidades Europeas, Luxemburgo (2007)
4. Schwaber, K., Beedle, M.: Agile Software Development with SCRUM, vol. 1. Prentice Hall, Upper Saddle River (2002)
5. Bates, A.W.: La Enseñanza en la Era Digital. Una guía para la enseñanza y el aprendizaje (2015)
6. Fernández, M.G., Godoy Guglielmone, M.V., Barrios, W.G., Sonia, M.: Diseño instruccional para fortalecer las competencias digitales en ingresantes: el caso de la FaCENA-UNNE. In: XXV Congreso Argentino de Ciencias de la Computación (2019)
7. Lobato, J.I.Z., Navarro, R.E., Noriega, J.L.: Competencias digitales y educación superior (2016)
8. Deseco, P.: La definición y selección de competencias clave. Executive Summary. OCDE, España (2015)
9. Piscitelli, A.: Nativos digitales. Contratexto **016**, 43–56 (2008)
10. Chiecher, A.C., Melgar, M.F.: ¿Lo saben todo? Innovaciones educativas orientadas a promover competencias digitales en universitarios. Apertura (Guadalajara, Jal.) **10**(2), 110–123 (2018)
11. Araújo Da Silva, K.K., Behari, P.A.: Competências Digitais Na Educação: Uma Discussão Acerca Do Conceito. Educ. Rev. (2019). https://doi.org/10.1590/0102-4698209940
12. Cabra Torres, F., Marciales-Vivas, G.P.: Mitos, realidades y preguntas de investigación sobre los 'nativos digitales': una revisión. Universitas Psychologica 8(2), 323–338 (2009). Accessed 7 Dec 2019
13. Bautista, G., Escofet, A., Forés Miravalles, A., López Costa, M., Marimon Martí, M.: Superando el concepto de nativo digital. Análisis de las prácticas digitales del estudiantado universitario (2013)
14. Zuñiga, J.I., Edel, R., Lau, J.: Competencias digitales y educación superior (2016). In de http://rete.mx/index.php/8-numero-tematico-educacion-mediada-por-tecnologia/7-competencias-digitales-y-educacion-superior. Accessed 4 Dec 2019
15. Márquez, E.F., Olivencia, J.J.L., Meneses, E.J.L.: Formación en competencias digitales en la universidad. Percepciones del alumnado. Campus Virtuales 6(2), 79–89 (2017)
16. UNESCO: Las competencias digitales son esenciales para el empleo y la inclusión social. https://es.unesco.org/news/competencias-digitales-son-esenciales-empleo-y-inclusion-social. Accessed 3 Nov 2019

17. Consejo Federal de Decanos de Ingeniería (CONFEDI): Propuesta de estándares de segunda generación para la acreditación de carreras de ingeniería en la República Argentina. Universidad FASTA Ed, Mar del Plata (2018)
18. Arcano, B.: Competencias digitales y videojuegos online. DIM: Didáctica, Innovación y Multimedia; Núm. 19 (2010)
19. Reis, C., Pessoa, T., Gallego-Arrufat, M.J.: Alfabetización y competencia digital en Educación Superior: una revisión sistemática. REDU. Revista de Docencia Universitaria 17(1), 45–58 (2019)
20. Díaz, F., Lule, M.C.: Metodología de diseño curricular para educación superior. Trillas (1990)
21. López-Alcarria, A., Olivares-Vicente, A., Poza-Vilches, F.: A systematic review of the use of agile methodologies in education to foster sustainability competencies. Sustainability 11(10), 2915 (2019)
22. Barrios, W.G., Guglielmone, M.V.G., Fernández, M.G., Mariño, S.I., Ferreira, F.M., Zarrabeitia, C.T.: SCRUM: application experience in a software development PyME in the NEA. J. Comput. Sci. Technol. 12(03), 110–115 (2012)
23. Kuz, A., Falco, M., Giandini, R.S.: Comprendiendo la aplicabilidad de SCRUM en el aula: herramientas y ejemplos. Revista Iberoamericana de Tecnología en Educación y Educación en Tecnología 21, e07 (2018)
24. Deemer, P., Benefield, G., Larman, C., Vodde, B.: The SCRUM Primer. A Lightweight Guide to the Theory and Practice of SCRUM, Version 2.0 (2013)
25. Mendes Calo, K., Estévez, E.C., Fillottrani, P.R.: Un framework para evaluación de metodologías ágiles. In: XV Congreso Argentino de Ciencias de la Computación (2009)
26. Feo, R., Guerra, C.: Propuesta de un modelo de diseño instruccional para la elaboración e implementación de cursos a distancia en el Instituto pedagógico de Miranda José Manuel Siso Martínez. Sapiens. Revista Universitaria de Investigación 14(1), 65–83 (2013)
27. González Sosa, O., Hennig Manzuoli, C.: Models for the pedagogical integration of information and communication technologies: a literature review. Ensaio Avaliação e Políticas Públicas em Educação (2019)
28. Mata, A.C.U.: Evaluación de modelos de diseño instruccional: una revisión de literatura. Innovaciones Educativas 16(21), 23–30 (2014)
29. Williams, P., Schrum, L., Sangrà, A., Guárdia, L.: Fundamentos del diseño técnico-pedagógico. Modelos de diseño instruccional en e-learning (2004)

Graphic Computation, Images and Visualization

Overview+Detail Visual Comparison of Karate Motion Captures

Dana K. Urribarri[1]([✉]), Martín L. Larrea[1,2], Silvia M. Castro[1,2], and Enrico Puppo[3]

[1] VyGLab (CIC-UNS), Depto de Cs. e Ing. de la Computación (UNS), San Andrés 800, 8000 Bahía Blanca, Buenos Aires, Argentina
{dku,mll,smc}@cs.uns.edu.ar
[2] ICIC (UNS-CONICET), Depto de Cs. e Ing. de la Computación (UNS), San Andrés 800, 8000 Bahía Blanca, Buenos Aires, Argentina
[3] DIBRIS, University of Genoa, Genoa, Italy
enrico.puppo@unige.it

Abstract. Motion capture (MoCap) data as time series provide a rich source of input for human movement analysis; however, their multidimensional nature makes them difficult to process and compare. In this paper, we propose a visual analysis technique that allows the comparison of MoCap data obtained from karate *katas*. These consist of a series of predefined movements that are executed independently by several subjects at different times and speeds. For the comparative analysis, the proposed solution presents a visual comparison of the misalignment between a set of time series, based on dynamic time warping. We propose an overview of the misalignment between the data corresponding to n different subjects. A detailed view focusing on the comparison between two of them can be obtain on demand. The proposed solution comes from a combination of signal processing and data visualization techniques. A web application implementing this proposal completes the contribution of this work.

Keywords: Dynamic time warping · Comparative visualization · Data visualization · Multidimensional data · Motion capture

1 Introduction

Many activities, such as sports or kinesiology [16,23,25], may benefit from the analysis and understanding of the human movement; in this context, motion capture data (MoCap) analysis becomes of great importance both for the recovery from databases [18] and for the comparison of the movement of different people [20]. While recovery, analysis, and comparison of movements, to a lesser extent, are appropriate tasks to perform automatically, they can also benefit considerably from visual techniques. In particular, Bernard et al. [5] emphasize the importance of visual comparison techniques and the challenge of designing

© Springer Nature Switzerland AG 2020
P. Pesado and M. Arroyo (Eds.): CACIC 2019, CCIS 1184, pp. 139–154, 2020.
https://doi.org/10.1007/978-3-030-48325-8_10

them. At first, a video may seem the most realistic visual technique; however, comparing movements of different videos is a very tedious and time-consuming task [19,20]. On the other hand, proper data visualization techniques can provide information on a full MoCap at a glance.

A detailed comparison of the time alignment of two similar sequences of movements was presented in [29]. In this paper, we present an overview+detail visual analysis tool that extends and improves that previous visualization by the addition of an overview comparison of the time alignment between all the sequences of the dataset. This overview visualization shows a quantitative summary of the misalignment between every two sequences of movements. The detailed visualization, based on Dynamic Time Warping, mainly shows how a *source* sequence of movements should be transformed to match a *reference* sequence. To address sequences represented by neat movements, we take karate *katas* performed by various participants as a case study. If we use the performance of the teacher as a reference, presumably the correct one, this visualization allows:

- An overview comparison of the time alignment between the karate students' and the teacher's performances.
- A detailed comparison between the performance of a particular student and the teacher. This allows the recognition of the moments when the student loses synchronization.

This paper continues with a discussion of the previous work in Sect. 2 and outlines the work that was carried out to complete and prepare the dataset in Sect. 3. Section 4 describes the Dynamic Time Warping (DTW) technique, which is the basis for the visual comparison of the temporal misalignment of sequences used in this work; misalignment measurements are also included. Sections 5 to 7 describe the proposed visual analysis technique, including a detailed view, an overview and some implementation notes. Finally, Sect. 8 draws some conclusions and presents possible future work.

2   Previous Work

Not only the comparison of two MoCaps is a challenging task, but also the visualization of a whole MoCap. Moreover, as Bernard et al. [5] state, the design of MoCap visual-comparison is full of challenges regarding data preprocessing, visualization design and interactions. This section presents the related work regarding different techniques that exist for visualizing and comparing MoCap data and 3D trajectories.

2.1   MoCap Visualization and Overview

Li et al. [19] present a review of MoCap-visualization techniques and classify them into *images summaries*, *interactive platforms*, and *animations or videos*. Image summaries rely mostly on key-frames [2,13], i.e., frames that best represent motion in a time window. Interactive platforms allow some customization of the visualization, avoiding the restriction of just one or a few images to summarize the whole MoCap [1,4,14,26]. Since the user has to watch the entire sequence, animations or videos are not suitable to visualize a complete MoCap at a glance.

Dimensionality reduction is proposed as a complementary technique to the visualization of time series and MoCaps [28]; however, it helps to expose meaningful information about groups within the data but not to interpret individual information or inspect changes over time. A dimensionality reduction technique used in MoCap analysis is the self-organizing map (SOM) [13,30]. The SOM reduces the dimensionality of the data and projects the frames onto a grid-like topology, where proximity of cells means similarity in the original frames. This grid supports both analyzing one motion sequence and comparing multiple motion sequences. Since each grid cell approximates a frame, the higher the resolution of the grid, the more accurate the approximation. However, the resolution of the grid can become unmanageable if it is sought to obtain a good approximation of large sequences of very different movements.

In image summaries, *motion belts* [31] transform a 2D motion sequence into a sequence of 2D keyframes. The result of projection strongly depends on the nature of the movement. Hu et al. [13] combine them with a subject-centered representation called *motion track* based on a self-organizing map (SOM). *Motion track* produces a matrix visualization that only represents angles between skeleton parts, without taking into account translation and orientation information.

The interactive platform presented by Malmstrom et al. [20] shows a skeletal view and a visualization to compare the angle, the angular speed and the angular acceleration between joints from two MoCaps. It also includes streamgraphs as an overview of the difference in angles between the joints. Wilhelm et al. [30] present a visual-interactive system for the exploration of horse motion data. This system provides multiple overviews: an overlap of schematic of the poses, a SOM with moving trajectories and a PCA projection of the poses.

Within the animations, Assa et al. [3] propose an algorithm to generate an overview video clip from human motion data analysis and Hajdin et al. [12] present an interactive visualization of folk dance. The later is oriented to learners and enables them to view any part of the dance from different angles and at different speeds.

Several visualization tools focus on providing an overview of the whole MoCap [1,4] or just of some attribute of the MoCap [20]. Bernard et al. [4] present an overview of the MoCap in the form of a dendrogram, which results from hierarchical clustering. Clusters are represented with a glyph composed of overlapping frames. As a complement of the dendrogram, they present a graph overview that links clusters according to the motion sequence. The Mova platform [1] includes a motion belt as an overview of the whole movement.

2.2   Comparison of MoCaps and 3D Trajectories

Most MoCaps visualizations focus on dimensionality reduction and compare only one 2D or 3D trajectory [6,10,13,18,30]. Others just focus on the comparison of patterns by overlapping frames [4,14]. More recently, Sedmidubsky et al. [27] compare the movements using convolutional neural networks, so the 3D position of the joints are represented as an image. However, they do not intend this image to be part of a visualization system.

In the field of signal processing, Dynamic Time Warping (DTW) [7] is a well-known technique for comparing two signals; for example, it is commonly used for speech recognition [24]. Bruderlin and Williams [8] stated that it is also appropriate to apply signal processing methods in general, and DTW in particular, to motion data represented by the length of the segments and the flexion angle of the joints.

Today, several approaches use DTW to synchronize and compare motion data [21]. Krüger et al. [18] use DTW as part of a larger system to find similarities between movements in a database from the comparison of the 3D position of the joints. Jiang et al. [15] use DTW to assess surgical skills in minimally invasive robot-assisted surgeries. They propose an additional indicator to include large deviations and speed changes in different phases of the training tasks under analysis. Hachaj et al. [11] analyze the repetitiveness of karate kicks using DTW distances. In a 3D plot, they visualize the comparison between the trajectories of two points and the overlapping of frames.

3   Data Preprocessing

As an extension of [29], this work is also based on the motion captures corresponding to the Bassai Dai kata of the karate dataset[1] [17,22]. This dataset consists of 20 MoCap sequences corresponding to 7 participants with different abilities and ages. Each MoCap sequence contains information about 25 markers placed on the participants' bodies (see Fig. 1a). Of the 7 participants, 4 are adults, and 3 are teenagers. Two of the adults have very high experience (one is a Karate teacher and the other a participant in international championships), and the other 2 are black belt with high experience. All the teenagers have a medium level of experience. Among all the participants, there is only one woman who is a black belt. See Fig. 1b for the correspondence between trials and years of expertise.

The data preprocessing consisted mainly of data completion and data normalization. Data normalization involves three stages: skeleton alignment, space normalization, and data reduction. A data completion strategy was necessary since MoCap sequences were affected by noise and missing data. Considering that markers are interconnected with bones, and the distance between two directly connected markers remains constant, the position of the missing markers was estimated by interpolation of the orientation of the joining bone.

---

[1] http://www.infomus.org/karate/eyesweb_dataset_karate_eng.php.

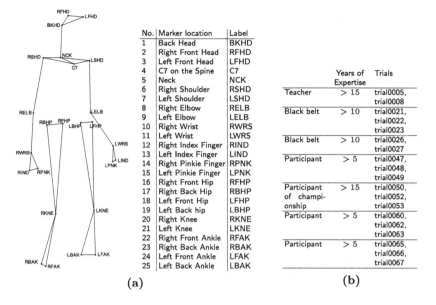

No.	Marker location	Label
1	Back Head	BKHD
2	Right Front Head	RFHD
3	Left Front Head	LFHD
4	C7 on the Spine	C7
5	Neck	NCK
6	Right Shoulder	RSHD
7	Left Shoulder	LSHD
8	Right Elbow	RELB
9	Left Elbow	LELB
10	Right Wrist	RWRS
11	Left Wrist	LWRS
12	Right Index Finger	RIND
13	Left Index Finger	LIND
14	Right Pinkie Finger	RPNK
15	Left Pinkie Finger	LPNK
16	Right Front Hip	RFHP
17	Right Back Hip	RBHP
18	Left Front Hip	LFHP
19	Left Back hip	LBHP
20	Right Knee	RKNE
21	Left Knee	LKNE
22	Right Front Ankle	RFAK
23	Right Back Ankle	RBAK
24	Left Front Ankle	LFAK
25	Left Back Ankle	LBAK

	Years of Expertise	Trials
Teacher	> 15	trial0005, trial0008
Black belt	> 10	trial0021, trial0022, trial0023
Black belt	> 10	trial0026, trial0027
Participant	> 5	trial0047, trial0048, trial0049
Participant of championship	> 15	trial0050, trial0052, trial0053
Participant	> 5	trial0060, trial0062, trial0063
Participant	> 5	trial0065, trial0066, trial0067

(a)   (b)

Fig. 1. (a) Labels and positions of the 25 markers that form the MoCaps. (b) Years of expertise of the each trial.

Since data normalization is an inherent problem in sequence comparison, several approaches exist in the literature. Following a simple method based on the one presented by Sedmidubsky et al. [27], we normalize the skeletons by changing the orientation and size through rotation, scaling, and translation transformations:

1. *Skeleton alignment*: the skeleton of every frame is roto-translated so that the marker NCK is placed at the origin $(0, 0, 0)$, the segment NCK–BKHD is aligned with axis z, and the triangle NCK–C7–BKHD is aligned with plane yz. The information about the roto-translation of the skeleton is lost; however, this information is not relevant to compare the timing of the poses.
2. *Space normalization*: to reduces distortions due to the different heights of participants, the skeleton-aligned MoCaps are translated and scaled to fit into the box $(0, 0, 0) - (1, 1, 1)$ and the marker NCK is placed at point $(0.5, 0.5, 0.5)$.
3. *Data reduction*: since the basic implementation of DTW requires both sequences to have the same number of frames, and the captures were taken at 250 Hz (producing sequences of approximately 25,000 frames), every sequence was reduced using the Lanczos sampling [9], to have the same number of frames and a frequency of at least 25 Hz. In this context, each frame represents a variable amount of time; this allows us to compare the movements of the sequence and their relative speeds, regardless of the actual performance speed.

4   Dynamic Time Warping

In this section, we outline the Dynamic Time Warping (DTW) technique [7,24], the basis of the visual comparison of time sequence misalignment presented in this work. DTW is combined with different visualization techniques to show how a MoCap S (the *source* sequence) is misaligned (delayed or early) with respect to a MoCap R (the *reference* sequence).

DTW is a method used in time series analysis for measuring the similarity (or dissimilarity) between two temporal sequences. In the process of computing this measure, DTW provides a mapping between the series that induces a warping function. This warping function transforms one of the sequences to obtain two time-aligned sequences, and thus, a misalignment function.

4.1   A Dissimilarity Measure

DTW compares all the frames from R with all the frames from S to compute the accumulated-distance matrix M (see Algorithm 1) and thus obtain a measure of dissimilarity between both sequences. The accumulated distance $M_{L,L}$ measures the cost of warping one sequence to match another. It therefore represents the dissimilarity between the two sequences. Any suitable distance function can be used to calculate the distance between frames. In this work, we have used Euclidean distance since it the most used in these cases.

Algorithm 1. Accumulated distance matrix M between sequences S and R

Input Two sequences R and S with L frames each one.
Output The accumulated distance matrix M between the two sequences.
   ▷ *The distance between the initial frames*
1: $M_{1,1} \leftarrow \text{dist}(R_1, S_1)$
2: **for all** $i \in [2, L]$ **do**
   ▷ *Accumulated distance between R_1 and every frame in S.*
3:      $M_{1,i} \leftarrow \text{dist}(R_1, S_i) + M_{1,i-1}$
   ▷ *Accumulated distance between S_1 and every frame in R.*
4:      $M_{i,1} \leftarrow \text{dist}(S_1, R_i) + M_{i-1,1}$
5: **for all** $i, j \in [2, L]$ **do**
   ▷ *Minimum accumulated distance between every other pair of frames*
6:      $M_{i,j} \leftarrow \text{dist}(R_i, S_j) + \min\{M_{i-1,j-1}, M_{i-1,j}, M_{i,j-1}\}$

4.2   Warping Function

The computation of the measure $M_{L,L}$ implies finding the minimal accumulated-distance path from $(1, 1)$ to (L, L). This *warping path* P is a list of pairs (i, j) that defines a warping between sequences R and S, where its first and second components are the numbers of frame in R and S (see Algorithm 2), respectively. Figure 2 shows the accumulated distance matrix between two sequences and the warping path between them. From this warping path, it is possible to obtain a function that warps S into R. This function should give, for each frame number in R, the number of the best matching frame in S. Since in the warping path there may exist several pairs warping different frame numbers in S into the same frame number in R, the warping function $F : N \rightarrow N$ is defined as:

$$F(n) = \lfloor \text{mean}_{(n,j) \in P} \{j\} \rfloor \tag{1}$$

Algorithm 2. Warping path P between sequences S and R

Input Accumulated-distance matrix M of $L \times L$ elements.
Output Warping path P between the two sequences.
1: P starts empty.
2: $i \leftarrow L, j \leftarrow L$
3: **while** $i \geq 1$ and $j \geq 1$ **do**
4:     Add (i, j) to the path P
5:     $(i, j) \leftarrow \begin{cases} (i, j - 1) & \text{if } i = 1, \\ (i - 1, j) & \text{if } j = 1, \\ (i, j - 1) & \text{if } M_{i,j-1} = \min\{M_{i-1,j-1}, M_{i-1,j}, M_{i,j-1}\}, \\ (i - 1, j) & \text{if } M_{i-1,j} = \min\{M_{i-1,j-1}, M_{i-1,j}, M_{i,j-1}\}, \\ (i - 1, j - 1) & \text{otherwise.} \end{cases}$

4.3   The Misalignment Function

Given a frame number n in the sequence R, the function $F(n)$ returns the frame number in S that match the best with it. The misalignment function $G(n)$, given by Eq. 2, is the distance from $F(n)$ to n:

$$G(n) = F(n) - n \tag{2}$$

The relation between $G(n - 1)$ and $G(n)$ gives a hint about whether S is delayed, on-time, or early with respect to R. If $G(n - 1) = G(n)$, then S is on-time. If $G(n - 1) < G(n)$, then S is delayed. Finally, if $G(n - 1) > G(n)$, then S is early. Depending on whether S is early, delayed, or on time, $G(n)$ has a negative, positive, or flat slope, respectively.

Figure 3 shows an example of the warping function $F(n)$ and the corresponding misalignment function $G(n)$ for the sequences A and B from the example of Fig. 2a. Finally, Fig. 4 shows the accumulated-distance matrix and the warping and misalignment functions for MoCaps *trial0021* as source and *trial0008* as reference, each one of 2675 frames. In Fig. 4a, columns of the matrix represent the frame times from the source and rows, the ones from the reference. The gray level represents the Euclidean distance between frames: the darker it is, the larger the distance. The value of $M_{2675,2675}$ provides a measure of dissimilarity between the

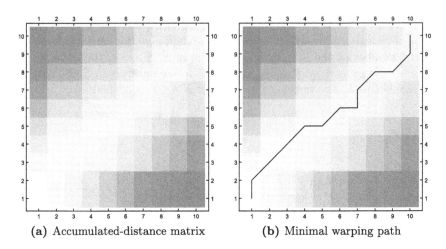

(a) Accumulated-distance matrix   (b) Minimal warping path

Fig. 2. (a) Accumulated distance matrix and (b) warping path for two sequences $A = \{10, 10, 40, 40, 50, 70, 70, 80, 90, 100\}$ and $B = \{10, 30, 30, 50, 50, 60, 70, 80, 80, 100\}$. Columns of the matrices represent the frame times from source B and rows, the ones from reference A. The gray level represents the Euclidean distance between frames: the darker it is, the larger the distance. The value of $M_{10,10}$ provides a measure of dissimilarity between A and B.

reference and the source. Figure 4b shows the warping function $F(n)$. This is a function that, given a frame number n in the reference MoCap, returns the number of the frame in the source one that is the best match following the warping path. Figure 4c shows the misalignment function $G(n)$ of the warping between the two MoCaps. The sequence of positive, flat and negative slopes indicates whether the source MoCap is delayed, on time, or early with respect to the reference one.

5 Detailed View

In this section, we present the detailed view that compares the misalignment between two MoCaps. This is an improved version of the one presented in [29]. Given two MoCaps, the source S and the reference R, this view combines different visualization techniques to show how S is misaligned (delayed or early) with respect to R. The detailed view consists of three visualizations showing different aspects of the misalignment between two sequences by using different techniques (see Fig. 5):

- At the top, a line and area graph that shows both the misalignment and the difference between the poses of time-aligned frames.
- In the middle, a line graph of the misalignment function $G(n)$.
- At the bottom, a parallel heat-map visualization that includes a complete image view of both MoCaps and the visualization of the misalignment between them.

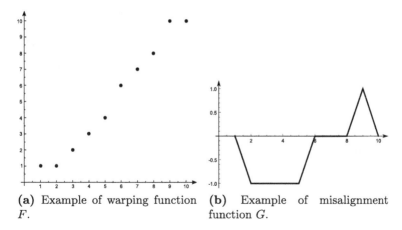

(a) Example of warping function F.

(b) Example of misalignment function G.

Fig. 3. Warping and misalignment functions. Figure (a) shows the warping function F resulting from the warping path from Fig. 2. Figure (b) shows the corresponding misalignment function. (Color figure online)

This detailed view and the overview (see Sect. 6) use the same color coding. The color of lines, connections or areas shows whether a frame of the reference sequence R was performed delayed (blue), on time (yellow) or early (red) in the source sequence S. A delayed frame means that the sequence S takes more time to complete it, an early frame means that the sequence S completes it too fast, and yellow means the the subsequence is performed at the same rhythm in sequence R and S.

The combination of these three representations of the temporal misalignment of both MoCaps allows us to interpret how synchronized the two participants are and how similar the sequences of movements they perform are.

5.1   Line and Area Graph to Show Misalignment and Differences

The first visualization shows not only the misalignment between the sequences but also the difference between the matching frames. The x axis is the timeline of the reference sequence and the y axis represents the absolute difference between the poses of time-aligned frames. The color of the area below a (x, y) point encodes, for each frame of the reference, how delayed (blue), on time (yellow) or early (red) was performed by the source. The difference mapped to the y axis is the Euclidean distance between markers, considering the collection of N markers as a unique point in a $3N$-dimensional space. This graph gives insight not only on the changes of rhythm between the sequences, but also on the similarity of the poses.

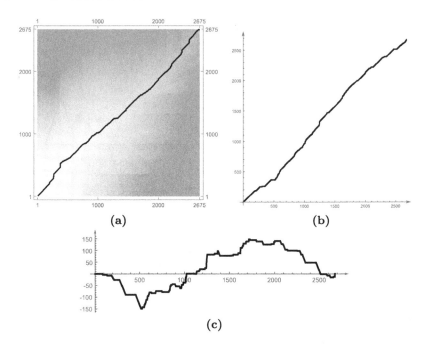

Fig. 4. (a) Accumulated distance matrix and warping path of two MoCaps: *trial0021* as source and *trial0008* as reference. Columns of the matrices represent the frame times from the source and rows, the ones from the reference. The gray level represents the Euclidean distance between frames: the darker, the larger. The value of $M_{2675,2675}$ provides a measure of dissimilarity between the reference and the source. (b) Warping function $F(n)$ that, given a frame number n in the reference MoCap, returns the number of the frame in the source one that is the best match following the warping path. (c) Misalignment function $G(n)$ of the warping between the two MoCaps. The sequence of positive, flat and negative slopes indicates whether the source MoCap is delayed, on time, or early with respect to the reference one.

5.2   Line Graph of Function $G(n)$

The middle visualization is a line graph that shows the misalignment function $G(n)$ between source and reference (Eq. 2). The x-axis corresponds to the time-line of the reference MoCap. The slope changes show the accelerations or the slowing down of the source sequence with respect to the reference. A positive slope means that the source is delayed, negative slope means that it is more accelerated and a zero slope indicates that both sequences are on time.

5.3   Parallel Heat-Map Visualization

To visualize the warping between the two MoCaps, we propose a parallel time-relationship visualization that uses as timeline a heat-map representation. This visualization includes both the MoCaps corresponding to the two sequences and

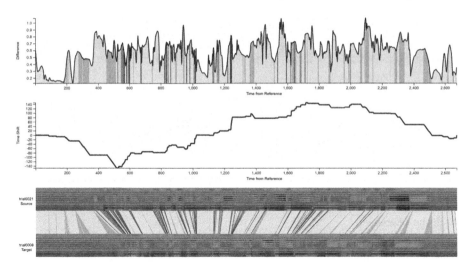

Fig. 5. Comparison between MoCaps *trial0021* (source) and *trial0008* (reference). The upper graph shows, with colors, the misalignment between the MoCaps and the absolute difference between time-aligned frames. The middle graph is the misalignment function. The graph at the bottom shows a heat-map visualization of the two MoCaps and how they are aligned in time. The color coding uses blue for delayed frames, yellow for on-time ones, and red for early ones. (Color figure online)

the misalignment between them. Figure 6 shows a comparison between *trial0021* as source and *trial0008* as reference. Each component of this visualization is described below.

Parallel Time-Relationship Visualization. To visualize the misalignment between two MoCaps, we propose a parallel time-relationship visualization. Inspired on parallel coordinates, each axis represents the timeline of a MoCap, and the connection between frame numbers represents the required warping to align both MoCaps. Figure 7a shows the same example than Fig. 3a using a parallel time-relationship visualization. The top line represents the frame numbers of the source sequence, while the bottom line represents the frame number of the reference sequence. Besides, the color of the connections indicates the temporal relationship between source and reference sequences, that is, whether the frames of the source sequence S is delayed (red), on time (yellow), or early (blue) respect to the reference sequence R.

Heat-Map Visualization. As described in Sect. 3, the space normalization of MoCaps causes every marker to lie in the box $(0, 0, 0) - (1, 1, 1)$, and, therefore, the position of each marker can be converted directly to a color. A *heat-map visualization*, where the color of each pixel encodes positional information, represents the whole MoCap [27]: the red, green, and blue channels encode the x, y, and z coordinates, respectively. The width of the image represents the timeline and the height, the markers. Adjacent pixels along the width of the image

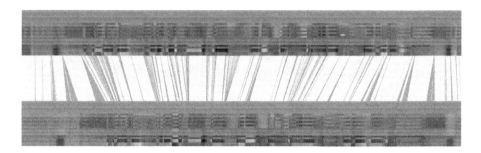

Fig. 6. Parallel heat-map visualization of MoCaps *trial0021* as source and *trial0008* as reference. The one on the top is the source MoCap and the one below is the reference MoCap. Connections between them represent the warping of the source MoCap to match the reference.

represent consecutive positions of the same marker; however, the adjacency of pixels along the height is not meaningful. Figure 7b shows the color representation of the pose of Fig. 1, which is a column in the image representation of a complete MoCap (Fig. 7c).

6 Overview

The overview shows a matrix visualization of the comparison between all possible sequence pairs. A rough visualization of the comparison between to sequences is presented as a *percentage summary*. It shows the percentages of the reference sequence that the source performs slower, at the same rate, or faster than the reference (see Fig. 8). The columns represent the reference sequences and the rows the source sequences.

Each cell of the matrix presents with a glyph the percentage summary of a pair of sequences. A tooltip shows, on demand, the exact values of the percentage summary at a given cell. Figure 9 shows the percentage summary of the comparison between *trial0021* (source) and *trial0008* (reference). Those numbers suggest that 17% of the performance from *trial0008* was accelerated in *trial0021*, 77% was at the same rate and 6% was decelerated.

Since the percentage-summary shows the percentages of one sequence that the other performs slower, at the same rate, or faster, the matrix is not symmetric despite resembling one. At first, from the matrix it can be noticed that something is wrong with *trial0050*. In particular, this performance was done very slowly but incompletely. Secondly, all the performances, when compared with *trial0005* of the teacher, show similar results. Thirdly, it can be seen that the performances of the teenagers are very similar to each other. On the other hand, comparisons with very experienced participants present more diverse results.

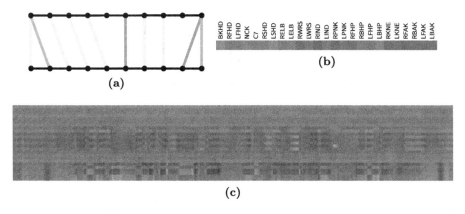

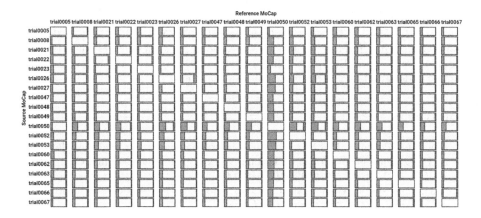

Fig. 7. Parallel heat-map visualization components. (a) Parallel time-relationship visualization of the warping of Fig. 3a. The top line represents frames from the source sequence A and the bottom line, frames from the reference sequence B. The color of the connections shows whether the frames of B was performed delayed (blue), on time (yellow) or early (red). (b) Color representation of the pose of Figure 1. The color of each pixel is given by the position of the marker inside the $(0,0,0) - (1,1,1)$ box. (c) Color representation as heat-map of the MoCap *trial0021*. The row at the top corresponds to marker BKHD and the one at the bottom, to marker LBAK. Times increases from left to right: the first column on the left corresponds to the first frame of the MoCap, and the last column on the right, to the last frame of the MoCap. (Color figure online)

7 Implementation Notes

The MoCap comparison tool presented in this work is available at http://cs.uns.edu.ar/~dku/mocap-synchromparator, while the previous version is maintained at http://cs.uns.edu.ar/~dku/mocap-synchromparator-v1. The prototype was

Fig. 8. Matrix visualization of the percentage summaries of every pair of sequences.

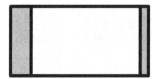

Fig. 9. Cell glyph and corresponding tooltip of the comparison between *trial0021* (source) and *trial0008* (reference). The red, blue, and yellow portions indicate the percentages of the reference sequence that the source performs slower, at the same rate, or faster than the reference, respectively. (Color figure online)

implemented using Javascript and the D3.js library. The input sequences for the application are the preprocessed results of Sect. 3 *Data Preprocessing* and the result for Eq. 1 for each possible DTW between the sequences.

8   Conclusions and Future Work

We have presented a comparative visualization of MoCap sequences that focuses on the time dimension. The visualization starts with an overview of the misalignment between the data corresponding to different subjects. Details on the comparison between two particular sequences can be obtained on demand. The detail view provides an overview of the misalignment between the selected sequences and visual information about when one of them is delayed or early with respect to the other. The time frames where the sequences differ are easily perceptible due to color-coding.

Currently, the detail visualization is static and provides no interactions. We plan to add suitable interactions for explorations (for example, semantic zoom). The possibility to compare more than two sequences at a time and the inclusion of multiresolution DTW are both worth exploring. Moreover, finding a meaningful order for the markers in the heat map is desirable. The extension for this tool to other time datasets beside MoCap data is also under study.

Acknowledgments. This work was funded by PGI 24/ZN33 and PGI 24/ZN35, Secretaría General de Ciencia y Tecnología, Universidad Nacional del Sur, Bahía Blanca, Argentina; and by the European Union's Horizon 2020 research and innovation programme under grant agreement n. 824160 (EnTimeMent).

References

1. Alemi, O., Pasquier, P., Shaw, C.: Mova: interactive movement analytics platform. In: Proceedings of the 2014 International Workshop on Movement and Computing, MOCO 2014, pp. 37:37–37:42. ACM (2014)
2. Assa, J., Caspi, Y., Cohen-Or, D.: Action synopsis: pose selection and illustration. ACM Trans. Graph. **24**(3), 667–676 (2005)
3. Assa, J., Cohen-Or, D., Yeh, I.C., Lee, T.Y.: Motion overview of human actions. ACM Trans. Graph. **27**(5), 115:1–115:10 (2008)

Overview+Detail Visual Comparison of Karate MoCaps   153

4. Bernard, J., Wilhelm, N., Krüger, B., May, T., Schreck, T., Kohlhammer, J.: Motionexplorer: exploratory search in human motion capture data based on hierarchical aggregation. IEEE Trans. Vis. Comput. Graph. **19**(12), 2257–2266 (2013)
5. Bernard, J., Vögele, A., Klein, R., Fellner, D.: Approaches and challenges in the visual-interactive comparison of human motion data. In: Proceedings of the 12th International Joint Conference on Computer Vision, Imaging and Computer Graphics Theory and Applications, vol. 3, pp. 217–224. SciTePress (2017)
6. Bernard, J., Wilhelm, N., Scherer, M., May, T., Schreck, T.: TimeSeriesPaths: projection-based explorative analysis of multivariate time series data. J. WSCG **20**(2), 97–106 (2012)
7. Berndt, D.J., Clifford, J.: Using dynamic time warping to find patterns in time series. In: Proceedings of the 3rd International Conference on Knowledge Discovery and Data Mining, AAAIWS 1994, pp. 359–370. AAAI Press (1994)
8. Bruderlin, A., Williams, L.: Motion signal processing. In: Proceedings of the 22nd Annual Conference on Computer Graphics and Interactive Techniques, SIGGRAPH 1995, pp. 97–104. ACM (1995)
9. Burger, W., Burge, M.J.: Principles of Digital Image Processing. Core Algorithms. Springer, London (2009). https://doi.org/10.1007/978-1-84800-195-4
10. Cho, K., Chen, X.: Classifying and visualizing motion capture sequences using deep neural networks. CoRR abs/1306.3874 (2013)
11. Hachaj, T., Piekarczyk, M., Ogiela, M.R.: How repetitive are karate kicks performed by skilled practitioners? In: Proceedings of the 2018 10th International Conference on Computer and Automation Engineering, ICCAE 2018, Brisbane, Australia, 24–26 February 2018, pp. 62–65. ACM (2018)
12. Hajdin, M., Kico, I., Dolezal, M., Chmelik, J., Doulamis, A., Liarokapis, F.: Digitization and visualization of movements of slovak folk dances. In: Auer, M.E., Tsiatsos, T. (eds.) ICL 2018. AISC, vol. 917, pp. 245–256. Springer, Cham (2019). https://doi.org/10.1007/978-3-030-11935-5_24
13. Hu, Y., Wu, S., Xia, S., Fu, J., Chen, W.: Motion track: visualizing variations of human motion data. In: 2010 IEEE Pacific Visualization Symposium (PacificVis), pp. 153–160 (2010)
14. Jang, S., Elmqvist, N., Ramani, K.: MotionFlow: visual abstraction and aggregation of sequential patterns in human motion tracking data. IEEE Trans. Vis. Comput. Graph. **22**(1), 21–30 (2016)
15. Jiang, J., Xing, Y., Wang, S., Liang, K.: Evaluation of robotic surgery skills using dynamic time warping. Comput. Methods Programs Biomed. **152**(Suppl. C), 71–83 (2017)
16. John Ward, D., Jesse Coats, D., DAAPM, C., Amir, P., Sarmiento, T., DeLeon, C., Moskop, J.: The impact of kinesiology tape over the posterior lower limb on runner fatigue. Top. Integr. Health Care **6**, 1–5 (2015)
17. Kolykhalova, K., Camurri, A., Volpe, G., Sanguineti, M., Puppo, E., Niewiadomski, R.: A multimodal dataset for the analysis of movement qualities in karate martial art. In: Proceedings of the 2015 7th International Conference on Intelligent Technologies for Interactive Entertainment (INTETAIN), INTETAIN 2015, pp. 74–78. IEEE Computer Society (2015)
18. Krüger, B., Tautges, J., Weber, A., Zinke, A.: Fast local and global similarity searches in large motion capture databases. In: Proceedings of the 2010 ACM SIGGRAPH/Eurographics Symposium on Computer Animation, SCA 2010, pp. 1–10. Eurographics Association (2010)

19. Li, W., Bartram, L., Pasquier, P.: Techniques and approaches in static visualization of motion capture data. In: Proceedings of the 3rd International Symposium on Movement and Computing, MOCO 2016, pp. 14:1–14:8. ACM (2016)
20. Malmstrom, C., Zhang, Y., Pasquier, P., Schiphorst, T., Bartram, L.: MoComp: a tool for comparative visualization between takes of motion capture data. In: Proceedings of the 3rd International Symposium on Movement and Computing, MOCO 2016, pp. 11:1–11:8. ACM (2016)
21. Müller, M.: Information Retrieval for Music and Motion. Springer, Heidelberg (2007). https://doi.org/10.1007/978-3-540-74048-3
22. Niewiadomski, R., Kolykhalova, K., Piana, S., Alborno, P., Volpe, G., Camurri, A.: Analysis of movement quality in full-body physical activities. ACM Trans. Interact. Intell. Syst. **9**(1), 1:1–1:20 (2019)
23. Noiumkar, S., Tirakoat, S.: Use of optical motion capture in sports science: a case study of golf swing. In: 2013 International Conference on Informatics and Creative Multimedia, pp. 310–313. IEEE (2013)
24. Rabiner, L., Juang, B.H.: Fundamentals of Speech Recognition. Prentice-Hall Inc., Upper Saddle River (1993)
25. Rallis, I., Langis, A., Georgoulas, I., Voulodimos, A., Doulamis, N., Doulamis, A.: An embodied learning game using kinect and labanotation for analysis and visualization of dance kinesiology. In: 2018 10th International Conference on Virtual Worlds and Games for Serious Applications (VS-Games), pp. 1–8. IEEE (2018)
26. Samy, V., Ayusawa, K., Yoshida, E.: Real-time musculoskeletal visualization of muscle tension and joint reaction forces. In: 2019 IEEE/SICE International Symposium on System Integration (SII), pp. 396–400 (2019)
27. Sedmidubsky, J., Elias, P., Zezula, P.: Effective and efficient similarity searching in motion capture data. Multimed. Tools Appl. **77**(10), 12073–12094 (2017). https://doi.org/10.1007/s11042-017-4859-7
28. Tanisaro, P., Heidemann, G.: Dimensionality reduction for visualization of time series and trajectories. In: Felsberg, M., Forssén, P.-E., Sintorn, I.-M., Unger, J. (eds.) SCIA 2019. LNCS, vol. 11482, pp. 246–257. Springer, Cham (2019). https://doi.org/10.1007/978-3-030-20205-7_21
29. Urribarri, D.K., Larrea, M.L., Castro, S.M., Puppo, E.: Visualization to compare karate motion captures. In: Anales del XXV Congreso Argentino de Ciencias de la Computación (CACIC 2019), pp. 446–455. Universidad Nacional de Río Cuarto, October 2019
30. Wilhelm, N., Vögele, A., Zsoldos, R., Licka, T., Krüger, B., Bernard, J.: FuryExplorer: visual-interactive exploration of horse motion capture data. In: Visualization and Data Analysis (VDA 2015) (2015)
31. Yasuda, H., Kaihara, R., Saito, S., Nakajima, M.: Motion belts: visualization of human motion data on a timeline. IEICE Trans. **91**(D), 1159–1167 (2008)

Software Engineering

Exploiting Anti-scenarios for the Non Realizability Problem

Fernando Asteasuain[1,2]([✉]) [ID], Federico Calonge[1], and Pablo Gamboa[2]

[1] Universidad Nacional de Avellaneda, Avellaneda, Argentina
{fasteasuain,fcalonge}@undav.edu.ar
[2] Centro de Altos Estudios CAETI, CABA, Universidad Abierta Interamericana,
Buenos Aires, Argentina
pgamboa@uai.edu.ar

Abstract. Behavioral synthesis is a technique that automatically builds a controller for a system given its specification. This is achieved by obtaining a winning strategy in a game between the system and the environment. Behavioral synthesis has been successfully applied in modern modularization techniques such as Aspect Orientation to compose each particular view of the system in a single piece. When a controller can not be found the engineer faces the Non Realizability Problem. In this work we exploit FVS a distinguishable feature in the FVS specification language called anti-scenarios to address this problem. Several case studies are introduced to show our proposal in action. Additionally, a performance analysis is introduced to further validate our approach.

Keywords: Aspect Orientation · Behavioral synthesis

1 Introduction

Modern modularization techniques have emerged in the past years aiming to improve how the different features supported by a system interact to provide its expected behavior. Among them, Aspect Orientation [18,22] or Feature Oriented Programming [3,29] earned a distinguished reputation since they have been applied successfully in several challenging domains such as software protocols, software architectures, hardware and robotic controllers or artificial intelligence [3,11,16,24,36], just to mention a few.

In essence what these techniques propose is to conceive a system as the interaction and combination of its individual features. These features are also called view or aspects, depending on the particular methodology to be employed. For example, in the classic ATM example the system is built combining diverse views such as security, availability, efficiency, data integrity or transaction management. Each view captures a portion of the behavior of the system. In this way the software engineer can focus on each one without being distracted with other irrelevant details that do not correspond to the view in turn being specified. This kind of approach is also present in multiple ways in other software engineering tools and techniques. Actors when defining use cases or roles when defining user

© Springer Nature Switzerland AG 2020
P. Pesado and M. Arroyo (Eds.): CACIC 2019, CCIS 1184, pp. 157–171, 2020.
https://doi.org/10.1007/978-3-030-48325-8_11

stories represent different ways (views) of interacting with the system. Similarly, UML's sequence diagrams aim to model localized behavior and also can be seen as a mechanism to specify a particular behavioral perspective of the system.

The critical point when developing system is to articulate and combine each particular view in order to produce the complete behavior of the system. This is indeed tricky since most of the times these views interfere with each other constituting a possible source of conflicts, problems and bugs. These conflicts should not be underestimated since the correct behavior of the system may depend on how they are addressed. For example, in the ATM system the encryption view must act (i.e., must encrypt the message) before any message is sent from the ATM to the bank. Similarly, the encryption perspective may constitute a menace to achieve successfully the efficiency view, since delays are introduced when performing transactions.

In the Aspect Orientation approach each view is named an *Aspect* and the process of combining aspects behavior is named *Weaving*. The problem of detecting and resolving aspects interaction has been addressed by the software engineering community [7,14,26,30,33]. Nonetheless, most of them rely on syntactic mechanisms and the semantic application of aspects is hard to analyze, explore or reason about [6,21,32]. In this sense, some approaches [6,28] have taken a different road to weave aspects employing a technique known as behavioral synthesis [8,13]. Contrary to the usual development of systems, where the implementation of the system is analyzed whether its fulfills its specification or not, when employing behavioral synthesis the system is built in such a way that the specification is satisfied by construction. In general, the output of the synthesis procedure is an automaton called the controller of the system that receives input from the environment (typically this information is provided by sensors) and produces instructions to actuators and then waits to receive the new information from the environment to initiate the loop one more time. The controller is obtained employing algorithms from the artificial intelligence and game theory domains. The objective is to produce a winning strategy that no matters what action is taken by the environment the systems always find a way to achieve its goals. Efficient symbolic algorithms for controller synthesis have been presented in [8,27].

A key issue when dealing with behavioral synthesis is how to proceed when a controller can not be derived from the specification. This is known as realizability checking. When the specification is non realizable the specifier must identify the source of the problem. Generally, this is achieved manually or employing sophisticated tools. Some approaches like [2] rely on inductive logics, work in [23] employs the concept of *counterstrategies* and work in [25] adds additional information into the specification as *conflict* and *recovery* sets of requirements. However, the specification language used in these approaches does not provide by itself a mechanism to help the specifier to identify the problem.

Given this context in this work we propose to exploit a distinguishable feature of the FVS language to address non realizability in the aspect oriented synthesis world. FVS can automatically build anti-scenarios from any property described in the language. This gives to the specifier an intuitive, visual and crucial information about all the possible ways things can go wrong and violate a property. This work illustrates how anti-scenarios can be employed to tackle non realizability in a friendly manner.

FVS is a declarative language based on graphical scenarios and features a flexible and expressive notation with clear and solid language semantics. In [6] we showed how FVS can be used to denote, compose and synthesize aspect oriented behavior, including dealing with properties that can not be expressed with Deterministic Büchi automata, which are excluded in other approaches like [27]. We now introduce a new edge on our methodology by exploiting FVS's anti-scenarios to alleviate the non realizability problem.

We also conducted a performance analysis to measure the effectiveness of our approach and explored a new tool named Acacia+ [9] to achieve our goals. The results show that FVS turns out to be a competitive framework among others known approaches.

To sum up, the contributions of this work can be summarized as follows:

- FVS anti-acenarios are employed to address the non realizability problem in behavioral synthesis.
- A performance analysis is shown to compare FVS efficiency against other tools.
- A new external tool is explored to obtain controllers.
- FVS is shown in action in new case studies in several applications and relevant domains.

The rest of this work is structured as follows. Section 2 briefly introduces the FVS language, its usage in the Aspect Orientation domain and how the behavioral synthesis is achieved. Section 3 presents the case studies and also discusses related work. Section 4 introduces the performance analysis. Finally, Sect. 5 enumerates future work whereas Sect. 6 present the conclusions of this work.

2   Background

In this section we will informally describe the standing features of FVS [4,5]. The reader is referred to [5] for a formal characterization of the language.

FVS is a graphical scenarios where scenarios and rules shape the expected behavior of the system. FVS scenarios consists of points and relationships between them. Points can be labeled with the events that occur in those points. In fact, a points' label consist of a logic formula that summarizes the events occurring on that moment. Two kind of relationships relate points: precedence, to indicate that an event occurs before another one, and constraining, which is used to restrict behavior between points. Finally, two special points are introduced to indicate the beginning and the end of a trace. For example Fig. 1 shows a typical FVS scenario modeling the behavior of a load-balancer server example. The big black point in the left extreme represents the beginning of the execution

and the last point, which is double rounded, represents the end of the execution. In particular the scenario describes a situation where the server is ready
once the execution started and afterwards a task is assigned such that the server
never reaches its full capacity from the moment was ready until the end of the
execution.

Fig. 1. A simple scenario in FVS

FVS rules can be seen as an implication relationship. They consist of an
scenario playing the role of the antecedent and two or more scenarios playing the
role of the consequent. The intuition is that whenever a trace "matches" a given
antecedent scenario, then it must also match at least one of the consequents.
When this happen we say that the rule is satisfied. The semantics of the language
is given by the set of traces that fulfills every rule. Graphically, the antecedent
is shown in black, and consequents in grey. Each item of consequents are labeled
to indicate to whom consequent they belong. As an example, an FVS rule is
shown in Fig. 2. This rule says that if an *TaskAssigned* event occurs, then the
Server-Ready event must occurred in the past (in other words, the server was in
the *ready* state) and between these points the *Server-Full* event that indicates
that the serves reached its maximum capacity did not occur.

Fig. 2. A simple FVS rule

We now introduce the concept of anti-scenarios. Anti-scenarios can be automatically generated from rule scenarios. Roughly speaking, they provide valuable
information for the developer since they represent a sketch of how things could go
wrong and violate the rule. The complete procedure is detailed in [10], but informally the algorithm obtains all the situations where the antecedent is found but
none of the consequents is feasible. For example, for the previous rule in Fig. 2
two anti-scenarios are found. In one situation a task is assigned, but the server
was never ready before since the beginning of the execution. In the other situation, the server was indeed ready, but it reaches its maximum capacity before
the task is assigned. These two anti-scenarios are shown in Fig. 3.

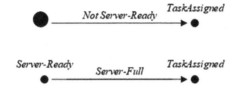

Fig. 3. Two anti-scenarios for the specified rule

2.1 FVS in Aspect Orientation and Behavioral Synthesis

Our previous work in [6] describes how FVS can be seen as an aspect oriented specification language and also how it can be connected to external tools to obtain a controller that satisfies the specification by construction. In few words, FVS rules can be seen as aspects, where the antecedent of the rule constitutes the *poincut* (those points where the aspect behavior is to be added) and the consequent represent the behavior to be introduced by the aspect.

FVS specifications are used to obtain a controller using different tools depending on the type of the property. Using the tableau algorithm detailed in [5] FVS scenarios are translated into Büchi automata. If the automata represent one of the specification patterns (excludings those that can not be represented by Deterministic Büchi automata) then we obtain a controller using a technique [27] based on the specification patterns [17] and the GR(1) subset of LTL. If that is not the case, but the automata is a Deterministic Büchi automata we either employ the GOAL [34] or the Acacia+ tool [9]. The performance analysis in Sect. 4 discusses the efficiency of these two tools. If the automaton is non deterministic we obtain a controller using only the GOAL tool using an intermediate translation from Büchi automata to *Rabin* automata.

3 Case Studies

In this section we show in action our approach to address non realizability in aspect oriented behavioral synthesis by modeling three different and challenging case studies. These examples are shown next in the following sub sections. Finally, Sect. 3.4 presents some considerations and conclusions and briefly discusses related work.

3.1 The Vessel Example

This case of study is based on the functioning of several navigation transports introduced in [25]. In particular we consider the requirements from the vessel example. We suppose that the basic specification describing the main behavior of a vessel denote the base system and then we introduce some security restrictions through the specification of an aspect named *SafeNavigation*. In particular, the *SafeNavigation* aspect considers three requirements:

1. The vessel can be in the *UnderWay* state either by starting on an engine or by sailing, but not on both modes at the same time. That is, the vessel navigates through the river either by using a engine or blowned by the wind.
2. A vessel can be constrained by her draught, but only when is navigating.
3. The vessel can be moored, but only when using the engine.

We modeled the *SafeNavigation* aspect in FVS. It contemplates three rules, one for each requirement of the aspect. The first rule says that if the *UnderWay* event occurs, then either the sailing mode was selected in the past and the engine has not been turned on since then, or viceversa, the engine was turned on in the past and the sailing mode has not occurred during that period. The FVS rule for this requirement is shown in Fig. 4.

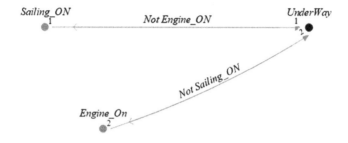

Fig. 4. FVS rule for requirement number one

The FVS rule in Fig. 5 addresses the second and third requirements. The rule in the top of Figure corresponds to the second requirement whereas the rule in the bottom corresponds to the third one. In the former rule, the *Constrained by her draught* event (named *CbyDraught* to simplify) occurs, then the *UnderWay* event must had occurred in the past. The latter rule indicates that if the *Moored* event occurs then the engine was turned on in the past (consequent 1), or it was turned on later on (consequent 2).

When the *SafeNavigation* aspect is weaved with the base system a controller can not be found. This is because the environment can introduce the *Moored* event and then activate the sailing mode execution of the vessel. A trace like that

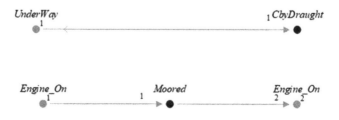

Fig. 5. FVS rule for requirements number two and three

requires the vessel to turn on the engine (because of requirement number three), but turning on the engine would be in conflict with requirement number one since the sailing mode was active. This behavior can be noted when exploring the anti-scenarios that the FVS tool generates from the rules shaping the *SafeNavigation* aspect easing the job for the specifier when faced to the non realizability problem. Three possible anti-scenarios are shown in Fig. 6. The anti-scenarios in the top of the Figure corresponds to behavior that violate requirement number one: in the first one, the sailing mode is activated, afterwards the engine is turned on and finally the vessel starts to navigate. This is a behavior violation since both modes are active simultaneously. The second one is the analogous behavior but just considering the engine was turned on first. The anti-scenario at the bottom of Fig. 6 violates requirement number three: the vessel is moored but the engine was neither turned on before or after its occurrence.

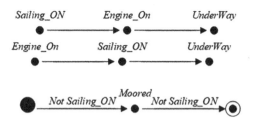

Fig. 6. Some anti-scenarios for the Safe Navigation Aspect

By just looking at the graphical information provided by these anti-scenarios the specifier can explore possible reasons that lead to the non realizability of the specification. In this case it can be noted that a trace like { *Moored, Sailing_ON* } would converge to a conflict since a occurrence of the *Engine_ON* event would match the first anti-scenario in Fig. 6 (and therefore a violation to the specification) and at the same time the absence of the *Engine_ON* event would match the third anti-scenario in Fig. 6, leading also to violation of the expected behavior. After this analysis the specifier can infer that the *Moored* event and the sailing mode are mutually exclusive. Introducing new rules for this extra requirement make the specification realizable and a controller con be found. These new rules are shown in Fig. 7.

3.2   The Halt-Exception Example

This example is inspired in the case of study shown in [35]. It consists of a typical buffer implementation in a distributed environment. A producer puts data in the buffer, it waits when the buffer is complete and sets a *Halt* flag on when it puts its last data. The consumer gets data from the buffer and waits when the buffer is empty. An exception is raised when the buffer is empty, the halt flag is on and the consumer attempts to get a data. This exception is specified with an

Fig. 7. New rules are introduced after exploring the anti-scenarios

aspect named *Halt Exception* aspect. Following the strategy presented in [35] we suppose that the specifier makes a mistake and the empty buffer condition is not included in the rule shaping this aspect. This incomplete rule is shown in Fig. 8

Fig. 8. The incomplete FVS rule for the Halt Exception Aspect

This error makes the specification non realizable. As in the previous case the specifier can then look at the anti-scenario that FVS can automatically generate. The anti-scenario is shown in Fig. 9. It shows how the aspect specification can be violated. In this case the sequence of events *Halt_ON* and *Get* on which the Halt Exception does not occur until the end of the execution is a violation of the rule.

Fig. 9. Anti-scenarios for the Halt Exception Aspect

By just looking at the sequence the specifier might detect that the empty buffer condition is not included and therefore spot the error in the specification. Adding this condition lead to the realizability of the specification and a controller is now found. The fixed rule is shown in Fig. 10.

3.3 The Exam System

This example is analyzed in [6] based on the case study presented in [28]. It consists on a Exam system which monitors and regulates students taking exams. The system starts in a *Wait* state and when a students arrives it shows a welcome screen. Then, the student takes the exam. The student can fail or pass the exam, the systems shows an exit screen and enters the *Wait* state once again. Two aspects are added next: the *Tuition* aspect and the *Availability* aspect. The first one validates that only students that have paid their tuition take the exam and

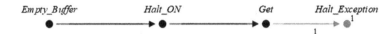

Fig. 10. Fixed Rule for the Halt Exception Aspect

the second one addresses a classic liveness requirement: the welcome screen will eventually be showed for every student. The rules for these two aspects are shown in Fig. 11.

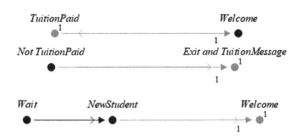

Fig. 11. Tuition and Availability aspects in the Exam System

As explained in [6] the specification containing both aspects in non realizable. If infinitely many students are received such that only a finite number of them have paid their tuition will lead the system not to enter the welcome state infinitely often, which violates its specification. Faced with this problem, the specifier might inspect anti-scenarios for both aspects. In particular, by analyzing the anti-scenario in Fig. 12 the specifier could realize that not visiting the *Welcome* state infinitely often might be a too strong condition and observing that it is enough that the systems leaves the *Wait* state but not necessarily enters the *Welcome* state.

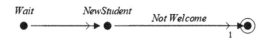

Fig. 12. An anti-scenario for the Availability aspect

The new rule introducing a more relaxed *Availability* aspect is shown in Fig. 13. With this new rule a controller is found for the *Exam* system.

Fig. 13. A more general Availability Aspect solving non the realizability problem

3.4 Remarks, Observations and Related Work

In all of the examples anti-scenarios provide meaningful information to solve the non realizability problem. We believe that is an appealing feature since it is provided by the specification language itself and there is no need to interact with external tools. Others technique such as [23,27] involves exchanging roles between environment and the system and try to discover in the winning strategy for the environment what behavior is obstructing the finding of a controller. Naturally, this can be achieved if anti-scenarios do not result in an effective weapon to solve the problem. Work in [25] provides a interesting solution to non realizability defining extra definitions such as *Conflict Sets* and *Recovery Sets* of Requirements. These definitions and the use of coloured automata allow the detection of possible conflicts between requirements that might lead to the non realizability of the specification. Finally, work in [2] proposes the us of inductive logic to solve non realizability. Inductive logics infers some missing information in the specification based on negative ans positive examples and its output could be used to solve non-realizability. We consider that our approach is orthogonal to these other works and could be easily combined. However, we affirm that taking the advantage of exploring anti-scenarios which are automatically obtained from the specification itself (win non costs or efforts for the specifier) is an captivating first step to address the non realizability problem in behavioral synthesis.

4 Performance Analysis

In this section we describe some performance analysis regarding employing FVS as an aspect oriented behavioral synthesis. Since we relay on external tools to solve the game between the environment and the system to obtain a controller we are in particular interested on measuring if the automata produced by our approach is comparable and competitive with other approaches. To achieve this objective we compare the time taken to obtain a controller taken as input FVS specifications versus other approaches since the algorithms involved depend on the size of the automata.

Also, we compare the performance of the two tools used to obtain a controller in our work: *GOAL* and *Acacia+*. In previous work such as [6] we employed the GOAL tool to resolve the behavioral synthesis problem. GOAL is a very powerful tool to rely on during the verification phase since it can handle several formalisms for automata and temporal logics and also, it implements several game solving algorithms such as [19,20,31,37]. For this paper we also employ an attractive tool called *Acacia+*, an efficient tool for solving synthesis specifications implemented in Python and C. It can be easily downloaded from its site [1] and also can be executed online. Instead of employing BDDs (Binary Decision Diagrams) as the main structure of data is uses the concept of antichains [12,15] with satisfactory results in some domains [9]. It takes as input LTL formulae as well as automata notations.

The rest of this section is structured as follows. Section 4.1 analyzes the performance of the external tools interacting with FVS, Sect. 4.2 compares FVS against other two approaches whereas Sect. 4.3 includes some final considerations regarding this performance experiment.

4.1 GOAL vs Acacia+ vs Specification Patterns

In this section we compare FVS performance using different external tools and kinds of specifications. As it is mentioned earlier in Sect. 2 we rely on several techniques to realize the behavioral synthesis: using the GR(1) technique in [27] if the properties modeling the expected behavior of the system can be denoted with most of the specifications patterns [17], using GOAL and Acacia+ with Deterministic Büchi and finally, using GOAL with Non Deterministic Büchi.

Table 1 resumes this performance analysis. The time is measured in seconds taking the average time to obtain the controller for all the case of studies introduced in Sect. 3. For all the problems we divided the set of requirements as follows: set 1 contains only properties denoted by specification patterns (excepting those ones that can not be represented by Deterministic Büchi), set 2 contains properties beyond specification patterns but still represented by Deterministic Büchi automata and finally, set 3 contains properties expressible only by Non Deterministic Büchi automata.

Table 1. FVS performance with external tools

Set-tool	FVS-GOAL	FVS-Acacia+	FVS-GR(1)
Set 1 s	4 s	2 s	1 s
Set 2 s	7 s	5 s	–
Set 3 s	20 s	–	–

It can be observed that the technique introduced by [27] (denoted by the column FVS-GR(1) in Table 1) is the most efficient in time when the behavior can be expressed by most of the specification patterns. In the same row, *Acacia+* comes in second place while the *GOAL* tool ends at the bottom but close to *Acacia+*. *Acacia+* leverages the advantage moving on to the second row, using Deterministic Büchi automata. Finally, only GOAL is able to handle requirements in set 3, which includes Non Deterministic Büchi automata. The GR(1) technique in [27] is only available for behavior denoted in the first set of requirements. These results can definitely guide the specifier when choosing the external tool to perform the behavioral synthesis using as input FVS specifications.

4.2 Efficiency Comparison

We now compare FVS against other approaches in those cases where performance times are available or can be obtained. We use only properties can could be expressed by Deterministic Büchi automata.

For the *Exam* System paper in [27] reports that 3.5 s is taken to obtain a controller using their approach based on the use of specification patterns. Employing FVS we obtained 4.5 s, since larger automata are used in our case. However, the difference is not a significative one. In [6] we add some extra requirement using specification patterns not covered in [27] since they can only be expressed with: the *Precedence pattern with After Q scope, the Response Chain pattern (with one stimuli and two responses) with After q until r scope* and *the Constrained Chain pattern with After q until r scope and the Precedence pattern with After Q scope.* In this case it took FVS-GOAL 33 s to obtain the controller.

For the *Vessel* System using *Acacia+* with its own specification language a controller is obtained in 7 s, whereas the tool took 11 to obtain the controller when using FVS-Specifications as input. It is worth noticing that *Acacia+* specifications language is more complex since *Conflicting* and *Recovery* set of requirements need to be specified. This extra effort added to the specification was not measured for the performance experiment. In FVS no additional information need to be provided besides the rules shaping the behavior of the system.

For the *Halt-Exception* example no comparison can be made since in [35] the bug in the specification is detected using traditional model checking whereas in this work we employed a behavioral synthesis approach. Nonetheless, FVS specification can be used in a traditional model checking approach. In this domain we do not expect great differences in the elapsed time of execution since the size of the automata involved are similar [5]. Table 2 summarizes the performance analysis of this section.

Table 2. Comparison against other approaches

Example-tool	Acacia+	Patterns	FVS
Vessel example	7 s	–	11 s
Exam system	–	3.5 s	4.5 s

4.3 Final Observations

From the performance analysis several interesting conclusions can be taken. For one side, FVS is behind in time execution against other approaches. However, the difference is not a significative one and barely has impact in the analyzed examples. On the other side, it is the only one that is able to handle all type of specifications, specially considering Non Deterministic Büchi automata. We believe this power expression enrichment of the specification language outweighs the loss in performance. Regarding anti-scenarios and the non realizability problem we believe the information provided by the anti-scenarios can solve faster the problem than feeding external tools. However, this must be concluded after an empiric study that is out of scope of this paper and addressed as future work.

5   Future Work

This work pinpoints several research line to further continue our proposal. In the first place we would like to measure the effectiveness of the use of anti-scenarios to solve the non realizability problem. This would imply the realization of an experiment that compares the results obtained by employing anti-scenarios against the usage of other techniques. The experiment should be designed to asses the percentage of non realizability problems solved and the time and resources taken to solve the problem. Secondly, we would like to employ our technique in the hardware verification and software architecture domain to take advantage of FVS's flexibility and expressive power. Finally, we would like to improve the efficiency of our tool. In order to achieve this goal the algorithm that translates FVS scenarios into Büchi automata must be analyzed aiming to reduce the size of the automata given as output.

6   Conclusions

In this work we exploit FVS's capability of automatically building anti-scenarios to address the non realizability problem when performing behavioral synthesis in aspect orientation. Anti-scenarios represent a meaningful graphical descriptions of situations and executions of the system that violates the specification and thus can be analyzed in order to solve the non realizability problem. The main advantage of this approach is that this information is provided by the specification language and there exists no need to interact with external tools that might make the process more complex. The proposal is validated with several and relevant case studies. Finally, a performance analysis is introduced to compare FVS interaction with synthesis tools and with other approaches as well.

References

1. Acacia+ web site. http://lit2.ulb.ac.be/acaciaplus/
2. Alrajeh, D., Kramer, J., Russo, A., Uchitel, S.: Learning operational requirements from goal models. In: 2009 IEEE 31st International Conference on Software Engineering, pp. 265–275. IEEE (2009)
3. Apel, S., Batory, D., Kästner, C., Saake, G.: Feature-Oriented Software Product Lines. Springer, Heidelberg (2016)
4. Asteasuain, F., Braberman, V.: Specification patterns: formal and easy. IJSEKE **25**(04), 669–700 (2015)
5. Asteasuain, F., Braberman, V.: Declaratively building behavior by means of scenario clauses. Requir. Eng. **22**(2), 239–274 (2016). https://doi.org/10.1007/s00766-015-0242-2
6. Asteasuain, F., Calonge, F., Gamboa, P.: Aspect oriented behavioral synthesis. In: CACIC, pp. 622–631 (2019). ISBN 978-987-688-377-1
7. Bergmans, L.M.: Towards detection of semantic conflicts between crosscutting concerns. In: Analysis of Aspect-Oriented Software (ECOOP 2003) (2003)

8. Bloem, R., Jobstmann, B., Piterman, N., Pnueli, A., Sa'Ar, Y.: Synthesis of reactive (1) designs (2011)
9. Bohy, A., Bruyère, V., Filiot, E., Jin, N., Raskin, J.-F.: Acacia+, a tool for LTL synthesis. In: Madhusudan, P., Seshia, S.A. (eds.) CAV 2012. LNCS, vol. 7358, pp. 652–657. Springer, Heidelberg (2012). https://doi.org/10.1007/978-3-642-31424-7_45
10. Braberman, V., Garbervestky, D., Kicillof, N., Monteverde, D., Olivero, A.: Speeding up model checking of timed-models by combining scenario specialization and live component analysis. In: Ouaknine, J., Vaandrager, F.W. (eds.) FORMATS 2009. LNCS, vol. 5813, pp. 58–72. Springer, Heidelberg (2009). https://doi.org/10.1007/978-3-642-04368-0_7
11. Cerny, T.: Aspect-oriented challenges in system integration with microservices, SOA and IoT. Enterp. Inf. Syst. **13**(4), 467–489 (2019)
12. De Wulf, M., Doyen, L., Henzinger, T.A., Raskin, J.-F.: Antichains: a new algorithm for checking universality of finite automata. In: Ball, T., Jones, R.B. (eds.) CAV 2006. LNCS, vol. 4144, pp. 17–30. Springer, Heidelberg (2006). https://doi.org/10.1007/11817963_5
13. D'Ippolito, N., Braberman, V., Piterman, N., Uchitel, S.: Synthesising non-anomalous event-based controllers for liveness goals. ACM Trans. Softw. Eng. Methodol. (TOSEM) **22**(9), 1–36 (2013)
14. Disenfeld, C., Katz, S.: A closer look at aspect interference and cooperation. In: AOSD, pp. 107–118. ACM (2012)
15. Doyen, L., Raskin, J.-F.: Improved algorithms for the automata-based approach to model-checking. In: Grumberg, O., Huth, M. (eds.) TACAS 2007. LNCS, vol. 4424, pp. 451–465. Springer, Heidelberg (2007). https://doi.org/10.1007/978-3-540-71209-1_34
16. Duhoux, B., Mens, K., Dumas, B.: Implementation of a feature-based context-oriented programming language. In: Proceedings of the Workshop on Context-Oriented Programming, pp. 9–16 (2019)
17. Dwyer, M., Avrunin, M., Corbett, M.: Patterns in property specifications for finite-state verification. In: ICSE, pp. 411–420 (1999)
18. Filman, R., Elrad, T., Clarke, S., Akşit, M.: Aspect-Oriented Software Development. Addison-Wesley Professional, Boston (2004)
19. Friedmann, O., Lange, M.: Solving parity games in practice. In: Liu, Z., Ravn, A.P. (eds.) ATVA 2009. LNCS, vol. 5799, pp. 182–196. Springer, Heidelberg (2009). https://doi.org/10.1007/978-3-642-04761-9_15
20. Jurdziński, M.: Small progress measures for solving parity games. In: Reichel, H., Tison, S. (eds.) STACS 2000. LNCS, vol. 1770, pp. 290–301. Springer, Heidelberg (2000). https://doi.org/10.1007/3-540-46541-3_24
21. Katz, S.: Aspect categories and classes of temporal properties. In: Rashid, A., Aksit, M. (eds.) Transactions on Aspect-Oriented Software Development I. LNCS, vol. 3880, pp. 106–134. Springer, Heidelberg (2006). https://doi.org/10.1007/11687061_4
22. Kiczales, G., et al.: Aspect-oriented programming. In: Akşit, M., Matsuoka, S. (eds.) ECOOP 1997. LNCS, vol. 1241, pp. 220–242. Springer, Heidelberg (1997). https://doi.org/10.1007/BFb0053381
23. Könighofer, R., Hofferek, G., Bloem, R.: Debugging formal specifications using simple counterstrategies. In: 2009 Formal Methods in Computer-Aided Design, pp. 152–159. IEEE (2009)
24. Krüger, J.: Separation of concerns: experiences of the crowd. In: ACM Symposium on Applied Computing, pp. 2076–2077. ACM (2018)

25. Maggi, F.M., Westergaard, M., Montali, M., van der Aalst, W.M.P.: Runtime verification of LTL-based declarative process models. In: Khurshid, S., Sen, K. (eds.) RV 2011. LNCS, vol. 7186, pp. 131–146. Springer, Heidelberg (2012). https://doi.org/10.1007/978-3-642-29860-8_11
26. Malakuti, S., Aksit, M.: Event-based modularization: how emergent behavioral patterns must be modularized? In: FOAL, pp. 7–12 (2014)
27. Maoz, S., Ringert, J.O.: Synthesizing a lego forklift controller in GR (1): a case study. arXiv preprint arXiv:1602.01172 (2016)
28. Maoz, S., Sa'ar, Y.: AspectLTL: an aspect language for LTL specifications. In: AOSD, pp. 19–30. ACM (2011)
29. Mezini, M., Ostermann, K.: Variability management with feature-oriented programming and aspects. In: ACM SEN, vol. 29, pp. 127–136. ACM (2004)
30. Casas, S.I., Perez-Schofield, J.B.G., Marcos, C.A.: MEDIATOR: an AOP tool to support conflicts among aspects. Int. J. Softw. Eng. Appl. (IJSEIA) 3(3), 33–44 (2009)
31. Schewe, S.: Solving parity games in big steps. In: Arvind, V., Prasad, S. (eds.) FSTTCS 2007. LNCS, vol. 4855, pp. 449–460. Springer, Heidelberg (2007). https://doi.org/10.1007/978-3-540-77050-3_37
32. Tahara, Y., Ohsuga, A., Honiden, S.: Formal verification of dynamic evolution processes of UML models using aspects. In: Proceedings of the 12th International Symposium on Software Engineering for Adaptive and Self-Managing Systems, pp. 152–162. IEEE Press (2017)
33. Tourwé, T., Brichau, J., Gybels, K.: On the existence of the AOSD-evolution paradox. SPLAT (2003)
34. Tsay, Y.-K., Chen, Y.-F., Tsai, M.-H., Wu, K.-N., Chan, W.-C.: GOAL: a graphical tool for manipulating Büchi automata and temporal formulae. In: Grumberg, O., Huth, M. (eds.) TACAS 2007. LNCS, vol. 4424, pp. 466–471. Springer, Heidelberg (2007). https://doi.org/10.1007/978-3-540-71209-1_35
35. Ubayashi, N., Tamai, T.: Aspect-oriented programming with model checking. In: Proceedings of the 1st International Conference on Aspect-Oriented Software Development, pp. 148–154. ACM (2002)
36. Velan, S.: Introducing artificial intelligence agents to the empirical measurement of design properties for aspect oriented software development. In: 2019 Amity International Conference on Artificial Intelligence (AICAI), pp. 80–85. IEEE (2019)
37. Zielonka, W.: Infinite games on finitely coloured graphs with applications to automata on infinite trees. Theor. Comput. Sci. 200(1–2), 135–183 (1998)

Software Product Line Development Based on Reusability at Subdomain Level

Agustina Buccella$^{(\boxtimes)}$, Alejandra Cechich, Gabriel Cancellieri, and Sofia Caballero

GIISCO Research Group, Departamento de Ingeniería de Sistemas, Facultad de Informática, Universidad Nacional del Comahue, Neuquen, Argentina
agustina.buccella@fi.uncoma.edu.ar

Abstract. Reusability is nowadays a highly valued attribute within the software engineering area. In particular, software product line (SPL) developments are focused on identifying similarities and variabilities within particular domains in order to be reused when new products are developed. It is also possible to reuse outside a domain, especially when the domains are related to each other. This fact allows us to develop SPLs by reusing assets that are hierarchically structured as domain/subdomain taxonomies. In this paper, we describe the process for developing new SPLs by reusing those most suitable assets. We exemplify the process for a case, and show similarity calculations that might facilitate systematic reuse.

Keywords: Software product line · Reusability · Mapping artifacts

1 Introduction

Benefits from reuse are obtained by means of a set of methodologies and techniques aimed at taking into account previously developed software artifacts and applying them to new developments. There are several approaches focused on software reuse, such as software product line development [12], component-based development [2], service-oriented software [4], etc. Each of them proposes specific techniques/methods based on maximizing the reuse, interoperability, and standardization. In particular, software product lines (SPLs) are focused on identifying similarities and variabilities within particular domains in order to be reused when new products are developed. At the same time, it is also possible to reuse outside a domain, specially when the domains are related to each other. In this sense, in previous works we have been working on the geographic domain as a generic domain, and specializing it into specific and related subdomains. Thus, we applied a subdomain-oriented development [5] in which each new software product line takes artifacts of other subdomains previously developed. In particular we have focused on the marine ecology [6] and paleobiology [7] subdomains. However, in order to continue developing new SPLs in other related subdomains, for example the *paleontology cultural heritage* one, it is important to generate the

© Springer Nature Switzerland AG 2020
P. Pesado and M. Arroyo (Eds.): CACIC 2019, CCIS 1184, pp. 172–187, 2020.
https://doi.org/10.1007/978-3-030-48325-8_12

mechanisms for identifying and reusing software artifacts previously developed maximizing the effective reuse.

Our work is related to those proposals in the literature focused on reusing software artifacts in some of the development phases. For example, in [15] authors present a review of different techniques for reusing UML artifacts, such as graph-based similarities, case-based reasoning, ontologies etc. Among the graph-based techniques, we can cite the work presented in [14]. Here, authors apply a graph mapping algorithm in order to identify reuse among UML sequence diagrams. In [16] authors calculate a structural similarity over class diagrams by using a genetic algorithm. Also in [13] an effort estimation model is proposed based on reuse of use cases. Finally, in [1] the authors present structural, functional and behavioral functions for mapping several UML diagrams. In contrast with these works and other related ones in the literature, we are focused on identifying and retrieving design software artifacts but based on a subdomain development. This is an important difference because our artifacts have been created for other related subdomains, and now they are considered as resources for finding the most suitable to be reused. Therefore, in this work we present a development process based on reusability at subdomain level, and describe its application on the development of a new SPL in the *paleontology cultural heritage* subdomain. At the same time, this work is an extension of the work presented in [9] in which we extend the reuse possibilities to other software artifacts and include them into the previous methodology.

This paper is organized as follows. The next section presents the background of our previous experiences on SPL development together with our previously developed software artifacts. Section 3 details our development process based on reusability at domain level. Section 4 presents a preliminary evaluation. Finally, future work and conclusions are discussed afterwards.

2 Background and Previous Works

In previous works [5–7] we have defined a methodology for SPL development based on a domain hierarchy. This hierarchy starts from the geography domain and it is specialized into set of subdomains sharing some services. For the development of the hierarchy we have created a service taxonomy [6] beginning from the ISO 19119 std[1], which is used as a structure by semantically defining service categories. The taxonomy includes five service categories: (HI) Human interaction, (MMS) Model/information management, (WTS) Workflow/Task, and (PS) Processing services, which is subdivided also into five subcategories involving thematic, spatial and communication services. From there, our work has extended these categories into a set of services for particular subdomains, specifically into marine ecology, oceanography [6] and paleobiology [7]. For each of these subdomains, we also took advantage from other standard information available; for

---

[1] Services International Standard 19119, ISO/IEC, 2005.

example the ISO 21127[2] and the CIDOC Conceptual Reference Model (CRM)[3] have been applied for the paleobiology subdomain.

In Fig. 1 we show the 3-layer reference architecture (based on the ISO 19109[4] std) for developing geographic systems, which is used as a reference architecture for our SPL developments. At the same time, the figure shows information from the ISO 19119 std for defining the type of services that must be included in each layer. For example, the *(HI) human interaction services* must be defined in the *human interaction layer*. Also, in Fig. 1 we can see the set of service categories (of ISO 19119 std - in italics) together with new services obtained from specific requirements of the GIS systems. For example, we define *(HI-MM) map manipulation* services for grouping those related to interactions with maps, or *(HI-LM) layer manipulation* for services related to interactions with layers. Finally, in Fig. 1 we show more specializations according to the marine ecology (in gray) and paleobiology (in bold-black) subdomains.

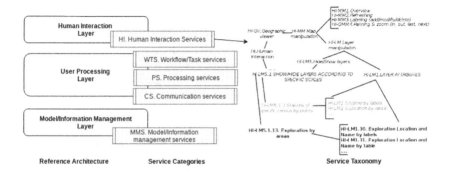

Fig. 1. Reference architecture and service taxonomy involving subdomains

Another important design artifact developed in previous works is the functional datasheet, which is used for designing the functionalities on each subdomain. Each datasheet contains five items: (1) an *identification* which is unique, a *name* with a description of the main function, a *domain* in which the functionality is included or it was firstly created, a list of *services* (from the service taxonomy) used to represent the functionality, and a set of *variability models* showing the service interactions (as common and variant services). For the last item, any graphical diagram could be used; however, in our work we use a graphical notation based on variability annotation of collaboration diagrams (of UML). The required variability, according to the functionality to be represented, is attached to the diagrams by using the OVM notation [12].

---

[2] Information and documentation—A reference ontology for the interchange of cultural heritage information, 2014.

[3] Conceptual Reference Model Version 6.0 http://www.cidoc-crm.org.

[4] ISO 19109 std - Rules for Application Schema 19109, ISO/IEC, 2005.

3   Development Process Based on Reusability at Subdomain Level

The *paleontology cultural heritage* subdomain involves information about the management of paleontological pieces with respect to the way they are found (on an exploration process), acquired (from other museums), and/or showed (on exhibitions). For the development of an SPL in this new subdomain, we must to extend previously developed artifacts (service taxonomy and functional datasheets) in order to include the commonalities and variabilities of this subdomain. Figure 2 shows our development process based on reusing the pregenerated artifacts for other subdomains. As we can see, the process contains three steps in which two of them (steps 2 and 3) are subdivided into two different activities considering the reuse of artifacts or the development of new ones. The three steps are:

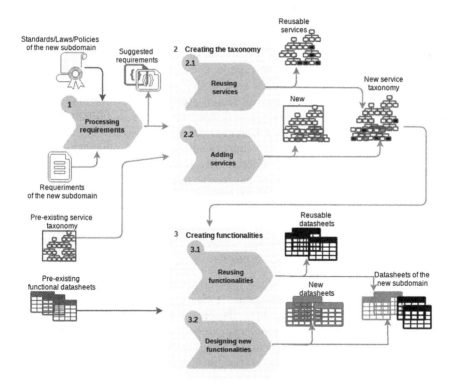

Fig. 2. Development process for new functionalities based on reusability at subdomain level

1. *Processing requirements:* The inputs of this step are the *requirements of the new subdomain* provided by expert users in the area; and *standards, laws and/or policies.* This last information is useful for determining regulations

which must be fulfilled for all products generated in the subdomain; so it is a useful source of information for extracting commonalities. The output of this step is a list of the *suggested requirements* that must be included in the SPL.

2. *Creating the taxonomy:* The inputs of this step are the *suggested requirements* obtained in the last step, and the *pre-existing taxonomy* created during the development of other SPLs in other subdomains. The output of this step is the new taxonomy containing the list of added/reused services of the new subdomain. This step is subdivided into two substeps:

   (a) *Reusing services:* Here, it is important to determine which of the suggested requirements can be translated into a service already defined by the pre-existing taxonomy (for other subdomains). In this way, the service can be reused.

   (b) *Adding services:* When the suggested requirements cannot be matched to a service of the pre-existing taxonomy, the requirements must be added. This addition is not trivial because they can be added as a completely new category of the taxonomy or as a new specialization of another pre-existing service (or category).

3. *Creating functionalities:* In this step, the functionalities of the new subdomain must be defined. Based on the output of the last step (list of services added/reused in the new taxonomy), the functional datasheets must be designed. The output of this step is the set of added/reused functional datasheets for the new subdomain. As in step 2, it is important to analyze whether the functionality is already defined for previous subdomains or it is a new one. Thus, this step is subdivided into two substeps:

   (a) *Reusing functionalities:* We must identify the functionalities that can be reused. For reusing a functionality the set of pre-existing functional datasheets must be analyzed in order to determine whether the new functionality can be reused completely, partially or it is not possible.

   (b) *Designing new functionalities:* A new functionality is designed when it cannot be reused completely. Sometimes, it is possible to reuse a functionality only partially, in which case it is necessary to create also a new one with the set of reused services.

Steps 2 and 3 of the development process are described in detail in the next sections, focusing on the way reusable artifacts are identified and selected to be part of a new development. It is important to denote that each of these steps, as in every software development, can be performed by different software engineers even in different moments. Thus, for example, the new and reused services defined in step 2 are stored (in repositories) along with the subdomain information in order to be retrieved during step 3.

3.1 Step 2: Creating the Taxonomy

As we have described in the previous section, the requirements of a new subdomain, which are written in natural language, must be mapped to some services of the taxonomy. In Fig. 3, we show the workflow for mapping requirements in which the output, for each requirement, is an ordered list of pairs

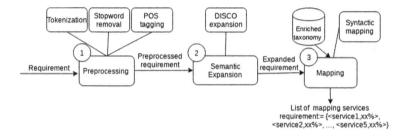

Fig. 3. Workflow for mapping requirements to services of the taxonomy

$<service, percentage>$ showing the first five services with better mapping results. In order to build this list, the workflow specifies three main activities:

1. *Preprocessing:* In this activity, each requirement is preprocessed in order to translate each specific word (tokenization) to a list of tokens, which will be then filtered by removing stopwords (symbols, letters, or other unwanted or useless elements). Finally, each of the remaining words are tagged (part-of-speech tagging) in order to determine the context in which they are used. We apply here the 36 categories defined by the Penn Treebank Project[5]. The output of this activity is a set of tokens, each of them with its category.
2. *Semantic Expansion:* In this activity, each requirement is enriched by adding semantic relationships to other similar words. To do so, we use DISCO (extracting DIstributionally related words using CO-occurrences)[6]. The selection of this tool was based on a previous work, presented in [3], in which DISCO obtained the better results when comparing queries to requirements in natural language. We use the tool to retrieve the first k semantically most similar words for each of the tokens extracted in the previous activity. Thus, the output of this activity is a list of tokens with associated k terms.
3. *Mapping:* In this activity the enriched requirement is compared to each of the services of the taxonomy in order to determine the percentage of similarity matching obtained. We also use DISCO to retrieve the value of semantic similarity between two input words, which are selected from the list of tokens with the associated terms and the enriched taxonomy. It is our pre-existing taxonomy which has been enriched and stored in a new database (stored previously in a repository). As Fig. 3 shows, the output of the activity is a new list containing the five better results obtained.

As this step is defined as semi-automatic, the results must be showed to the software engineers and they must decide whether the requirement matches completely to some candidate service of the list or not. When a mapping is agreed, the requirement is translated to the service in the taxonomy (so the service is reused). However, if the software engineers do not agree the mapping,

---

[5] https://catalog.ldc.upenn.edu/docs/LDC95T7/cl93.html.
[6] https://www.linguatools.de/disco/disco.html.

they should decide whether the requirement must be added as a specialization of a pre-existing service (the most similar one), or as a new category (with the requirement as a service) in the taxonomy. In these last two cases, the taxonomy is changed to contain this new requirement/service. In Fig. 4 we can see (highlighted in gray) some new services added for the paleontology cultural heritage subdomain as category or service specialization, such as PS-T2.56 and PS-T4.2.35 respectively.

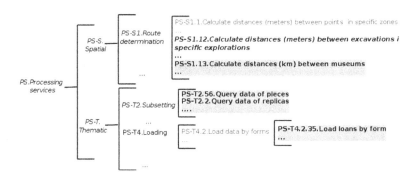

Fig. 4. Part of the service taxonomy with some of the new services added

Finally, the last activity is to classify these reusable/new services as: *Completely reusable*, when the requirement is mapped to a pre-existing service (total mapping); *Partially reusable*, when the requirement is added as an specialization of some pre-existing service (partial mapping); and *Non reusable*, when the requirement is added as a new service (no mapping). This *service classification* is stored in a repository and used for searching reusable functionalities (as we will describe in the next section).

3.2   Step 3: Creating Functionalities

Based on the new taxonomy containing the specific services used in the new subdomain, the functionalities must be designed as functional datasheets. At the same time, the pre-existing datasheets must be analyzed in order to determine the reuse possibility. To do so, we apply the algorithm showed in Fig. 5.

This algorithm is similar to another one we presented in a previous work [9], with some modifications for considering the inputs of step 2. Let us describe some instructions deeply.

Input: A New Datasheet. The input of the algorithm is a datasheet for the new subdomain containing the list of services used and the variability model representing the functionality.

```
 1   Input: A new datasheet
 2       Translate the datasheet to a graph (Dn)
 3       Select the most related pre-existing datasheets wrt to Dn and retrieve the
             associated graphs (ListDes)
 4       For each graph in ListDes (De):
 5           For each node in Dn (Dn.node):
 6               For each node in De (De.node):
 7                   Apply service classification and variability (Eq 2)
 8               Match De.node <=> Dn.node with the best substitution cost
 9           Calculate deleted costs
10   Output: The 5 best De's costs
```

Fig. 5. Algorithm for reusing functionalities

Translate the Datasheet to a Graph (Dn). The instruction 2 translates the variability model of the functional datasheet to a graph. In Fig. 6a) we can see the variability model for *Add a new piece* for the paleontology cultural heritage subdomain together with the translated graph representing the same information in a different notation (Fig. 6b)).

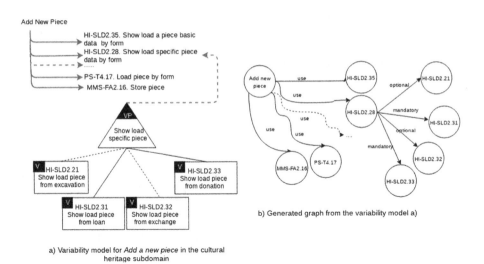

a) Variability model for *Add a new piece* in the cultural heritage subdomain

b) Generated graph from the variability model a)

Fig. 6. Variability model and translated graph for the *Add a new piece* functionality

Select the Most Related Pre-existing Datasheets wrt to Dn and Retrieve the Associated Graphs (ListDes). In instruction 3 the algorithm selects, from our repository, the most related pre-existing datasheets and retrieves their associated graphs. The first task is performed by matching the list of used services for the new datasheet with respect to the list of used services for the pre-existing datasheets. When the matching is 0 (that is, the intersection of services is null), the matching is performed by considering their parents in the hierarchy. In this way, the output is a list of the first five most related datasheets that will be used to make the comparisons. At the same time, the algorithm also retrieves, from our repository, the associated graphs for each of the selected pre-existing datasheets (which have been previously created).

Cost Calculation. The cost calculation (based on the graph distance metric presented in [8,10]) is based on the edition steps (insertion/substitution/deletion) needed to transform one graph to another. In this case, the cost of transforming Dn to De. We only consider substitutions and deletions because insertions are not relevant in this context. We are looking for which services (nodes) of the pre-existing datasheet can be reused, so extra nodes of De are not important. The formula for calculating the general cost is defined as (Eq. 1):

$$cost_{total}(Dn, De) = \frac{min}{e_1, ..., e_k \epsilon P(Dn, De)} \sum_{i=1}^{k} c(e_i) \qquad (1)$$

in which $P(Dn, De)$ refers to the set of edition steps required to transform Dn to De, and $c(e) \geq 0$ is the cost for each edition operation e.

Cost Calculation For Substitution. For the substitution cost (instructions 5–8), for each similar node we assign a substitution cost. We take one node of the new graph ($Dn.node$ - instruction 5) and compare it to each node of the selected pre-existing graph ($De.node$ - instruction 6). This node-by-node comparison allows us to calculate the associated cost. The formula for calculating the substitution cost is defined as (Eq. 2):

$$cost_{sust}(n1, n2) = \frac{cla_{ser}(n1, n2) + cla_{var}(n1, n2)}{2} \qquad (2)$$

in which $n1$ is $Dn.nodo$ and $n2$ is $De.nodo$. The equation returns the average cost after analyzing the result of the *service classification* (cla_{ser}) for the nodes according to the taxonomy, and the *variability classification* (cla_{var}) according to node interactions in the graphs. Both functions return a value between 0 and 1.

For the *service classification* we use the information previously stored during the step 2, in which we classified each service of the new subdomain as *completely reusable*, *partially reusable* and *non reusable*. In this activity we must to determine, based on that service classification (of a $Dn.node$), if the $De.node$ is the node for which the mapping was done. For example, for the case of a *partially reusable* classification, we must determine if $De.node$ is a generalization of $Dn.node$.

At the same time, depending on this, we assign the following costs:

– $Dn.nodo$ is a service *completely reusable* of $De.nodo$, so the cost is equal to 0, and a mapping $Dn.node <= SCR => De.node$ is added. We are assuming a null cost for reusability.
– $Dn.nodo$ is a service *partially reusable* of $De.nodo$, so the cost is equal to 0.5, and a mapping $Dn.node <= SRE => De.node$ is added. We are assuming that some reuse could be applied.
– Otherwise, the cost is equal to 1 assuming no reuse is possible.

These costs have been determined by considering hypothetically the efforts of implementing partially and non-reusable services. Thus, for partially reusable services, we are assuming that developers will need to make some re-implementations or adaptations for development; and in the case of non-reusable services, the implementation must be total. An example of a partial mapping is when comparing the service PS-T4.2 belonging to the marine biology subdomain to the service PS-T2.35 of the paleontology cultural heritage (Fig. 4).

For the *variability classification* (cla_{var}) we analyze the variability dependencies involved in each node. These dependencies are: *mandatory, optional, alternative, variant* and *use*. For example in Fig. 6 the PS-T4.17 node is a *use* dependency, HI-SLD2.21 is *optional*, and HI-SLD2.33 *mandatory*. Thus, each node is classified and compared according to these dependencies. The specific costs assigned according to the variability classification of the dependencies is defined in Table 1.

Table 1. Variability dependency costs

$Dn.node.variability$	$De.node.variability$	Cost
Use	Mandatory	0,2
Use	Optional	0,7
	Variant	
	Alternative	
Mandatory	Optional	0,7
	Variant	
	Alternative	
Optional	Variant	0,3
	Alternative	
Opcional	Use	0,2
	Mandatorio	

As in service classification, these costs were defined hypothetically assuming: (1) a low cost when dependencies are *use* and *mandatory* in *De.node.variability*; and (2) a higher cost when dependencies are *use* and *mandatory* in *Dn.node.varia bility*; and *optional, alternative*, and *variant* in *De.node.variability*. In (1) we consider that the services can be reused because they were developed in previous LPSs; and in (2) we consider that the service could not be implemented because we do not know if some derived product (of previous LPSs) has instantiated it.

Finally, as we can see in instruction 7, we select the best cost (the lower one) from all comparisons of *Dn.nodo* to each *De.nodo* generating a final mapping *Dn.nodo* <=> *De.nodo*. For example, considering two nodes (*Dn.nodeA* and *De.nodoB*) representing the same service in the taxonomy (with an SCR mapping *Dn.nodeA* <= *SCR* => *De.nodeB*) and related by the same variability dependency (*use* dependency), the cost is null – they are representing the same service and the same variability dependency.

Calculate Deleted Costs. Our algorithm must also determine the deleted costs for those nodes that cannot be mapped. (instruction 9). These non-mapping nodes returned 1 in cla_{ser} ($Dn.node, De.node$) because $Dn.node$ is a completely new service in the taxonomy. Thus, the cost of deleting it is 0.2 considering that developers make the effort of analyzing which parts must be deleted or ignored from previous implementations [9].

Output: The 5 Best De's Costs. Finally, we apply Eq. 1 in order to obtain the 5 *De's* with the lower costs (instruction 10). These 5 *De's* are showed to the software engineers to select one for reusability.

As an example, in Fig. 7 we can see two graphs to be compared. The first one (Fig. 7) represents the *Add a new piece* functionality for the paleontology cultural heritage subdomain; and the second one represents the same functionality (Fig. 7b) but defined for the paleobiology subdomain. When these two graphs are compared to each other, the final result from Eq. 1 is 0.9 obtained from four nodes completely mapped (only one with a different cla_{var} classification) and from the elimination of other four nodes that are not present in the second graph. Although this final value does not have an associated cost function measuring some attributes such as effort, adaptability, etc., it is comparative in terms of the result generated by each comparison of the new graph to each of the existing ones. That is, the result of 0.9 is useful when the ranked list is generated.

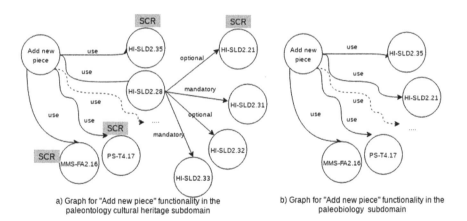

a) Graph for "Add new piece" functionality in the paleontology cultural heritage subdomain

b) Graph for "Add new piece" functionality in the paleobiology subdomain

Fig. 7. Graphs for two different subdomains

4   Preliminary Evaluation

In order to evaluate our process for domain reusability, we have developed a prototype containing the main automatic activities of the two steps. The prototype is implemented in Angular[7], Nodejs[8] and MongoDB[9]. The evaluation is designed as an experiment according to guidelines from [17]. Following we describe the experiment and the generated results.

4.1   Selection of Inputs and Available Artifacts

The experiment takes as input a controlled subset of the requirements for the *cultural heritage* subdomain. These requirements were selected from the large set of requirements we analyzed during our SPL development for this subdomain. At the same time, for evaluating the step 3 of the process the experiment takes as input a set of functional datasheets of the new subdomain. Also, repositories containing the pre-existing taxonomy and functional datasheets are stored in MongoDB databases.

4.2   Evaluation Design

As our proposal is focused on helping software engineers and developers with the identification of services and functionalities to be reused, we designed experiments to analyze the correctness of this identification. So, our main hypotheses are:

Hypothesis 1 (H1). *Is our process useful for software engineers and developers on finding the best reusable services in the pre-existing taxonomy during the taxonomy construction for a new subdomain?*

Hypothesis 2 (H2). *Is our process useful for software engineers and developers on finding the best reusable functionalities during an SPL development for a new subdomain?*

4.3   Expected Results

After defining the controlled set of requirements and datasheets as inputs, it is necessary to define which are the expected results. Thus, we established which services and functionalities are expected to be retrieved from the inputs.

To do so, we divided the expected results in two sets according to the outputs of steps 2 and 3 of our process (Fig. 2). Firstly we created two groups of students from the Software Engineering Department (of the National University of Comahue), who are elaborating their graduation thesis in the paleontology cultural heritage subdomain. The first group was responsible for manually matching 120 requirements to some service in the taxonomy. They had to define a full, partial and null mapping to one (or none) service of the taxonomy. Then, the second group defined matches between the inputs (22 functional datasheets for

---

[7] https://angular.io/.
[8] https://nodejs.org/es/.
[9] https://www.mongodb.com/.

the new subdomain) to one (or none) pre-existing functional datasheet. Thus, each requirement and datasheet was matched manually to one (or none) of the pre-existing services (of the taxonomy) and datasheet (of other subdomain), respectively. These results were compared to the results provided by our proto-type.

4.4 Evaluation Results

Here, we performed a correctness analysis by applying information retrieval (IR) techniques [11] in terms of *recall* and *DCG* (Discounted Cumulative Gain) in the reuse identification. *Recall* is the fraction of relevant items that are retrieved, and it is defined as (Eq. 3):

$$Recall = \frac{\#(relevant services retrieved)}{\#(relevant services)} \tag{3}$$

DCG is a function for measuring relevant items according to a ranked list. This last function is useful here because in both, step 2 and 3, we return a ranked list of the best 5 matched items (pre-existing services and datasheets respectively). So, the function returns better values when the relevant items are obtained in first position of the ranked list and then penalizes those items obtained in the following positions. This function is defined as (Eq. 4):

$$DCG_n = \sum_{i=1}^{n} \frac{rel_i}{\log_2(i+1)} \tag{4}$$

In both functions relevant items (services and datasheets) are considered as the expected items to be matched (previously described in Subsect. 4.3).

To analyze the two hypotheses defined in Subsect. 4.2 and apply these two functions, we divided our analysis into the results of the two steps, one for reusing services and the other for reusing datasheets.

4.5 Results of Step 2 - Hypothesis 1

Here, we applied the two functions, *recall* and *DCG*, by taking as inputs 120 requirements, 120 mapping results defined manually by software engineers, and the list of the five ranked results for each requirement provided by the prototype (denoting a total of 600 services).

For the *recall* function we considered the position in which the relevant ser-vices are found by adding these results during the next positions. Thus, after analyzing the five positions in the list, it is natural the *recall* function is closer to 1 (when all requirements are correctly mapped). For example, if the expected service of one requirement was found in position 3 of the ranked link, it will be added to the number of matched requirements in positions 1 and 2. In the first graphic of Fig. 8, we can see the *recall* function according to the position in the list the expected services were found. From the total of 120 requirement, 45 were found in position 1, 31 in position 2, 22 in position 3, 16 in position 4, and 5

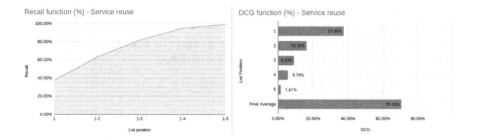

Fig. 8. Recall and DCG for step 2 - Service reusability

in the last position. Only one requirement was not found on any position of the list; and for that the function was not 100% at the final position.

Following, we applied the *DCG* in the same way as for the *recall* function, but analyzing and penalizing when the expected services are found in the last positions on the list. In the second graphic of Fig. 8, we show the results obtained on each position together with the final average of the function considering the 120 requirements. As we can see, this final average was approx. 70% denoting the penalties of finding the matches later on the list.

4.6 Results of Step 3 - Hypothesis 2

Here, we applied the same two functions as before, but considering as inputs 22 new datasheets, 22 matching results defined manually by software engineers, and the list of the five ranked results for each requirement provided by the prototype (denoting a total of 110 datasheets). As before, the *recall* function considered the matches found on each position. In this case, from the total of 22 new datasheets, 6 were found in position 1, 4 in position 2, 6 in position 3, 2 in position 4, and 2 in the last position. Two datasheets were not found on any position of the list; and because of that the function was not 100% at the final position. In the first graphic of Fig. 9, we can see the *recall* according to the place the matches were found.

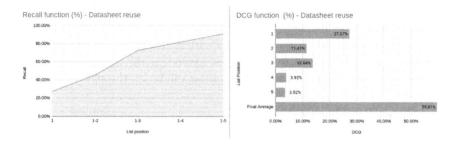

Fig. 9. Recall and DCG for step 3 - Datasheet reusability

Following, we also applied the DCG function for the same inputs, obtaining the results showed in the second graphic of Fig. 9. As we can see, this final average is approx. 60% denoting the penalties of finding the matches late on the list and the fact that two datasheets could not be matched.

4.7 Discussion

By considering the results previously described and the hypotheses defined, we can see that our process obtained good results for both metrics and for both steps. However, we can see better results for the step 2 (service reusability) because we are performing a (syntactic and semantic) string comparison against a graph comparison of step 3. In this last step (datasheet mapping), we must compare two structures combining different services with different interactions among them, so the final results are worse. However, considering the penalties of the DCG function, the final average is also good.

At the same time, as our development process is defined as semi-automatic, the outputs of the two steps return a ranked list of possible mapped services/datasheet, so software engineers must make the final decisions. During our evaluation, we could see a very low percentage of not found services/datasheets (only one in step 2 and two in step 3), so the possibility of finding the correct service/datasheet to be reused is really high. Obviously we are working on improvements for making best results appear firstly in the ranked lists, then reducing the number of trustable results to be analyzed, and consequently the selection effort.

5 Conclusions

We have introduced a process for developing SPLs based on reusing functionalities from a domain hierarchy, which embodies commonalities and variabilities of several subdomains. Building a new SPL means understanding and probably extending a service taxonomy and functionality in the form of reusable assets. In this paper, we have shown the case for the paleontology cultural heritage subdomain, which is modeled from existing SPLs in a geographic-oriented hierarchy. Our proposal implies determining similarity among these reusable assets, which is a complex process itself. We have shown a preliminary approach with promissory results; however, more complex similarity cases should be addressed, such us the analysis of services in the taxonomy with no corresponding functionality in datasheets. We are currently working on extending the approach as well as developing a supporting tool, which would allow validation through case studies.

References

1. Adamu, A., Zainon, W.M.N.W.: Multiview similarity assessment technique of UML diagrams. Procedia Comput. Sci. **124**, 311–318 (2017). 4th Information Systems International Conference (ISICO)

2. Aksit, M.: Software Architectures and Component Technology. Kluwer Academic Publishers, Norwell (2001)
3. Arias, M., Buccella, A., Cechich, A.: A framework for managing requirements of software product lines. Electron. Notes Theor. Comput. Sci. **339**, 5–20 (2018). http://www.sciencedirect.com/science/article/pii/S157106611830046X. The XLII Latin American Computing Conference
4. Bell, M.: Service-Oriented Modeling: Service Analysis, Design, and Architecture. Wiley Publishing, Indianapolis (2008)
5. Buccella, A., Cechich, A., Arias, M., Pol'la, M., Doldan, S., Morsan, E.: Towards systematic software reuse of GIS: Insights from a case study. Comput. Geosci. **54**, 9–20 (2013)
6. Buccella, A., Cechich, A., Pol'la, M., Arias, M., Doldan, S., Morsan, E.: Marine ecology service reuse through taxonomy-oriented SPL development. Comput. Geosci. **73**, 108–121 (2014)
7. Buccella, A., Cechich, A., Porfiri, J., Diniz Dos Santos, D.: Taxonomy-oriented domain analysis of GIS: a case study for paleontological software systems. ISPRS Int. J. Geo-Inf. **8**(6) (2019). https://www.mdpi.com/2220-9964/8/6/270
8. Bunke, H., Shearer, K.: A graph distance metric based on the maximal common subgraph. Pattern Recogn. Lett. **19**(3), 255–259 (1998)
9. Caballero, S., Buccella, A., Cechich, A.: Reuso de funcionalidades en el subdominio de patrimonio cultural. In: Computer Science - CACIC 2019. RedUnci (2019)
10. Dijkman, R., Dumas, M., van Dongen, B., Käärik, R., Mendling, J.: Similarity of business process models: metrics and evaluation. Inf. Syst. **36**(2), 498–516 (2011). https://doi.org/10.1016/j.is.2010.09.006
11. Manning, C.D., Raghavan, P., Schütze, H.: Introduction to Information Retrieval. Cambridge University Press, Cambridge (2008)
12. Pohl, K., Böckle, G., van der Linden, F.J.: Software Product Line Engineering: Foundations, Principles and Techniques. Springer, Heidelberg (2005). https://doi.org/10.1007/3-540-28901-1
13. Rak, K., Car, Z., Lovrek, I.: Effort estimation model for software development projects based on use case reuse. J. Softw. Evol. Process **31**(2), 2119 (2019)
14. Robinson, W.N., Woo, H.G.: Finding reusable UML sequence diagrams automatically. IEEE Softw. **21**(5), 60–67 (2004)
15. Salami, H., Ahmed, M.A.: UML artifacts reuse: state of the art. Int. J. Soft Comput. Softw. Eng. **3**, February 2014
16. Salami, H.O., Ahmed, M.A.: A framework for class diagram retrieval using genetic algorithm. In: SEKE (2012)
17. Wohlin, C., Runeson, P., Hst, M., Ohlsson, M., Regnell, B., Wessln, A.: Experimentation in Software Engineering. Springer, New York (2012). https://doi.org/10.1007/978-1-4615-4625-2

Evaluation of Open Source Tools for Requirements Management

Sonia R. Santana[1]([✉]), Lucrecia R. Perero[1], Amalia G. Delduca[1], and Gladys N. Dapozo[2]

[1] Facultad de Ciencias de la Administración, Universidad Nacional de Entre Ríos, Concordia, Entre Ríos, Argentina
sr.santana675@gmail.com, rmlperero@gmail.com,
amadel.agd@gmail.com
[2] Facultad de Ciencias Exactas y Naturales y Agrimensura,
Universidad Nacional del Nordeste, Corrientes, Argentina
gndapozo@exa.unne.edu.ar

Abstract. Requirements management is a critical task in any Software Engineering project. It implies both a technological defy and a complex social process. Engineering Requirements tools (ER) help speed up and optimize ER processes through a formal and systematical management of requirements, change management and traceability. In general, tools available for that use are proprietary software, costly and difficult to work with. Open source tools offer a great potential to cover these needs. This work aims to analyze open source requirements management tools to evaluate their capabilities and contribution for each step of the ER process. It includes a comparative analysis of their performance in three scenarios, representing different levels of software development organizations' requests. Results show that development of open source requirements management tools is more oriented towards elicitation and requirements analysis phases than modeling.

Keywords: Requirements engineering · Requirements management · Requirements engineering management tools · Open source software

1 Introduction

Requirements management is fundamental for software delivering and project life cycle success. Software development is not only a technological defy but also a complex social process. During this process, which leads to a correct and consistent requirements gathering, effective communication between all interested parties plays a vital role on the software development project.

Errors in requirements, such as inconsistencies, incompleteness or incorrectness may cause extensive reworking and irrecoverable failures [1]. Also, detecting these errors at a later phase of the software development project is slower, more difficult and expensive [2, 3].

According to [4], 56% of errors in software projects are caused by errors originated during requirements phase, as shown in Fig. 1. Half of these errors is due to incomplete and ambiguous requirements while the other half is due to omitted requirements.

© Springer Nature Switzerland AG 2020
P. Pesado and M. Arroyo (Eds.): CACIC 2019, CCIS 1184, pp. 188–204, 2020.
https://doi.org/10.1007/978-3-030-48325-8_13

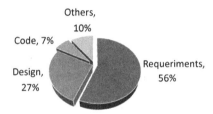

Fig. 1. Error distribution.

Error prevention is a matter of good practice in Software Engineering, however, it is prudent to assume that errors will occur. Fortunately, this type of errors can be avoided with a proper requirements management that gets errors detected, corrected and minimized as soon as possible.

Requirements management is fundamental to software quality assurance and can be a key factor in the success or failure of a computer system.

Requirements management is defined as: "The process of managing changes to requirements to ensure that the changes made are properly analyzed and tracked throughout the system" [4].

Requirements Engineering (RE) tools are an integral part of most requirements management solutions, and are needed to streamline and facilitate the optimization of RE processes through more systematic and formal requirements management, change management and traceability.

Today, tools are evolving rapidly. The demand for flexibility, agile development, global collaboration and advanced software is changing the way requirements are managed. ER tools are adapting to these demands with changes in design and architecture. Traditionally, they have been geared towards different environments and market niches (e.g. automotive, medical and defense) and development processes (agile, development management and prototyping) [5].

From company surveys, the "divide and conquer" approach is found to be particularly ineffective. Requirements specify needs and solutions. Data from the projects evaluated showed that only 52% of the originally assigned requirements appear in the final released version of the software product [6, 7].

The market for RE tools is changing. The classic tools that used to dominate the market are becoming more complex and difficult to use. Many expensive tools are not sufficiently open to other suppliers' tools, such as modeling or traceability [5]. This encourages free tools to introduce interesting functionalities, especially for collaboration.

Based on the results obtained in [8], this paper seeks to deepen the analysis of free tools for requirements management with the incorporation of new tools and the evaluation of their performance based on certain functionalities and scenarios that show their capacity.

2   Methodology

This section provides detailed information about the methodology used to carry out the evaluation of the ER-free tools for requirements management.

The methodology consist of three stages. The first stage is a review of documentation from different bibliographic sources and is carried out with the objective of identifying the existence of free tools related to requirements management during the development of a software project.

Then, the tools are classified and their main characteristics, functionalities and limitations are described, identifying the main information inputs required for their operation.

Once tools have been analyzed, in the second stage their functionalities are defined according to different data sources that allow the evaluation of them.

Finally, in the third and last stage, many of the identified tools are evaluated according to their functionalities and in different scenarios to find out how they work, information needs and restrictions.

2.1   Survey of Tools

To start the literature review, the following question was posed: What are the open source tools mentioned in the literature that allow to manage requirements? What functionalities and what scope do they have? As a result of this survey, Table 1 presents a summary of the outstanding free RE tools, indicating for each one of them, which RE functionality it fulfills. It is indicated Y when it contributes to the functionality and N, otherwise. The dash (−) represents that no data related to the functionality was obtained.

The RE functions that are contemplated in this analysis are the following:

El: Elicitation, **An**: Analysis, **Sp**: Specification, **Vv**: Validation & Verification, **Tr**: Traceability, **Do**: Documentation, **Gr**: Graphic representation, **Ti**: Tool integration.

Through this review it was possible to check basic RE capabilities of the tools as well as other aspects like traceability, integration with other platforms, documentation functionalities and graphical representations. All these aspects are relevant for the investigation since they allow to make an idea of the completeness with which a requirements management system must operate.

Table 1. ER Open source tools functionalities.

Tools	El	An	Sp	Vv	Tr	Do	Gr	Ti
aNimble [9]	Y	Y	Y	Y	Y	Y	N	–
Controla [10]	Y	Y	Y	Y	Y	Y	Y	N
CSRML [11]	Y	Y	Y	Y	N	Y	N	Y
Heler [12]	Y	N	Y	Y	Y	Y	N	–
Jeremia [13]	Y	Y	Y	Y	Y	Y	N	–
Let's req [14]	Y	Y	Y	Y	Y	Y	N	–
OpenOME [15]	N	Y	N	Y	N	Y	Y	Y
OpenReq Live [16]	Y	Y	Y	Y	–	–	–	N
OSRMT [17]	Y	Y	Y	Y	Y	Y	N	–
Rambutan [18]	Y	Y	Y	N	N	Y	N	N
REASEM [19]	Y	Y	Y	N	N	Y	Y	–
REM [20]	Y	Y	Y	Y	N	Y	Y	N
Remas [21]	Y	Y	Y	Y	Y	Y	N	–
Rmtoo [22]	Y	N	Y	N	N	Y	Y	N
ReqHeap [23]	Y	Y	N	Y	N	Y	N	–
ReqMan [24]	Y	Y	N	N	N	Y	N	–
ReqT [25]	Y	Y	N	N	N	N	N	N
Retro [26]	N	N	N	Y	Y	Y	N	N
Sigerar [27]	Y	Y	Y	Y	Y	Y	Y	N
TestMeReQ [28]	N	N	N	Y	N	Y	N	–

2.2 Definition of Tool Functionalities

Table 2, which was prepared by the authors based on the following two data source, presents the required functionalities of the tools to ensure their evaluation.

- The ISO/IEC TR 24766: 2009 "Guía para las capacidades de las herramientas de ingeniería de requerimientos".
  In [29] a list of required capabilities for RE tools is provided, which are organized according to the activities and requirements of a software system mentioned in ISO/IEC 12207: 2008, ISO/IEC 15288: 2008 and ISO/IEC TR 19759 (SWEBOK).
- Information gathered in the first stage and its analysis in terms of the inputs requested by the tools and the functionalities that a tool must provide in the requirements management phase during the whole life cycle of system development.

This way, the functionalities defined in Table 2 belong to more than one of the categories detailed below:

- **Elicitation.** It means functionalities that focus on supporting the identification of stakeholders and on the capture and follow-up of business/user requirements, functional and non-functional requirements.
- **Analysis.** Covers functionalities aimed at breaking down requirements into details, assessing feasibility, negotiating priorities and identifying conflicts. It also includes

functionalities to identify unclear, incomplete, ambiguous or contradictory requirements and to resolve these problems.

- **Specification**. Includes features that focus on documenting the functionalities a system should provide and the constraints it should respect. These functionalities and constraints must be specified in a consistent, accessible and reviewable manner to achieve that objective.
- **Verification and Validation**. Includes functionalities to support various tests and evaluation means to verify and validate requirements.
- **Traceability**. It includes functionalities focused on documenting the life cycle of a requirement, providing mechanisms for linking the associated requirements and tracking changes made to each requirement.
- **Documentation**. Covers functions focused on generating documents related to requirements modeling.
- **Graphic representation**. Involves functions aimed at generating graphic representations related to requirements modeling.
- **Tool integration**. It includes features related to the integration of the tool in the system and the software development environment.
- **Other capabilities**. It contains functions related to the security, portability, usability and integrity of the tool.

Table 2. Required tool functions. Own elaboration.

Identifier	Description	Identifier	Description
F000	Create project	F036	Describe requirement
F001	Delete project	F037	Assign requirement to user
F002	Modify project	F038	Prioritize requirement
F003	Check project	F039	Assign risk to requirement
F004	Create project date-time	F040	Set requirement complexity
F005	Set project date-time	F041	Set requirement dependency
F006	Create multiple projects	F042	Set requirement conflict
F007	Create sub-project	F043	Import requirement
F008	Delete sub-project	F044	Export requirement
F009	Modify sub-project	F045	Classify requirements
F010	Check sub-project	F046	Comment requirements
F011	Create sub-project date-time	F047	Create requirement date-time
F012	Set sub-project date-time	F048	Set requirement date-time
F013	Create user	F049	Check requirement report
F014	Delete user	F050	Help write a requirement
F015	Modify user	F051	Escalate requirements
F016	Check user	F052	Version requirements
F017	Set user	F053	Generate requirements specifications
F018	Grant user permissions	F054	Manage diagrams
F019	Create stakeholder	F055	Manage prototypes
F020	Delete stakeholder	F056	Manage models
F021	Modify stakeholder	F057	Requirements review

(continued)

Table 2. (*continued*)

Identifier	Description	Identifier	Description
F022	Check stakeholder	F058	Requirements inspection
F023	Set stakeholder	F059	Perform test-case
F024	Create release	F060	Test-case inspection
F025	Delete release	F061	Perform statistics
F026	Set release	F062	Requirements traceability
F027	Create keyword	F063	Emit reports
F028	Delete keyword	F064	Graphic representations
F029	Set keyword	F065	Import diagrams/models
F030	Project versioning	F066	Export diagrams/models
F031	Send messages	F067	Portability
F032	Create requirement	F068	Security
F033	Delete requirement	F069	Integrity
F034	Modify requirement	F070	Usability
F035	Check requirement		

2.3   Evaluation of Tools According to Their Functionalities

This step describes the evaluation of a selected set of open source tools.

Tool Filtering. Previously, the set of tools listed in Table 1 was analyzed and those that, for various reasons, did not meet the conditions required for the evaluation were excluded.

Table 3 shows the tools that were excluded due to different problems detailed below:

- Not-working tool: The tool could not be evaluated due to problems during the installation and/or difficulties in its configuration caused by the lack of sufficient information.
- Download link out of service: The link to obtain the tool is damaged or does not exist. The tool was requested to the author without further notice.
- It was not rated in the evaluation: The tool was not considered because it does not comply with the functionalities for requirements management, or they are aimed at managing requirements of specific systems.
- Error while working with the tool: The tool has an error that prevents its operation. The tool was requested to the author without further notice.

Table 3. Tools excluded from the evaluation.

Tool	Problem
aNimble	Not-working tool
Heler y Controla	Download link out of service
CSRML	It was not rated in the evaluation because it performs the modeling and analysis of Collaborative Systems requirements
Jeremía	Not-working tool
Let's req	Download link out of service
OpenOME	It was not rated in the evaluation because it performs the modeling and analysis of Collaborative Systems requirements
Rambutan	Error while working with the tool
Rmtoo	It was not rated in the evaluation because it is intended for developers and does not have a graphical user interface
REASEM	Performs management of Embedded Systems requirements only
ReqMan	Not-working tool
ReqT	The tool was not rated in the evaluation because it performs requirements elicitation only
Retro y TestMeReq	The tools were not rated in the evaluation because they only perform validation and verification of requirements
Sigerar	Not-working tool. Abandoned project

Tool Selection. After the filtering process, five open source software tools were selected:

- **OSRMT** (*Open Source Requirements Management Tool*). Manages requirements and its main characteristics are: it has client/server architecture; it is developed in Java; from version 1.3 it introduces change management traceability; it generates requirements documentation. The project is currently abandoned as aNimble came as its successor.
- **REM** (*REquisite Management*). Facilitates the elicitation of requirements, allows to easily generate a standardized document where to include necessary requirements for a computer system development. It is simple to use. It is based on **XML** and **XSLT**. It generates documentation in HTML format. Last updated in 2004.
- **Remas** (*RElease MAnagement System*). Manages requirements and process definition, supports standard elements such as use cases, traceability matrix and also calculates function point metrics based on visual interface requirements. Last updated in 2011.
- **ReqHeap** (*Requirement Heap*). It is a web application oriented to requirements management. It allows rich text requirements edition, supports version control and requirements management. It supports use cases, interviews and test cases. It is possible to work with multiple projects. Users, stakeholders and glossaries can be managed globally or per project. Last updated in 2010.

- **OpenReq Live** (*Open Requirement Live*) is an online web application oriented to requirements management, created as a result of the OpenReq project funded by the European Union's Horizon 2020 Research and Innovation program. It maintains a requirements base through its own editor, records the requirements modeled in sentences, performs version control, allows access to its base through a browser and supports change control process.

Evaluation of Tools. A software requirements specification of a case study was elaborated in order to carry out the evaluation, based on an evaluation processing system. A project named "Evaluation System" was developed where users, stakeholders, releases, keywords and requirements were defined. Then, priority, risk, complexity, dependencies, conflicts, type and comments were specified for each requirement. Finally, the project was introduced in each tool to evaluate its functionalities.

A table of compliance categories was previously defined for each functionality, as shown in Table 4.

Table 4. Compliance categories of the condition evaluated in the tools.

Acronym	Meaning	Description
Y	Appropriate	The item is adequately fulfilled
N	Not appropriate	The item is partially or not fulfilled at all
N/I	Needs improvement	The item is fulfilled, but can be optimized
N/A	Not accepted	The item does not apply to the tool

The evaluation consisted of the compliance verification of the 5 selected tools: **OSRMT**, **REM**, **Remas**, **ReqHeap** and **OpenReq Live**, with each of the functionalities detailed in Table 2 and then applying the rating determined in Table 4.

Table 5 shows the results.

Table 5. Tools evaluation.

Identifier	Description	OSRMT	REM	Remas	ReqHeap	OpenReq Live
F000	Create project	Y	Y	Y	Y	Y
F001	Delete project	N	N	Y	Y	Y
F002	Modify project	N	Y	Y	Y	Y
F003	Check project	Y	Y	Y	Y	Y
F004	Create date-time project	N/I	N/I	N/I	Y	Y
F005	Set date-time project	N/I	N/I	N/I	Y	N

(*continued*)

Table 5. (*continued*)

Identifier	Description	OSRMT	REM	Remas	ReqHeap	OpenReq Live
F006	Create multiple projects	Y	Y	N/A	Y	Y
F007	Create sub-project	N/A	N/A	N/A	Y	N/A
F008	Delete sub-project	N/A	N/A	N/A	Y	N/A
F009	Modify sub-project	N/A	N/A	N/A	Y	N/A
F010	Check sub-project	N/A	N/A	N/A	Y	N/A
F011	Create date-time sub-project	N/A	N/A	N/A	Y	N/A
F012	Set date-time sub-project	N/A	N/A	N/A	Y	N/A
F013	Create user	Y	Y	N/I	Y	Y
F014	Delete user	N	N	N/I	Y	Y
F015	Modify user	Y	Y	N/I	Y	Y
F016	Check user	Y	Y	N/I	Y	Y
F017	Set user	Y	Y	N/A	Y	Y
F018	Grant user permissions	Y	N/A	N/A	Y	Y
F019	Create stakeholder	Y	Y	N/A	Y	Y
F020	Delete stakeholder	N/A	Y	N/A	Y	Y
F021	Modify stakeholder	Y	Y	N/A	Y	Y
F022	Check stakeholder	Y	Y	N/A	Y	Y
F023	Set stakeholder	Y	Y	N/A	Y	Y
F024	Create release	N/A	Y	N/A	Y	Y
F025	Delete release	N/A	N/A	N/A	Y	Y
F026	Set release	N/A	Y	N/A	Y	Y
F027	Create keyword	N/A	Y	N/A	Y	N/A
F028	Delete keyword	N/A	Y	N/A	Y	N/A
F029	Set keyword	N/A	Y	N/A	Y	N/A
F030	Project versioning	N/A	Y	N/A	Y	Y
F031	Send messages	N/I	N/A	N/A	Y	N/I
F032	Create requirement	Y	Y	Y	Y	Y
F033	Delete requirement	Y	Y	Y	Y	Y
F034	Modify requirement	Y	Y	Y	Y	Y
F035	Check requirement	Y	Y	Y	Y	Y
F036	Describe requirement	Y	N/I	N/I	Y	Y
F037	Assign requirement to user	Y	Y	N/A	Y	Y
F038	Prioritize requirement	Y	Y	N/A	Y	Y

(*continued*)

Table 5. (*continued*)

Identifier	Description	OSRMT	REM	Remas	ReqHeap	OpenReq Live
F039	Assign risk to requirement	N/A	Y	N/A	Y	Y
F040	Set requirement complexity	Y	N/A	N/A	Y	Y
F041	Set requirement dependency	Y	Y	N/I	Y	Y
F042	Set requirement conflict	N/A	Y	N/A	Y	Y
F043	Import requirement	N/I	N/A	N/A	N/A	Y
F044	Export requirement	N/I	N/A	N/A	N/A	N
F045	Classify requirements	N/A	Y	N/I	Y	Y
F046	Comment requirements	Y	Y	Y	Y	Y
F047	Create requirement date-time	Y	N/I	N/I	Y	N
F048	Set requirement date-time	Y	N/I	N/I	Y	N
F049	Check requirement report	Y	Y	Y	Y	N
F050	Help write a requirement	N/A	N/A	N/A	Y	Y
F051	Escalate requirements	N/A	Y	N/A	Y	N
F052	Version requirements	Y	Y	N/A	Y	N
F053	Generate requirements specifications	N/I	N/I	N/I	N/A	N
F054	Manage diagrams	N/A	N/I	N/I	Y	N/A
F055	Manage prototypes	N/A	N/A	N/A	N/A	N/A
F056	Manage models	N/A	N/A	N/A	N/A	N/A
F057	Requirements review	N/I	N/I	N/I	Y	Y
F058	Requirements inspection	N/I	N/I	N/I	Y	Y
F059	Perform test-case	N/I	N/I	N/A	Y	Y
F060	Test-case inspection	N/I	N/I	N/A	Y	Y
F061	Perform statistics	N/A	N/A	N/A	Y	Y
F062	Requirements traceability	N/I	N/I	N/I	N/A	N/I

(*continued*)

Table 5. (*continued*)

Identifier	Description	OSRMT	REM	Remas	ReqHeap	OpenReq Live
F063	Emit reports	N/I	N/I	N/I	N/I	Y
F064	Graphic representations	N/A	N/I	N/I	N/A	Y
F065	Import diagrams/models	N/A	N/A	N/A	N/A	N/A
F066	Export diagrams/models	N/A	N/A	N/A	N/A	N/A
F067	Portability	N/A	N/A	N/A	Y	Y
F068	Security	N/I	N	N/A	Y	Y
F069	Integrity	N/I	N/I	N/I	N/I	N/I
F070	Usability	N/I	N/I	N/I	N/I	N/I

2.4   Evaluation of Tools in Scenarios

The idea of combining scenarios with the tools comes from the fact that the scenario is extremely effective when exchanging ideas and concepts. The scenario serves as a way to provide information about implementation constraints, conditions of the problem domain and system objectives at different levels of relevance. It allows to analyze the system from the customer or user's perspective and to obtain concrete information about the user activity at the moment of carrying out a specific task.

The functionality of the RE tools in specific use case scenarios can help determine what tools are best suited for which activities. To this end, three different scenarios were defined, each of which projects a description of an organization's activity and defines a set of tool functionalities (based on Table 2), according to the categories defined for each of them.

Scenario 1. This scenario describes organizations where it is critical to determine user needs in their development project and ensure that the final product meets specifications and expectations. The activities include the elicitation and the validation and verification (V&V) of requirements.

Tools support elicitation if they are able to:

- Store and manage projects and sub-projects
- Store and manage users.
- Store and manage stakeholders.
- Store and manage release and keyword.
- Store and manage messaging.
- Store and manage requirements.

Tools support V&V if they are able to:

- Store and manage diagrams, models and prototypes.
- Review and inspect requirements.

- Perform and inspection test cases.
- Perform requirement traceability.
- Generate charts and reports.

Scenario 2. This scenario refers to organizations that want to establish a solid foundation for design and implementation, including modeling and requirements specification.

Tools support modelling if they are able to:

- Store and manage diagrams, models and prototypes.
- Import and export diagrams and models
- Generate charts and reports.

Tools support specification if they are able to:

- Generate requirements specification.
- Generate reports.

Scenario 3. The last scenario is related to organizations seeking a high level of project control and quality assurance. This can only be achieved through requirement management.

Tools support elicitation if they are able to:

- Store and manage projects and sub-projects
- Store and manage users.
- Store and manage stakeholders.
- Store and manage release and keyword.
- Store and manage messaging.
- Store and manage requirements.

Tools support modelling if they are able to:

- Store and manage diagrams, models and prototypes.
- Import and export diagrams and models
- Generate charts and reports.

Tools support specification if they are able to:

- Generate requirements specification.
- Generate reports.

Tools support V&V if they are able to:

- Store and manage diagrams, models and prototypes.
- Review and inspect requirements.
- Perform and inspection testcases.
- Perform requirement traceability.
- Generate charts and reports.

Tools support portability, security, integrity and usability if they:

- Allow execution on different platforms.
- Protect the integrity and security of stored information.
- Ensure the accuracy and reliability of data.
- Provide an easy to use tool.

3   Results

3.1   Analysis of the Tools Evaluated by Functionality

With the results of the tool evaluation, it was possible to quantify the compliance of functionalities for each category of RE considered, which is shown in Table 6. For each category, the total of the functionalities foreseen in Table 4 is indicated, as well as the number of them that each tool complies with (considering that there are functionalities that belong to more than one category) and the percentage that they represent of the total.

The ER functionalities included in Table 6 correspond to the following categories: **El**: Elicitation, **An**: Analysis, **Sp**: Specification, **Vv**: Validation and Verification, **Tr**: Traceability, **Do**: Documentation, **Gr**: Graphic representation, **Ti**: Tool integration, **Oc**: Other capabilities.

Table 6. Functionalities met by each tool.

Categories	Total	OSRMT	%	REM	%	Remas	%	ReqHeap	%	OpenReq Live	%
El	38	14	37%	25	66%	14	37%	36	95%	26	68%
An	20	7	35%	13	65%	7	35%	15	75%	11	55%
Sp	3	1	33%	1	33%	1	33%	0	0%	0	0%
Vv	11	3	27%	5	45%	3	27%	5	45%	5	45%
Tr	3	1	33%	0	0%	1	33%	1	33%	2	67%
Do	5	5	100%	4	80%	5	100%	2	40%	1	20%
Gr	5	1	20%	1	20%	1	20%	0	0%	1	20%
Ti	4	0	0%	0	0%	0	0%	0	0%	1	25%
Oc	4	4	100%	2	50%	4	100%	4	100%	2	50%
Total	**93**	**36**	**39%**	**51**	**55%**	**36**	**39%**	**63**	**68%**	**49**	**53%**

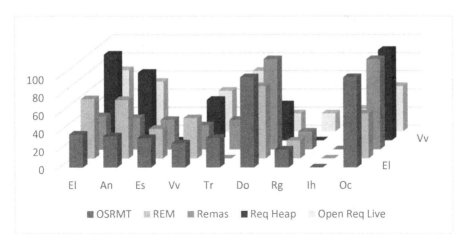

Fig. 2. Number of functionalities of each tool by categories

Figure 2 shows the percentage contribution of each tool in the categories.

3.2 Analysis of the Tools Evaluated in the Scenarios

With the findings shown in Table 6, the performance of tools in the proposed scenarios was measured, the results were summarized and useful characteristics were highlighted along with the percentage in the tools that support them. These characteristics represent the capacities tools shown in the scenarios, i.e. capacities with a high percentage of tools that support them.

Evaluation of Tools in Scenario 1. Table 7 shows the compliance of the functionalities of each tool in Scenario 1. The tools are scored with the following percentages: ReqHeap 79%, OpenReq Live 61%, Rem 60%, Remas 35% and OSRMT 35%.

Table 7. Functionalities fulfilled by each tool for scenario 1

Categories	Total	OSRMT %		REM %		Remas %		ReqHeap %		OpenReq Live %	
El	38	14	37%	25	66%	14	37%	36	95%	26	68%
An	20	7	35%	13	65%	7	35%	15	75%	11	55%
Vv	11	3	27%	5	45%	3	27%	5	45%	5	45%
Tr	3	1	33%	0	0%	1	33%	1	33%	2	67%
Total	72	25	35%	43	60%	25	35%	57	79%	44	61%

Evaluation of Tools in Scenario 2. Table 8 shows the compliance of the functionalities of each tool in Scenario 2. The tools are scored with the following percentages: OSRMT 41%, Remas 41%, Rem 35%, OpenReq Live 18% and ReqHeap 12%.

Table 8. Functionalities fulfilled by each tool for scenario 2

Categories	Total	OSRMT %		REM %		Remas %		ReqHeap %		OpenReq Live %	
Sp	3	1	33%	1	33%	1	33%	0	0%	0	0%
Do	5	5	100%	4	80%	5	100%	2	40%	1	20%
Gr	5	1	20%	1	20%	1	20%	0	0%	1	20%
Ti	4	0	0%	0	0%	0	0%	0	0%	1	25%
Total	**17**	**7**	**41%**	**6**	**35%**	**7**	**41%**	**2**	**12%**	**3**	**18%**

Evaluation of Tools in Scenario 3. Table 9 shows the compliance of the functionalities of each tool in Scenario 3. The tools are scored with the following percentages: ReqHeap 68%, Rem 55%, OpenReq Live 53%, Remas 39% and OSRMT 39%.

Table 9. Functionalities fulfilled by each tool for scenario 3

Categories	Total	OSRMT %		REM %		Remas %		ReqHeap %		OpenReq Live %	
El	38	14	37%	25	66%	14	37%	36	95%	26	68%
An	20	7	35%	13	65%	7	35%	15	75%	11	55%
Sp	3	1	33%	1	33%	1	33%	0	0%	0	0%
Vv	11	3	27%	5	45%	3	27%	5	45%	5	45%
Tr	3	1	33%	0	0%	1	33%	1	33%	2	67%
Do	5	5	100%	4	80%	5	100%	2	40%	1	20%
Gr	5	1	20%	1	20%	1	20%	0	0%	1	20%
Ti	4	0	0%	0	0%	0	0%	0	0%	1	25%
Oc	4	4	100%	2	50%	4	100%	4	100%	2	50%
Total	**93**	**36**	**39%**	**51**	**55%**	**36**	**39%**	**63**	**68%**	**49**	**53%**

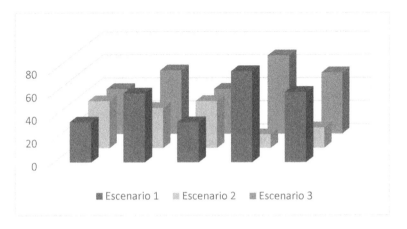

Fig. 3. Compliance of each tool in the scenarios

The level of compliance of each tool in the scenarios is summarized in Fig. 3. From the results obtained from Fig. 3 it was possible to quantify the tools that have a high percentage of compliance for each scenario, which are shown in Table 10.

Table 10. Scenario tool capabilities.

Scenario	Tool capacity	Tool name
Scenario 1 (Requirements Elicitation and V&V)	79%	ReqHeap
Scenario 2 (Requirements modeling and specification)	41%	OSRMT
Scenario 3 (Requirements management)	68%	ReqHeap

After the characterization of some of the free tools for requirements management based on certain functionalities, high percentages were obtained in the evaluation, as shown in Table 6, for ReqHeap 68%, Rem 55%, OpenReq Live 53%, OSRMT and Remas 39%.

In terms of the scenario-based evaluation, the tools with the best results are located in the scenario focused on elicitation and V&V requirements, ReqHeap 79%. Then, there is the scenario oriented to requirements management, ReqHeap 68%, and finally the scenario oriented to modeling, OSRMT 41%.

The results indicate that the development of open-source tools for requirements management is more oriented to requirements elicitation and analysis than to modeling. This can be considered as a gap in the field of development of open-source ER tools.

References

1. Zhou, J.: An observer-based technique with trace links for requirements validation in embedded real-time systems. In: International. Conference on Research in Engineering and Technology, vol. 177, pp. 1–52 (2014)
2. Aceituna, D., Do, H., Lee, S.W.: SQ^(2) E: An approach to requirements validation with scenario question. In: Asia Pacific Software Engineering Conference, pp. 33–42 (2010)
3. Kof, L., Gacitua, R., Rouncefield, M., Sawyer, P.: Ontology and model alignment as a means for requirements validation. In: IEEE Fourth International Conference on Semantic Computing, pp. 46–51 (2010)
4. Kotonya, G., Sommerville, I.: Requirements Engineering Processes and Techniques. Wiley, New York (1998)
5. De Gea, J.M.C., Nicolas, J., Aleman, J.L.F., Toval, A., Ebert, C., Vizcaino, A.: Requirements engineering tools. IEEE Softw. **28**(4), 86–91 (2011)
6. Ebert, C., Dumke, R.: Software Measurement. Springer, Heidelberg (2007). https://doi.org/10.1007/978-3-540-71649-5
7. What Are Your Requirements? Technical report, Standish Group (2003)

8. Santana, S., Perero, L., Delduca, A., Dapozo, G.: Evaluación de las herramientas libres para la gestión de requerimientos. CACIC 2019. ISBN 978-987-688-377-1
9. aNimble Platform. https://sourceforge.net/projects/nimble/
10. Fraga Filho, C.V., Dos Reis, J.M.: CONTROLA: Herramienta de apoyo al proceso de desarrollo de software en las pequeñas compañías. Revista Ingeniería Informática, edn.12 (2006)
11. Teruel, M., Navarro, E., López-Jaquero, V., Montero, F., González, P.: CSRML Tool: una Herramienta para el Modelado de Requisitos de Sistemas Colaborativos (2012)
12. Callejas Cuervo, M., Castillo Estupiñán, L.Y., Fernández Álvarez, R.M.: HELER: una herramienta para la ingeniería de requisitos automatizada, ISSN 1900-3803 (2010)
13. Jeremia: Sistema de Gestión de Requerimientos. http://jeremia.sourceforge.net/
14. Let's req. http://www.dicyt.com/noticias/una-herramienta-facilita-el-desarrollo-de-proyectos-informaticos
15. Horkoff, J., Yu, Y., Yu, E.: OpenOME: an open-source goal and agent-oriented model drawing and analysis tool. iStar (2010)
16. Grings, C., Sayão, M.: OpenReq: uma Ferramenta para Auxílio à Gerência de Requisitos (2009)
17. OSRMT Open Source Requirements Management Tool. https://sourceforge.net/projects/osrmt/
18. Rambutan: Requirements Management Tool for Busy System Analysts. http://rambutan.sourceforge.net/
19. Gómez, M., Jorge, E., Urrego, G., González Palacio, L.: REASEM: Herramienta para la gestión de requisitos. Revista Avances en Sistemas e Informática, pp. 59–67 (2009). ISSN: 1657-7663
20. Durán Toro, A.: Herramienta REM, Universidad De Sevilla. http://www.lsi.us.es/descargas/descarga_programas.php?id=3&lang=en
21. Remas: Release Management System. https://sourceforge.net/projects/remas/
22. Rmtoo: Requirements Management Tool. http://rmtoo.florath.net/
23. ReqHeap: Requirement Heap. https://sourceforge.net/projects/reqheap/
24. ReqMan: Requirements Manager. https://sourceforge.net/projects/reqman/
25. Regnell, B.: reqT.org – towards a semi-formal, open and scalable requirements modeling tool. In: Doerr, J., Opdahl, A.L. (eds.) REFSQ 2013. LNCS, vol. 7830, pp. 112–118. Springer, Heidelberg (2013). https://doi.org/10.1007/978-3-642-37422-7_8
26. Hayes, J., Dekhtyar, A., Sundaram, S., Holbrook, E., Vadlamudi, S., April, A.: REquirements TRacing On target (RETRO): improving software maintenance through traceability recovery. Innovations Syst. Softw. Eng. 3(3), 193–202 (2007). https://doi.org/10.1007/s11334-007-0024-1
27. Grande, J., Martins, L.E.: SIGERAR: Uma Ferramenta para Gerenciamento de Requisitos, pp. 75–83 (2006)
28. Moketar, N.A., Kamalrudin, M., Sidek, S., Robinson, M.: TestMEReq: automated acceptance testing tool for requirements validation. In: International Symposium on Research in Innovation and Sustainability, vol. 2014, pp. 15–16 (2014)
29. ISO/IEC TR 24766:2009: Information technology. Systems and software engineering. Guide for requirements engineering tool capabilities

PWA and TWA: Recent Development Trends

Verónica Aguirre[1,2(✉)], Lisandro Delía[1,2], Pablo Thomas[1,2],
Leonardo Corbalán[1,2], Germán Cáseres[1,2],
and Juan Fernández Sosa[1,2]

[1] Instituto de Investigación en Informática LIDI (III-LIDI), Facultad
de Informática, Universidad Nacional de La Plata, La Plata, Argentina
{vaguirre, ldelia, pthomas, corbalan, gcaseres,
jfernandez}@lidi.info.unlp.edu.ar
[2] Centro Asociado a la Comisión de Investigaciones Científicas de la Provincia
de Buenos Aires (CIC), La Plata, Argentina

Abstract. The continuous growth of the computing power of mobile devices
and their relative low cost are some of the reasons for their great expansion.
Currently, for example, in Argentina 9 out of 10 people own a smartphone. This
trend, locally and globally, has been accompanied by the evolution of the
software industry for these devices with the leadership of two operating systems:
Android and iOS. This segmentation has generated the need to have mobile
applications for both platforms and consequently different development
approaches have emerged in response to this need.

This paper presents the analysis of a recently emerged approach to mobile
application development, called Progressive Web Applications or PWA, as a
novel alternative to existing approaches. Additionally, the basics of TWA
(Trusted Web Activities), used as a complement to PWA, are also introduced.

Keywords: PWA · Progressive Web Applications · TWA · Trusted Web
Activities · Mobile web applications · Multiplatform development

1 Introduction

Mobile applications are present in multiple domains, they are characterized by providing access to information and are available at all times from any mobile device with
Internet access. Most of the activities that used to be done from a computer, such as
checking emails or visiting a social network, are now done from mobile devices [1].

Currently, for the development of software applications, the various existing
devices (desktop computers, notebooks, smartphones, tablets, wearables, etc.) and the
available operating systems (Android, iOS, Windows, among others) must be considered. The specific development for each platform may require expensive work, so
software providers look for alternatives, more economical solutions with similar quality
in the final product [2]. There are two types of mobile applications: native and multi-
platform.

Native applications are developed using specific technologies, resulting in a new
development project for each platform to be covered.

© Springer Nature Switzerland AG 2020
P. Pesado and M. Arroyo (Eds.): CACIC 2019, CCIS 1184, pp. 205–214, 2020.
https://doi.org/10.1007/978-3-030-48325-8_14

On the contrary, there are different development approaches that start from a single base project and allow to cover multiple platforms [3, 4]: mobile web applications, hybrid applications, interpreted applications and cross-compiled applications; they have been accepted by both academic and industrial fields several years ago [1, 3–5]. These approaches have been analyzed by the authors of this paper in [1, 2, 6–8], however, the scenario is constantly evolving.

A new alternative for mobile web application development, called Progressive Web Applications (PWA), has recently emerged. This new alternative was first introduced at the Google I/O developers' conference in May 2016 in San Francisco, California, USA [9].

This article is an extension of [10] with new information, analysis and references. In addition to presenting PWA with its main characteristics, the concept of TWA is introduced. The use of PWA is exemplified through 2 case studies and various aspects of web applications, PWA and PWA + TWA, are comparatively analyzed.

This paper is structured as follows: Sect. 2 summarizes mobile web application development, while Sect. 3 introduces the PWA approach. Section 4 describes the TWA. Section 4 presents a detailed comparative analysis between mobile web applications, PWAs, and the transformation of a PWA into a TWA. Finally, conclusions are presented and future work is proposed.

2 Mobile Web Applications

Mobile web applications are developed using standard web technology such as HTML, CSS and Javascript. For this reason, development, distribution and testing are relatively simple, being an option to consider to have presence in the mobile devices scenario. These applications do not need any manufacturer's approval for publication and are platform-independent: all you need is a web browser and internet access [2]. The great challenge presented by the development of this type of application is to achieve a satisfactory user experience, considering that there is a wide variety of devices (computers, smartphones of different sizes, tablets, video game consoles, intelligent televisions, cable TVs, among others) on which the application can be used [11].

The concept of an "adaptive" mobile web application (known as "web responsive"), which means that the site can be adapted to the different screen sizes of the devices, has emerged as a mechanism to avoid building the same application for each type of device. There are currently several web development frameworks that facilitate this work, such as Bootstrap [12], Foundation [13], Bulma [14], among others.

As presented in [2] and [3], mobile web applications can slow down response time as they require client-server interaction. They are also less attractive than an application installed on the device, since the web browser is used as an intermediary. Moreover, it is not possible to use all the features of the device (sensors, battery status, storage, etc.) or to have the application running in the background [2].

3   PWA

The applications called PWA are mobile web applications that take advantage of the new possibilities and APIs provided by new web technologies, such as the Service Worker (script that runs in the background and allows the implementation of functionalities that do not require a web page or user interaction) [15] and Web App Manifest (JSON file that allows the specification of application metadata such as name, color and distinguishing icon) [16–18], among others. This allows a web application to incorporate some of the historically unique features of native applications, such as offline operation, push notification as well as an access icon in the application launcher.

PWA uses a set of technologies that allow a web application to overcome some of the limitations underlying the mobile web approach, and give the user the feeling of using a native application [19].

Although this approach is oriented towards mobile devices, it allows for installations on desktop computers, thus constituting a possibility to unify application development, regardless of the type of device [20]. This feature puts PWAs ahead of all other approaches to mobile application development.

However, because PWAs are installed via a web browser, their availability is limited to the support of that browser. For example, Apple's web browser, Safari, does not support all of the APIs required to run PWAs [21].

Regardless of the technologies required for its implementation, Google proposes a series of basic requirements that a web application must meet in order to be considered a PWA: (a) to operate offline (without connectivity, the information from the last access must be retrieved), (b) to respond to any request in less than 5 s, (c) to provide a user experience similar to a native application, (d) to use adaptive design and (e) to use the HTTPS protocol [15, 22, 23]. A complete list of desirable features for a well-designed and implemented PWA is provided in [24].

4   TWA

TWA (Trusted Web Activities) is the strategy implemented by Google to integrate a PWA with an Android application. This way, companies do not lose customers who already use the store. TWA's are executed from an APK and distributed from the Play Store. They show, in full screen, a web browser inside an Android application without showing the browser interface.

In order to publish a TWA in the Application Store, the PWA must meet all the requirements described above, plus 80/100 scores in the Lighthouse application and all current Google Play Store rules validated from the Digital Assets Links [25].

Digital Assets Links allows you to establish a relationship between a web page and an APK, denoting that the owner of both is the same person. This strategy allows that when accessing a link from a mobile device, the associated mobile application is automatically opened, if installed, instead of the web browser [26].

In case the user's version of Chrome does not support TWA, Chrome will use a custom toolbar.

The advantages of installing a TWA are that it provides a home screen widget, direct access to applications and operating system integrations, will get automatically reinstalled after a full reset or a backup restore to a new phone, and it has a better internationalization support. The size in bytes of an application's APK with respect to a PWA's APK does not vary.

The main disadvantage is that it presents a bad first load experience in the event of no internet connexion, since the real files are not available until visiting the page at least once.

Chrome formally announced that TWA only works from Android 4.4 KitKat versions onwards [26].

Some companies have already published PWA in Google Play Store, such as YouTube Go, Maps Go, Twitter Lite, among others.

5   Case Studies

This section presents two case studies about this new technology. The first one consists of the transformation of an existing website into a PWA, and the second case is based on the creation of a PWA using a framework for the development of hybrid mobile applications.

5.1   Transforming a Website into a PWA

The website of the UNLP School of Computer Science was used for this case study [27]. This site is developed with the Wordpress content management system [28] and through the installation of the Super PWA plugin [29], it was converted to a PWA. The configuration of this Plugin required setting a name and icon to identify the application in the device's application launcher; the home URL, the page to be displayed in case of no connectivity, and the default startup orientation were defined.

Figure 1a shows the site accessed from a browser. At the bottom of the screen, a banner for installing the PWA is displayed on the main screen of the device. Once installed, a login icon is generated in the application launcher. Figure 1b shows the PWA interface of the UNLP School of Computer Science.

5.2   Development of a PWA + TWA

The Center for Innovation and Technology Transfer (CIyTT) of the School of Computer Science of the University of La Plata hosted a Science and Technology exhibition in which different innovative technological developments were exhibited. The exhibition consisted of 10 stations, distributed throughout the center, which contained different projects that could be visited by the general public.

A PWA called "InnovApp" was developed for a guided tour. Its main functionality was to describe, through text and multimedia content (images, audio and video), each of the projects within the different stations. Figure 2 shows the application interface for 2 projects of station 3. This PWA was distributed in a set of tablets with which the public could interact. In addition, a QR code was provided so that people could have

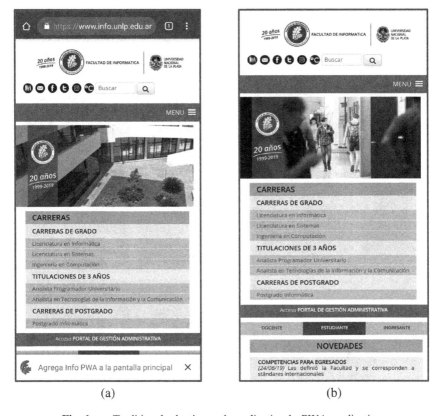

(a)   (b)

Fig. 1. a. Traditional adaptive web application b. PWA application

the same software application on their mobile devices, regardless of the Operating System they have. The application is available at [30].

For the implementation of this application, the Ionic framework [31] was used, which allows the creation of high performance multi-platform and desktop mobile applications using web technologies (HTML, CSS, JavaScript). This framework provides visual components that offer the user an experience similar to that of a native application. The logic and behavior of the application was implemented with Angular [32].

Since 2016 Ionic began providing support for PWA using Angular or React. In order to transform the development into a PWA, it was necessary to create two files: one for the configuration of the service worker and another for the manifest. This can be automated by installing an Angular package called "@angular/pwa". The service worker file configures the application cache strategy for offline operation, while the manifest provides information to the web browser, for example, the application name and icon.

Once InnovApp was developed, the IDE Android Studio [33] was required, through which the configurations indicated by Google [34] were made and an APK file was generated from it, constituting a TWA. In this way, InnovApp could be distributed in the Android applications store.

Fig. 2. InnovApp PWA.

5.3 Case Study Analysis

From the previous experiences, we can conclude that there are tools for the development of web applications that are beginning to offer the possibility of creating PWA applications or transforming the existing web applications into this new technology, being able to take advantage of its benefits in a simple way, besides being available in the store of Android applications like TWA.

6 Mobile Web Applications, PWA and PWA + TWA

As regards institutions, developing and maintaining specific mobile applications for each operating system is a significant effort. For this reason it is important to evaluate multi-platform development approaches and decide which one suits best the needs of the project. The choice of the approach to be used affects the life cycle of the application. Changing the focus in an advanced project has a high re-engineering cost.

In [2] the authors of the present paper made a thorough comparative analysis of the characteristics that should be evaluated to determine which development approach that suits the needs of a project, without considering PWA.

This section deepens the analysis of mobile web applications using the taxonomy of characteristics and scale of possible values proposed in [2]. The result consists of three tables comparing traditional mobile web applications, PWA and the combination of PWA with TWA.

Table 1 presents non-functional characteristics to be considered in mobile application development; Table 2 describes technical aspects of interest to developers; and Table 3 synthesizes characteristics related to software project management.

Table 1. Comparative analysis of non-functional features.

Technology feature	Mobile web applications	PWA	PWA + TWA
User experience	Very low	High	High
Interfaz de usuario	Web	Web	Web
Performance	Very low	Medium	Medium
Installation mode	No installation required. Accessed through a web browser	Requires installation through a web browser	Download through the Play Store and installation
Battery consumption	Low	Low	Low
Disk usage/Application size	Very low	Low	Medium
Image rendering	Very high	Very high	Very high
Start time	Low	Very low	Very low

Table 2. Comparative analysis of development features.

Technology feature	Mobile web applications	PWA	PWA + TWA
Integrated development environment (IDE)	Multiple options. There is no official IDE	Multiple options. There is no official IDE	Android Studio
Programming language	HTML, CSS, JavaScript and another server-side language	HTML, CSS, JavaScript and another server-side language	HTML, CSS, JavaScript and another server-side language
Open source/License and cost	Free	Free	Free
User interface design	HTML, CSS, JavaScript	HTML, CSS, JavaScript	HTML, CSS, JavaScript
Learning curve	Very low	low	Medium
Access to device-specific features	Very low	Medium	Medium

Table 3. Comparative analysis of software project management features

Technology feature	Mobile web applications	PWA	PWA + TWA
Target platforms	All	All (iOS has some limitations)	Android
Speed and development cost	Very low	Low	Low
Maintenance	Very low	Very low	Very low
Maturity level	Very high	Medium	Medium
Long-term viability	Very high	High	High
Application category	Social, tourist or institutional	Social, tourist or institutional	Social, tourist or institutional
Offline use	No	Yes	Yes
Code reusability	Total	Total	Total
Distribution	Through a web browser	Through a web browser	Through the Play Store
Access	Through a web browser	Start from the application launcher	Start from the application launcher
Potential users	Unlimited	Unlimited	Unlimited

It is clear that the values in many characteristics are exactly the same. However, there are differences that are worth highlighting. PWAs offer advantages in the following areas: (a) access is made directly from the application launcher without the need for a browser, (b) the user experience is enhanced because it runs in full screen mode, hiding the browser elements, (c) performance is superior because they are installed on the device and use cached content, (d) they allow access to device-specific features such as the ability to receive push notifications, and (e) they operate without connectivity.

On the other hand, traditional mobile web applications are a better alternative in the following aspects: (a) they are more viable in the long term since they are not platform-driven, (b) the learning curve and development effort is lower since they do not require the requirements presented in Sect. 3 for PWAs, and (c) the degree of maturity is higher given the recent emergence of PWAs.

Finally, by combining PWA and TWA, it is possible to add the PWA in the Android application store.

7 Conclusions and Future Work

This paper discusses PWA, a new approach to multi-platform application development that allows traditional web applications to incorporate features that are unique to the native mobile approach.

As case studies of this new approach, the website of the Faculty of Informatics of the UNLP and the App for the Center for Innovation and Technology Transfer (CIyTT) of the Faculty of Informatics of the University of La Plata were used.

Since a PWA is built from a mobile web application, it is of great interest a comparative analysis between them. From this analysis, aspects of PWAs that make them a better option can be pointed out:

a) They are installed in the application launcher
b) They are executed from the application launcher
c) They operate without connectivity
d) They improve the user experience
e) They allow the incorporation of native application features, such as the receipt of push notifications

On the other hand, due to their recent appearance, they present the following disadvantages compared to traditional web applications:

a) lower degree of maturity
b) increased learning curve and development effort
c) have incompatibilities on some platforms, e.g. iOS [21]

However, this approach is oriented to mobile devices, it is noteworthy that it allows installations on desktop computers, so it is a possibility to unify the development of applications, regardless of the type of device and operating system.

In order to maximize the use of PWA, the possibility of uploading them to the Google application store was generated, through the TWA technology.

From the above, it is concluded that PWAs have the potential to establish themselves as a solid alternative in software development.

In order to deepen the study of this work, we propose to extend the comparative analysis of PWA with the other development approaches considered in [2].

References

1. Delia, L., Galdamez, N., Thomas, P., Corbalan, L., Pesado, P.: Multi-platform mobile application development analysis. In: 2015 IEEE 9th International Conference on Research Challenges in Information Science (RCIS), pp. 181–186. IEEE, May 2015
2. Delia, L., et al.: Development approaches for mobile applications: comparative analysis of features. In: Arai, K., Kapoor, S., Bhatia, R. (eds.) SAI 2018. AISC, vol. 857, pp. 470–484. Springer, Cham (2019). https://doi.org/10.1007/978-3-030-01177-2_34
3. Xanthopoulos, S., Xinogalos, S.: A comparative analysis of cross-platform development approaches for mobile applications. In: BCI 2013, Greece (2013)
4. Biørn-Hansen, A., Grønli, T.-M., Ghinea, G.: A survey and taxonomy of core concepts and research challenges in cross-platform mobile development. ACM Comput. Surv. **51**(5), 1–34 (2018). https://doi.org/10.1145/3241739
5. Dalmasso, I., Datta, S.K., Bonnet, C., Nikaein, N.: Survey, comparison and evaluation of cross platform mobile application development tools. In: 2013 9th International Wireless Communications and Mobile Computing Conference (IWCMC) (2013)
6. Delía, L., Galdamez, N., Corbalan, L., Pesado, P., Thomas, P.: Approaches to mobile application development: comparative performance analysis. In: 2017 Computing Conference, London (2017)

7. Corbalán, L., et al.: A study of non-functional requirements in apps for mobile devices. In: Naiouf, M., Chichizola, F., Rucci, E. (eds.) JCC&BD 2019. CCIS, vol. 1050, pp. 125–136. Springer, Cham (2019). https://doi.org/10.1007/978-3-030-27713-0_11

8. Corbalan, L., et al.: Development frameworks for mobile devices: a comparative study about energy consumption. In: 5th IEEE/ACM International Conference on Mobile Software Engineering and Systems (ICSE), MobileSoft 2018, Gothenburg, Sweden (2018)

9. https://events.google.com/io2016/

10. Aguirre, V., et al.: PWA para unificar el desarrollo Desktop, Web y Mobile. In: XXV Congreso Argentino de Ciencias de la Computación, CACIC (2019)

11. https://developers.google.com/web/fundamentals/design-and-ux/responsive/

12. https://getbootstrap.com/

13. https://foundation.zurb.com/

14. https://bulma.io/

15. Gaunt, M.: Introducción a los service workers

16. https://developers.google.com/web/fundamentals/web-app-manifest/

17. https://www.w3.org/TR/appmanifest/

18. https://developer.mozilla.org/en-US/docs/Web/Manifest

19. Fortunato, D., Bernardino, J.: Progressive web apps: an alternative to the native mobile apps (Portugués). In: 2018 13th Iberian Conference on Information Systems and Technologies (CISTI) (2018)

20. https://developers.google.com/web/progressive-web-apps/desktop

21. Biørn-Hansen, A., Majchrzak, T.A., Grønli, T.-M.: Progressive web apps for the unified development of mobile applications. In: Majchrzak, T.A., Traverso, P., Krempels, K.-H., Monfort, V. (eds.) WEBIST 2017. LNBIP, vol. 322, pp. 64–86. Springer, Cham (2018). https://doi.org/10.1007/978-3-319-93527-0_4

22. https://developers.google.com/web/fundamentals/codelabs/your-first-pwapp/

23. https://developers.google.com/web/progressive-web-apps

24. https://developers.google.com/web/progressive-web-apps/checklist

25. https://developers.google.com/digital-asset-links/v1/getting-started

26. https://medium.com/@firt/google-play-store-now-open-for-progressive-web-apps-ec6f3c6ff3cc

27. https://info.unlp.edu.ar

28. https://es.wordpress.com/

29. https://superpwa.com/

30. https://innovapp-pwa.firebaseapp.com/

31. https://ionicframework.com/

32. https://angular.io/

33. https://developer.android.com/studio

34. https://developers.google.com/web/updates/2019/02/using-twa

Databases and Data Mining

An Adaptive and Efficient Method for Detecting First Signs of Depression with Information from the Social Web

Leticia C. Cagnina[1,2(✉)], Marcelo L. Errecalde[1], Ma. José Garciarena Ucelay[1],
Dario G. Funez[1], and Ma. Paula Villegas[1,2]

[1] Laboratorio de Investigación y Desarrollo en Inteligencia Computacional,
Universidad Nacional de San Luis, Ej. de los Andes 950, San Luis, Argentina
lcagnina@gmail.com, merrecalde@gmail.com, mjgarciarenaucelay@gmail.com,
funezdario@gmail.com, villegasmariapaula74@gmail.com
[2] Consejo Nacional de Investigaciones Científicas y Técnicas (CONICET),
Buenos Aires, Argentina

Abstract. Depression is one of the most prevalent mental disorders in the world. At present, there are more than 264 million people of all ages suffering depression and close to 800000 ends up in suicide (World Health Organization (Jannuary 2020)). The early recognition of depression can lead to timely treatment and save lives. In this context, the use of information from social media platforms can be a valuable resource for the early detection of depression. Previously, we presented k-TVT, a method able to set the level of urgency for the detection of this mental disorder. This adaptive method considers the variation of the vocabulary along the time step line for representing the documents. The results obtained with k-TVT using publicly available data sets demonstrated its flexibility and effectiveness over state-of-the-art methods. In this extended work, we confirm the previous conclusions with a more elaborated analysis of results.

Keywords: Early depression detection · Document representations · Concise Semantic Analysis · Temporal variation of terms

1 Introduction

Mental disorder detection based on social media information is a complex task that has been studied in the last decade [8]. Platforms like Facebook, Twitter and Reddit are daily used to express feelings, emotions, preferences, activities, and behaviours. Even more, many people suffering some kind of disease or mental illness share their own experience looking for support, attention or just understanding. In that context, the development of computational methods that take advantage of that information to detect people with signs of depression is becoming an important research area. The quick detection of depression is very useful because can limit the worsening of the disease and suggest a treatment.

© Springer Nature Switzerland AG 2020
P. Pesado and M. Arroyo (Eds.): CACIC 2019, CCIS 1184, pp. 217–233, 2020.
https://doi.org/10.1007/978-3-030-48325-8_15

We previously presented an effective method for the early risk detection (ERD) on Internet, named TVT [11]. The proposal participated of the early depression detection (EDD) pilot task [21] and with the information of only 4 "chunks" (short pieces of text) addressed the problem of balancing the minority class (depressive persons). The analysis of the impact of varying the number of chunks, the relation of the number of chunks versus the urgency level of the problem, and other TVT parameters were beyond the scope of that publication.

Later, we proposed k-TVT [5] with the aim of improving the analysis and conclusions about the good performance of TVT on EDD. k-TVT is a generalization of its predecessor TVT with the advantage of setting the number of chunks k considered for the minority class. Depending on the urgency (earliness) required in a particular scenario (specified by the σ parameter), it is possible to select for k-TVT a proper number of chunks k that obtains acceptable Early Risk Detection Error ($ERDE_\sigma$) values. We also provided some guidance about which could be robust learning algorithms and appropriate probability thresholds τ to be combined with the specific selected k value.

In this extended version of [5] we present a detailed review of the more relevant works for ERD problems, and we provide a more complete description of the collections and the error measure used in the experimentation. Finally, we show a more elaborate analysis of results.

The structure of the paper is as follows. In Sect. 2 we present a review of works that address ERD problems. Section 3 explains in detail k-TVT. In Sect. 4 we describe the data sets used in our experiments and the definition of the error measure. Section 5 shows the experimental study settings, a comparison with state-of-the-art methods and the analysis of results. Finally, Sect. 6 summarizes the main conclusions obtained and possible future works.

2   Related Work

For many years, psychologists have used tests or carefully designed questionnaires to assess different psychological constructs. Nowadays all the information available in social media, such as Twitter and Facebook, enables novel measurement approaches applying automated methods [33]. In that context, methods for automatic depression detection (ADD) have gained increasing interest in the last years. Given the close relationship of depression with the problem of suicide, we will review not only ADD but also related suicide studies.

A pioneering work in these areas [34] uses the Linguistic Inquiry and Word Count (LIWC) software and shows that it is possible to characterize depression through natural language use. Besides, it is suggested that suicidal poets use more first-person pronouns (e.g., I, me, mine) and less first plural pronouns (e.g., we, ours) throughout their writing careers than non-suicidal poets. In a similar study [31], depressed students are observed to use more first person singular pronouns, more negative emotion words and fewer positive emotion words in their essays in comparison to students who has never suffered this disease. Suicide prevention is a major challenge on the global public health agenda.

In [28], the authors estimate the risk of suicide (with an accuracy of 65%) by examining the clinical notes taken from a national sample of United States Veterans Administration medical records. They generated datasets of single keywords and multiword phrases and then built a 3-bin classification scheme (three matched cohorts: veterans who committed suicide, veterans who used mental health services and did not commit suicide, and veterans who did not use mental health services and did not commit suicide during the observation period). In [10] emotions are analyzed in suicidal notes and different studies have tried to detect suicidal ideation in social media with more complex techniques such as deep learning based [6, 16, 35].

Regarding social media postings, the posts on Twitter shared by subjects diagnosed with clinical depression are analyzed in [8] and a Support Vector Machine (SVM) classifier is developed to predict if a post is depression-indicative (with an accuracy of 73%). Furthermore, they suggest that the timestamp would help to predict if the post is depression-indicative because one characteristic of depressed subjects is the nightly activity on the Internet due to insomnia. Other research work indicates that subjects with major depressive disorder show lower social activity, greater negative emotion, high self-attentional focus, increased relational and medicinal concerns, heightened expression of religious thoughts and belong to highly clustered close-knit networks [15].

Even though notable research has been published on the area of Text and Social Analytics, where several studies have attempted to predict or analyze depression [2, 8, 26] no one has attempted to build a dataset where a large chronological sequence of writings leading to that disorder is properly stored and analyzed [20]. This is mainly due to the fact that text is often extracted from social media sites, such as Twitter or Facebook, that do not allow re-distribution. Besides, in the machine learning community, it is well known the importance of having publicly available datasets to foster research on a particular topic, in this case, predicting depression based on language use. That is why the primary objective in [20] was to provide the first collection to study the relationship between depression and language usage by means of machine learning techniques.

The work developed in [20] was important for ADD, not only for generating a data set for experimentation in this area, but also because they proposed a measure ($ERDE$) that simultaneously evaluates the accuracy of the classifiers and the delay in making a prediction. Both tools (the data set and the evaluation measure) were later used in the first task of eRisk [21], with the participation of 8 different research groups. Then, the task continued in 2018 [22] adding early anorexia detection and continued in 2019 [23] where automatic self-harm detection was added and it also included a new form of depression evaluation by filling out a questionnaire. In that regard, in those works ([20, 21] and its extensions [22, 23]) the proposals of all the groups participating in the early risk detection task and our preliminary report on TVT [11] are the closest antecedents to the proposal presented in this work.

Some interesting approaches (which had the best results) from the three eRisk editions are [32, 37, 39] from 2017, [4, 12, 27, 38] from 2018 and [1, 3] from

2019. As observed in the summary of results of eRisk editions [21–23], a wide range of different document representations and classification models were used.

Regarding document representations some research groups used simple features like standard Bag of Words [12,37,39], bigrams and trigrams [39], lexicon-based features [1,3,32,37,38], LIWC features [1,12,37–39], Part-of-Speech tags, statistical features (average number of posts or words per post, the hour of the posts, etc.) or even hand-crafted features [37]. Some other groups made use of more sophisticated features such as Latent Semantic Analysis [4,9,37,38], Concise Semantic Analysis [12,39], Paragraph to Vector [37,38] or even graph-based representations [40].

With respect to classification models, some groups used standard classifiers (such as Multinomial Naive Bayes (MNB), Logistic Regression, Support Vector Machine(SVM), Random Forest, Decision Trees), graph-based models, or even combinations or ensemble of different classifiers [1,4,12,32,37–39]. Taking into account that EDD is basically a sequential classification problem, it was not surprising that also were used several neural network methods for sequence classifications that have received increasing interest in the last years in many sequential NLP tasks [14,24,25,29,30,40] and some tasks that involve sequence classification like sentiment classification [36]. In regards to this, [27,32,37,38] made use of more complex methods such as different types of Recurrent and Convolutional Neural Networks.

Another interesting aspect of this evaluation task was the wide variety of mechanisms used to decide *when* to make each prediction. Many works apply a simple policy in which, the same way as in [20], a subject is classified as depressed when the classifier outputs a value p greater than a fixed threshold [12,32,37–39]. Some other groups applied no policy at all and no early classification was performed, i.e. their classifiers made their predictions only after seeing the entire subject's history[1]. It is worth mentioning that some groups [12,37–39] added extra conditions to the given policy, for instance [37,38] used a list of manually-crafted rules of the form: "if output $\geq \alpha_n$ and number of writings $\geq n$, then classify as positive", "if output $\leq \beta_n$ and number of writings $\geq n$, then classify as non-depressed", etc.

Finally, although our preliminary ideas about TVT presented in [11] were not used as an independent method, they were integrated in the ensemble method proposed in [39] obtaining the best $ERDE_{50}$ value over the 30 systems presented. These last two works are the closest antecedents to our proposal and we will focus here on different extensions and improvements of them.

3   The Proposed Method

Our method is based on the *Concise Semantic Analysis* (CSA) technique proposed in [18] and later extended in [19] for author profiling tasks. Therefore, we first present the key aspects of CSA in Sect. 3.1 and then, we explain in

---

[1] Note that this is not a realistic approach, usually there is no such thing as a subject's "last writing" in real life since subjects are able to create new writings over time.

Sect. 3.2 how we instantiate CSA with concepts derived from the terms used in the temporal chunks analyzed by an ERD system at different time steps.

3.1   Concise Semantic Analysis

Standard text representation methods such as *Bag of Words* (BoW) suffer of two well-known drawbacks. First, their high dimensionality and sparsity; second, they do not capture relationships among words. CSA is a semantic analysis technique that aims at dealing with those shortcomings by interpreting words and documents in a space of *concepts*. Differently from other semantic analysis approaches such as *Latent Semantic Analysis* (LSA) [9] and *Explicit Semantic Analysis* (ESA) [13] which usually require huge computing costs, CSA interprets words and text fragments in a space of concepts that are close (or equal) to the category labels. For instance, if documents in the data set are labeled with q different category labels (usually no more than 100 elements), words and documents will be represented in a q-dimensional space. That space size is usually much smaller than standard BoW representations which directly depend on the vocabulary size (more than 10000 or 20000 elements in general). To explain the main concepts of the CSA technique we first introduce some basic notation that will be used in the rest of this work.

Let $\mathcal{D} = \{\langle d_1, y_1 \rangle, \ldots, \langle d_n, y_n \rangle\}$ be a training set formed by n pairs of documents (d_i) and variables (y_i) that indicate the concept the document is associated with, $y_i \in \mathcal{C}$ where $\mathcal{C} = \{c_1, \ldots, c_q\}$ is the *concept space*. Consider that these concepts correspond to standard category labels although, as we will see later, they might represent more elaborate aspects. In this context, we will denote as $\mathcal{V} = \{t_1, \ldots, t_v\}$ to the vocabulary of terms of the collection being analyzed.

Representing Terms in the Concept Space. In CSA, each term $t_i \in \mathcal{V}$ is represented as a vector $\mathbf{t_i} \in \mathbb{R}^q$, $\mathbf{t_i} = \langle t_{i,1}, \ldots, t_{i,q} \rangle$. Here, $t_{i,j}$ represents the degree of association between the term t_i and the concept c_j and its computation requires some basic steps that are explained below. First, the raw term-concept association between the ith term and the jth concept, denoted w_{ij}, will be obtained. If $D_{c_u} \subseteq \mathcal{D}$, $D_{c_u} = \{d_r \mid \langle d_r, y_s \rangle \in \mathcal{D} \wedge y_s = c_u\}$ is the subset of the training instances whose label is the concept c_u, then w_{ij} might be defined as Eq. 1 shows.

$$w_{ij} = \sum_{\forall d_m \in D_{c_j}} \log_2 \left(1 + \frac{tf_{im}}{len(d_m)} \right) \tag{1}$$

where tf_{im} is the number of occurrences of the term t_i in the document d_m and $len(d_m)$ is the length (number of terms) of d_m.

As noted in [18] and [19], direct use of w_{ij} to represent terms in the vector $\mathbf{t_i}$ could be sensible to highly unbalanced data. Thus, some kind of normalization is required and, in our case, we selected the one proposed in [19] (see below).

$$t'_{ij} = \frac{w_{ij}}{\sum\limits_{i=1}^{|\mathcal{V}|} w_{ij}} \tag{2}$$

$$t_{ij} = \frac{t'_{ij}}{\sum\limits_{j=1}^{|\mathcal{C}|} w_{ij}} \tag{3}$$

Equation 2 normalizes weights in proportion to the $|\mathcal{V}|$ terms of each class and Eq. 3 normalizes term weights in order to make them comparable among the $|\mathcal{C}| = q$ categories/concepts. With this last conversion we finally obtain, for each term $t_i \in \mathcal{V}$, a q-dimensional vector $\mathbf{t_i}$, $\mathbf{t_i} = \langle t_{i,1}, \ldots, t_{i,q} \rangle$ defined over a space of q concepts. Up to now, those concepts correspond to the original categories used to label the documents.

Representing Documents in the Concept Space. Once the terms are represented in the q-dimensional concept space, those vectors can be used to represent documents in the same concept space. In CSA, documents are represented as the central vector of all the term vectors they contain [18]. Terms have distinct importance for different documents so it is not a good idea computing that vector for the document as the simple average of all its term vectors. A previous work in BoW [17] has considered different statistic techniques to weight the importance of terms in a document such as $tfidf$, $tfig$, $tf\chi^2$ or $tfrf$ among others. Here, we will use the approach used in [19] for author profiling that represents each document d_m as the weighted aggregation of the representations (vectors) of terms that it contains (see Eq. 4).

$$\mathbf{d_m} = \sum_{t_i \in d_m} \left(\frac{tf_{im}}{len(d_m)} \times \mathbf{t_i} \right) \tag{4}$$

Thus, documents are also represented in a q-dimensional concept space (i.e., $\mathbf{d_m} \in \mathbb{R}^q$) which is much smaller in dimensionality than the one required by standard BoW approaches ($q \ll v$).

3.2 k-Temporal Variation of Terms

In Subsect. 3.1 we said that the concept space $\mathcal{C}$ usually corresponds to standard category names used to label the training instances in supervised text categorization tasks. In this scenario, which in [18] is referred as *direct derivation*, each category label simply corresponds to a concept. However, in [18] also are proposed other alternatives like *split derivation* and *combined derivation*. The former uses the low-level labels in hierarchical corpora and the latter is based on combining semantically related labels in a unique concept. In [19] those ideas are extended by first clustering each category of the corpora and then using those subgroups (sub-clusters) as new concept space.[2]

---

[2] In that work, concepts are referred as *profiles* and subgroups as *sub-profiles*.

As we can see, the common idea to all the above approaches is that once a set of documents is identified as belonging to a group/category, that category can be considered as a concept and CSA can be applied in the usual way. We take a similar view to those works by considering that the positive (minority) class in ERD problems can be augmented with the concepts derived from the sets of partial documents read along the different time steps. In order to understand this idea, it is necessary to first introduce a sequential work scheme as the one proposed in [20] for research in ERD systems for depression cases.

Following [20], we will assume a corpus of documents written by p different individuals ($\{I_1, \ldots, I_p\}$). For each individual I_l ($l \in \{1, \ldots, p\}$), the n_l documents that he has written are provided in chronological order (from the oldest text to the most recent one): $D_{I_l,1}, D_{I_l,2}, \ldots, D_{I_l,n_l}$. In this context, given these p streams of messages, the ERD system has to process every sequence of messages (in the chronological order they are produced) and has to make a binary decision (as early as possible) on whether or not the individual might be a positive case of depression. Evaluation metrics on this task must be time-aware, so an early risk detection error (ERDE) is proposed. This metric not only takes into account the correctness of the (binary) decision but also the delay taken by the system to make the decision.

In a usual supervised text categorization task, we would only have two category labels: *positive* (risk/depressive case) and *negative* (non-risk/non-depressive case). That would only give two concepts for a CSA representation. However, in ERD problems there is additional temporal information that could be used to obtain an improved concept space. For instance, the training set could be split in h "chunks", $\hat{C}_1, \hat{C}_2, \ldots, \hat{C}_h$, in such a way that $\hat{C}_1$ contains the oldest writings of all users (first $(100/h)\%$ of submitted posts or comments), chunk $\hat{C}_2$ contains the second oldest writings, and so forth. Each chunk $\hat{C}_m$ can be partitioned in two subsets $\hat{C}_m^+$ and $\hat{C}_m^-$, $\hat{C}_m = \hat{C}_m^+ \bigcup \hat{C}_m^-$ where $\hat{C}_m^+$ contains the positive cases of chunk $\hat{C}_m$ and $\hat{C}_m^-$ the negatives ones of this chunk.

It is interesting to note that we can also consider the data sets that result of concatenating chunks that are contiguous in time and using the notation $\hat{C}_{i-j}$ to refer to the chunk obtained from concatenating all the (original) chunks from the ith chunk to the jth chunk (inclusive). Thus, $\hat{C}_{1-h}$ will represent the data set with the complete stream of messages of all the p individuals. In this case, $\hat{C}_{1-h}^+$ and $\hat{C}_{1-h}^-$ will have the obvious semantic specified above for the complete documents of the training set.

The classic way of constructing a classifier would be to take the complete documents of the p individuals ($\hat{C}_{1-h}$) and use an inductive learning algorithm such as SVM to obtain that classifier. As we mentioned earlier, another important aspect in EDS systems is that the classification problem being addressed is usually highly unbalanced. That is, the number of documents of the majority/negative class ("non-depression") is significantly larger than of the minority/positive class ("depression"). More formally, following the previously specified notation $\mid \hat{C}_{1-h}^- \mid \gg \mid \hat{C}_{1-h}^+ \mid$.

An alternative to balance the classes would be to consider that the minority class is formed not only by the complete documents of the individuals but also by the partial documents obtained in the different chunks. Following the general ideas posed in CSA, we could consider that the partial documents read in the different chunks represent "temporal" concepts that should be taken into account. In this context, one might think that variations of the terms used in these different sequential stages of the documents may have relevant information for the classification task. With this idea in mind, the method proposed in this work named *k-temporal variation of terms* (*k*-TVT) arises, which consists in enriching the documents of the minority class with the partial documents read in the first k chunks. These first chunks of the minority class, along with their complete documents, will be considered as a new concept space for a CSA method.

Therefore, in k-TVT we first determine the number k of initial chunks that will be used to enrich the minority (positive) class. Then, we use the document sets $\hat{C}_1^+, \hat{C}_{1-2}^+, \ldots, \hat{C}_{1-k}^+$ and $\hat{C}_{1-h}^+$ as concepts for the positive class and $\hat{C}_{1-h}^-$ for the negative class. Finally, we represent terms as documents in this new $(k+2)$-dimensional space using the CSA approach explained in Sect. 3.1.

4   Data Sets and Error Measure

We employed the data sets supplied by *eRisk 2017 pilot task*[3] and *eRisk 2018 Lab*[4] on *early risk prediction* for *depression* to execute our study. They are compounded of writings (posts) of Social Media users (or subjects) taken from *Reddit*. There are two kind of users: "depressed" (or positive) and "non-depressed/control" (or negative). For each user, the data sets consist of a sequence of writings (in chronological order) divided into 10 chunks. The first chunk contains the oldest 10% of the messages, the second chunk contains the second oldest 10%, and so forth. The subjects labelled as positive are those that have explicitly mentioned that they have been diagnosed with depression.

Both collections were split into training and test sets. The training set of eRisk 2017 corpus is composed of 486 users (83 positive versus 403 negative) and the test set contains 401 users (52 positive versus 349 negative). Meanwhile, eRisk 2018 training set is the join of eRisk 2017 training and test sets, that is, 135 positive users (83 from eRisk 2017 training set plus 52 from eRisk 2017 test set) and 752 negative users (403 plus 349 from training and test set of eRisk 2017 corpus respectively). Similarly, eRisk 2018 test set consists of 79 depressed subjects and 741 non-depressed ones. Table 1 summarizes, for both data sets, the number of users for each class.

These depression prediction tasks were divided into a training and a testing stage. In the training stage, the participating teams had access to the training set with all chunks of all training users. They could therefore tune their systems with this data. Then, during the testing stage, classifiers must decide, as *early*

---

[3] http://early.irlab.org/2017/index.html.
[4] http://early.irlab.org/2018/index.html.

Table 1. Data sets for depression task.

	Training		Total	Test		Total
	Depressed	Non-depressed		Depressed	Non-depressed	
eRisk 2017	83	403	486	52	349	401
eRisk 2018	135	752	887	79	741	820

as possible, whether each user is 'depressed' or not based on his/her writings. In order to accomplish this, the user's writings were divided into 10 *chunks* —thus each *chunk* contained 10% of the user's history. Hence, classifiers were given the user's history, one chunk at a time, and after each chunk submission the classifiers were asked to decide whether the subject was depressed, not depressed or that more chunks needed to be read.

Standard classification measures such as F_1-measure (F_1), Precision (π) and Recall (ρ) are time-unaware, that is, they do not take into account the amount of time (or information) the classifier need to take a decision. Therefore, an important aspect introduced in [20] to evaluate classifiers considering time was the *Early Risk Detection Error* (ERDE) measure defined in Eq. 5.

$$ERDE_\sigma(d,k) = \begin{cases} c_{fp} & if \ d = p \ \& \ truth = n \\ c_{fn} & if \ d = n \ \& \ truth = p \\ lc_\sigma(k) \cdot c_{tp} & if \ d = p \ \& \ truth = p \\ 0 & if \ d = n \ \& \ truth = n \end{cases} \qquad (5)$$

where the sigmoid *latency cost function*, $lc_\sigma(k)$ is defined in Eq. 6.

$$lc_\sigma(k) = 1 - \frac{1}{1 + e^{k-\sigma}} \qquad (6)$$

c_{fn}, c_{tp} and c_{fp} refer to the *cost of false negative, true positive* and *false positive*, respectively. The delay is measured by counting the number (k) of distinct textual items seen before making the binary decision (d) which could be positive (p) or negative (n). The o parameter serves as the "deadline" for decision making, i.e. if a correct positive decision is made in time $k > \sigma$, it will be taken by $ERDE_\sigma$ as if it were incorrect (false positive). Additionally, it was also set $c_{fn} = c_{tp} = 1$ and c_{fp} was calculated by the number of depressed subjects divided by the total subjects in the test set.

5   Experimental Study

Our experimental study scheme consisted in evaluating if it is possible to select an appropiate number k of chunks to obtain good $ERDE_\sigma$ values for different levels of urgency σ. This is addressed in Sect. 5.1 by performing a cross-validation study on the whole data set eRisk2017 (training and test corpus) described in the previous section. Besides, the incidence of the probability threshold τ on the classifier's performance is deeply analyzed. Then, in Subsect. 5.2, results are compared with the ones previously published in [21,22]. Lastly, in Subsect. 5.3 we examine to what extent the predictions made by the approaches of k-TVT with SVM, to see how differ (or coincide) depending on the value of the k value and the confidence level τ.

5.1   Setting the k Parameter

We present an exploratory analysis that allows us to understand in greater depth the relationship between the number of initial chunks k used by k-TVT and the urgency level specified by σ. In that way, we could give some guidance about a reasonable number k for the different thresholds σ.

First, we joint train and test sets of 2017 eRisk corpus in order to obtain a larger data set to perform a 5-fold cross validation with different versions of k-TVT. Thus, we randomly split the 887 users (135 positives and 752 negative) into 5 parts. We got 3 folds with 177 users each (27 positive and 150 negative) and 2 folds of 178 users each (27 positive and 151 negative). In addition, we used 3 learning algorithms: Support Vector Machine (SVM), Naïve Bayes (NB) and Random Forest. The implementations of these algorithms were provided by the Python scikit-learn library with the default parameters.

The performance of the classifiers was assessed using the $ERDE_\sigma$ measure and the parameter σ was varied considering the values: 5, 10, 25, 50 and 75. Because σ represents some type of "urgency" in detecting depression cases, we analyzed how k-TVT performs under different levels of σ. Note that $\sigma = 5$ means a high urgency (a quick decision should be made) and $\sigma = 75$ represents the lowest urgency (there is more time for a decision) to detect positive cases.

As we stated before, k-TVT defines concepts that capture the sequential aspects of the ERD problems and the variations of vocabulary observed in the distinct stages of the writings. Thus, different number k of chunks that will enrich the minority (positive) class could have an impact in the $ERDE_\sigma$ measure. In this study, the k value was varied in the (integer) range $[0, 5]$.

In each chunk, classifiers usually produce their predictions with some "confidence" (in general, the estimated probability of the predicted class). Therefore, we can select different thresholds τ considering that an instance is assigned to the target class when its associated probability p is greater (or equal) than certain threshold τ ($p \geq \tau$). We taken into account 4 different settings for the probabilities assigned by each classifier: $p \geq 0.9$, $p \geq 0.8$, $p \geq 0.7$ and $p \geq 0.6$. Once a classifier determines that an instance is positive in a specific chunk, that decision remains unchanged until chunk 10. Due to space constraints, only the best results are shown (Table 2).

The performance of k-TVT was compared with that of a standard bag of words (BoW) representation with different weighting schemes: boolean, term-frequency (tf) and tf-inverse document frequency (tfidf). The best results with BoW were achieved with tfidf scheme, SVM as learning algorithm and different thresholds τ. These results were adopted as a baseline.

Table 2. Best results of 5-fold cross validation on the whole eRisk2017 data set.

			ERDE				
		τ	5	10	25	50	75
Best $ERDE_{5-10}$	0-TVT-SVM	0.8	**13.58**	**12.48**	12.04	11.40	11.08
	BOW-SVM	0.7	14.13	13.18	11.75	10.97	10.49
Best $ERDE_{25-50}$	4-TVT-SVM	0.7	14.10	12.51	**11.00**	**9.59**	9.17
	BOW-SVM	0.6	14.42	13.20	11.28	10.38	9.70
Best $ERDE_{75}$	4-TVT-NB	0.7	14.49	12.72	11.05	9.67	**8.74**
	BOW-SVM	0.6	14.42	13.20	11.28	10.38	9.70

Table 2 shows the best values obtained by k-TVT for the temporal-aware measure $ERDE_\sigma$ with the different urgency levels σ. As we can see in the first row of the table, for the lowest σ ($\sigma = 5$ and $\sigma = 10$), k-TVT obtained the best $ERDE_5$ and $ERDE_{10}$ (highlighted in boldface) with the minimum k value, that is, $k = 0$ and the SVM classifier using $p \geq 0.8$. Those two numbers are around a 5% better than the ones corresponding to the baseline (BoW-SVM, $p \geq 0.7$). However, it is interesting to notice in the same row, the baseline was better than 0-TVT when $\sigma = 25, 50$ and 75 are used. Those results were a preliminary evidence that k-TVT performance, as measured by $ERDE_\sigma$, effectively depends on the selected number of chunks k. That is, 0-TVT does not seem to produce as good results for higher σ values as the ones obtained with $\sigma = 5$ and 10. The same fact is confirmed by the best $ERDE_{25}$ and $ERDE_{50}$ obtained by k-TVT using the first 4 initial chunks ($k = 4$), SVM as learning algorithm and a lower probability, $p \geq 0.7$. Finally, the best $ERDE_{75}$ was obtained with 4-TVT using Naïve Bayes with the same probability ($p \geq 0.7$). Here, the lowest $ERDE_{75}$ indicates that 4-TVT-NB outperformed the baseline in almost 1 unit which constitutes a good value.

In summary, from this study we can conclude that when there is a high urgency level (low σ values) in detecting depression cases, the best performance is obtained with 0-TVT. As the level of urgency in the detection decreases ($\sigma \geq 0.25$), 4-TVT performs well and it can detect the positive cases with enough accuracy. It seems that while more information enriches the k-TVT representation, more confident can be the classifier, therefore better $ERDE_\sigma$ can be obtained. It is also worth to note that for $\sigma \in \{5, 10, 25, 50\}$ SVM classifier obtained the best results demonstrating thus enough robustness. Using k-TVT the classifiers obtained the predictions with highest probability: 0.8 and 0.7 while if BoW is used, the threshold is lower (around 0.7 and 0.6).

Since SVM performs well in most of the cases, we can suggest it as an acceptable algorithm to be combined with generic k-TVT and it will be used in next subsection.

5.2   Performance of k-TVT - eRisk's Train and Testing Sets

Here our approach was analyzed against some of the state-of-the-art methods. In this way, k-TVT results were directly compared with those obtained by the different groups participating in the tasks and published in [21,22]. Thus, the same conditions that participants faced were reproduced: first, we worked on the data set released on the training stage for obtaining the models and then, these were tested on the test sets. Note that only $ERDE_5$ and $ERDE_{50}$ values were reported because those two σ were evaluated in the tasks and a lower value of $ERDE$ is always preferable.

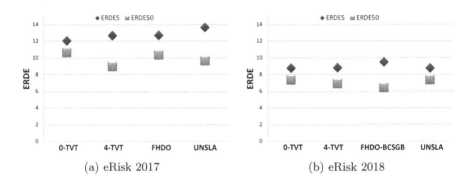

(a) eRisk 2017   (b) eRisk 2018

Fig. 1. Comparison among best results

Figure 1 shows the results obtained with k-TVT and SVM considering $\sigma \geq 0.7$ (4-TVT) and $p \geq 0.8$ (0-TVT) in comparison to the results obtained by the best approaches employing each collection. The complete description of those methods can be found in [21,22]. In Fig. 1(a), UNSLA is an assembly of several methods which includes 4-TVT representation. Meanwhile in Fig. 1(b), UNSLA is effectively 0-TVT representation with SVM classifier.

The figures reveal several interesting aspects. First of all, we can confirm the hypothesis originated from the previous study regarding that lower k values for k-TVT produce better $ERDE_\sigma$ when σ is low (high urgency level). Also, when there are low urgency levels, it is better to set k with higher values. With both k-TVT and probability thresholds ($\tau \geq 0.7$ and 0.8), the $ERDE_5$ measures are better than the best published for the eRisk 2017 task. For $ERDE_{50}$ the 4-TVT outperforms the best published for eRisk 2017, while 4-TVT obtains a value slightly worse in eRisk 2018, although it is better than 0-TVT.

5.3   Final Discussion

Even though the previous study gave significative evidence of the relationship between the number of chunks k and the level of urgency σ, some aspects deserve a more detailed analysis. One of them is to determine to what extent the predictions made by the approaches k-TVT with SVM as classifier differ (or coincide) depending on the value of the k value and the probability threshold τ.

A popular method to determine this kind of agreement is taking into account the Cohen's kappa (κ) coefficient [7], which provides a robust measure of agreement. It attempts to correct the degree of agreements, subtracting the portion of predictions that could be attributed to chance. If the classifiers completely agree, then $\kappa = 1$ whereas if there is no coincidence, the predictions would be by chance and $\kappa = 0$.

As we saw before, SVM demonstrated to be robust with k-TVT, particularly for probabilities $p \geq 0.7$ and $p \geq 0.8$. Therefore, we perform a pairwise comparison between the k-TVTs (with $k = 0 \dots 5$) and we obtained the κ coefficients.

Figure 2 shows the comparison of the same k-TVT-SVM but considering how they vary between different probabilities (0.7 and 0.8), for example, 0-TVT-SVM with $p \geq 0.7$ vs. 0-TVT-SVM with $p \geq 0.8$. Here, it is worth to note that all κ values are higher than 0.65 and, in some cases, quite similar (with 0.937 as the highest value). Thus, we could conclude that the difference in the performance of our proposals regarding ERDE metric (see Table 2) are mainly due to the contribution of the k value in the representation rather than the classifier or the probability used for the predictions.

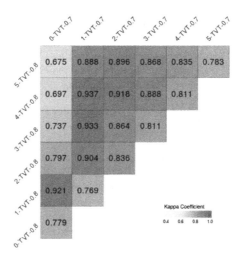

Fig. 2. Kappa coefficient for k-TVT with SVM ($p \geq 0.7$ and $p \geq 0.8$)

6 Conclusions and Future Work

This work describes an adaptive and flexible method for early detection of depression. The proposal, named *k-temporal variation of terms* (k-TVT), is effective due to the variation of the vocabulary along the different time steps as concept space for the representation of the documents. k-TVT is also an adaptable method because of the possibility of setting a parameter (the k value) depending on the urgency level (the threshold σ) required to detect the risky cases.

We obtained interesting evidence about the relationship between the k parameter and the required level of earliness σ in the predictions. For low σ values (high urgency) a low number of chunks ($k = 0$) is an adequate representation while for low urgency (higher σ), the use of a higher value ($k = 4$) seems to be more adequate.

The 0-TVT and 4-TVT versions show to be competitive and better, in some cases, than state-of-the-art methods in EDD problems. A very relevant aspect of the k-TVT representation is the complete domain independence because it is only based on the vocabulary present in the training corpus. Besides, it does not depend on features specifically derived for the depression problem or other costly hand-crafted features. Even more, the mechanism used to determine the classification time does not need to be adapted to a particular domain. This makes k-TVT suitable for implementation in other early risk tasks such as the early detection of anorexia or pedophiles without virtually any cost of migrating from one domain to another.

In that context, as future work, we plan to apply k-TVT approach to other problems that can be directly tackled as early risk detection such as sexual predation, suicide discourse identification or other kinds of mental disorders. We also plan to evaluate deep neural networks for the same problems and compare the performance of k-TVT against those RNN-based models.

Acknowledgments. This work was partially funded by CONICET and Universidad Nacional de San Luis (UNSL) - Argentina. For several experiments of this research, we used a Titan Xp donated by the NVIDIA Corporation.

References

1. Abed-Esfahani, P., et al.: Transfer learning for depression: early detection and severity prediction from social media postings. In: Working Notes of the Conference and Labs of the Evaluation Forum - CEUR Workshop Proceedings, vol. 2380 (2019)
2. Arora, P., Arora, P.: Mining twitter data for depression detection. In: 2019 International Conference on Signal Processing and Communication, pp. 186–189 (2019)
3. Burdisso, S.G., Errecalde, M.L., Montes y Gómez, M.: UNSL at eRisk 2019: a unified approach for anorexia, self-harm and depression detection in social media. In: Working Notes of the Conference and Labs of the Evaluation Forum - CEUR Workshop Proceedings, vol. 2380 (2019)
4. Cacheda, F., Iglesias, D.F., Nóvoa, F.J., Carneiro, V.: Analysis and experiments on early detection of depression. In: Working Notes of the Conference and Labs of the Evaluation Forum - CEUR Workshop Proceedings, vol. 2125 (2018)
5. Cagnina, L.C., Errecalde, M.L., Garciarena Ucelay, M.J., Funez, D.G., Villegas, M.P.: k-TVT: a flexible and effective method for early depression detection. In: XXV Congreso Argentino de Ciencias de la Computación. CACIC 2019. Libro de actas, pp. 547–556 (2019)

6. Chiroma, F., Cocea, M., Liu, H.: Detection of suicidal Twitter posts. In: Ju, Z., Yang, L., Yang, C., Gegov, A., Zhou, D. (eds.) UKCI 2019. AISC, vol. 1043, pp. 307–318. Springer, Cham (2020). https://doi.org/10.1007/978-3-030-29933-0_26
7. Cohen, J.: A coefficient of agreement for nominal scales. Educ. Psychol. Measur. **20**(1), 37 (1960)
8. De Choudhury, M., Counts, S., Horvitz, E.: Social media as a measurement tool of depression in populations. In: Proceedings of the 5th Annual ACM Web Science Conference, pp. 47–56. ACM (2013)
9. Deerwester, S., Dumais, S.T., Furnas, G.W., Landauer, T.K., Harshman, R.: Indexing by latent semantic analysis. J. Am. Soc. Inform. Sci. Technol. **41**(6), 391–407 (1990)
10. Desmet, B., Hoste, V.: Emotion detection in suicide notes. Expert Syst. Appl. **40**(16), 6351–6358 (2013)
11. Errecalde, M.L., Villegas, M.P., Funez, D.G., Garciarena Ucelay, M.J., Cagnina, L.C.: Temporal variation of terms as concept space for early risk prediction. In: Working Notes of the Conference and Labs of the Evaluation Forum - CEUR Workshop Proceedings, vol. 1866 (2017)
12. Funez, D.G., et al.: UNSL's participation at eRisk 2018 lab. In: Working Notes of the Conference and Labs of the Evaluation Forum - CEUR Workshop Proceedings, vol. 2125 (2018)
13. Gabrilovich, E., Markovitch, S.: Wikipedia-based semantic interpretation for natural language processing. J. Artif. Intell. Res. **34**, 443–498 (2009)
14. Gu, J., Lu, Z., Li, H., Li, V.O.: Incorporating copying mechanism in sequence-to-sequence learning. In: Proceedings of the 54th Annual Meeting of the Association for Computational Linguistics (Volume 1: Long Papers), pp. 1631–1640. Association for Computational Linguistics (2016)
15. Jalonen, H.: Negative emotions in social media as a managerial challenge. In: European Conference on Management Leadership and Governance (2014)
16. Ji, S.: Suicidal ideation detection in online social content. Ph.D. thesis, School of Information Technology and Electrical Engineering, The University of Queensland (2020)
17. Lan, M., Tan, C., Su, J., Lu, Y.: Supervised and traditional term weighting methods for automatic text categorization. IEEE Trans. Pattern Anal. Mach. Intell. **31**(4), 721–735 (2009)
18. Li, Z., Xiong, Z., Zhang, Y., Liu, C., Li, K.: Fast text categorization using concise semantic analysis. Pattern Recogn. Lett. **32**(3), 441–448 (2011)
19. López-Monroy, A.P., Montes-y-Gómez, M., Escalante, H.J., Villaseñor-Pineda, L., Stamatatos, E.: Discriminative subprofile-specific representations for author profiling in social media. Knowl.-Based Syst. **89**, 134–147 (2015)
20. Losada, D.E., Crestani, F.: A test collection for research on depression and language use. In: Fuhr, N., Quaresma, P., Gonçalves, T., Larsen, B., Balog, K., Macdonald, C., Cappellato, L., Ferro, N. (eds.) CLEF 2016. LNCS, vol. 9822, pp. 28–39. Springer, Cham (2016). https://doi.org/10.1007/978-3-319-44564-9_3
21. Losada, D.E., Crestani, F., Parapar, J.: eRISK 2017: CLEF lab on early risk prediction on the internet: experimental foundations. In: Jones, G.J.F., et al. (eds.) CLEF 2017. LNCS, vol. 10456, pp. 346–360. Springer, Cham (2017). https://doi.org/10.1007/978-3-319-65813-1_30

22. Losada, D.E., Crestani, F., Parapar, J.: Overview of eRisk: early risk prediction on the internet. In: Bellot, P., et al. (eds.) CLEF 2018. LNCS, vol. 11018, pp. 343–361. Springer, Cham (2018). https://doi.org/10.1007/978-3-319-98932-7_30

23. Losada, D.E., Crestani, F., Parapar, J.: Overview of eRisk at CLEF 2019: early risk prediction on the internet (extended overview). In: Working Notes of the Conference and Labs of the Evaluation Forum - CEUR Workshop Proceedings, vol. 2125 (2019)

24. Ma, X., Hovy, E.: End-to-end sequence labeling via bi-directional LSTM-CNNs-CRF. In: Proceedings of the 54th Annual Meeting of the Association for Computational Linguistics (Volume 1: Long Papers), pp. 1064–1074 (2016)

25. Melamud, O., Goldberger, J., Dagan, I.: context2vec: learning generic context embedding with bidirectional LSTM. In: Proceedings of The 20th SIGNLL Conference on Computational Natural Language Learning, pp. 51–61 (2016)

26. Park, M., McDonald, D.W., Cha, M.: Perception differences between the depressed and non-depressed users in Twitter. The International AAAI Conference on Web and Social Media, vol. 9, pp. 217–226 (2013)

27. Paul, S., Kalyani, J., Basu, T.: Early detection of signs of anorexia and depression over social media using effective machine learning frameworks. In: Working Notes of the Conference and Labs of the Evaluation Forum - CEUR Workshop Proceedings, vol. 2125 (2018)

28. Poulin, C., et al.: Predicting the risk of suicide by analyzing the text of clinical notes. PLoS ONE 9(1), e85733 (2014)

29. Raganato, A., Bovi, C.D., Navigli, R.: Neural sequence learning models for word sense disambiguation. In: Proceedings of the 2017 Conference on Empirical Methods in Natural Language Processing, pp. 1156–1167 (2017)

30. Rodrigues Makiuchi, M., Warnita, T., Uto, K., Shinoda, K.: Multimodal fusion of BERT-CNN and gated CNN representations for depression detection. In: Proceedings of the 9th International on Audio/Visual Emotion Challenge and Workshop, AVEC 2019, pp. 55–63. Association for Computing Machinery (2019)

31. Rude, S., Gortner, E.M., Pennebaker, J.: Language use of depressed and depression-vulnerable college students. Cogn. Emot. 18(8), 1121–1133 (2004)

32. Sadeque, F., Xu, D., Bethard, S.: UArizona at the CLEF eRisk 2017 pilot task: linear and recurrent models for early depression detection. In: Working Notes of the Conference and Labs of the Evaluation Forum - CEUR Workshop Proceedings, vol. 1866 (2017)

33. Schwartz, H.A., Ungar, L.H.: Data-driven content analysis of social media: a systematic overview of automated methods. ANNALS Am. Acad. Polit. Soc. Sci. 659(1), 78–94 (2015)

34. Stirman, S.W., Pennebaker, J.W.: Word use in the poetry of suicidal and nonsuicidal poets. Psychosom. Med. 63(4), 517–522 (2001)

35. Tadesse, M., Lin, H., Xu, B., Yang, L.: Detection of suicide ideation in social media forums using deep learning. Algorithms 13, 7 (2019)

36. Tang, D., Qin, B., Liu, T.: Document modeling with gated recurrent neural network for sentiment classification. In: Proceedings of the 2015 Conference on Empirical Methods in Natural Language Processing, pp. 1422–1432 (2015)

37. Trotzek, M., Koitka, S., Friedrich, C.: Linguistic metadata augmented classifiers at the CLEF 2017 task for early detection of depression. In: Working Notes of the Conference and Labs of the Evaluation Forum - CEUR Workshop Proceedings, vol. 1866 (2017)
38. Trotzek, M., Koitka, S., Friedrich, C.: Word embeddings and linguistic metadata at the CLEF 2018 tasks for early detection of depression and anorexia. In: Working Notes of the Conference and Labs of the Evaluation Forum - CEUR Workshop Proceedings, vol. 2125 (2018)
39. Villegas, M.P., Funez, D.G., Garciarena Ucelay, M.J., Cagnina, L.C., Errecalde, M.L.: LIDIC - UNSL's participation at eRisk 2017: pilot task on early detection of depression. In: Working Notes of CLEF 2017 - CEUR Workshop Proceedings, vol. 1866 (2017)
40. Wang, W., Chang, B.: Graph-based dependency parsing with bidirectional LSTM. In: Proceedings of the 54th Annual Meeting of the Association for Computational Linguistics (Volume 1: Long Papers), vol. 1, pp. 2306–2315 (2016)

Heuristics for Computing k-Nearest Neighbors Graphs

Edgar Chávez[2], Verónica Ludueña[1(✉)], and Nora Reyes[1]

[1] Departamento de Informática, Universidad Nacional de San Luis,
San Luis, Argentina
{vlud,nreyes}@unsl.edu.ar
[2] Centro de Investigación Científica y de Educación Superior de Ensenada, Ensenada, Mexico
elchavez@cicese.mx

Abstract. The k-Nearest Neighbors Graph (kNNG) consists of links from an object to its k-Nearest Neighbors. This graph is of interest in diverse applications ranging from statistics, machine learning, clustering and outlier detection, computational biology, and even indexing. Obtaining the kNNG is challenging because intrinsically high dimensional spaces are known to be unindexable, even in the approximate case. The cost of building an index is not well amortized over just all the objects in the database. In this paper, we introduce a method to compute the kNNG without building an index. While our approach is sequential, we show experimental evidence that the number of distance computations is a fraction of the $n^2/2$ used in the naïve solution. We make heavy use of the notion of *pivot*, that is, database objects with full distance knowledge to all other database objects. From a group of pivots, it is possible to infer upper bounds of distance to other objects.

Keywords: Near neighbor graph · Proximity search · Metric spaces

1 Introduction

Metric space searching addresses the problem of efficient similarity searching in many applications, such as multimedia databases, text retrieval, function prediction, machine learning, and classification; information retrieval; image quantization and compression; computational biology; text searching; and function prediction; between others, and many others. Thus, it has become an essential operation in applications that deal with unstructured data sources. All those applications can be formalized with the *metric space model* [8]. Formally, a metric space is composed by a universe of objects $\mathbb{U}$ and a distance function d. The distance function gives us a dissimilarity criterion to compare objects from $\mathbb{U}$. A database is a subset $S \subseteq \mathbb{U}$, whose cardinality is named $n = |S|$.

In the metric space model the similarity queries in S of any $q \in \mathbb{U}$ are usually of two types:

- *range query*: given $r \in \mathbb{R}^+$ it retrieves all the elements in S within distance r to q ($R(q, r)$), and
- *k-nearest neighbors query*: given $k \in \mathbb{N}$ it retrieves the k closest elements to q in S-$\{q\}$ (k-$NN(q)$).

© Springer Nature Switzerland AG 2020
P. Pesado and M. Arroyo (Eds.): CACIC 2019, CCIS 1184, pp. 234–249, 2020.
https://doi.org/10.1007/978-3-030-48325-8_16

The k-NN(q) query is a building block for a large number of problems in a vast number of application areas. For instance, in pattern classification, the nearest-neighbor rule can be implemented with 1-NN(q) [9]. Another known application is the *Nearest Neighbor Graph*. Formally, the Nearest Neighbor Graph (NNG) is a graph whose vertex set is S and with one edge from u to v whenever v is the nearest neighbor of u in S. The problem of determining the nearest neighbor of any element is often called the *all-nearest neighbor problem*. It could be generalized to obtain the k-NN of *all* elements of database as the *All-k-NN* problem. It is a useful operation for batch-based processing of a large distributed point dataset when we need to report the closest points for every element. In this paper, we focus on the k-Nearest Neighbors Graph (kNNG), where each element connects with its $k - \mathrm{NN}$.

Metric spaces are characterized, from an indexing point of view, by its intrinsic dimensionality. Real-world datasets tend to be high dimensional, difficult to index. Furthermore, a recent result on the hardness of indexing establish that for datasets with $O(\log n)$ intrinsic dimensions, with n the size of the database, every indexing method requires a linear scan over the data, even in the approximate sense of searching $1 + \epsilon$ approximations to the actual nearest neighbors [15]. Hence we pursue lowering the constant, that is, revising just a fraction of the database in each $k - \mathrm{NN}$ query. Furthermore, we focus on lowering the number of distance computations, as they represent the leading cost in indexing.

The conventional wisdom in indexing consists of building an index to avoid exhaustive search at query time. However, competitive indexes are costly to build, and they will probably not be amortized over just $O(n)$ queries. While our approach does not use an index, its total cost is significantly lower than the $n^2/2$ distance computations of the naïve solution. Our proposal computes some distances between database objects and ingeniously takes advantage of the properties that distance function satisfies. A preliminary version of this paper appeared in [5]. This new version includes another heuristic for computing kNNG and a more detailed analysis of how the curse of dimensionality affects our proposals.

The paper organization is as follows: Sect. 2 presents a brief description of some useful concepts. Section 3 introduces our proposals, and Sect. 4 contains the empirical evaluation of our proposed solutions. Finally, in Sect. 5 we conclude and discuss about possible extensions for our work.

2 Previous Concepts

In this section, we formally state the problem to continue the discussion. A metric space is composed of a universe of objects $\mathbb{U}$, and a distance function $d : \mathbb{U} \times \mathbb{U} \to \mathbb{R}^+$, such that for any $x, y, z \in \mathbb{U}$, $d(x, y) > 0$ (strict positiveness), $d(x, y) = 0 \iff x = y$ (reflexity), $d(x, y) = d(y, x)$ (symmetry), and obeying the triangle inequality: $d(x, z) + d(z, y) \geq d(x, y)$. The smaller the distance between two objects is, the more *similar* they are. We have a finite database S, a subset $S \subseteq \mathbb{U}$. Let $n = |S|$. At a later stage, a new object q from $\mathbb{U}$ is the query, and we must retrieve all the elements in S close enough to q using as few distance computations as possible.

In the metric space model, the most common similarity queries are range queries and k-nearest neighbors queries. For a given database S, $q \in \mathbb{U}$ and $r \in \mathbb{R}^+$: $(q, r) = \{x \in S \mid d(q, x) \leq r\}$ is known as a *range query*; and k-NN(q), denotes the *k-nearest neighbors* query of q, and formally it retrieves the set $R \subseteq S$ such that $|R| = k$ and $\forall u \in R, v \in S - R, d(q, u) \leq d(q, v)$. This last primitive is a fundamental tool in cluster and outlier detection [3, 10], image segmentation [1], query or document recommendation systems [2], VLSI design, spin glass and other physical process simulations [4], pattern recognition [9], and so on.

Interesting distances are expensive to compute (think, for example, in comparing two fingerprints). Thus, the ultimate goal is to build *offline* an index to speed up *online* queries. Differents techniques to solve the problem of similarity queries have arisen to reduce these costs, usually based on data preprocessing and storing some distances in the index. All those structures work based on discarding elements using the triangle inequality, and most of them use the classical divide-and-conquer approach.

A related version of the k-NN problem, perhaps less studied, is the *All-k-NN* problem. That is, if $|S| = n$, we solve the *All-k-NN* problem by efficiently retrieving the k-NN(u_i) for each u_i in S and performing less than $O(n^2)$ distance evaluations. Consider, for example, a location-based service that recommends each user his or her nearby users, who may be the candidates of new friends. Since the locations of users are stored in the underlying database, we can generate such recommendation lists by issuing an *All-k-NN* query on the database. This operation is also useful to build a kNNG, that is one of the available indexes for metric space.

Most of the solutions that have been proposed and developed for this problem use indexes. Some of them, for general metric spaces [13, 14], are based on the construction of k-nearest neighbors graphs (kNNG). The kNNG is a weighted directed graph connecting each object from the metric space to its k-nearest neighbors; that is, $G(S, E)$ such that $E = \{(u, v), u, v \in S \wedge v \in k\text{-NN}(u)\}$. G connects each element through a set of arcs whose weights are computed according to the distance of the corresponding space. In the same way, the *All-k-NN* problem is a direct generalization of All-1-NN) problem, building the kNNG can be seen as a direct generalization of building the 1NNG. The kNNG offers an indexing alternative, which requires a moderate amount of memory, obtaining reasonably good performance in the search process [13]. In fact, in low-memory scenarios, which only allow small values of k, the search performance of kNNG is better than using classical pivot-based indexing. Besides, graph-based techniques offer great potential for improvements, ranging from fully dynamic graph-based indexes to specific optimizations for metric space search.

The naïve algorithm for *All-k-NN* calculates the distance function d between each $u_i \in S$ and every element of S, so its complexity is quadratic $(n^2/2)$.

3   Our Proposals

Performing similarity queries on a database using a sequential scan can become non-scalable, either because of the size of the database or because of the cost of distance computations. Under this cost model, the ultimate goal of a similarity search technique is to solve queries doing the fewest number of distance computations. We took into account this objective in our new proposals. We stress that our proposals reduce the number of distance computations for each query without using an index.

The general gist of our approaches consists in selecting some objects $x_i \in S$, computing the distance from every database element x_j in the database ($x_j \in S - \{x_i\}$). The elements x_i have full distance knowledge in S. We can use that to filter the database when searching the k-nearest neighbors of other database elements. Furthermore, our heuristic consists of computing the k-nearest neighbors of objects already close to a pivot x_i. The rationale is that we can expect some kind of transitivity in the k-nearest neighbors relationship.

After computing the $n-1$ distances from x_i to the other $n-1$ objects in S, we obtain the set of distances: $\{d(x_i, x_1), d(x_i, x_2), d(x_i, x_3), \ldots, d(x_i, x_{n-1})\}$. The elements $\{x_1, x_2, x_3, \ldots, x_{n-1}\}$ are sorted by distance to x_i, resulting in the sequence of objects $x_{j_1}, x_{j_2}, \ldots, x_{j_{n-1}}$. The first k elements of this sequence, $x_{j_1}, x_{j_2}, \ldots, x_{j_k}$, are the k objects more similar to x_i, therefore their k-nearest neighbors, and at this time they can be reported.

Next, we calculate the k-NN of the objects $x_{j_i} \in S$ that do not have them yet. For this purpose, we consider solving the k-NN query by a range query with decreasing radius, and to use the known fact that the search is more efficient as we reduce the search radius quickly. Assuming, furthermore, that very close objects possibly share some of their closest neighbors with x_i. That is, it takes the first neighbor of x_i, which is x_{j_1}, and starts the computation of its k-NN by comparing it with the k-NN$(x_i)-\{x_{j_1}\}$. We notice that x_{j_1} already knows one distance; that is, its distance to x_i because of the simmetric property of d. In this way, by adding x_i to this group, we get the first k candidates for being its closest neighbors, and an initial covering radius, which is the distance of x_{j_1} to its furthest neighbor:

$$r_k(x_{j_1}) = \max\{d(x_{j_1}, x_i), d(x_{j_1}, x_{j_2}), \ldots, d(x_{j_1}, x_{j_k})\} \tag{1}$$

The knowledge acquired by x_i, when compared to all objects in the database, allows estimating the distances between x_{j_1} and the other elements in S using the triangular inequality. This estimate defines a lower bound of the actual distance between x_{j_1} and any other element of S; that is, how close an object x_j could be to x_{j_1}. Then, we sort database elements from highest to lowest estimation value.

By knowing the covering radius (Eq. 1) and the estimates of distances it is possible to discard some objects of S, avoiding its actual comparison with x_{j_1}. If the above lower bound is greater than the current radius enclosing the k candidates for k-NN(x_{j_1}); that is, $|d(x_j, x_i) - d(x_i, x_{j_1})| > r_k(x_{j_1})$, this object will be discarded because it will not be closer to x_{j_1} than the current neighbors. Otherwise, those objects x_j whose estimated distance is less than the current covering radius; that is, they satisfy $|d(x_j, x_i) - d(x_i, x_{j_1})| < r_k(x_{j_1})$, will be directly compared with x_{j_1}.

The elements that when they are compared with x_{j_1} verify $d(x_j, x_{j_1}) < r_k(x_{j_1})$; that is, their real distance is smaller than the covering radius, will become part of the k-NN(x_{j_1}), since they are closer than any of the present neighbors. Hence, the element whose distance was $r_k(x_{j_1})$, which is the current farthest one from x_{j_1}, will be discarded and it implies that the covering radius $r_k(x_{j_1})$ should be shrink. When we update the covering radius, reducing it, we also recheck to determine if we can discard some other objects. If the elements that remained as promising when they are directly compared with x_{j_1} verify $d(x_j, x_{j_1}) > r_k(x_{j_1})$, they must be discarded, since they are farther away than their neighbors current and cannot contribute to the set k-NN(x_{j_1}) or reduce the covering radius $r_k(x_{j_1})$.

When all the objects in S are reviewed, or when the next estimate distance analyzed is greater than the covering radius, the process end. At this time, all elements from S are not part of the k-NN. The above is true because we sorted objects in ascending order by their estimated distance, and if the object analyzed does not improve the neighbors that are already known for x_{j_1}, then no elements will ever enter the covering radius. At the end of this process, we report the k-NN(x_{j_1}), and it will be turn of the next unprocessed object in the list of x_i, until all the elements in the database are processed.

As the elements to which k-NN are calculated move away from x_i, the number of objects that can be discarded from the list of promising ones, using triangular inequality, will decrease; that is, the amount of elements to compare directly with x_{j_1} will increase. Therefore reducing the filtering ability of the pivot. But, as our goal is to reduce this number, at that time we must look for a new element helping in the remaining calculation of k-NN.

A parameter α helps us to decide when an object becomes useful in helping to discard candidates. Each time we finish the process of associating an object with its k-nearest neighbors, we check whether the element x_i used as support still produces a good discard. When an element x_i allows rejecting less than α elements, its discard capability is considered insufficient. Therefore, we must replace this element by another database object, which can discard a larger quantity of members from the list of promising elements. Then, we select a new object between the elements in S, this new x_i replace the old one. So, the necessary distances to the members of S are computed. Now this new x_i will be used to assist in the calculation of k-NN(x_{j_i}) for some x_{j_i}, while this x_i allows to discard more than α elements.

We try different ways to choose a new distinguished object, x_i. One heuristic is to select them randomly; this alternative only verifies that the chosen object has not been still associated with its k-NN. So, we calculate the $(n-1)$ distances to the remaining elements of S, obtain k-NN(x_i), and use x_i as support in the calculation of the neighbors of some closest objects. Another way to choose a new x_i is using the last object x_{j_i} to which we compute its k-NN. We call this alternative as *Latest*. This election considers that due to the low discard capacity of the current x_i, x_{j_i} had to be compared with most of the elements of S. Thus, we expect that some more comparisons reach the necessary $(n-1)$ to assist in the calculation of the k-NN of some x_j in the database.

In every alternative of selection proposed, we repeat the process until all the elements in S have their k-nearest neighbors. In this way, we have all the needed information to build the kNNG.

4   Experimental Results

To evaluate our proposals, we perform some experiments over different metric databases having widely different histograms of distances. For each database, we run the process over different database permutations. Besides, we test different values for the α parameter. First, we analyze the different alternatives of the proposal presented; that is, the two ways to select the objects used as support for the calculation of the k-NN (x_i). Then we contrast the most competitive option with known indexes of proven efficiency.

We consider a set of some real-life metric spaces, all of them with a low intrinsic dimension, and a set of some synthetic metric spaces, where we can control their intrinsic dimensionality.

The real-life metric spaces considered are:

NASA images: a set of 40,150 20-dimensional feature vectors, generated from images downloaded from NASA[1]. The Euclidean distance is used.

Strings: a dictionary of 69,069 English words. The distance is the *edit distance*; that is, the minimum number of character insertions, deletions and substitutions needed to make equal the two strings.

Color histograms: a set of 112,682 8-D color histograms (112-dimensional vectors) from an image database[2]. Any quadratic form can be used as a distance, so we chose Euclidean distance.

To analyze how intrinsic dimensionality affects the behavior of our approach, we evaluated it over synthetic metric spaces. We use collections of 100,000 vectors, uniformly distributed in the unit hypercube, in dimensions 4, 8, 12, 16, 20, 24, 28 and 32. We consider the vectors in these spaces as metric objects. Thus, we do not use the information on the coordinates of each vector explicitly. In these spaces, we also use Euclidean distance. All these metric databases are available from www.sisap.org [11].

We tested different values of the parameter α: $\frac{n}{10}$, $\frac{n}{5}$, $\frac{n}{4}$, $\frac{n}{3}$, and $\frac{n}{2}$. Moreover, we evaluate several values of the number k of nearest neighbors to be obtained: 1, 2, 5, 10, 50, and 100. Our performance meter is the number of computed distances, as discussed above. To summarize the results, we report the average number of distance computations for a database element, as the fraction of the database revised to compute the neighbors.

The Fig. 1 shows the costs of answering to *All-k-NN* in the space of NASA Images (Fig. 1(a)), Strings (Fig. 1(b)) and Color histograms (Fig. 1(c)), respectively. In this case, the x_i were randomly selected from the database. Each line represents the costs of obtaining k-nearest neighbors with a certain α. As it can be seen, better results are obtained when α is smaller (e.g. $\frac{n}{10}$). Possibly, in this case the distinguished objects x_i are not changed quickly and this allows reducing the number of distance calculations. However, as it can be noticed, all our alternatives need to perform much less than n distance evaluations in average by element. Therefore, the speedup obtained respect to the naïve solution is very significant.

It can be regarded from these results that for higher values of α. For example, if we consider $\alpha = \frac{n}{2}$, it is difficult to find an element able to discard one half of the database. Higher values of α cause replacing more frequently the distinguished element owing to it does not satisfy the discard quality. Consequently, the new candidate must calculate again its $(n-1)$ distances. Surprisingly, it do not occur in the String space, where the distance takes discrete values. In this case, all costs are very similar, no matter the value of α.

---

[1] At http://www.dimacs.rutgers.edu/Challenges/Sixth/software.html.
[2] At http://www.dbs.informatik.uni-muenchen.de/~seidl/DATA/histo112.112682.gz.

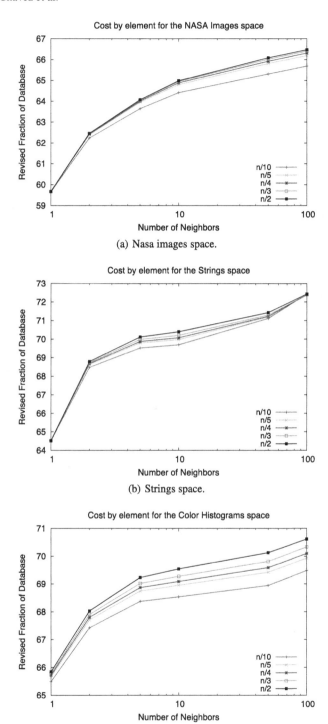

Fig. 1. Costs of *All-k*-NN in real spaces (random selection).

Please note that for around half of the database, the number of distinguished objects used is approximately half the k used for k-NN. That is, each distinguished element is useful for computing, on the average, the k-NN for two more objects, and then it loses its discard quality. When the process achieves the last database elements; that is, most of the objects already have their k-NN, the remaining objects to be used as distinguished elements are not so good to discard. Hence, we must replace them more quickly, increasing, in consequence, the number of distance calculations.

The Fig. 2 depicts the costs of answering to *All-k-NN* in the three real-life spaces, but in this experiments the x_i were choosen using the last object x_{j_i} to which we compute its k-NN. The Fig. 2(a) illustrates the results for the space of NASA images, the Fig. 2(b) for Strings, and the Fig. 2(c) for Color histograms. It should be noticed that, in this alternative, there are valid the same considerations made in the case of random choice: with small values of α, less distance comparisons are performed. The best results are obtained when we consider an $\alpha = \frac{n}{10}$. In this situation, for the distinguished object, it is also easier to discard small parts of the database, but it is not able to discard half of it, causing its frequent replacement. This behavior is held in these three spaces used.

Despite the expectations set in this strategy, the costs by each element are higher than those presented by the random selection version of the distinct elements. Experiments over the latest selection policy showed that, on average, distinguished objects only allow computing the neighbors of one more object. That is, it takes many more x_i to compute the k-nearest neighbors to all database elements. The distinct element must be continuously changed. Consequently, this strategy needs to perform more distance calculations to solve the problem. The degradation of this variant is due, probably, because the new object selected as a replacement is too close to the previous one distinguished object. Therefore, its "perspective" of space is not very different from that of the element it replaces. This similar perspective causes its discard capacity is also similar; that is, it is also reduced.

As discussed and empirically shown, the best strategy of the two evaluated alternatives is the random selection of the distinguished element. On the other hand, from the different values of α used in the experiments, those showing better performance were the lower ones considered; that is $\frac{n}{10}$ and $\frac{n}{5}$. Therefore, in the following sections, we only consider the selection as random. We evaluate this option with some well-known indexes to fairly compare its performance.

4.1 Comparison with Methods Using Indexes

Exact indexes belong to one of two families: Partition-based algorithms and Pivot-based algorithms. We compared the performance of our better technique with respect solutions that use representative indexes: List of Clusters [7], Distal SpatialApproximationn Trees [6], and a generic pivot index [8]. List of Clusters and Distal Spatial Approximation Trees belongs to Partition-based algorithms, and the other index is a generic representative of the Pivot-based family. All of them have their implementation available from www.sisap.org [11]. As the other methods considered need to build the index, and then perform the searches, we compute their costs considering both the construction cost and the search cost of all k-NN operations.

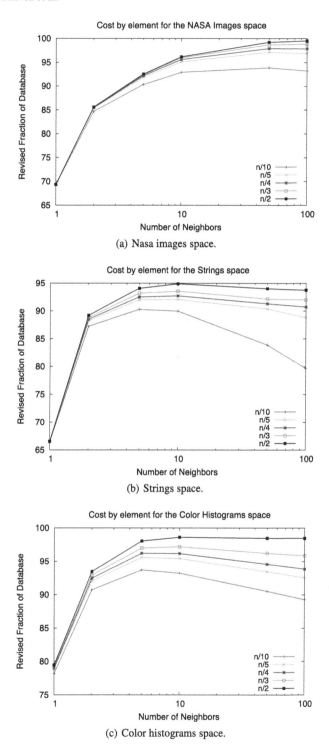

(a) Nasa images space.

(b) Strings space.

(c) Color histograms space.

Fig. 2. Costs of *All-k*-NN in real spaces (latest selection).

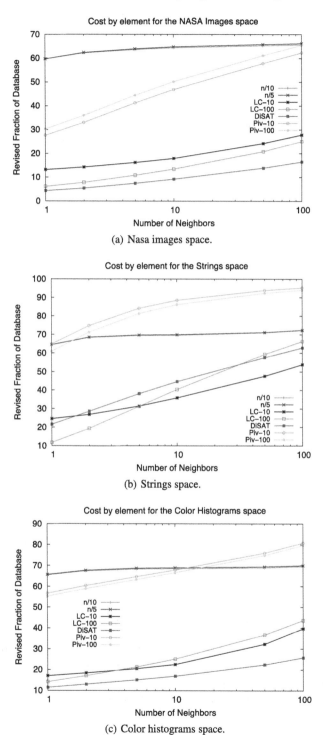

Fig. 3. Comparison of costs to solve *All-k*-NN on real spaces.

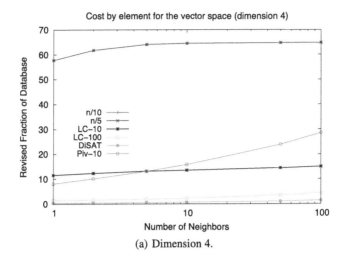

(a) Dimension 4.

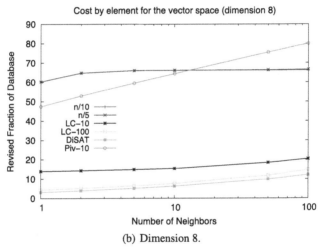

(b) Dimension 8.

Fig. 4. Comparison of costs to obtain *All-k*-NN in synthetic spaces, in dimensions 4 and 8.

The Fig. 3 illustrates the comparison of the costs of our proposal and the other considered indexes. The Fig. 3(a) shows the results for the space of NASA images, the Fig. 3(b) for Strings, and the Fig. 3(c) for Color histograms. We use LC for the List of Clusters, DiSAT for the Distal Spatial Approximation Trees, and Piv for the general pivot index, as names in the plots. In particular, the values for LC indicate the different cluster sizes used to build the index, and for Piv the number of pivots. We choose to show for each index its better alternatives. For our approach we use the better values of α empirically determined: $\frac{n}{10}$ and $\frac{n}{5}$. We label each α option with the corresponding value.

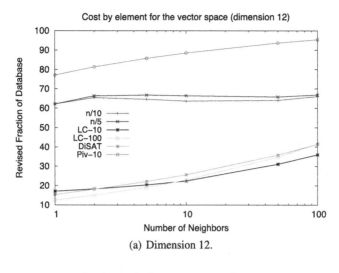

(a) Dimension 12.

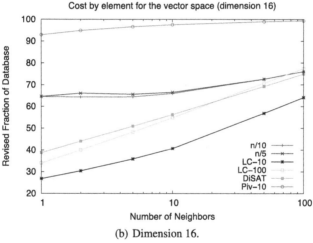

(b) Dimension 16.

Fig. 5. Comparison of costs to obtain *All-k-*NN in synthetic spaces, in dimensions 12 and 16.

In the Strings space, only the pivot-based index is more expensive than our method. The other indexes beat us for all the k values used. We only get closer to LC and DiSAT for $k = 100$. For the Nasa images space, our technique is surpassed by all indexes and for all the values of k. We guess that it is because this space has the lowest intrinsic dimensionality. Moreover, in the Color histograms space, we again beat the pivot index but only for $k > 10$. LC and DiSAT always are better than us. It is remarkable that despite the distance histograms for the three real-spaces considered are widely different, all of them have low intrinsic dimensionality [12].

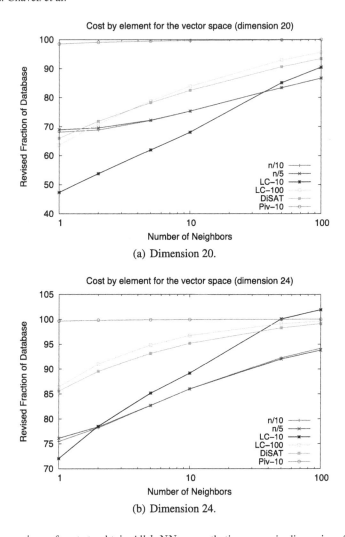

(a) Dimension 20.

(b) Dimension 24.

Fig. 6. Comparison of costs to obtain *All-k*-NN on synthetic spaces, in dimensions 20 and 24.

To analyze how intrinsic dimensionality affects the performance of our solution, we use a set of synthetic metric spaces. As we mentioned, we can manage the intrinsic dimensionality of these spaces. We consider spaces in dimension 4 (very low dimensionality) through dimension 32 (very high dimensionality).

The Figs. 4, 5, 6, and 7 depict the same experiments on the synthetic spaces, considering dimensions 4 and 8, 12 and 16, 20 and 24, and finally 28 and 32, respectively. As we can see, in low dimensions, the performance of our proposal is similar to those obtained on the real-life metric spaces. However, as the dimension grows, our proposal becomes better and better than the other alternatives. If we analyze the costs of the space in dimension 20, Fig. 6(a), we can observe that the LC index, with cluster size 10, is the only one that exceeds our proposal. For dimensions from 24 (Figs. 6(b), 7(a), and 7(b)), we can overcome all the other indexes, for almost all number of neighbors retrieved.

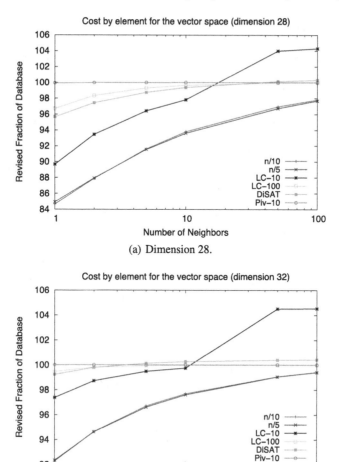

Fig. 7. Comparison of costs to obtain *All-k-*NN on synthetic spaces, in dimensions 28 and 32.

Although LC and DiSAT are indexes that have good behavior on medium to high dimensional metric space, they also degrade their performance when dimension is higher than 24. Hence, it is important to remark that our approach seems more resistant to the curse of dimensionality.

5   Conclusions

An extended version of determining the k-NN of an element, is to solve the *All-k-NN* problem. Solving this problem is useful, for example, to build the metric index named the k-nearest neighbors graph. To this moment, the only way to solve this problem, without using an auxiliary index, is via the naïve solution of comparing each database element with one other. In this paper, we propose and test two alternative approaches to solve this problem. One of them is very efficient concerning this naïve solution because it needs to compute a fraction of the n distance evaluations by element.

Our results are preliminary, although encouraging. We can say with confidence that, on low dimensional metric spaces, an index is a better solution than our proposal. However, in medium and high dimensional spaces, where the curse of dimensionality effect is evident, our approach is superior. Therefore, as the dimension grows, our proposal achieves a better performance than other alternatives to this problem.

As future work, we consider analyzing different options to select the unique elements or pivots for each process step, and characterize how this selection affects the method performance. We also plan to study how to take advantage of the available memory space to cache some distances computed avoiding recalculation.

References

1. Archip, N., Rohling, R., Cooperberg, P., Tahmasebpour, H., Warfield, S.K.: Spectral clustering algorithms for ultrasound image segmentation. In: Duncan, J.S., Gerig, G. (eds.) MICCAI 2005. LNCS, vol. 3750, pp. 862–869. Springer, Heidelberg (2005). https://doi.org/10.1007/11566489_106
2. Baeza-Yates, R., Hurtado, C., Mendoza, M.: Query clustering for boosting web page ranking. In: Favela, J., Menasalvas, E., Chávez, E. (eds.) AWIC 2004. LNCS (LNAI), vol. 3034, pp. 164–175. Springer, Heidelberg (2004). https://doi.org/10.1007/978-3-540-24681-7_19
3. Brito, M., Chávez, E., Quiroz, A., Yukich, J.: Connectivity of the mutual k-nearest neighbor graph in clustering and outlier detection. Stat. Probab. Lett. **35**(4), 33–42 (1996)
4. Callahan, P., Kosaraju, R.: A decomposition of multidimensional point sets with applications to k nearest neighbors and n body potential fields. JACM **42**(1), 67–90 (1995)
5. Chávez, E., Ludueña, V., Reyes, N.: Solving all-k-nearest neighbor problem without an index. In: Procs. del XXV Congreso Argentino de Ciencias de la Computación (CACIC 2019), pp. 567–576. UniRío editora (2019)
6. Chávez, E., Ludueña, V., Reyes, N., Roggero, P.: Faster proximity searching with the distal sat. Inf. Syst. **59**, 15–47 (2016)
7. Chávez, E., Navarro, G.: A compact space decomposition for effective metric indexing. Pattern Recogn. Lett. **26**(9), 1363–1376 (2005)
8. Chávez, E., Navarro, G., Baeza-Yates, R., Marroquín, J.: Searching in metric spaces. ACM Comput. Surv. **33**(3), 273–321 (2001)
9. Duda, R., Hart, P.: Pattern Classification and Scene Analysis. Wiley, New York (1973)
10. Eppstein, D., Erickson, J.: Iterated nearest neighbors and finding minimal polytopes. Int. J. Math. Comput. Sci. **11–3**, 321–350 (1994)

11. Figueroa, K., Navarro, G., Chávez, E.: Metric spaces library (2007). http://www.sisap.org/Metric_Space_Library.html
12. Navarro, G., Paredes, R., Reyes, N., Bustos, C.: An empirical evaluation of intrinsic dimension estimators. Inf. Syst. **64**, 206–218 (2017)
13. Paredes, R.: Graphs for Metric Space Searching. Ph.D. thesis, University of Chile, Chile, July 2008
14. Paredes, R., Chávez, E., Figueroa, K., Navarro, G.: Practical construction of k-nearest neighbor graphs in metric spaces. In: Àlvarez, C., Serna, M. (eds.) WEA 2006. LNCS, vol. 4007, pp. 85–97. Springer, Heidelberg (2006). https://doi.org/10.1007/11764298_8
15. Rubinstein, A.: Hardness of approximate nearest neighbor search. In: Proceedings of the 50th Annual ACM SIGACT Symposium on Theory of Computing, pp. 1260–1268. ACM (2018)

MeTree: A Metric Spatial Index

Adrián Planas[1], Andrés Pascal[1]([⊠]) [iD], and Norma Herrera[2]

[1] UTN-FRCU, Concepción del Uruguay, Argentina
pladnic@gmail.com, andrespascal2003@yahoo.com.ar
[2] UNSL-Departamento de Informática, San Luis, Argentina
nherrera@unsl.edu.ar

Abstract. Metric Spaces model databases allowing similarity searching. e.g., looking for objects similar to a given one. Spatial databases are used to store and efficiently retrieve data with some spatial attribute. Some applications need to search both by similarity and space at the same time. This kind of queries cannot be solved efficiently using spatial o metric indexes separately. Recently, Metric Spatial queries were formalized and a new access method, the MeTree, was proposed to solve them. In this article, we present new experiments that show the performance of this index.

Keywords: Metric spatial queries · Similarity searching · Metric index · Spatial index

1 Introduction

In the last three decades, databases have gradually incorporated the ability to store unstructured data types such as images, sound, text, video, geometric elements, etc. The problem of storage and search these objects differs markedly from structured types of classic databases. These types of data do not have a fixed length, therefore they are more difficult to organize within a structure; normally they cannot be ordered, and exact searching has no utility in this area. In this context new database models have emerged to effectively and efficiently covering the storage and searching needs of these applications. These models include spatial databases, which allow keeping a record of the location of an object in an n-dimensional space, and metric spaces, which constitute a generic model that allows similarity searching.

The goal of similarity searching [1] is to find objects with similar characteristics to one given under certain criteria. This kind of functionality has been used in many areas of computing. For example, in pattern recognition similarity queries can be used to classify new objects according to already classified nearby objects; in recommendation systems they can be used to generate personalized recommendations; in image databases they can be used for content searching.

Since the data types of these systems can vary considerably (images, strings, protein sequences, sound, free text, etc.), it is desirable to have a generic model that encompasses them, and that allows different distance functions. In this aspect, the most used model is Metric Spaces, which allows any similarity function that meets certain properties.

© Springer Nature Switzerland AG 2020
P. Pesado and M. Arroyo (Eds.): CACIC 2019, CCIS 1184, pp. 250–261, 2020.
https://doi.org/10.1007/978-3-030-48325-8_17

A metric space is a pair (U, d) where U is a universe of objects and $d: UxU \rightarrow R+$ is a distance function defined between the elements of U, measuring the similarity (dissimilarity, actually) between them; i.e., the closer the objects are, the similar they are. This function d complies with the characteristic properties of a metric function:

(a) $\forall x, y \in U, d(x, y) \geq 0$ (positivity)
(b) $\forall x, y \in U, d(x, y) = d(y, x)$ (simetry)
(c) $\forall x \in U, d(x, x) = 0$ (reflexivity)
(d) $\forall x, y, z \in U, d(x, y) \leq d(x, z) + d(z, y)$ (triangle inequality)

This last property, triangle inequality, is the most important to discard items during the search. The database then, will be a finite subset $X \in U$ of cardinality n. One of the typical queries in this model is searching by range, which is denoted by $(q, r)_d$. Given an element $q \in U$ that we will call query and a radius of tolerance r, a search by range consists of retrieving all the objects of X that are at most r from q, that is:

$$(q, r)_d = \{x \in X / d(q, x) \leq r\}$$

On the other hand, the spatial model has significantly increased its use since the 90's, mainly as a support for Geographic Information Systems (GIS). With the growth of Internet, the number of objects that have a spatial location has increased exponentially. For example, mobile devices have enabled the generation of huge amounts of geo-referenced data that is shared over the Web, e.g., photos with location.

Spatial databases are made up of structured information which geometric objects added: points, polylines or polygons, under a predefined reference system. Such databases can contain hundreds of thousands or millions of these objects on which queries are performed with operations such as intersection, adjacency, inclusion and many others. Such operations are usually computationally expensive, so access methods are required to greatly decrease the number of comparisons required to solve a query.

There are applications in which is interesting to search for similarity but also taking into account a spatial component. Typical cases are GIS, where elements with spatial location in many cases need to be consulted also for similarity. For example, on a map with photos of widely known buildings and constructions, it would be of interest, given an image of a building, to find similar images within a particular geographic area. Or instead of an image, simply search by similarity the name of the point of interest closest to the present location, since sometimes it is not known how it is well written. These queries involve a search that needs both spatial and metric aspects. The second example is very common when using Global Positioning Systems (GPS). A particular case of this problem, searching for geographic documents, has been previously studied giving rise to indexes such as the IR-Tree [2], but that are designed only to work on documents and they are not suitable for other kind of objects.

While these queries can be solved using spatial and metric indices separately, it is more efficient to have access methods that are specifically designed to solve them. This article shows new experiment results of the MeTree access method presented previously in CACIC conference [3], and it is organized as follows. Section 2 presents a brief summary of related work. In Sects. 3 and 4 the problem of metric-spatial queries is defined and MeTree is descripted. In Sect. 5 new experimental evaluation is presented, and finally conclusions and future work are shown in Sect. 6.

2 Related Work

This section summarizes the most important developments about metric and spatial access methods.

2.1 Metric Indexes

There are several access methods designed to speed up the search for similarity in generic metric spaces. In general, they can be classified into two categories: methods based on compact partitions [4–7] and methods based on pivots [8–11]. The firsts divide the space into regions represented by centers and try to discard the regions far from the object being queried. While pivot-based ones store pre-calculated distances of each object to pivots and use them for the same purpose. In both cases, triangle inequality is used to reduce the number of elements to be compared with the query. In general, pivot-based methods perform better in terms of query performance.

Within compact partition-based methods, BST [12, 13] is a recursively constructed binary tree that use a center with a radius of coverage to represent each partition. GHT [14] uses two centers for each node in the tree and groups the elements according to the center closest to each one. GNAT [15] is a generalization of GHT. It uses Voronoi partitions to split the space in groups. EGNAT [16] is a dynamic version of this last. SAT [17] uses a complementary model to the Voronoi diagrams, the Delaunay graphs. There is also a dynamic extension for SAT [18], and a variation for secondary memory [19]. M-tree [5] is a balanced tree optimized for secondary memory, which arises as a natural adaptation of the family of B-Trees to many dimensions. There are several variants of the M-Tree, such as Slim-Tree [7], DBM-Tree [20] and CM-Tree [21]. D-index [6] is a structure that uses a hash function to map objects into buckets. LC [4] uses a list of clusters that improves search efficiency at the cost of making its construction less efficient. BP [22] is an unbalanced tree designed for high dimensional metric spaces.

About pivot-based methods, AESA [23] uses a table that records all the distances between the objects in the database. To reduce the size of that table, different variants have been proposed. For example, LAESA [10] only saves distances to a set of selected pivots. EP [24] selects a set of pivots without redundancy, which cover the entire database. Clustered Pivot-Table [25] groups pre-calculated distances to further improve search efficiency. The BKT [8] was one of the first pivot-based metric indices, and is designed for discrete distances. It is a tree where each node contains a different pivot and all the elements that are at the same distance of this, are located on the same child node. The FQT [26] is similar to the BKT, but uses the same pivot for all nodes at the same level, reducing the number of comparisons between the query and the pivots. VPT [11] is a binary tree designed for continuous distances and its r-ary version is MVPT [27].

There are also hybrid methods that combine compact partitions with pivots, e.g., PM-Tree [28], which uses pivots on regions defined by an M-Tree, or the M-Index [29], which groups objects using pre-calculated distances to its closest pivots.

2.2 Spatial Indexes

Spatial query processing involves executing complex and expensive geometric operations. Considering that spatial databases usually contain large amounts of geometric objects, performing a sequential search to solve a spatial query is not a practical solution in most cases, so in real applications the use of spatial indexes is required.

Spatial access methods can also be classified into two categories [30]: space-driven structures, and data-driven structures. The firsts are based on partitioning a 2D space into rectangular regions. Objects are mapped into regions according to some geometric criteria. In the second case, partitions are based on the distribution of the set of objects being indexed.

The Grid File [31] divides the space into fixed cells to index points. Each cell is associated with a disk page, where the objects contained in that cell are sequentially stored. If the cell fills up, it splits in two. There are variants to index rectangles. QuadTree [32] subdivides the plane into four quadrants of the same size, and performs this same operation on each quadrant, resulting in a 4-ary tree. Each node represents all the objects contained in its quadrant. QuadTree has been widely used for both spatial search and various image processing tasks. Bittree Quadtree (BQ-Tree) [33] is a variant designed for large-scale geospatial data. K-D-Tree [34] stores k-dimensional points by subdividing the space alternatively into parallelepiped rectangles orthogonal to each coordinate axis. There is a family of methods called "Space Filling Curve", which are based on functions that transform an n-dimensional space into a single dimension, preserving certain proximity properties. An example of this is the Hilbert Space Filling Curve [35].

Regarding data-driven methods, the most important are the family of R-Tree indexes [36], which constitute a generalization of the B-Tree to two or more dimensions. They are M-ary trees of rectangles where each node spatially contains all the elements of the corresponding sub-tree. This tree is balanced and each interior node except the root contains between m and M children and is stored on a disk page. They are the most commonly used spatial indexes in commercial database engines.

3 Metric Spatial Model

This new model [3] allows the design of access methods that solve efficiently queries with spatial and similarity requirements. Applications where metric-spatial queries make sense have the following characteristics:

- Exact searching cannot be performed on objects: the elements of the database do not have an identifier (or a group of attributes) that can be used as a search key.
- Objects have a spatial location (and/or shape).
- The results of a query must satisfy both similarity and spatial requirements.

- The database contains a large number of objects, or the response time to a query must be short enough that is not possible to perform a sequential search.

Let U be the universe of valid objects, the Metric-Spatial model is defined by the pair (U, d), where for all $o \in U$, the function $s(o) \in S$ returns the metric component of the object (a string, image, sound, text, etc.) and $e(o) \in E$ its spatial aspect (usually a point, line or polygon). The metric function d, is the measure of dissimilarity and is defined as $d: SxS \rightarrow R+$. A query by metric range and spatial intersection, is denoted then, by the 3-upla $(q, r, g)_d$ and is formally defined as follows:

$$(q, r, g)_d = \{o \in X/d(s(o), q) \leq r \wedge \mathit{intersects}(e(o), g)\}$$

where $X \in U$ is the database, q is the metric aspect of the query, r is the search radius that represents the maximum value of accepted dissimilarity, and g is its geometric aspect (point, polyline or polygon).

A trivial way to solve a metric-spatial query is to use two indexes, one of them metric and the other spatial. Then, for a query $(q, r, g)_d$, we proceed as follows:

1. Perform the search $(q, r)_d$ by similarity on the metric index and return the set L as result,
2. Search for the elements that intersect g using the spatial index, returning the set M as result,
3. Finally, perform the intersection $L \cap M$ to obtain the final result.

From now on we will call it *Trivial Solution*. The disadvantage of this solution is that it does not take advantage of the metric and spatial information at the same time to discard elements. A better strategy is to design an index that integrates both aspects and that allows metric, spatial and metric-spatial queries.

4   MeTree: A Metric Spatial Access Method

MeTree combines a variant of the FQT metric index (which allows continuous distances and where all the leaves are at the same level) and R-Tree family of spatial indexes. MeTree is an r-ary tree in which each node has a rectangle that spatially contains all its children, just like the R-Tree. But in addition, each node has a metric interval that represents the minimum and maximum value of the distances of all the elements of the subtree to the pivot corresponding to the node level (like a FQT). The height of the tree is fixed in principle, and it is determined by the number of pivots of the index. However, this number can be extended at any time adding new pivots and therefore new levels. A tree leaf will contain pointers to similar objects that are also spatially close.

A major problem is that similar elements could be very far spatially. In the lower levels of the tree, this situation would produce rectangles too large, reducing the efficiency of the index. To solve this problem, restrictions were established to allow two elements to belong to the same leaf. Besides, metric intervals of sibling nodes are not exclusive.

An inner node of the MeTree is a 3-upla *(i_m, f_m, rect)*, where $i_m.f_m$ is the metric interval and *rect* is the rectangle that spatially contains all the children of that node. In turn, each level of the tree (except the root) has an associated pivot.

An example of the structure of a MeTree is presented in Fig. 1. The tree nodes and the metric intervals of each node are shown in the upper part, according to the distances of the elements to the pivot of each level. For readability reasons, the rectangles of each node are shown separately, at the bottom of the figure. As you can see, there can be overlap both between metric intervals of the sibling nodes and between rectangles that represent the space they occupy.

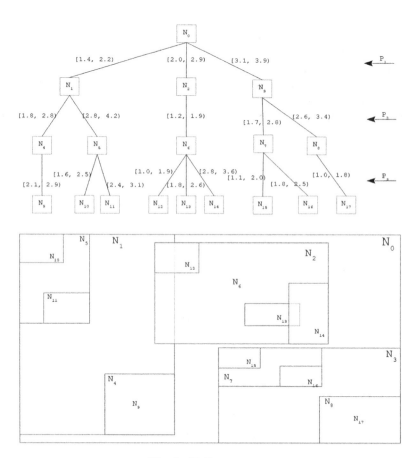

Fig. 1. MeTree structure

An insertion is done as follows. Let *o* be the object to insert and p_n the pivot corresponding to level *n*, the cost of adding the object to each of the child nodes of the current node is calculated, and the minimum is obtained. If this cost is less than *infinite*, the object is added to the minimum cost child, and otherwise a new child is added. The cost is calculated as the weighted sum of the metric cost and the spatial cost. The metric cost is zero if $i_m \leq d(s(o), p_n) \leq f_m$, i.e., if the distance from the object to the pivot of the level is within the node's metric range. Otherwise it is equal to the smallest increment of the interval, necessary to include $d(s(o), p_n)$. If the increased interval is greater than the maximum size allowed, the cost is *infinite*. A similar procedure is used to calculate the spatial cost. If the spatial aspect of the object to be inserted is located inside the rectangle of the node, the cost is zero. To calculate the cost of increasing the rectangle to include the object, the necessary increase in its diagonal is calculated, and if it is greater than a maximum value, it is again considered *infinite*. When an element is added to an existing node, both its metric range and its rectangle can increase in size. The maximum size of the metric intervals is a parameter set in advance. In the case of rectangles, the maximum diagonal depends on the level of the node. The root contains the entire space where the elements can exist. At each level the maximum diagonal is half the diagonal of the parent level. In other words, the sizes decrease logarithmically.

When performing a metric-spatial $(q, r, g)_d$, the nodes that meet the conditions $im-r \leq d(q, p_n) \leq fm + r$ and *intersects(g, rect)* are visited until reaching the leaves, obtaining a set of candidates. This set is then traversed sequentially and the elements are compared with the query to obtain the final result. Figure 2 shows the pseudocode of the searching algorithm.

```
MeTreeSearch(q, r, g)
  nodes2visit:=childrenOf(root)
  level:=1
  WHILE |nodes2visit|>0 AND level<=MaxLevel:
    children:=[]
    dist:=metricDistance(q, pivotOf(level))
    FOR node IN nodes2visit:
      FOR child IN childsOf(node):
        IF (dist BETWEEN child.im-r AND child.fm+r):
          IF intersects(g, child.rect):
            children.add(child)
    nodes2visit:= children
    level+= 1

  results:=[]
  FOR leaf IN nodes2visit:
    elements:=elementsOf(leaf)
    FOR elem IN elements:
      dist:= metricDistance(q, s(elem))
      IF (dist<=r) AND (intersects(g, e(elem))):
        results.add(e)
  Return results
```

Fig. 2. Similarity-spatial searching using a MeTree

This mechanism takes advantage of both the metric and spatial aspects to discard tree branches, which increases significantly the efficiency, compared to the trivial solution.

5 Experimental Evaluation

In [3], preliminary results over a 1514 elements database were shown. In this article new experiments on a bigger database are presented, showing variations of performance when size of the database and number of pivots of the tree is changed.

MeTree was tested on a GIS database of 20,000 points of interest (POI) corresponding to the Autonomous City of Buenos Aires. Some of them were randomly generated and the others are real POIs. Similarity queries were carried out on the names of the POIs, using Levenshtein distance as metric function and their geographical location (points) as spatial aspect. 100 range-intersection-queries consisting of strings, random radii, and polygons of different sizes and shapes were defined. 10 elements from the database were chosen at random to be used as pivots, and the maximum size of the metric intervals was set.

These queries were executed using the *Trivial Solution* outlined in Sect. 3 and the MeTree. Their results were compared for different numbers of elements: 5000, 10000, 15000 and 20000, and different numbers of pivots: 2, 4, 6, 8 and 10. Since both metric distance function and intersection operation are usually expensive, performance was measured as the number of those operations needed to solve each query.

First, we compare the efficiency of the MeTree against the trivial solution for 20,000 elements and 10 pivots. Results for the 100 queries are illustrated in Fig. 3. Average query cost using MeTree was around 15% of cost of the Trivial Solution. This is because this new method uses both spatial and metric aspect to discard elements at the same time. If a query has a wide metric range but a small rectangle, many elements are discarded by the spatial aspect. In the same way, if a query has a small metric range but a big rectangle, elements will be removed from the candidates by the metric aspect. The average cost for the 100 queries was 1,486.44 for the MeTree, and 10,237.29 for the trivial solution.

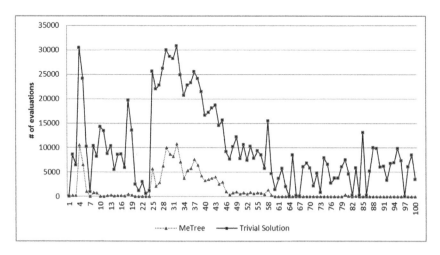

Fig. 3. Cost of MeTree and Trivial Solution for 100 queries.

The second experiment was testing the effects of the number of elements in the database over the performance. Figure 4 shows the increase of the average cost of both methods for 5,000, 10,000, 15,000 and 20,000 objects. As observed, both curves seem to have a linear behavior, but the slope of our method is significantly less than the trivial solution. This means that the more elements exist in the database, the greater the difference in efficiency.

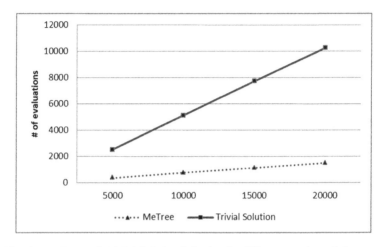

Fig. 4. MeTree and Trivial Solution behavior for different number of elements.

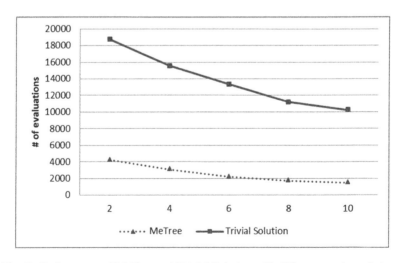

Fig. 5. Performance of MeTree and Trivial Solution with different number of pivots

Finally, the effectiveness of the number of pivots was investigated. Figure 5 shows the decreasing of the cost when more pivots are added to the tree. Increasing the number of them, has a significant good impact on the performance of the queries, but requires much more storage space. In the biggest tree tested (10 levels), the number of nodes was around 113,000. It is known that pivot selection methods are critical to choose a good set of pivots, but that is beyond the scope of this article, in particular because for this problem they must be adapted to include as a criterion also the spatial aspect.

Although the results are promising, more experiments are needed to provide greater detail and confidence about the behavior of the index under different situations and with greater number of data.

6 Conclusions and Future Work

In this work, we show the metric-spatial model and MeTree access method, which solves generic queries with similarity and spatial constraints at the same time, and we present results of new experiments that show its performance under different situations. In all cases the MeTree significantly exceeded the efficiency of the Trivial Solution.

This index can be used too, to perform separates similarity searches or spatial searches as well, although further studies are required to determine its efficiency for those cases.

6.1 Future Work

Some important tasks left to do are:

1. Calculate the temporal complexity of the method in an analytical way, a topic we are currently working on.
2. Carry out experiments with other types of data (images, for example), with more complex distance functions and a greater amount of data (we are preparing a database of around a million of elements).
3. Analyze and improve the insertion procedure, to decrease the size of rectangles and metric intervals, and reduce the overlaping.
4. Design pivot selection methods including both metric and spatial aspects as criteria.

References

1. Chávez, E., Navarro, G., Baeza-Yates, R., Marroquín, J.L.: Searching in metric spaces. ACM Comput. Surv. **33**(3), 273–321 (2001)
2. Li, Z., Lee, K.C.K., Zheng, B., Lee, W.-C., Lee, D.L., Wang, X.: IR-tree: an efficient index for geographic document search. IEEE Trans. Knowl. Data Eng. **23**, 585–599 (2011)
3. Planas, A., Pascal, A., Herrera, N.: Consultas Métrico Espaciales. XXV Congreso Argentino de Ciencias de la Computación. Universidad Nacional de Río Cuarto (2019)
4. Chavez, E., Navarro, G.: A compact space decomposition for effective metric indexing. Pattern Recogn. Lett. **26**(9), 1363–1376 (2005)
5. Ciaccia, P., Patella, M., Zezula, P.: M-tree: an efficient access method for similarity search in metric spaces. In: VLDB, pp. 426–435 (1997)

6. Dohnal, V., Gennaro, C., Savino, P., Zezula, P.: D-index: distance searching index for metric data sets. Multimedia Tools Appl. **21**(1), 9–33 (2003). https://doi.org/10.1023/A:1025026030880

7. Traina, C., Traina, A., Seeger, B., Faloutsos, C.: Slim-trees: high performance metric trees minimizing overlap between nodes. In: Zaniolo, C., Lockemann, P.C., Scholl, M.H., Grust, T. (eds.) EDBT 2000. LNCS, vol. 1777, pp. 51–65. Springer, Heidelberg (2000). https://doi.org/10.1007/3-540-46439-5_4

8. Burkhard, W., Keller, R.: Some approaches to best-match file searching. Commun. ACM **16**(4), 230–236 (1973)

9. Traina, C., Filho, R.F.S., Traina, A.J.M., et al.: The Omni-family of all-purpose access methods: a simple and effective way to make similarity search more efficient. VLDB J. **16**(4), 483–505 (2007). https://doi.org/10.1007/s00778-005-0178-0

10. Mico, L., Oncina, J., Carrasco, R.C.: A fast branch & bound nearest neighbour classifier in metric spaces. Pattern Recogn. Lett. **17**(7), 731–739 (1996)

11. Yianilos, P.N.: Data structures and algorithms for nearest neighbor search in general metric spaces. In: SODA, pp. 311–321 (1993)

12. Kalantari, I., McDonald, G.: A data structure and an algorithm for the nearest point problem. IEEE Trans. Software Eng. **9**(5), 631–634 (1983)

13. Noltemeier, H., Verbarg, K., Zirkelbach, C.: Monotonous Bisector* Trees—a tool for efficient partitioning of complex scenes of geometric objects. In: Monien, B., Ottmann, T. (eds.) Data structures and efficient algorithms. LNCS, vol. 594, pp. 186–203. Springer, Heidelberg (1992). https://doi.org/10.1007/3-540-55488-2_27

14. Uhlmann, J.K.: Satisfying general proximity/similarity queries with metric trees. Inf. Process. Lett. **40**(4), 175–179 (1991)

15. Brin, S.: Near neighbor search in large metric spaces. In: VLDB, pp. 574–584 (1995)

16. Navarro, G., Paredes, R.U.: Fully dynamic metric access methods based on hyperplane partitioning. Inf. Syst. **36**(4), 734–747 (2011)

17. Navarro, G.: Searching in metric spaces by spatial approximation. VLDB J. **11**(1), 28–46 (2002). https://doi.org/10.1007/s007780200060

18. Britos, L., Printista, A.M., Reyes, N.: *DSACL+-tree*: a dynamic data structure for similarity search in secondary memory. In: Navarro, G., Pestov, V. (eds.) SISAP 2012. LNCS, vol. 7404, pp. 116–131. Springer, Heidelberg (2012). https://doi.org/10.1007/978-3-642-32153-5_9

19. Navarro, G., Reyes, N.: Dynamic spatial approximation trees for massive data. In: SISAP, pp. 81–88 (2009)

20. Vieira, M.R., Traina, C., Jr., Chino, F.J.T., Traina, A.J.M.: DBM-tree: a dynamic metric access method sensitive to local density data. J. Inf. Data Manage. **1**(1), 111–128 (2010)

21. Aronovich, L., Spiegler, I.: CM-tree: a dynamic clustered index for similarity search in metric databases. Data Knowl. Eng. **63**(3), 919–946 (2007)

22. Almeida, J., Torres, R.D.S., Leite, N.J.: BP-tree: an efficient index for similarity search in high-dimensional metric spaces. In: CIKM, pp. 1365–1368 (2010)

23. Vidal, E.: An algorithm for finding nearest neighbors in (approximately) constant average time. Pattern Recogn. Lett. **4**(3), 145–157 (1986)

24. Ruiz, G., Santoyo, F., Chávez, E., Figueroa, K., Tellez, E.S.: Extreme pivots for faster metric indexes. In: Brisaboa, N., Pedreira, O., Zezula, P. (eds.) SISAP 2013. LNCS, vol. 8199, pp. 115–126. Springer, Heidelberg (2013). https://doi.org/10.1007/978-3-642-41062-8_12

25. Mosko, J., Lokoc, J., Skopal, T.: Clustered pivot tables for I/O optimized similarity search. In: SISAP, pp. 17–24 (2011)

26. Baeza-Yates, R., Cunto, W., Manber, U., Wu, S.: Proximity matching using fixed-queries trees. In: Crochemore, M., Gusfield, D. (eds.) CPM 1994. LNCS, vol. 807, pp. 198–212. Springer, Heidelberg (1994). https://doi.org/10.1007/3-540-58094-8_18

27. Bozkaya, T., Ozsoyoglu, M.: Distance-based indexing for high dimensional metric spaces. In: SIGMOD, pp. 357–368 (1997)

28. Skopal, T., Pokorny, J., Snasel, V.: PM-tree: pivoting metric tree for similarity search in multimedia databases. In: ADBIS, pp. 803–815 (2004)

29. Novak, D., Batko, M., Zezula, P.: Metric Index: an efficient and scalable solution for precise and approximate similarity search. Inf. Syst. 36(4), 721–733 (2011)

30. Rigaux, P., Scholl, M., Voisard, A.: 6 - Spatial Access Methods. In: Spatial Databases, pp 201–266. Morgan Kaufmann, San Francisco (2002)

31. Nievergelt, J., Hinterberger, H., Sevcik, K.C.: The grid file: an adaptable, symmetric multikey file structure. ACM Trans. Database Syst. 9(1), 38–71 (1984)

32. Finkel, R.A., Bentley, J.L.: Quad trees a data structure for retrieval on composite keys. Acta Informatica 4, 1–9 (1974). https://doi.org/10.1007/BF00288933

33. Zhang, J., You, S., Gruenwald, L.: Parallel quadtree coding of large-scale raster geospatial data on GPGPUs. In: Proceedings of the 19th ACM SIGSPATIAL International Conference on Advances in Geographic Information Systems, pp. 457–460. ACM, New York (2011)

34. Bentley, J.L.: Multidimensional binary search trees used for associative searching. Commun. ACM 18(9), 509–517 (1975)

35. Castro, J., Burns, S.: Online data visualization of multidimensional databases using the Hilbert space–filling curve. In: Lévy, P.P., Le Grand, B., Poulet, F., Soto, M., Darago, L., Toubiana, L., Vibert, J.-F. (eds.) VIEW 2006. LNCS, vol. 4370, pp. 92–109. Springer, Heidelberg (2007). https://doi.org/10.1007/978-3-540-71027-1_9

36. Guttman, A.: R-trees: a dynamic index structure for spatial searching. SIGMOD Rec. 14(2), 47–57 (1984)

Hardware Architectures, Networks and Operating Systems

Study of Video Traffic in IPv6 Multicast IEEE 802.11ac Test Bed

Santiago Pérez[1](✉) ⓘ, Higinio Facchini[1], Alejandro Dantiacq[1],
Gabriel Quiroga Salomón[1,2], Fabián Hidalgo[1], Gastón Cangemi[1],
Mauricio Muñoz[1], and Adrián Cárdenas[1]

[1] CeReCoN – Department of Electronics – Regional Mendoza, National
Technological University, Rodríguez 273, M5502AJE Mendoza, Argentina
santiagocp@frm.utn.edu.ar
[2] Department of ICT, National University of Chilecito, 9 de Julio 22,
5360 Chilecito, La Rioja, Argentina
hgquiroga@undec.edu.ar

Abstract. The increasing number of multimedia users on networks entails an exponential growth in the demand for bandwidth. End users and applications pose increasing demands on Traffic Engineering, QoS and QoE of video-based products. This paper reports an experimental study of multicast video traffic in an actual laboratory network, in a controlled environment, as a testbed, with IEEE 802.11ac IPv6 wireless clients. Experiments were conducted using a Star Trek movie trailer. Alternatively, for contrast purposes, a video of equal length taken from a video conference on Adobe Connect was used. The videos were coded using H.264, H.265, VP8 and Theora. This study is the sequel to an earlier experimental study conducted on video traffic for wired networks. The main conclusions seek to guide and help simulation analysts, network administrators, designers and planners in determining the best settings to take into account in order to properly manage similar networks, efficiently using available resources without compromising the expected quality and performance levels.

Keywords: Multicast traffic · Codecs · IEEE 802.11ac · IPv6 networks

1 Introduction

Video traffic has grown exponentially in the last few years, especially as a result of new mobile device applications. According to Cisco [1], by 2021, smartphone data traffic will surpass PC data traffic, bandwidth speeds will almost double those in 2016, video traffic will account for 82% of total IP traffic, and Internet video and Video on Demand (VoD) will continue to grow. Additionally, IEEE 802.11 (Wi-Fi) networks are currently the most used points of access to networks and services in most of the usual areas, including video traffic.

However, for video traffic applications, bandwidth availability in Wi-Fi networks as well as the availability of other shared resources need to be taken into account. Wi-Fi networks have improved their service with the adoption of new sets of standards, such as IEEE 802.11n and IEEE 802.11ac. IPv6 multicast traffic in these networks is a convenient way to reduce the impact of a video being streamed simultaneously to a

P. Pesado and M. Arroyo (Eds.): CACIC 2019, CCIS 1184, pp. 265–282, 2020.
https://doi.org/10.1007/978-3-030-48325-8_18

group of users, thus saving network resources by having a single data flow for all receivers. This issue proves very relevant since the traffic of each video flow may be, in proportion, the largest network load when compared to other traffic flows, such as voice traffic, best-effort delivery or background delivery. Furthermore, when analyzing multimedia priority traffic and real-time traffic, video and voice traffic are not alike. The quantification of the load introduced by voice over IP (VoIP) inside the network is deterministic. Quantifying video traffic is a more complex task, one that is specifically dependent on the video in question. Finally, video compression serves as another valuable means to reduce video traffic load. The variety of available codecs makes for differences with one another. They all continue to show increasingly better services and continue to evolve over time. In this scenario, comparing and knowing about codecs in connection with video traffic compression becomes very important, as well as assessing its impact on network load.

This paper describes an experimental study on multicast video traffic as performed on an actual laboratory network used as a testbed. To that end, a new topology of wired and wireless networks was used, featuring IEEE 802.11ac wireless clients, IPv6 protocol, FFmpeg Server and Client software as video server and clients, and WireShark traffic analysis tool. Video traffic was then coded using H.264, H.265, VP8 and Theora, with the goal of assessing, comparing and understanding their impact. The experiments were conducted using a Star Trek film video trailer and, for contrast purposes, a video from a video conference on Adobe Connect, both of the same length and resolution. The experiences correspond to specific cases of pre-recorded, low-demand videos. This study is the continuation of a series of similar experiments conducted on IPv4 wired networks.

The main contributions of this study include: (i) showing, on the basis of detailed direct quantitative data and averages, that the values for the analyzed performance metrics are those expected for the behavior of multicast video traffic, and that they depend on the characteristics of the streamed video and, to a lesser extent, on the video codec that is being used; and (ii) specifying a new testbed comprising eight experimental sub-scenarios (changing the video and codec being tested), as well as a new methodology that uses comparative mechanisms to determine the differences among the sub-scenarios.

The rest of this document is structured as follows: Sect. 2 analyzes the State of the Art; Sect. 3, Scenarios and Experimental Resources, describes the topology and tools that were used; Sect. 4, Results, shows the main results arising from this study; and Sect. 5, Conclusions, covers the main conclusions and contributions arising from this work.

2   State of the Art

A number of earlier research papers and publications have been taken into account for this study. Unfortunately, experimental studies on these topics often fail to display uniformed, standardized topologies for the scenarios being under study, resulting in discrepancies in the methodology, video(s), or video codecs being used. This situation hinders the comparison and contrast of measurements and conclusions of contemporary studies and/or studies conducted over time by the same or different authors.

This study has especially taken into account the contributions specifically related to the field, such as those resulting from analyzing multicast traffic and video streaming across a variety of networks [2–4], papers on compression techniques and video codecs [5–8], and our own contributions from earlier studies on video traffic in WAN networks [9, 10] and Wi-Fi networks [11], which are now enhanced by new results and a fuller, more detailed discussion.

The rest of this section offers a brief description of the main features of the tools and protocols that were used.

2.1 IP Multicast

In general, applications resort to either one of two models of data transmission over IP networks: the unicast model and the multicast one. In the unicast model, a one-to-one association is needed between the source and the receiver in order to send a given flow of data. Therefore, the network needs to be configured in such a way to allow supporting as many flows as receivers potentially interested in receiving the content exist. On the contrary, the multicast model is adaptable to content distribution models such as one-to-many and many-to-many, among other variants. In this case, the network will transport a single flow of data for each source, and the first source is responsible for delivering the flow of data to those receivers who are interested in receiving it. This design offers the possibility to improve in particular scalability and performance.

Routers are responsible for replicating and distributing the multicast content to all the receivers within a multicast group. Routers resort to multicast protocols that create distribution trees in order to transmit multicast content. IPv6 uses PIM-SM, PIM-SSM or other protocols. For this study, in an attempt to keep in line with the research conducted on IPv4, PIM-SM (Protocol Independent Multicast – Sparse Mode) was used.

2.2 Video Codec

Codecs are used to digitally compress or reduce the size of a video in order to improve service delivery as well as transmission or storage efficiency. A large number of algorithms or codecs are available, be they standard or proprietary. Oftentimes, video compression may compromise quality image and other application requirements.

The video codecs that were used in this study are listed and described below:

- H.264/MPEG-4 AVC: A video compression standard promoted jointly by the ITU and the ISO, offering significant advances in terms of compression efficiency, which result in half or lower bit rate when compared to MPEG-2 and MPEG-4 Simple Profile.
- H.265/MPEG-H Part 2/High Efficiency Video Coding (HEVC): A video compression format following H.264/MPEG-4 AVC, developed jointly by the ISO/IEC Moving Picture Experts Group (MPEG) and ITU-T Video Coding Experts Group (VCEG), corresponding to ISO/IEC CD 23008-2 High Efficiency Video Coding.

This standard may be used to deliver higher quality, low bit-rate video while requiring the same bit rate. It is compatible with ultra-high-definition television and 8192 × 4320 display resolution.

- VP8: A video codec by On2 Technologies, released on September 13, 2008. On May 19, 2010, Google, having acquired On2 Technologies back in 2009, released VP8 as an open-source codec (under a BSD-like license).
- Theora: A free video compression format developed by the Xiph.Org Foundation as part of the Ogg project. It derives from VP3 codec. In 2010, Google began funding part of the Ogg Theora Vorbis project. Theora stands for a general purpose video codec requiring low CPU usage.

2.3   Video Streaming

A broad range of video streaming options are available, each of which may display different sets of behavior. Video traffic may be point-to-point, multicast or broadcast. Additionally, videos may be precoded (stored) or they may be coded in real time (for example, while an interactive videophone communication or video conference ensues). Video channels may be static or dynamic, and require a packet-based or a circuit-based switching system. Additionally, channels may withstand a constant or a variable bit rate speed. They may have also reserved a number of resources in advance or they may simply be offering best-effort capacity.

Clearly, a few basic issues are at play here, since only best-effort delivery is generally offered, which means that there are no guarantees regarding bandwidth, jitter or potential packet losses. Therefore, a key goal in video streaming involves designing a reliable system that delivers high quality video and takes into account Traffic Engineering, QoS (Quality of Service) and QoE (Quality of Experience).

2.4   IEEE 802.11ac Standard

In 1990, the IEEE 802 Committee created the IEEE 802.11 working group, which concerned wireless LAN networks specifically, with a view to developing specifications for medium access control (MAC) and physical layer (PHY) functions. Although IEEE 802.11 was the first standard to become widely known, it was only in 1999 that wide industry adoption was gained, with 802.11a and 802.11b. More recently, in an attempt to meet new and increasing demands, new IEEE projects were created with a view to providing a VHT (Very High Throughput) system. The Task Group TGac has specified IEEE 802.11ac as an extension of IEEE 802.11n.

The IEEE 802.11ac standard works on a 5 GHz band, which shows much less saturation, resulting in a cleaner signal and reduced interference. It also offers greater performance by using up to eight MIMO flows at 160 MHz, improving signal intensity by means of Beamforming technology, and accelerating data transmission by means of 256-QAM modulation.

2.5   Internet Protocol Version 6 – IPv6

IPv6 represents the evolution of IPv4. In most devices and operating systems, this protocol is installed as a software update. In early 2011, IPv6 native users represented about 0.2%. In 2014, IPv6 was used by almost 3% of Internet users, representing about 72 million people. As of early 2020, IPv6 has achieved 30% penetration. The number of IPv6 Internet users has been doubling steadily every nine months approximately.

IPv6's main advantage is its extended address mode (represented in 128 bits). Furthermore, it offers several additional features, such as allocating an IP address from the client's end, allocating several addresses to the same device, integrated encryption and IPsec, enhanced performance, faster connection and much reduced latency, among others.

3   Scenarios and Experimental Resources

The main objective of the experiment reported in this paper has been studying Wi-Fi video traffic streaming by assessing on a testbed both the limitations imposed by these networks as well as issues derived from varying the type of video or codec being used, and the use of IPv6 multicast in combination with IEEE 802.11ac.

3.1   Network Topology

The topology that has been put forward includes a general scenario featuring a streaming server, mobile devices, and desktop PCs, IEEE 802.11ac Wi-Fi connectivity, and users connected to the ends of the network. The network comprises a series of routers and switches with different types of links interconnecting them. Figure 1 shows the experiment topology, where solid lines depict Fast Ethernet links with a transmission speed of up to 100 Mbps, while the end users' devices are connected by means of the IEEE 802.11ac standard. For the operation between routers, the unicast OSPFv2 and the multicast PIM-SM routing protocols were set. Cisco 2811 routers and Cisco Linksys LAPAC 1200 APs were used. The software used as the streaming server and the receiving clients are based on FFmpeg [12].

3.2   Videos

Two on-demand video files were used, which were coded alternatively using the codecs selected for this experiment. One of the videos was a Star Trek movie trailer (Fig. 2-Video 1) [13], while the other one was an extract from a video conference using Adobe Connect (Fig. 3-Video 2) [14], which will be referenced to as Video 2, of the same length and quality as Video 1. Tables 1 and 2 compare the features of each codec for each video.

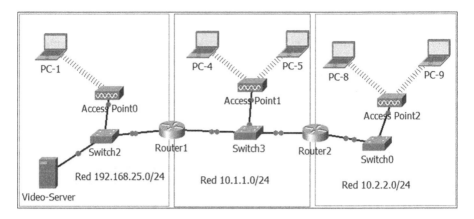

Fig. 1. Network topology.

Fig. 2. Screenshot of the Star Trek movie trailer – Video 1.

Fig. 3. Screenshot of VC on Adobe Connect – Video 2.

Table 1. Video 1 Properties – Star Trek movie trailer.

Video 1	H.264	H.265	Theora	VP8
Format	MPEG-4	MPEG-4	Ogg	WebM v2
File size	79.9 MiB	72.3 MiB	83.3 MiB	78.6 MiB
Length	2 min 11 s	2 min 11 s	2 min 11 s	2 min 11 s
Bit rate mode	Variable	Variable	Variable	Variable
Bit rate	5,109 kb/s	4,620 kb/s	5,329 kb/s	5,028 kb/s
Video				
Format	AVC	HEVC	Theora	VP8
Bit rate	5,011 kb/s	4,514 kb/s	5,010 kb/s	4,721 kb/s
Width [in pixels]	1,280 pixels	1,280 pixels	1,280 pixels	1,280 pixels
Height [in pixels]	528 pixels	528 pixels	528 pixels	528 pixels
Aspect ratio	2.4:1	2.4:1	2.4:1	2.4:1
Frame rate mode	constant	constant	constant	constant
Frame rate [in fps]	23.976 fps	23.976 fps	23.976 fps	23.976 fps
Bits/(pixel*frame)	0.309	0.279	0.309	0.291
Audio				
Format	AAC LC	AAC LC	Vorbis	Vorbis
Bit rate mode	Variable	constant	Variable	Variable
Bit rate	98.7 kb/s	99.7 kb/s	98.7 kb/s	98.7 kb/s
Maximum bit rate	167 kb/s	167 kb/s	167 kb/s	167 kb/s
Channel	2 channels	2 channels	2 channels	2 channels
Sampling rate	44.1 kHz	44.1 kHz	44.1 kHz	44.1 kHz
Track size	1.54 MiB (2%)	1.56 MiB (2%)	1.54 MiB (2%)	1.54 MiB (2%)

Table 2. Properties of Video 2 – Adobe Connect video conference

Video 2	H.264	H.265	Theora	VP8
Format	MPEG-4	MPEG-4	Ogg	WebM v2
File size	6.02 MiB	6.10 MiB	8.84 MiB	11.5 MiB
Length	2 min 11 s	2 min 11 s	2 min 11 s	2 min 11 s
Bit rate mode	Variable	Variable	Variable	Variable
Bit rate	385 kb/s	390 kb/s	565 kb/s	733 kb/s
Video				
Format	AVC	HEVC	Theora	VP8
Bit rate	256 kb/s	256 kb/s	407 kb/s	568 kb/s
Width [in pixels]	1,280 pixels	1,280 pixels	1,280 pixels	1,280 pixels
Height [in pixels]	720 pixels	720 pixels	720 pixels	720 pixels
Aspect ratio	16:9	16:9	16:9	16:9
Frame rate mode	constant	constant	constant	constant

(*continued*)

Table 2. (*continued*)

Video 2	H.264	H.265	Theora	VP8
Frame rate [in fps]	30.000 fps	30.000 fps	30.000 fps	30.000 fps
Bits/ (pixel*frame)	0.009	0.009	0.015	0.021
Audio				
Format	AAC LC	AAC LC	Vorbis	Vorbis
Bit rate mode	Variable	Variable	Variable	Variable
Bit rate	126 kb/s	126 kb/s	127 kb/s	127 kb/s
Maximum bit rate	257 kb/s	127 kb/s	257 kb/s	257 kb/s
Channel	2 channels	2 channels	2 channels	2 channels
Sampling rate	44.1 kHz	44.1 kHz	44.1 kHz	44.1 kHz
Track size	43.066 fps (1024 SPF)	43.066 fps (1024 SPF)	1.99 MiB (22%)	1.99 MiB (17%)

3.3   Methods and Procedures

Based on the previous topology, the tasks in this experiment comprised the steps and considerations listed below:

a) Video 1 files were coded in the streaming server using the 4 formats;
b) Prior to being measured, all equipment items in the topology were synchronized by means of an NTP local server.
c) Video 1 was streamed to the network in multicast format, from the server, and using a specific codec.
d) Step c) was repeated until Video 1 was assessed using all codecs.
e) The same process was followed for Video 2.

In each of the 8 experiments that were conducted (which involved 4 codecs per video), measurements were made by capturing traffic on the server as well as on each of the end devices connected through Wi-Fi. Traffic capture was achieved by means of Wireshark sniffer software [15]. Using this software, a capture file was created at each point of measurement (the streaming server and the end devices) for each of the 8 tests. Each capture file contained the data on individual video traffic frames. These files contained data for each of the frames captured during the test, including the exact date and time of frame capture, origin and destination MAC and IP addresses, transport and/or application layer protocol, frame size, etc.

3.4   Metrics

The experiments resulted in a series of metrics for server and for clients. The data for each metric were determined individually for each device, after which, measurement averages were computed.

The metrics obtained were as follows:

- Total running time of video [Tt],
- Total number of packets (or frames) [NP],
- Total numbers of bytes [NB],
- Packet average size [PAS],
- Interframe space or Time between frames or packets [IFS], and
- Effective data transfer rate [BR]: Defined as NB divided by Tt.

Additionally, other metrics and measurements were recorded, such as:

- Streaming timing delay [Td],
- Timing delay difference (or jitter) [DD],
- Amount of errors obtained [Eo], and
- Statistical distribution.

4   Results

Table 3 briefly summarizes the average metrics of the most relevant metrics as defined above. Since the work involved a controlled laboratory topology, no streaming errors or significant frame losses occurred. Additionally, the load of control traffic for protocols OSPFv2 and PIM-SM was non-significant. The values at individual measurement points proved very similar.

Table 3. Average metrics per codec for each video.

Codec	Number of frames NP	Average interframe space IFS [s]	Number of bytes NB [Mbytes]	Packet average size PAS [bytes]	Bit Rate BR [Mbits/s]
Video 1 – *Star Trek* Movie Trailer					
H264	111,203	0.00097	82.80746	806.62	5.04901
H265	87,852	0.00147	70.85176	806.02	4.34782
Theora	82,292	0.00145	60.37944	802.72	3.69813
VP8	117,826	0.00109	82.28519	802.38	5.01721
Video 2 – Adobe Connect Video Conference					
H264	8,067	0.01582	6.90888	856.44	0.42142
H265	7,943	0.01618	6.91067	870.03	0.42150
Theora	6,782	0.01652	9.78550	1442.86	0.59661
VP8	10,090	0.01274	12.76103	1264.72	0.77831

High levels of dependency were observed between the characteristics of the video type that was streamed and the codec that was used. In bit rate, the video conference represents a traffic load volume around 90% lower than a movie of similar resolution, which will consequently exhibit fewer frames, greater average interframe space, or a smaller number of bytes in similar proportion.

Table 4. Average metrics for each video.

Average between codecs	Number of frames NP	Average interframe space IFS [s]	Number of bytes NB [Mbytes]	Packet average size PAS [bytes]	Bit Rate BR [Mbits/s]
Video 1 – *Star Trek* Movie Trailer					
Video 1	99,793	0.00124	74.08096	804.43	4.52804
Video 2 – Adobe Connect Video Conference					
Video 2	8,220	0.01531	9.09152	1104.01	0.55446
Difference	82.37%	12.34 times +	88.91%	25.44%	88.91%

Additionally, it is worth highlighting in Table 4 that the average across all codecs amounted to 99,793 frames to be streamed for Video 1. For Video 2, on its part, it took 8,220 frames to stream the video conference, which had the same length as Video 1. This means Video 2 required almost 82% fewer frames. Since both videos have the same length, it should be expected that the interframe space in Video 1 would be substantially lower. Indeed, the average codec interframe time for Video 1 was 1.24 ms, while for Video 2 it was 15.31 ms, i.e. about 12.34 times more.

4.1   H.264 Codec Behavior

Figure 4 and 5 respectively show the distribution of frame sizes and interframe spaces for Video 1. Figure 4 shows high frame concentration, of around 54,000 frames for each case, for a length below 100 bytes and above 1,500 bytes (almost the total of frames). In Fig. 5, on its part, it should be pointed out that almost 97% of the frames have an interframe space under 1 ms.

Figure 6 and 7 respectively show the distribution of frame sizes and interframe spaces. Figure 6 shows greater frame distribution depending on the size; where 24% correspond to frames above 1,500 bytes, 26% to frames around 1,150 bytes, and about 25% to frames below 150 bytes. In Fig. 7, 50% of the frames display an interframe space under 3 ms, 26% around 30 ms, 9.5% around 39 ms, and the remainder is distributed within the work range.

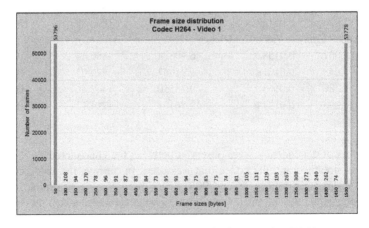

Fig. 4. Frame size distribution of Video 1 using H264.

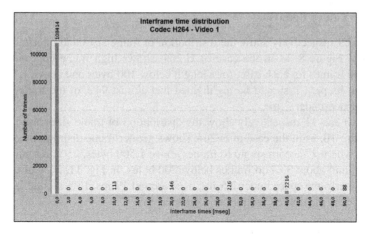

Fig. 5. Interframe space distribution of Video 1 using H264.

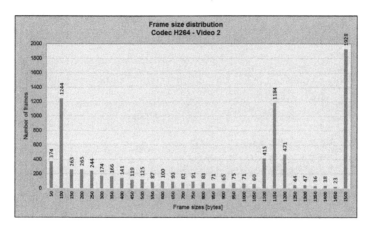

Fig. 6. Frame size distribution of Video 2 using H264.

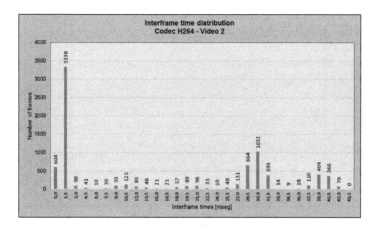

Fig. 7. Interframe space distribution of Video 2 using H264.

4.2   H.265 Codec Behavior

Figure 8 and 9 respectively show the distribution of frame sizes and interframe spaces for Video 1. Figure 8, as in the case of H.264, shows high frame concentration, of about 42,000 frames for each case, for a length below 100 bytes and above 1,500 bytes. In Fig. 9, on its part, it should be highlighted that almost 94% of the frames have an interframe space under 2 ms.

Figure 10 and 11 respectively show the distribution of frame sizes and interframe spaces. Figure 10, as in the case of H.264, shows greater frame distribution depending on the size; where 27% correspond to frames above 1,500 bytes, 25% to frames around 1,150 bytes, and about 33% to frames below 200 bytes. In Fig. 11, 32% of the frames display an interframe space under 2.5 ms, 31% around 19 ms, 13% around 29 ms, and the remainder is distributed within the work range.

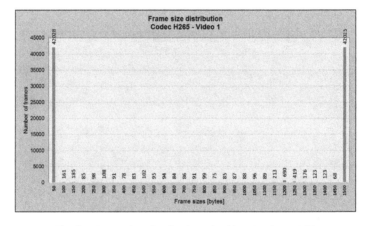

Fig. 8. Frame size distribution of Video 1 using H265.

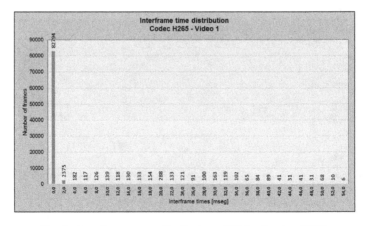

Fig. 9. Interframe space distribution of Video 1 using H265.

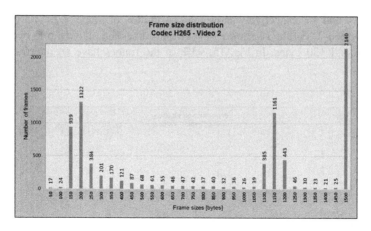

Fig. 10. Frame size distribution of Video 2 using H265.

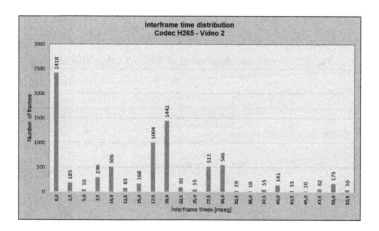

Fig. 11. Interframe space distribution of Video 2 using H265.

4.3 Theora Codec Behavior

Figure 12 and 13 respectively show the distribution of frame sizes and interframe spaces for Video 1. In Fig. 12, almost the total amount of frames is distributed into two groups, of around 42,300 frames each, for a length below 100 bytes and above 1,500 bytes. In Fig. 13, on its part, it should be pointed out that almost 97% of the frames have an interframe space under 2 ms.

Figure 14 and 15 respectively show the distribution of frame sizes and interframe spaces for Video 2. Figure 14 shows 74% of the frames are above 1,500 bytes, while 13% are around 130 bytes. In Fig. 15, 93% of the frames have an interframe space under 3 ms.

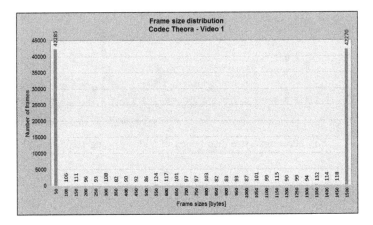

Fig. 12. Frame size distribution of Video 1 using Theora.

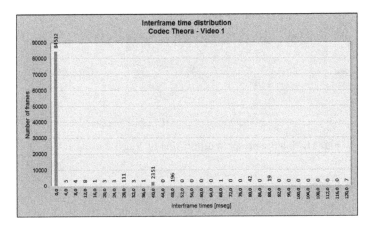

Fig. 13. Frame size distribution of Video 1 using Theora.

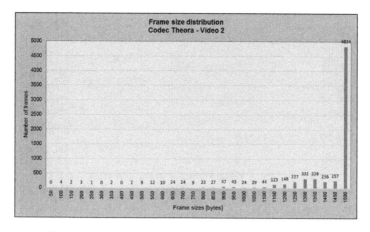

Fig. 14. Frame size distribution of Video 2 using Theora.

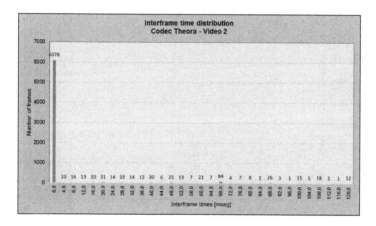

Fig. 15. Frame size distribution of Video 2 using Theora.

4.4 VP8 Codec Behavior

Figure 16 and 17 respectively show the distribution of frame sizes and interframe spaces for Video 1. In Fig. 16, virtually all the frames (97.4%) are distributed into two size groups, of around 57,390 frames each, for lengths below 100 bytes and above 1,500 bytes. In Fig. 17, on its part, it should be pointed out that almost 97.3% of the frames have an interframe space under 0.3 ms.

Figure 18 and 19 respectively show the distribution of frame sizes and interframe spaces for Video 2. Figure 18 shows a group represented by 45% of the frames above 1,500 bytes, and another one, represented by 40% of the frames, evenly distributed between 1,000 and 1,450 bytes. Finally, in Fig. 19, 50% of the frames have an interframe space below 3 ms, 19% have one around 19 ms, and the rest are distributed mostly between 9 and 29 ms.

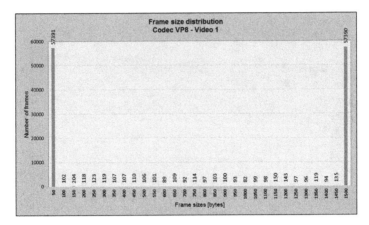

Fig. 16. Frame size distribution of Video 1 using VP8.

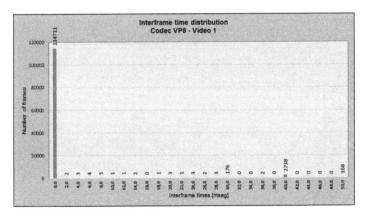

Fig. 17. Interframe space distribution of Video 1 using VP8.

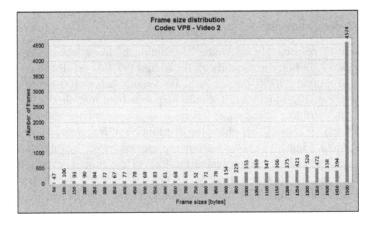

Fig. 18. Frame size distribution of Video 2 using VP8.

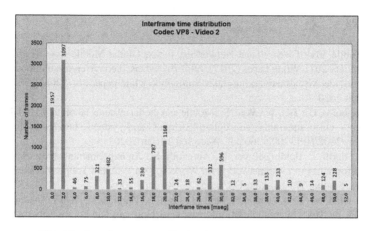

Fig. 19. Interframe space distribution of Video 2 using VP8.

5   Conclusions

The primary motivation behind this study was learning about the behavior of video traffic on Wi-Fi networks while using IPv6, and understanding the requirements needed by the network, contrasting two clearly different cases: a movie trailer (Video 1) and a video conference video (Video 2). Using a detailed multicast scenario, a series of tests were conducted, where 8 sub-scenarios were set up. The results include values of direct and average metrics, as well as the distribution as per frame size and interframe space for each of the 4 codecs that were used for Videos 1 and 2.

The videos being compared clearly showed similar characteristics between them in terms of length and resolution, but they were quite different in terms of the dynamics at play.

A quantitative conclusion was made as to the existence of high levels of dependency between the characteristics of the video type being streamed (whether it was a movie or a video conference) and, to a lesser extent, the codec that was used. An additional conclusion is that neither the network topology nor the equipment type exercise significant impact, since their behavior is virtually identical for clients located at different network nodes.

This case study will prove useful to administrators, designers, planners, analysts, and Wi-Fi video traffic simulators for improving the execution of their tests. Although it is not possible to ensure the same type of behavior for all movies and video conferences, for codecs other than those used in this study, or for a standard different from IEEE 802.11, simulation analysts may use the metrics obtained experimentally in this paper as a guide as to the network demands made by video conferences, movies, etc. as well as their characteristics and features. Designers, planners, and network administrators, on their part, with a keener interest in bandwidth data, may use the 4.52 Mbps from the Star Trek movie trailer and the 0.55 Mbps for the video conference on Adobe Connect as reference data.

References

1. Cisco Mobile VNI: Cisco Visual Networking Index: Global Mobile Data Traffic Forecast Update, 2016–2021 White Paper (2017). https://www.cisco.com/c/en/us/solutions/collateral/service-provider/visual-networking-index-vni/mobile-white-paper-c11-520862.html. Accessed 18 Jan 2020

2. Apostolopoulos, G., Tan, W., Wee, S.: Mobile and media systems laboratory HP laboratories Palo Alto - video streaming: concepts, algorithms, and systems. http://www.hpl.hp.com/techreports/2002/HPL-2002-260.pdf. Accessed 18 Jan 2020

3. Sun, Y., Sheriff, I., Belding-Royer, E., Almeroth, K.: An experimental study of multimedia traffic performance in mesh networks. In: Workshop on Wireless Traffic Measurements and Modeling, Seattle, Washington, USA, pp. 25–30, June 2005

4. Shin, Y., Choi, M., Koo, J., Kim, Y., Ihm, J., Choi, S.: Empirical analysis of video multicast over WiFi. In: Third International Conference on Ubiquitous and Future Networks, ICUFN, China, pp. 381–386 (2011)

5. Abdalla, A., Mazhar, A., Salah M., Khalaf, S.: Comparative study of compression techniques for synthetic videos. Int. J. Multimedia Its Appl. (IJMA) 6(2) (2014)

6. Grois, D., Marpea, D., Nguyena, T., Hadarb, O.: Comparative assessment of H.265/MPEG-HEVC, VP9, and H.264/MPEG-AVC encoders for low-delay video applications. In: SPIE Proceedings, vol. 9217, Applications of Digital Image Processing XXXVII, California, USA, September 2014

7. Addu, R., Potuvardanam, V.: Effect of codec performance on video QoE for videos encoded with Xvid, H.264 and WebM/VP8. Master thesis, Blekinge Institute of Technology, Karlskrona, Sweden, August 2014

8. Tanwir, S., Perros, H., Anjum, B.: A QoS evaluation of video traffic models for H.264 AVC video. In: Fifth International Conference on Next Generation Networks and Services (NGNS), pp. 313–320, Casablanca, Morocco, May 2014

9. Pérez, S., Campos, J., Facchini, H., Dantiacq, A.: Experimental study of unicast and multicast video traffic using WAN test bed. https://ieeexplore.ieee.org/document/7585260. Accessed 18 Jan 2020

10. Pérez, S., Marrone, L., Facchini, H., Hidalgo, F.: Experimental study of multicast and unicast video traffic in WAN links. IEEE Latin American Transactions 15(10), 1847–1855 (2017). ISSN: 1548-0992

11. Pérez, S., et al.: Estudio experimental de tráfico de video en redes IPv6 multicast IEEE 802.11ac. In: Congreso Argentino de Ciencias de la Computación 2019, CACIC 2019, Libro de Actas, Rio Cuarto, Córdoba, Argentina, pp. 847–856 (2019). ISBN: 978-987-688-377-1

12. FFmpeg. https://www.ffmpeg.org/. Accessed 18 Jan 2020

13. Video 1, Star Trek. https://www.youtube.com/watch?v=g5lWao2gVpc. Accessed 18 Jan 2020

14. Video 2, Videoconference Adobe Connect. https://www.youtube.com/watch?v=4ZFsIqxpbAc. Accessed 18 Jan 2020

15. Wireshark Foundation. https://www.wireshark.org/. Accessed 18 Jan 2020

Innovation in Software Systems

Materialization of OWL Ontologies from Relational Databases: A Practical Approach

Sergio Alejandro Gómez[1,2(✉)] and Pablo Rubén Fillottrani[1,2]

[1] Laboratorio de I+D en Ingeniería de Software, Departamento de Ciencias e Ingeniería de la Computación, Universidad Nacional del Sur, San Andrés 800, Bahía Blanca, Argentina
{sag,prf}@cs.uns.edu.ar
[2] Comisión de Investigaciones Científicas de la Provincia de Buenos Aires (CIC-PBA), La Plata, Argentina
https://lissi.cs.uns.edu.ar/

Abstract. Providing both end-users and applications with a uniform way to query legacy databases through a high-level ontology that models both the business logic and the underlying data sources is the main concern in Ontology-based Data Access (OBDA). Our goal in this research is providing tools for performing OBDA with relational and non-relational data sources. Within the OBDA framework, in this work, we present a prototype tool that can access an H2 database, allowing the user to explicitly express mappings, and populating an ontology that can be saved for later querying. We report on the current functionality of our tool, which includes creating, loading, saving a global ontology populated with a database or a CSV file. For the latter, we devised a language for specifying the underlying schema of the CSV file. We argue that this language is better suited than current alternatives such as JSON. Also, the system allows the user to visually express mappings from the database to the ontology and the ability to create databases for testing the behavior of the system in the presence of increasing workloads. Our tests indicate that the system can handle a moderate workload of tables of tens of thousands of records but fails to handle tables of millions of records.

Keywords: Ontology-based data access · Ontologies · Description Logics · Web Ontology Language · Relational databases

1 Introduction

Ontology-based Data Access (OBDA) [1,2] is concerned with providing end-users and applications with a way to query legacy databases through a high-level ontology that models both the business logic and the underlying data sources. Modern knowledge-based applications have replaced the representation of business logic by using a high-level representation of the business intelligence which is decoupled from the application code. This allows for improved flexibility. In Semantic Web applications [3], the business intelligence is represented by ontologies expressed in the Web Ontology Language 2 (OWL 2) [4]. Briefly, an ontology

© Springer Nature Switzerland AG 2020
P. Pesado and M. Arroyo (Eds.): CACIC 2019, CCIS 1184, pp. 285–301, 2020.
https://doi.org/10.1007/978-3-030-48325-8_19

is a logical theory formed by a collection of concepts and roles and also a set of concept and role assertions [5]. The relationship holding among the concepts and roles in the ontology are described in terms of inclusion and equality axioms. Ontologies used to represent business logic are then used by ontology reasoners to conclude implicit knowledge (i.e. not present in the database). The conclusions that can be got include making explicit the implicit terminology of concepts defined by the ontology, determining if a certain individual is a member of a concept, or determining if two individuals are related through a role, determining if a concept is subsumed by another concept, or if a role is subsumed by another role.

Thus, the classic OBDA architecture [1] is composed of a global database, a legacy database and a bridge between the ontology and the database. The bridge between the ontology and the data sources is addressed by mappings that define how to express records of the database as ontological assertions. Relational databases are comprised of relations (tables), that in term are defined by data schemas, which define the names and domains of table attributes as well as any integrity constraints that might apply to them, and are composed of records. Ontologies, on the other hand, are composed of axioms, and concept and roles assertions. The mappings define how to populate the ontology in terms of the elements of the database. Basically, the concept and role fillers are defined by SQL queries that indicate how to populate them. Notice that in the case of having several databases, a federation system can be used that allows to see the set of databases as a unified database. In this work, however, we will not take this possibility into account.

In this research, we are concerned with providing tools for performing OBDA with relational and non-relational data sources. Several tools have been developed by other research groups (see for instance [6–9] that we reviewed in [10]). Some of those tools are closed-source while others are open-source, some are downloadable and can be used as stand-alone applications or as programming libraries. While many times they are a good starting point for building applications, many times they are not flexible enough. In that regard, we are developing a tool, which nowadays is in a prototypical state, that can access an H2 database, allowing the user to explicitly formulate mappings, and populating an ontology that can be saved for later querying and visualization. See [10,11] for previous reports on the functionality of the application and its prospective application areas.

We present the advances we have made on the development of such a tool. In particular, we have added a form that allows end-users to fully specify in a high-level manner the nature of mappings and by writing SQL queries as well. We also added a module that allows testing on how our application behaves in the presence of increasing demands. We introduce a language that allows the user to precisely define the contents of a CSV file, we use that information to interpret the contents of a CSV file and then translating into OWL. We also discuss how this materialization tool could be used in the context of an e-government application. We provide with a downloadable prototype and a user manual at http://cs.uns.edu.ar/~sag/obda-v4. We assume that the reader has a basic knowledge of Description Logics (DL) [12], relational databases [13] and the Web Ontology Language [4].

This work consolidates and extends results presented in [14]. We have included a new language for specifying the underlying schema of a CSV file, its implementation and an analysis of its performance. Also, we have also included an analysis of how this prototypical application could be integrated with an electronic government setting where public open data has to be machine processed.

The rest of the paper is structured as follows. In Sect. 2, we briefly recapitulate the concepts associated with materializing ontologies from tables. In Sect. 3, we present a novel development in the system that allows a naïve user to define a mapping from tables to ontologies in a visual manner. In Sect. 4, we present an alternative language for describing CSV meta information. In Sect. 5, we show an empirical evaluation of the performance of the prototype creating tables and ontologies. In Sect. 6, we present a case study where we show how the proposed application could be used for supporting data handling in an e-government application in a municipality. In Sect. 7, we review related work. In Sect. 8, we conclude and foresee future work.

2 Materialization of OWL Ontologies from Relational Databases

An ontology is a logical theory formed by set of axioms and assertions describing the business logic. The mappings describe how to map relational views into ontological vocabulary. Given a data access instance formed by a relational database $\mathcal{D}$, an ontological vocabulary $\mathcal{V}$, a set of ontological axioms $\mathcal{O}$ over $\mathcal{V}$, and a set of mappings $\mathcal{M}$ between $\mathcal{V}$ and $\mathcal{D}$, there are two approaches to answer a query Q over $\mathcal{V}$: (i) *materialization*: ontological facts are materialized (i.e. classes and properties participating in mappings are populated with individuals by evaluating SQL queries participating in mappings) and this gives a set of ontological facts $\mathcal{A}$ and then Q is evaluated against $\mathcal{O}$ and $\mathcal{A}$ with standard query-answering engines for ontologies, or (ii) *virtualization*: Q should be first rewritten into SQL using $\mathcal{O}$ and $\mathcal{M}$ and then SQL should be executed over $\mathcal{D}$.

In this work, we will only use the materialization approach. Materializing an OWL ontology from a relational database requires exporting the database contents as a text file in OWL format. For doing this, we need to export the schema information of each table as Tbox axioms and the instance data of the tables as Abox assertions. Here, we review the formalization for exporting database relations as ontologies as we presented it in [10] according to the directions given by [1,15]. Building an ontology from a database requires creating at least a class C_T for every table T, and for every attribute a of domain d in T we need two inclusion DL axioms $C_T \sqsubseteq \exists a$ and $\exists a^- \sqsubseteq d$. Primary key values k_i serve the purpose of establishing the membership of individuals to classes as DL Abox assertions of the form $C_T(C_T\#k^j)$. For indicating that a^j is the value of attribute a, we will use a role expression of the form $C_T\#a(C_T\#k^j, C_T\#a^j)$.

When it is clear from context, we might drop the prefix $C_T\#$ for simplifying our notation. A foreign key fk in table T_1 referencing a primary key field in table T_2 will also require to add two Tbox axioms $C_{T_1} \sqsubseteq \exists ref\_fk$ and $\exists ref\_fk^- \sqsubseteq C_{T_2}$ and an Abox assertion $ref\_fk(k^j, fk^t)$ for expressing that the individual named k^j in C_{T_1} is related to the individual named fk^t in C_{T_2}. Besides, in any case, if we want to consider a subset of a table for its mapping into an ontology, we might define an SQL query that will act as an SQL filter. In this work, we will only deal with the translation into OWL of single tables and one-to-many relations (see [10] for details):

Definition 1 (Mapping of a table with a single primary key). *Let T be a table with schema $T(\underline{k}, a_1, \ldots, a_n)$ and instance $\{(k^1, a_1^1, \ldots, a_n^1), \ldots, (k^m, a_1^m, \ldots, a_n^m)\}$. To map T into a DL terminology $\mathcal{T}$, we have to create a class T and for each attribute a_i of domain D_i we have to add two axioms: $T \sqsubseteq \exists a_i$, indicating that every T has an attribute a_i, and $\exists a_i^- \sqsubseteq D_i$, meaning that the domain of a_i is D_i. The assertional box $\mathcal{A}$ for T will contain $\{T(k^1), \ldots, T(k^m)\}$. Given a key value k_j, $j = 1, \ldots, m$, for every attribute a_i, $i = 1, \ldots, n$, of the schema and instance value a_i^j (i.e. the value of i-th attribute of the j-th individual), produce a property $a_i(k^j, a_i^j)$.*

Example 1. Consider a table for representing people with schema Person (personID, name, sex, birthDate, weight) and instance as on the left side of Fig. (1). This table is created by the SQL script presented in the right side of Fig. (1).

personID	name	sex	birthDate	weight
1	John	true	2010-01-01	100.0
2	Mary	false	2009-01-01	60.0

```
create table "Person" (
    "personID" int unsigned not null
    auto_increment primary key,
    "name" varchar(20) not null,
    "sex" boolean, "birthDate" date,
    "weight" real );
insert into "Person"("name", "sex", "birthDate",
    "weight") values ('John', true, '2010-01-01', 100.0);
insert into "Person"("name", "sex", "birthDate",
    "weight") values ('Mary', false, '2009-01-01', 60.0);
```

Fig. 1. On the left, relational instance of the table Person and, on the right, SQL script for creating the table Person

The table Person is interpreted in Description Logics according to Definition 1, as $\Sigma = (\mathcal{T}, \mathcal{A})$ in Fig. 2. Description Logic ontologies are implemented in the OWL language, which includes an XML serialization which we partially present in Fig. 3 by showing the representation for John.

We now recall how to map two tables participating in a one-to-many relationship.

Definition 2 (Mapping of a one-to-many relationship). *Let $A(\underline{k_1}, a_1, \ldots, a_n)$ and $B(\underline{k_2}, b_1, \ldots, b_m, k_1)$ be two tables participating in a one-to-many relationship where k_1 is both the primary key in A and a foreign key in B.*

$$\mathcal{T} = \left\{ \begin{array}{ll} \text{Person} \sqsubseteq \exists \text{personID}, & \exists \text{personID}^- \sqsubseteq \text{Integer}, \\ \text{Person} \sqsubseteq \exists \text{name}, & \exists \text{name}^- \sqsubseteq \text{String}, \\ \text{Person} \sqsubseteq \exists \text{sex}, & \exists \text{sex}^- \sqsubseteq \text{Boolean}, \\ \text{Person} \sqsubseteq \exists \text{birthDate}, & \exists \text{birthDate}^- \sqsubseteq \text{Date}, \\ \text{Person} \sqsubseteq \exists \text{weight}, & \exists \text{weight}^- \sqsubseteq \text{Real} \end{array} \right\}$$

$$\mathcal{A} = \left\{ \begin{array}{ll} \text{Person}(\text{Person}\#1), & \text{personID}(\text{Person}\#1, 1), \\ \text{name}(\text{Person}\#1, \text{John}), & \text{sex}(\text{Person}\#1, \text{true}), \\ \text{birthDate}(\text{Person}\#1, 2001\text{-}01\text{-}01), & \text{weight}(\text{Person}\#1, 100.0), \\ \text{Person}(\text{Person}\#2), & \text{personID}(\text{Person}\#2, 2), \\ \text{name}(\text{Person}\#2, \text{Mary}), & \text{sex}(\text{Person}\#2, \text{false}), \\ \text{birthDate}(\text{Person}\#2, 2009\text{-}01\text{-}01), & \text{weight}(\text{Person}\#2, 60.0) \end{array} \right\}.$$

Fig. 2. Ontology $\Sigma = (\mathcal{T}, \mathcal{A})$ representing the table *Person* from Example 1

```
<owl:Class rdf:about="http://cs.uns.edu.ar/~sag#Person"/>
<!-- http://cs.uns.edu.ar/~sag/Person/personid=1 -->

<owl:NamedIndividual rdf:about="http://cs.uns.edu.ar/~sag/Person/personid=1">
<rdf:type rdf:resource="http://cs.uns.edu.ar/~sag#Person"/>
<Person:birthDate rdf:datatype="http://www.w3.org/2001/XMLSchema#dateTime">
2010-01-01T00:00:00</Person:birthDate>
<Person:name rdf:datatype="http://www.w3.org/2001/XMLSchema#string">John</Person:name>
<Person:personID rdf:datatype="http://www.w3.org/2001/XMLSchema#integer">1</Person:personID>
<Person:sex rdf:datatype="http://www.w3.org/2001/XMLSchema#boolean">true</Person:sex>
<Person:weight rdf:datatype="http://www.w3.org/2001/XMLSchema#double">100.0</Person:weight>
</owl:NamedIndividual>
```

Fig. 3. Part of the OWL code for the definition of the class Person from Example 1

Tables A and B are translated in DL according to Definition 1. Besides, the two axioms are added: $B \sqsubseteq \exists \text{ref\_}k_1.A$ and $\exists \text{ref\_}k_1^-.B \sqsubseteq A$. And for every tuple $(k_1^i, a_1^i, \ldots, a_n^i)$ of A related to a tuple $(k_2^j, b_1^j, \ldots, b_m^j, k_1^i)$ in B, an assertion $\text{ref\_}k_1(k_2^j, k_1^i)$ is added.

Example 2 (Continues Example 1). Consider a one-to-many relation of table Person from Example 1 with a table Phone(phoneNumber, personID), populated as shown in Fig. 4. Notice that personID is a foreign key referencing table Person.

phoneNumber (pk)	personID (fk)
555-0000	1
555-0001	1

Fig. 4. Relational instance of table Phone from Example 2

Notice that phoneNumber is the primary key while personID is a foreign key referencing key-values of the table Person. Concerning the one-to-many relation and according to Definition 2, two axioms are added to the ontology: Phone $\sqsubseteq \exists \text{ref\_personID.Person}$ and $\exists \text{ref\_personID}^-.\text{Phone} \sqsubseteq \text{Person}$. Let $p_1 = \text{Phone}\#$ 555-0000 be an IRI for the first phone and $p_2 = \text{Phone}\#555\text{-}0001$ for the second one. The assertions $\text{Phone}(p_1)$, $\text{phoneNumber}(p_1, 555\text{-}0000)$, $\text{personID}(p_1, 1)$, ref_personID(p_1, Person#1), Phone(p_2), phoneNumber(p_2, 555-0001), personID (p_2, 1), ref_personID (p_2, Person#1), are then added to the ontology indicating that 555-0001 and 555-0002 are phone numbers and that the person with id 1 owns these phone numbers. Notice how the IRIs for the phones are built concatenating both the name of the class and the value of the respective key values. Assertions prefixing the name of the field with ref_ that relate the person and his/her phone are added too.

3   Visual Mapping Specification

The specification of the mappings for obtaining the fillers of concept from a table is usually a complex matter for naïve end-users. Remember that a mapping is basically a SQL query that defines how the fillers of concept, property or role are computed in terms of the contents of a database. When there is no support for composing mappings, the user has to write such SQL from scratch. We believe that adding support for building the mappings will improve the user experience of a prospective user of OBDA technology.

With the idea of providing support to end-users in their quest of creating concepts for populating ontologies from database contents, we created a module that allows to visually specify a mapping from a table. The module retrieves the tables from the database, and allows to select a table. Once the table is selected, its fields can be selected too. The user can then introduce what conditions each field of the table has to satisfy. Besides, one field (usually the key field of the table) has to be selected to fill the concept. The module then will automatically generate the SQL filter for filling the concept by extracting the records from the table, and will also add a subclass axiom to the ontology.

Example 3. Consider again the table Person from Example 1 and suppose that some user of the system wants to define the concept "heavy, young, male individual". Suppose also that the user models a heavy individual as somebody who weighs at least a hundred kilograms, a young individual as someone who was born after 2001, and a male individual as someone of male sex. People of male sex are codified as having the column named sex as true while females are codified as false. Although this is a trivial example, it shows the complexities that run into database modeling that produce a degradation of the representation of the world and that are unretrievable afterwards. The user will then visually specify the conditions for an individual to be a member of the concept YoungHeavyMalePerson in a form like the one presented in Fig. 6. Notice how the user specifies which database field corresponds to the key (i.e. the name of the individuals), in this case personID. In turn, the system will generate a SQL query as shown in Fig. 5.

After the execution of the query that will compute the individuals that fill the concept, the system will add to the current ontology the triples expressing that those individuals are the fillers of the concept YoungHeavyMalePerson. Besides, in order to relate this concept to its superconcept, the axiom YoungHeavyMalePerson $\sqsubseteq$ Person will be added to the current ontology as well.

SELECT "Person"."personID" FROM "Person"
WHERE "Person"."birthDate" >= '2001-01-01'
AND "Person"."weight" >= 100 AND "Person"."sex" = true

Fig. 5. SQL query for the specification of the concept YoungHeavyMalePerson of Example 3

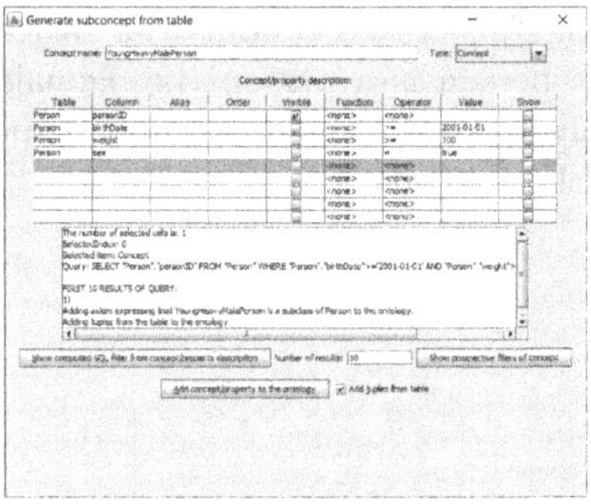

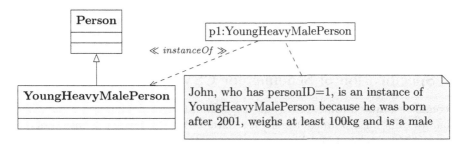

Fig. 6. Visual concept specification of the concept YoungHeavyMalePerson

This will lead to the situation presented in Fig. 7. The new class YoungHeavy-MalePerson is defined as a subclass of Person and John, whose personID role is "1" becomes a member of YoungHeavyMalePerson. Notice also that no new individuals are defined as John is already present in the ontology because he is a Person. In this sense, we adhere to the unique name assumption as much as we can although this is not required by the formalism. Also notice how the intensional definition of the concept is lost in the ontology (other than being a subclass of Person) and only its extension is maintained in the ontology (as the set of its fillers).

Person

≪ *instanceOf* ≫

p1:YoungHeavyMalePerson

YoungHeavyMalePerson

John, who has personID=1, is an instance of YoungHeavyMalePerson because he was born after 2001, weighs at least 100kg and is a male

Fig. 7. Situation arisen by specifying a subclass of Person named YoungHeavyMale Person

Another feature that the current version of the system includes is the possibility of specifying a subclass by means of an explicit SQL query.

Example 4. Continuing Example 3, the concept FemalePerson (which defines a subset of the table Person formed by women) is specified by means of the SQL query:

SELECT "personID" FROM "Person" WHERE "sex" = false

This can be done by using the form presented in Fig. 8. Notice the additional OWL code in the ontology generated by out tool which is presented in Fig. 9 expressing that a female person is a person (i.e. FemalePerson ⊑ Person is an axiom in the ontology) and that Mary is both a female person and a person (i.e. FemalePerson(Mary) and Person(Mary) are assertions in the ontology).

Fig. 8. Specification of the subclass FemalePerson of Person by a SQL query

```
<owl:Class rdf:about="http://cs.uns.edu.ar/~sag#FemalePerson">
<rdfs:subClassOf rdf:resource="http://cs.uns.edu.ar/~sag#Person"/>
</owl:Class>
...
<owl:NamedIndividual rdf:about="http://cs.uns.edu.ar/~sag/FemalePerson=2">
<rdf:type rdf:resource="http://cs.uns.edu.ar/~sag#FemalePerson"/>
...
</owl:NamedIndividual>
```

Fig. 9. Portion of OWL code for introducing subconcept FemalePerson

4   Specification of Schemas for CSV Files

A comma-separated values (CSV) file is a delimited text file that uses a comma to separate values. Each line of the file is a data record. Each record consists of one or more fields enclosed in delimiters and separated by commas. A CSV file stores tabular data (numbers and text) in plain text, in which case each line will have the same number of fields. Comma separated files are used for the interchange of database information between machines of two different architectures. The plain-text character of CSV files largely avoids incompatibilities such as byte-order and word size. The files are human-readable, so it is easier to deal with them in the absence of perfect documentation or communication.

Example 5. In Fig. 10, we show the CSV table for the table Person of Example 1.

```
"personID","name","sex","birthDate","weight"
"1","John","true","2010-01-01","100.00"
"2","Mary","false","2009-01-01","60.00"
```

Fig. 10. CSV file for the table Person of Example 1

Despite its simplicity, the lack of both standardization and schema information in CSV files poses a disadvantage, forcing application programs to guess or ask the user for delimiter and field-separators characters. For solving this problem, the W3C Working Group has proposed a format for specifying CSV metadata [16] based mostly in JSON (JavaScript Object Notation)[1]. Although this solution works in practice, we think that JSON files, although their human readability, are not simple enough for naive users. We then propose a simpler language for specifying the schema (or meta information) of a CSV file as defined by the BNF grammar presented in the left side of Fig. 11. We believe that our language is simple enough to be human-readable and complex enough for its purpose. The declarations have to be *sound* (i.e each declared field in CSV Meta information file must be present in the CSV file), *complete* (i.e. each field in the CSV file must be declared in the CSV meta information file) and *ordered* (i.e. the order in which fields appear in both the CSV file and the CSV meta information file must be the same).

In the right side of Fig. 11, we provide an example of a file for defining the schema of a CSV file that would represent the data provided in Example 5. Although the declarations for *number-of-key-fields* and *number-of-fields* seem redundant, we think that they offer a way for validating that the user is doing things correctly. Valid identifiers begin with a letter and continue with letters and numbers. For now we consider only the types: integer, real, string, boolean and date, but this can be easily extended. If the number of rows to be translated is not specified then *all* is assumed by default. If no field separator is specified, the comma is assumed by default. If no quotation character is specified, the double quotation mark is assumed by default. The parser validates that both the number of key-fields and fields declared matches those that were defined.

The contents of the CSV file are validated and processed according to the definitions given in the CSV schema file. Then the contents of the CSV file are loaded into an H2 database which is translated into OWL as explained in Sect. 2. Our implementation approach parses first the meta-information schema file and then the CSV file; it then generates a SQL script that is used to create an H2 table, that is translated into OWL.

---

[1] See https://www.w3schools.com/js/js_json_intro.asp (checked on 2020-02-20).

```
⟨list-commands⟩ ::=  ⟨command⟩
    |   ⟨command⟩⟨list-commands⟩

⟨command⟩ ::=  ⟨field-separator-def⟩
    |   ⟨quote-separator-def⟩
    |   ⟨class-def⟩
    |   ⟨number-of-key-fields-def⟩
    |   ⟨number-of-fields-def⟩
    |   ⟨key-field-def⟩
    |   ⟨field-def⟩
    |   ⟨number-of-rows-def⟩

⟨field-separator-def⟩ ::=  field-separator ⟨character⟩

⟨quotation-separator-def⟩ ::=  quotation-character-for-fields ⟨character⟩

⟨class-def⟩ ::=  class-name ⟨identifier⟩

⟨number-of-key-fields-def⟩ ::=  number-of-key-fields ⟨positive-integer⟩

⟨number-of-fields-def⟩ ::=  number-of-fields ⟨positive-integer⟩

⟨key-field-def⟩ ::=  keyfield ⟨identifier⟩ type ⟨type-id⟩

⟨field-def⟩ ::=  field ⟨identifier⟩ type ⟨type-id⟩

⟨number-of-rows-def⟩ ::=  number-of-rows-to-translate ⟨quantity-def⟩

⟨type-id⟩ ::=  integer
    |   real
    |   string
    |   boolean
    |   date

⟨quantity-def⟩ ::=  all
    |   ⟨positive-integer⟩
```

```
field-separator ,
quotation-character-for-fields "
class-name Person
number-of-key-fields 1
key-field personID type integer
number-of-fields 4
field name type string
field sex type boolean
field birthDate type date
field weight type real
number-of-rows-to-translate all
```

Fig. 11. On the left, BNF grammar for the meta information language for defining CSV schemas, and, on the right, example of providing schema information for the CSV file in Fig. 10

5   Experimental Evaluation

We now discuss some of the tests we have performed in order to test how our application handles increasing demands in database size. The performance of our system is affected mainly by the fact that we chose to materialize tables as triples (i.e. class membership, property and roles assertions) and also by three factors: (i) the system is implemented in the JAVA programming language; (ii) the database management system that we use is H2[2], and, (iii) the handling of the global ontology is done via the OWL API [17,18].

Our tests were conducted on an ASUS notebook having an Intel Core i7, 3.5 GHz CPU, 8 GB RAM, 1 TB HDD, Windows 10. They involved the creation of simple databases composed by a single table containing 100 fields of text type filled with an increasing number of records. Table 1 summarizes our results. As it can be seen, our implementation starts having problems at tables with 100,000 records; although an ontology can be generated and saved to the disk, when we try to load the ontology we saved previously, we get an error inside the code of the OWL API, indicating that library cannot handle such a data load. When running a test for creating a database of a million records, the H2 database produces an error (which is understandable as it is maintained in RAM). Likewise, in

---

[2] See http://www.h2database.com.

Table 1. Running times for ontology generation from H2 database

Number of records	Database file size [Megabytes]	Time for creating the ontology [seconds]	Ontology file size [Megabytes]	Time for loading the ontology [seconds]
1,000	0.80	1.029	8.65	4.014
10,000	8.82	5.345	87.26	15.106
100,000	98.11	66.48	19,053.36	Out of memory error
1,000,000	1,080.60	Out of memory error	–	–

Table 2. Running times for ontology generation from CSV file

Number of records	CSV file size [Megabytes]	Time for loading CSV file [seconds]	Time for creating ontology [seconds]	Size of ontology file [Megabytes]	Time for loading ontology from disk [seconds]
100	0.048	1.313	0.437	0.871	1.579
1,000	0.568	1.764	1.111	8.560	4.784
10,000	6.636	9.161	3.743	8.215	12.577
100,000	75.987	85.855	37.137	872.883	Out of memory error
1,000,000	856.188	936.473	–	–	–

Table 2, we can see the times for loading CSV files of 100 fields containing integer values and also an increasing number of records. Therefore, we conclude that our application can only handle tables with a size tens of thousands records and is not able of handling tables of a hundred thousand records. Because of this limitation, we think that we will be forced to use query-rewriting techniques [1] for delegating the evaluation of queries to the database management system instead of the ontology management library.

6 Case Study: Support for e-Gov in Municipalities

The importance of social policies has grown in recent years at all levels of government (whether municipal, provincial, national and international), since they represent one of the main tools to combat economic inequalities that occur globally [19] and serve to meet the needs of many vulnerable groups. The provision of public social action services to citizens become an obligation for governments, just as such services are a human right, such as are access to water, energy, health, education and other services.

Despite the global relevance, universality in the provision of public services is a challenge for each government due to the variety of contexts in which such services are provided, including the needs of specific social groups, the capacities of each government, and the context-specific conditions (such as territory, political, cultural, economic, etc.) [19, 20]. In some municipalities of the province of Buenos Aires in Argentina, the following challenges are observed for the provision of public social action services: (i) the services are provided by several municipal government agencies and there is no consolidated information on how the services are being delivered; (ii) currently, there are ad hoc applications that support the process for the delivery of each service, these applications work in isolation, without sharing data; (iii) there is no strategy for the delivery of these services using multiple channels; (iv) the digital channels that could be used are not being exploited properly; (v) there is no software infrastructure that allows the rapid development of applications for the delivery of social action services [21].

Based on these challenges, it is necessary to find a way to publish data contained in legacy and current applications and used in various state institutions in a way that can be integrated, accessed, modified and consulted in a format that is uniform, distributed and scalable. In this sense, the technologies of the Semantic Web have matured enough to be considered as a viable solution for the publication and integration of institutional data. In particular, using semantics implies conceiving systems where the meaning of the data is explicitly specified and is taken into account to design their functionalities. This idea has become crucial for a wide variety of information processing applications and has received much attention in the artificial intelligence, database, web and data mining communities.

As a case study of the operation of the application developed, we present an example loosely based on the public data available in the Municipality of Bahía Blanca. A preliminary version was presented in [11][3]. Let us take as an example three tables, presented in Fig. 12 with the details of the beneficiaries of all social assistance in the period selected in the Municipality of Bahía Blanca[4], where we have a table called *Program* representing social assistance programs, another with the beneficiaries called *Beneficiary* and a third called *Person* with the data of the people enrolled in the aid programs.

The program table schema contains the identifier (which is the primary key) and program name. The table of beneficiaries of aid programs contains the identification (id) of the benefit (which is the primary key of the table), the document number of the beneficiary (which is a foreign key), the amount received, the date of reception and the help program for which the help was received (which is a foreign key). The people table contains the person's social ID (personal document) number (which is the primary key) and his/her last and first name.

---

[3] The authors would like to thank funding from Comisión de Investigaciones Científicas (Project *Herramientas para el desarrollo y la entrega de servicios públicos digitales de acción social para municipios bonaerenses – PIT-AP-BA 2016*).

[4] See http://datos.bahiablanca.gob.ar/dataviews/74266/social-aids.

Program table	
id(pk)	*name*
0001	Municipal Occupational Training Program

Beneficiary table

id(pk)	*dni(fk)*	*amount*	*date receiving help*	*program(fk)*
1	22,000,000	12000	2019-03-10	0001
2	26,000,000	16000	2019-05-04	0001
3	22,000,000	13000	2019-05-04	0001

Person table

dni(pk)	*name*
22,000,000	Smith, John
26,000,000	Doe, Jane

Fig. 12. Relational tables from Bahia Blanca municipality public information site

The Tbox axioms in Fig. 13 represent the schema information of the tables in Fig. 12 and the Abox assertions in Fig. 14 represent the relational instance.

$Program \sqsubseteq \exists id^-,$
$\exists name^- \sqsubseteq String,$
$Beneficiary \sqsubseteq \exists dni,$
$\exists ref\_dni^- \sqsubseteq Beneficiary,$
$Beneficiary \sqsubseteq \exists dateReceivingHelp,$
$\exists program^- \sqsubseteq Integer,$
$Person \sqsubseteq \exists dni,$
$\exists name^- \sqsubseteq String.$

$\exists id^- \sqsubseteq String,$
$Beneficiary \sqsubseteq \exists id,$
$\exists dni^- \sqsubseteq Integer,$
$Beneficiary \sqsubseteq \exists amount,$
$\exists dateReceivingHelp^- \sqsubseteq Date,$
$Beneficiary \sqsubseteq \exists ref\_program . Program,$
$\exists dni^- \sqsubseteq Person,$

$Program \sqsubseteq \exists name,$
$\exists id^- \sqsubseteq Integer,$
$Beneficiary \sqsubseteq \exists ref\_dni . Person,$
$\exists amount^- \sqsubseteq Real,$
$Beneficiary \sqsubseteq \exists program,$
$\exists ref\_program^- \sqsubseteq Program.$
$Person \sqsubseteq \exists name,$

Fig. 13. Terminology for the schema of the data from the municipality

Next, we present the technology for querying the OWL ontologies materialized from this database. SPARQL (SPARQL Protocol and RDF Query Language) [22] is a declarative query language for RDF that allows to retrieve and manipulate data stored in the Semantic Web represented as RDF statements. A SPARQL endpoint accepts queries for any web-accessible RDF data and returns results via HTTP. The results of SPARQL queries can be returned in a variety of formats such as XML, JSON, RDF and HTML. Then, with this solution, data from the municipality's administration can be published in an uniform, public, modern, open format that can be queried both by people and by applications. For instance, finding who were the ten people who, during the year 2019, collected the most of a plan of at least $\$15,000$ could be done by means of the SPARQL query as shown in Fig. 15. This would allow both applications to use it as a web service or end-users users to query the data in a web page.

7 Related Work

With ViziQuer, Cerans et al. [23] provide an open source tool for web-based creation and execution of visual diagrammatic queries over RDF/SPARQL data. The tool supports the data instance level and statistics queries, providing visual counterparts for most of SPARQL 1.1 select query constructs, including aggregation and subqueries. A query environment can be created over a user-supplied SPARQL endpoint with known data schema. ViziQuer provides a visual interface for expressing user queries in SPARQL posed against an ontology. In contrast, we provide the user with an interface for describing subclass expressions and inclusion axioms by means of restrictions imposed on records of a relational table with the aim of populating an ontology that could later be exposed and queried as an SPARQL endpoint.

Program(0001),   name(0001, ' MunicipalOccupationalTrainingProgram'),
Beneficiary(1),   id(1, 1),   dni(1, 22000000),
amount(1, 12000),   dateReceivingHelp(1, '2019-03-10'),   program(1, 0001),
Beneficiary(2),   id(2, 2),   dni(2, 26000000),
amount(2, 16000),   dateReceivingHelp(2, '2019-05-04'),   program(2, 0001),
Beneficiary(3),   id(3, 3),   dni(3, 22000000),
amount(3, 13000),   dateReceivingHelp(2, '2019-05-04'),   program(2, 0001),
Person(22000000),   name(22000000, ' Smith, John'),   Person(26000000),
name(26000000, ' Doe, Jane').

Fig. 14. Relational instance from the data of the municipality

```
PREFIX mbb <http://www.mbb.gov.ar/>
SELECT ?name ?date ?amount
FROM <http://www.mbb.gov.ar>
WHERE
{
    ?beneficiary mbb:ref_dni ?person .
    ?beneficiary mbb:amount ?amount .
    ?beneficiary mbb:date_receiving_help ?date .
    ?person mbb:name ?name .
    BIND (YEAR(?date) as ?year)
    FILTER (?year = 2019 && ?amount >= 15000)
}
ORDER BY DESC(?amount)
LIMIT 10
```

```
---------------------------------------
| name        | date       | amount |
=======================================
| "Doe, Jane" | 2019-05-04 | 16,000 |
---------------------------------------
```

Fig. 15. On the left, the SPARQL query for finding who were the ten people who, during the year 2019, collected the most of a plan of at least $15,000$; and, on the right, the result of the execution of the query by a SPARQL engine against the ontology data in Fig. 14

Christodoulou et al. [24] make the case that structural summaries over linked-data sources can inform query formulation and provide support for data integration and query processing over multiple linked-data sources. To fulfil this aim, they propose an approach that builds on a hierarchical clustering algorithm for inferring structural summaries over linked-data sources. Thus, their approach takes as input an RDF repository and then reverse engineers an ontology using clustering techniques to detect prospective classes. In contrast, we take a database and the user proposes SQL queries to express subconcepts intensionally; when the SQL queries are executed, the fillers of the concept populate the ontology building an extensional de facto definition of the concept. In that regard, the work of Christodoulou et al. can be considered complementary to ours.

Barrasa et al. [25] propose R2O, an extensible and declarative language to describe mappings between relational DB schemas and ontologies implemented in RDF(S) or OWL. R2O provides an extensible set of primitives with well defined semantics. This language has been conceived expressive enough to cope with complex mapping cases arisen from situations of low similarity between the ontology and the DB models. R2O allows the user to express complex queries in terms of ontologies in a language that is similar to the relational algebra but aimed at ontologies. Therefore, this approach is complementary to ours because it allows to query the ontology once it is published in OWL format.

8 Conclusions and Future Work

We presented a framework for performing ontology-based data access by means of performing a materialization approach. Our implementation is JAVA-based and relies on a H2 database management system and a JAVA library called OWL-API for accessing and querying databases and maintaining an OWL database in main memory, respectively. We presented several enhancements that we have made to the previous iteration of our prototype implementation, which now includes a visual mapping specification functionality and allows to maintain a global database that can be either created from scratch or loaded from disk, modified and later saved again to disk. From the experimental evaluation to which we subjected our system, we conclude that our application is able to handle a moderate workload of a table of tens of thousands of records but fails to handle table of the order of millions of records. In this regard, we think that we will be forced to use query-rewriting techniques for delegating the evaluation of queries to the database management system instead of the ontology management library. Part of our current research efforts are aimed in this direction. Other form of improvement lies in the possibility of addressing the federation of databases for performing integration of multiple heterogeneous data sources. We introduced a language for defining the schema information of a CSV file, and then how to interpret the contents of a CSV file for performing its translation into OWL. We discussed how this materialization tool could be used in the context of an e-government application showing how relational data can be publish as open data in OWL.

Acknowledgments. This research is funded by Secretaría General de Ciencia y Técnica, Universidad Nacional del Sur, Argentina and by Comisión de Investigaciones Científicas de la Provincia de Buenos Aires (CIC-PBA).

References

1. Kontchakov, R., Rodríguez-Muro, M., Zakharyaschev, M.: Ontology-based data access with databases: a short course. In: Rudolph, S., Gottlob, G., Horrocks, I., van Harmelen, F. (eds.) Reasoning Web 2013. LNCS, vol. 8067, pp. 194–229. Springer, Heidelberg (2013). https://doi.org/10.1007/978-3-642-39784-4_5
2. Xiao, G., et al.: Ontology-based data access - a survey. In: Proceedings of the Twenty-Seventh International Joint Conference on Artificial Intelligence (IJCAI 2018), pp. 5511–5519 (2018)
3. Berners-Lee, T., Hendler, J., Lassila, O.: The Semantic Web. Sci. Am. **284**(5), 34–43 (2001)

4. Bao, J., Kendall, E.F., McGuinness, D.L., Patel-Schneider, P.F.: OWL 2 Web Ontology Language Quick Reference Guide, 2nd edn. W3C Recommendation, 11 December 2012
5. Gruber, T.R.: A translation approach to portable ontologies. Knowl. Acquisition **5**(2), 199–220 (1993)
6. Calvanese, D., Giacomo, G.D., Lembo, D., Savo, D.F.: The MASTRO system for ontology-based data access. Semantic Web **2**(1), 43–53 (2011)
7. Jimenez-Ruiz, E., et al.: BootOX: practical mapping of RDBs to OWL 2. In: The 14th International Semantic Web Conference, pp. 113–132 (2015)
8. de Medeiros, L.F., Priyatna, F., Corcho, O.: MIRROR: automatic R2RML mapping generation from relational databases (2015)
9. Pinkel, C., et al.: RODI: benchmarking relational-to-ontology mapping generation quality. Semantic Web, 1–26 (2016)
10. Gómez, S.A., Fillottrani, P.R.: Towards a framework for ontology-based data access: materialization of OWL ontologies from relational databases. In: Pesado, P., Aciti, C. (eds.) X Workshop en Innovación en Sistemas de Software (WISS 2018), XXIV Congreso Argentino de Ciencias de la Computación, CACIC 2018, pp. 857–866 (2018)
11. Gómez, S.A., et al.: Desarrollo de herramientas para acceso a bases de datos heterogéneas basado en ontologías en el contexto de la entrega de servicios públicos digitales. Primer Encuentro de Centros Propios y Asociados de la Comisión de Investigaciones Científicas de la Provincia de Buenos Aires, pp. 235–238 (2018)
12. Baader, F., Horrocks, I., Lutz, C., Sattler, U.: An Introduction to Description Logic. Cambridge University Press, Cambridge (2017)
13. Silberschatz, A., Korth, H.F., Sudarshan, S.: Database System Concepts, 6th edn. McGraw-Hill Education, New York (1983)
14. Gómez, S.A., Fillottrani, P.: A framework for OBDA - current state and perspectives. In: Actas del XXV Congreso Argentino de Ciencias de la Computación (CACIC 2019), pp. 920–929 (2019)
15. Arenas, M., Bertails, A., Prud'hommeaux, E., Sequeda, J.: A Direct Mapping of Relational Data to RDF. W3C Recommendation, 27 September 2012
16. Tennison, J.: CSV on the Web - A Primer, W3C working group note, 25 February 2016
17. Horridge, M., Bechhofer, S.: The OWL API: a Java API for OWL ontologies. Semantic Web **2**(1), 11–21 (2011)
18. Matentzoglu, N., Palmisano, I.: An Introduction to the OWL API. Technical report, The University of Manchester (2016)
19. Bertot, J., Estevez, E., Janowski, T.: Universal and contextualized public services - digital public service innovation framework. Gov. Inf. Q. **33**, 211–222 (2016)
20. Estévez, E., Fillottrani, P., Janowski, T., Ojo, A.: Government information sharing - a framework for policy formulation. In: Pin-Yu, C., Yu-Che, C. (eds.) E-Governance and Cross-boundary Collaboration - Innovations and Advancing Tools, pp. 23–55. IGI Global (2011)
21. Fillottrani, P., Estévez, E., Cenci, K., Pesado, P., Pasini, A., Thomas, P.: Herramientas para el desarrollo y la entrega de servicios públicos digitales de acción social para municipios bonaerenses. In: IV Congreso Internacional Científico y Tecnológico-CONCYT 2017 (2017)
22. Harris, S., Seaborne, A.: SPARQL 1.1 Query Language for RDF W3C recommendation, 21 March 2013. https://www.w3.org/TR/rdf-sparql-query/

23. Čerāns, K., et al.: ViziQuer: a web-based tool for visual diagrammatic queries over RDF data. In: Gangemi, A., et al. (eds.) ESWC 2018. LNCS, vol. 11155, pp. 158–163. Springer, Cham (2018). https://doi.org/10.1007/978-3-319-98192-5_30
24. Christodoulou, K., Paton, N.W., Fernandes, A.A.: Structure inference for linked data sources using clustering. In: Proceedings of the Joint EDBT/ICDT 2013 Workshops, EDBT 2013, pp. 60–67 (2013)
25. Barrasa, J., Corcho, Ó., Gómez-Pérez, A.: R2O, an extensible and semantically based database-to-ontology mapping language. In: Proceedings of the Second Workshop on Semantic Web and Databases, SWDB 2004, vol. 3372 (2004)

New Application of the Requirements Elicitation Process for the Construction of Intelligent System-Based Predictive Models

Cinthia Vegega$^{(\boxtimes)}$, Pablo Pytel, and María Florencia Pollo-Cattaneo

Information System Methodologies Research Group, National Technological University of Buenos Aires, Buenos Aires, Argentina
cinthiavg@yahoo.com.ar, ppytel@gmail.com,
flo.pollo@gmail.com

Abstract. Decision-making is an essential process in the life of organizations and is particularly important for managerial positions in charge of making decisions on resources allocation. These decisions must be based on predictions about time, effort and/or risks involved in their tasks. Currently, this situation is exacerbated by the complex environment surrounding the organizations, which makes them act beyond their traditional management systems incorporating new mechanisms such as those provided by Artificial Intelligence, leading to the development of an Intelligent Predictive Model. In this context, this work proposes a new case study where the proposed process is applied for the elicitation of the necessary requirements for the implementation an Intelligent System-based Predictive Model, in this case, one oriented to the construction of an Artificial Neural Network.

Keywords: Elicitation process · Intelligent systems · Machine learning · Training data

1 Introduction

Decision-making involves questioning the validity of the alternatives, their weightings, the selection criteria to be used and their future impact [1]. For this reason, Humanity has always sought mechanisms to make accurate predictions. Such need not only affects individuals but also organizations. Decision-making is an essential process in the life of organizations. While each member of an organization makes decisions, this process is particularly important for managerial positions. Consequently, managers are known as "decision makers" in their tasks of planning, organizing, directing and controlling [2]. Daily, they have to decide how to allocate valuable resources based on predictions [3] about time, effort and/or risks involved in their tasks. This situation is exacerbated by the highly complex and hardly predictable environment of the 21st century [4], which makes organizations act beyond their traditional management systems and incorporate new mechanisms for the "creation and enhancement of the organization's knowledge" such as those provided by Artificial Intelligence [5, 6].

© Springer Nature Switzerland AG 2020
P. Pesado and M. Arroyo (Eds.): CACIC 2019, CCIS 1184, pp. 302–318, 2020.
https://doi.org/10.1007/978-3-030-48325-8_20

An example of these new mechanisms can be found in the area of Predictive Models. Despite the fact that Statistical Techniques and Parametric Models have traditionally been used to generate predictions [7], in the last two decades diverse methods associated to Machine Learning have been incorporated [3, 8]. Consequently, it is possible to build models to find a relation between past and future situations using available historical data. In this sense, Artificial Neural Networks [9, 10] and Bayesian Networks [11, 12] can be mentioned as the main Intelligent Systems architectures to be used for this kind of problems [13–15]. These Intelligent System-based Predictive Models possess very useful features, such as generalization capacities, robustness, and self-organization [16].

However, unfortunately, Predictive Models are usually imprecise [3] or, in some cases, they fail, thus often generating incompatible answers [17]. In this regard, the quality of the information required is highly important to make accurate decisions [18]. It is possible to generate more accurate predictions if lack of knowledge on the problem and its context is reduced. Yet, it is almost impossible to have complete, accurate and precise information to make absolutely accurate predictions. There is always a risk related with trusting the available information to assess the situation so a prediction must be associated to a certain degree of probability [19]. Such probability is affected by what is known about the problem and what is not. Consequently, apart from collecting historical data that will be used to build the Predictive Model, it is also necessary to identify the general characteristics of the domain where the prediction is taking place thus being able to detect situations or events of which there are no data but which the model must consider.

In this context, a process has been proposed to assist the Information Systems Engineer in the difficult work of collecting, understanding, identifying and registering the necessary information to implement an Intelligent System-based Predictive Model. In [20] this proposed process has been applied to a case study developed at Facultad Regional Buenos Aires (FRBA), Universidad Tecnológica Nacional (UTN), Argentina. Specifically, it is carried out in a course of the first year of the "Information Systems Engineering" undergraduate program. The aim has been to implement an Intelligent System to predict the performance of students throughout the course. Because any error in the predictions can lead teachers or students to make wrong decisions, it is of great importance that the system presents consistent results taking into account the normal behavior of the students in the course.

This new work, then, presents the application of the process in a new case study within the context of a medical office. For that purpose, Sect. 2 presents a brief summary of the proposed process and Sect. 3 presents the results of applying this process in the new case study. Finally, Sect. 4 describes conclusions taking into account the contributions of the process identified from its application in both cases study, as well as future line of work.

2 Proposed Process

The proposed process aims to assist with the Information Systems Engineers (in their role of Functional Analyst) involved in the implementation of Intelligent Predictive Models, that is, it seeks to support them during the initial phases of the Project considering its particularities. This proposed Project is limited to contemplating the characteristics of two types of Intelligent Systems applied for the implementation of Predictive Models, Multi-layer Perceptron Artificial Neural Networks (ANN) with error Backpropagation training (BPNN) and Bayesian Networks (BN). Consequently, as a result of this proposal, the objectives, success criterion, constraints and assumptions of the Project are determined in order to identify the available information required to train the Intelligent System and to generate an initial specification of it. These results will help the development team start working on the construction, training and validation of the Intelligent Predictive Model to meet the expectations of the organization. The proposed process is structured into the following five phases:

1. **Project Definition Phase:** it aims to define the stakeholders who collaborate in the Project and its scope based on the objectives to be achieved. To do this, the following activities are carried out: "Identify the Objectives of the Project", "Identify the Project Stakeholders" and "Identify the Project Scope".
2. **Business Process Elicitation Phase:** its objective is to identify and collect the business processes that are relevant for the project, as well as the expert's task in the case of building a model that emulates their prediction capabilities. This is done through the activities of "Identify Business Processes" and "Collect Business Processes". Since the aim is to implement a Predictive Model based on the knowledge of experts available in the organization, the tasks corresponding to the third activity "Collect the Expert's Tasks", since they are not associated with any business process that is standardized within the domain. For this purpose, knowledge education techniques are used, such as Protocol Analysis, which allows to obtain the knowledge about how the experts perform their tasks.
3. **Business Process Data Elicitation Phase**: it seeks to identify the data repositories where the information of the different business processes is stored and to collect information about the characteristics of those repositories. This is achieved through the activities of "Identify Data Repositories" and "Collect Business Data". In this way, it is intended to reveal the characteristics of each of the data repositories.
4. **Business Data Conceptualization Phase:** its objective is to identify and evaluate the representativeness of the data available in the business for the construction of the intelligent predictive model. In order to carry out this evaluation, in the activity "Identify Data to Build the Predictive Model", Knowledge Extraction techniques are used to obtain the characteristics of each data and, Knowledge Education techniques (such as the Interview), to obtain the knowledge of those responsible for the repositories in each of these data. Taking into account the data obtained, the representativeness of these data is analyzed in the "Validate Data Representativeness" activity. For this purpose, a technique has been proposed to validate that the data to be used in the construction of a Predictive Model are representative of the domain of the problem. This technique is called Clustered Grid and its tasks are based on the

Grid technique but present some differences with respect to the original technique. The main difference is that the grids (matrices) are generated directly from the data collected and then the results generated by the formalization of the grids are contrasted with the vision of the experts or stakeholders of the business. In addition, three grids are used: one for the Elements (which allows the evaluation of already known classes) and two for the Characteristics (one direct and one opposite, to evaluate the rest of the attributes). In order to demonstrate the functioning of the applied technique, before being used in the proposed process model, in [21] it was employed in two sets of data recognized as being widely used for the verification and comparison of Machine Learning algorithms. The first set of data corresponds to the Iris flower data while the second set corresponds to the wine quality data.

5. **Intelligent System Initial Specification Phase:** based on the information obtained in previous phases, the most appropriate type of technology to implement the predictive model is determined, as well as a proposal of its initial topology. To achieve this, the activities of "Select the Type of Intelligent System" and "Define Initial Topology of the Intelligent System". In order to carry out the first of these activities, an ad-hoc technique is used to evaluate the suitability of each of the possible architectures (in this case, Artificial Neural Networks or Bayesian Networks) and thus determine which is the most appropriate. For this purpose, the characteristics of the project are considered. Therefore, this technique requires that a set of questions be answered to allow the project to be characterized. However, at the beginning of a project it is not easy to answer these questions with an adequate degree of certainty, so the technique proposed is based on the principle of Fuzzy Expert Systems, thus allowing to handle a range of five linguistic values and, in this way, to give an answer to each of the questions to be considered. By using a simple procedure it is possible to transform these linguistic values, indicated by the engineer, into diffuse intervals that will then be used to obtain an assessment of the suitability of each architecture. To demonstrate the functioning of this technique in [22], two proofs of concept and a statistical analysis using the Monte Carlo simulation method have been carried out.

3   Application of the Process in Case Study of a Medical Office

This section presents the implementation of the phases of the proposed model in a case in a medical office. Specifically within a pediatric medical office, which sees children from birth to adolescence on their 18th birthday. Office appointments are provided online, with the exception of prenatal or first-time telephone consultations. Despite not having an on-call service, unscheduled consultations from their own patients are often attended to. Appointments for such consultations (called "over-shifts" appointments) are granted by telephone on the same day as they are required. These over-shifts appointments are discharged by the secretary the same day they are requested, since if an over-shift is required, the office must be called to check availability. The over-shifts are registered between the normal office appointments. For example, between the 9:00 a.m. and 9:30 a.m. appointment there may be an over-shift appointment at 9:15 a.m. In this context, we seek to implement an intelligent system that allows us to predict the number of normal and over-shift appointments for a particular date and time, given that we wish to hire, when necessary, another paediatrician to assist in the care of patients.

The following Sects. 3.1 to 3.5 describe the results of each phase of the process along with the activities that are carried out in each one of them.

3.1 Application of the Project Definition Phase

The following activities are performed:

Activity: "Identify the Objectives of the Project". In this activity, the first conceptual meeting of the project is held with the paediatrician in charge of the office, in order to understand the objective of the project and its expectations. Likewise, the contact of the person responsible for the computer system is established, who will be one of the interested parties in the project, with whom the initial meeting is held. Hiring, when necessary, another paediatrician to assist in the care of the patients. The information obtained is analyzed and the main objectives of the Project are identified, which are documented in the project objectives form, as shown in Fig. 1.

OBJECTIVES OF THE PROJECT		
ID	*Objective Description*	*Priority*
OBJ1	To implement an Intelligent System to predict the number of patient's normal and over-shift appointments for the pediatric office.	High
Observations		
The priority is considered high because it is the only objective that originates the project.		

Fig. 1. Project objectives form.

Activity: "Identify the Project's Stakeholders". In this activity, the Functional Analyst, based on the information gathered from the organization, identifies the project participants and creates the form shown in Fig. 2.

PROJECT STAKEHOLDERS			
Position	*Org / Sector*	*Project Role*	*Knowledge Areas*
Doctor	Pediatric Office	Person in charge	Office Management
Secretary		Stakeholder	
IT System Manager			IT System Functionalities

Fig. 2. Project stakeholders form.

Activity: "Identify the Project Scope". Based on the collected information, the Functional Analyst defines the success criteria of the project as shown in Fig. 3 and determines the problems to be solved in order to establish what should be included as a result of the project. With this information, the project scope definition form is created, as shown in Fig. 4. This form must be validated by the doctor. Furthermore, the Functional Analyst also needs to identify the assumptions for the execution of the project. This project assumptions form is shown in Fig. 5. Finally, the information restrictions of the project are defined by the project restrictions form (Fig. 6).

PROJECT SUCESS CRITERIA		
ID	*Criterion Description*	*OBJ-ID*
CE1	You want to be able to predict by date (month and day) and time (morning, noon and evening), the number of normal and over-shift appointments granted.	OBJ1

Fig. 3. Project success criteria form.

PROJECT SCOPE DEFINITION		
ID	*Problems to solve*	*OBJ-ID*
P1	To analyze in a complete way the management of the appointments (normals and over-shifts) of the office identifying the states through which each one of the reserved appointments passes (from its creation until the patient has been attended).	OBJ1
Problems excluded from the Project		
Medical diagnoses per patient are excluded as they are considered confidential.		

Fig. 4. Project scope definition form.

PROJECT ASSUMPTIONS		
ID	*Assumption Description*	*OBJ-ID*
S1	There will be unrestricted access to the person responsible for the computer system and to the office secretary, and consultations can be made by e-mail or in person.	OBJ1
S2	The data are considered to be correct and complete.	OBJ1

Fig. 5. Project assumptions form.

PROJECT RESTRICTIONS			
ID	*Type*	*Description*	*OBJ-ID*
R1	Data	Patients' names, surnames, addresses, telephone numbers and documents cannot be used as they are considered confidential.	OBJ1
R2	Data	The data corresponding to the affiliations of the health insurance cannot be used because they are considered confidential.	OBJ1

Fig. 6. Project restrictions form.

3.2   Application of the Business Process Elicitation Phase

The following activities are performed:

Activity: "Identify Business Processes". From the minutes of the meetings held with project stakeholders, the Project Objectives form (Fig. 1), the Project Success Criteria form (Fig. 2) and the Project Scope Definition form (Fig. 3), the Functional Analyst defines the most significant business activities for the project and makes a use case diagram that is included in the business process diagram form (Fig. 7a).

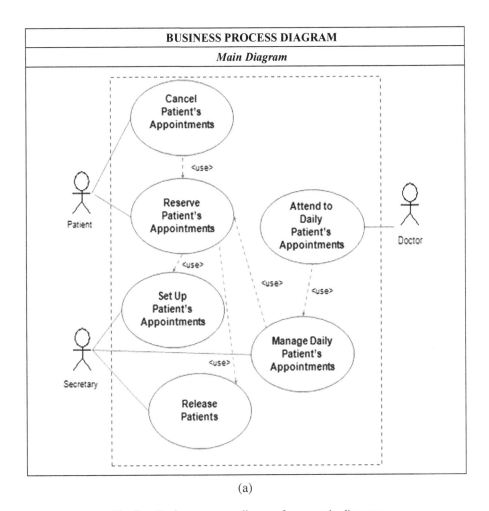

(a)

Fig. 7a. Business process diagram form - main diagram.

Activity: "Collect Business Processes". Taking into account the collected information associated with the identified business process, the Functional Analyst holds a new meeting with the secretary and IT system manager. In this way, information is collected to record how the processes work and how it is related to data repositories. This new information is registered also in the business process diagram form (Fig. 7b).

BUSINESS PROCESS DIAGRAM				
Business Process List				
ID	*Name*	*Description*	*Person in Charge*	*OBJ-ID*
P0001	Set Up Patient's Appointments	The goal of this process is to load the schedule of appointments for the doctors in the office. As a result, the appointments are recorded with "available" status.	Secretary	OBJ1
P0002	Reserve Patient's Appointments	The goal of this process is for the patient to book an appointment. The appointment's status is recorded as "booked".	Patient	OBJ1
P0003	Cancel Patient's Appointments	The goal of this process is the cancellation of an appointment by the patient. The appointment's status returns to "available".	Patient	OBJ1
P0004	Manage Daily Patient's Appointments	The objective of this process is to manage all the appointments that the office has reserved for the day. If the patient goes to the consultation room, he or she will be placed in "waiting" status, but if at the end of the day he or she hasn´t attended, he or she will be assigned "suspended" status.	Secretary	OBJ1
P0005	Attend to Daily Patient's Appointments	The aim of this process is to update the appointments once the paediatrician has seen his patients. Upon entering the office, the appointment changes to "attending" and then to "finished" to indicate that he or she has been attended to.	Doctor	OBJ1
P0006	Release Patients	The goal of this process is to discharge patients who are visiting the office for the first time.	Secretary	OBJ1

(b)

Fig. 7b. Business process diagram form - business process list.

3.3   Application of the Business Process Data Elicitation Phase

The following activities are performed:

Activity: "Identify Data Repositories". The Functional Analyst analyzes the information gathered from the interviews conducted with the business stakeholders. As a result, he detects that the main data to be used in the project are in the comma-separated values (CSV) file named *"patient_appointments.csv"* which describe the patient's appointments granted since November 2017 to the present. These data were extracted directly from the IT system database and were provided by the person responsible for that system. After defining such data repositories, the Functional Analyst registers this information and prepares the data repository form shown in Fig. 8.

DATA REPOSITORIES					
ID	*Name*	*Type*	*Description*	*Business Process /Task*	*Person in charge*
T_CONS	patient_ appointments.csv	CSV file	Patient's appointments granted since November 2017 to the present.	P0001, P0002, P0003, P0004, P0005	IT System Manager

Fig. 8. Data repository form.

Activity: "Collect Business Data". The Functional Analyst prepares the data structure form, shown in Fig. 9. It is clarified that the CSV file is a single file that has the non-standardized data of all the tables, where each record corresponds to a certain appointment (either normal or over-shift).

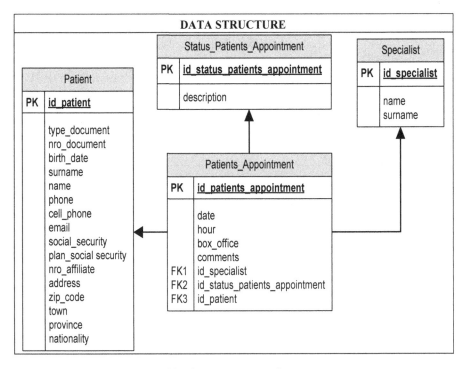

Fig. 9. Data structure form.

3.4   Application of the Business Data Conceptualization Phase

The purpose of this phase is to determine whether the data that will be used in the Predictive Model are representative. Therefore the following activities are performed:

Activity: "Identify Data to Build the Predictive Model". Based on the "Data Repository" form (Fig. 8), the "Data Structure" form (Fig. 9) and the information collected in the interviews conducted to the business stakeholders, the Functional Analyst documents the obtained data in the "Available Data" form (Fig. 10).

AVAILABLE DATA	
The data repositories named *patient_appointments.csv* has 10 attributes. In this case, one attribute is described as an example.	
Attribute:	*STATUS*
Description:	Status Patient's Appointments (field "id_status_patients_appointment" within the table "Status_Patients_Appointment" in the database)
Type of Data:	Numeric
Value Range:	- 1: Available - 2: Reserved - 3: Waiting - 4: Attending - 5: Finished - 6: Suspended

Fig. 10. Available data form.

Activity: "Validate Data Representativeness". Based on the available data obtained in the previous activity, the Functional Analyst analyzes whether such data are representative of the business in order to build the Predictive Model. Due to space constraints, all the tasks performed on the data set are specified in [23].

Firstly, the preparation of the data is carried out where tasks including formatting, cleaning and integration of the data are performed. Once prepared, the segmentation of the numerical attributes is carried out. Using the segmented data, the grids of elements and characteristics are generated, in order to obtain the ordered trees of elements and characteristics respectively. Taking into account these trees, a meeting is held with the paediatrician and the office secretary who take the role of experts in the domain to discuss the results generated.

- When they are presented with the ordered tree of elements, in view of the relationship between the completed and suspended normal appointments together with the completed over-shift appointments, they mention that this relationship is correct, since the behavior of the over-shifts is similar to the behavior of the normal appointments. The only difference is that over-shifts are requested on the same day by the patient and not in advance as normal appointments. On the other hand, they agree that it is correct that suspended over-shift appointments are not within the same relationship because it is very rare for over-shifts to be cancelled by patients.

In general, unless the patient requires a very urgent consultation and must attend an appointment, patients who ask for over-shifts attend the office at the time indicated by the secretary.

- Then, the ordered tree of characteristics is presented. In view of this, they express that they also agree on the relationships generated, since the specialist who attends the office always has a certain schedule. In this case, there are only two specialists in the office, but the objective is to incorporate even more at specific times. Likewise, there are times when the specialists take turns (for example, during vacation periods) so it is considered correct to relate this to the month and finally to the day of the month in which they attend. Likewise, the doctor tells us that he would have liked to know the season of the year, because depending on the season there can be more or less appointments. As the season can be calculated with the existing data, it is not necessary to carry out a new analysis and the interpretation of the tree is considered to be correct.

Based on the conclusions obtained, the data is representative and will be used to build the Predictive Model.

3.5   Application of the Initial Specification of the Intelligent System Phase

The following activities are performed

Activity: "Select Type of Intelligent System". The Functional Analyst answers the questions associated to each characteristic using the meeting minutes written in previous phases, formalizing them in Table 1 as shown below.

Table 1. Characteristics evaluated in order to define the most appropriate architecture.

Category	ID	Question associated to the characteristic	Value
Available data	D1	How much confidence is there as to the representativeness of the data?	Much
	D2	To what extent may the data be considered complex and with a nonlinear relationship between their attributes?	Little
	D3	How many examples do the data include?	Little
	D4	What percentage of data is there with continuous numeric values (in relation to non-numeric values or numeric discrete values)?	Nothing
Expected results	R1	To what extent is prediction accuracy considered critical?	Much
	R2	To what extent is it desirable to know and compare the predictions for different possibilities and scenarios?	Little
	R3	To what extent is it important to be able to explain how the results generated were obtained?	Nothing
Problem domain	P1	How stable is the problem to be solved?	Much
	P2	To what extent are the domain experts available to participate in the project?	Much
	P3	To what extent it is desirable to be able to manually adjust the network based on the knowledge about the data?	Nothing

Once the linguistic values ("Nothing", "Little", "Regular", "Much" or "All") corresponding to each characteristic defined in Table 1 are assigned, the Functional Analyst obtains the values corresponding to each architecture and selects the best architecture for the project. The operations made are presented in the spreadsheet available in [24]. As shown in Fig. 11, the type of technology selected in this case is a Multi-layer Perceptron Artificial Neural Networks with error Backpropagation training. This selection is registered in the predictive model architecture form, shown in Fig. 12.

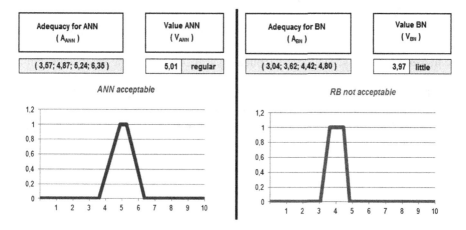

Fig. 11. Appropriateness values for each architecture.

PREDICTIVE MODEL ARCHITECTURE
The most suitable architecture for this project corresponds to the Artificial Neural Networks, while it is ruled out to use Bayesian Networks for the problem to be solved. The reasons for the score assigned to ANN are mainly related to the following factors: On the one hand, the available data includes examples from the year 2017. Although it would have been preferable to have more data, which is not feasible, given that the appointments prior to that year were made on paper agendas that have already been discarded, so they cannot be recreated. Similarly, with the available data, training can be carried out and the network can also be validated. However, first the available data must be transformed into numerical values in order to be used by this technology. For this purpose, there are experts in the field who can contribute their knowledge and participate in the project. However, this knowledge will not be used to make manual adjustments to the network. On the other hand, in this problem it is appropriate to apply an ANN because it is not necessary to know how the results were obtained, nor is it essential to compare the predictions for different scenarios. Furthermore, great importance is attached to the accuracy of the results generated.

Fig. 12. Predictive model architecture form.

Activity: "Define Initial Topology of the Intelligent System". Once the type of architecture to be used is selected, the Functional Analyst defines the initial characteristics of the topology and documents them in the initial topology of the predictive model architecture form.

For building the proposed model, the analysis used the NEAT4J [25] framework, which implements in Java the 'NeuroEvolution of Augmenting Topologies' or NEAT [26] algorithm for the construction of ANN using evolutionary algorithms. In this case, a fitness function provided by the framework called "MSE NEAT Fitness Function" is used to minimize the error when calculating the root mean square of the difference between the desired output and that generated by the network. Due to the requirements of this function, the values of the attributes had to be reformatted into decimal numbers (when divided by 100). This data is then stored in a new CSV file to be accessed from the framework. Finally, the file is supplied to NEAT4J, so that the latter can begin to evolve possible ANN topologies to generate the quantities corresponding to the date to be estimated. After several runs, the "species" with the best suitability value (i.e., the ANN topology that generates the least error in the prediction) is obtained in "time" (or cycle) 939 of the 3rd run with a suitability value of 0.0569. The topology thus generated is shown in Fig. 13.

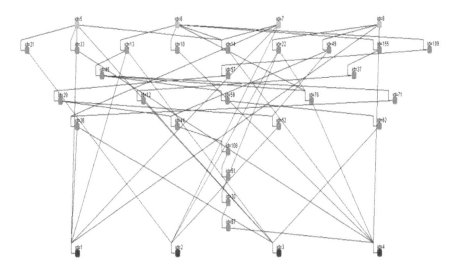

Fig. 13. Artificial Neural Networks.

Although the implementation of the final ANN is beyond the scope of this process, in order to confirm whether this initial topology was successfully defined, it is validated using the NeurophStudio tool [27]. A new project is then generated in which a Multi-Perceptron BackPropagation ANN is defined with the following topology, shown in Fig. 14: 4 neurons in the entry layer, 4 neurons in the first hidden layer, 4 neurons in the second hidden layer, 5 neurons in the third hidden layer, 3 neurons in the fourth hidden layer, 9 neurons in the fifth hidden layer and 4 neurons in the exit layer.

Although in a real project it would not make sense to validate an Intelligent System with the same data with which it was trained (given that the precision thus obtained is not reliable), here we only seek to confirm that the probabilities provided by the network can be considered as representative of the data used. In this case, an accuracy of 98.8% is obtained for completed normal appointments, 98.9% for suspended normal appointments, 95.3% for completed over-shift appointments and 97.8% for suspended over-shift appointments. From these results it is possible to assure that this initial topology is useful to be used as a base prototype of the Intelligent Model to predict the number of appointments in the doctor's office.

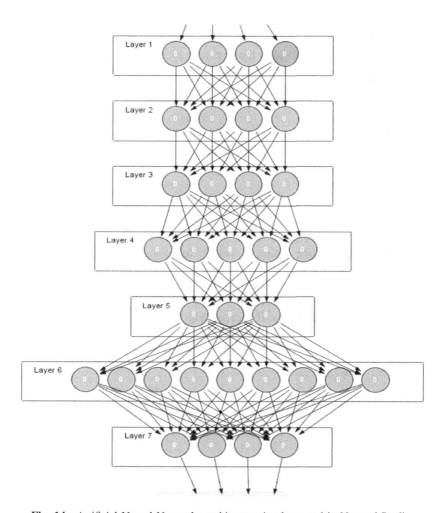

Fig. 14. Artificial Neural Networks architecture implemented in NeurophStudio.

4   Conclusions

The proposed process (including its phases and activities) has been validated in two different domains, one within the educational field and the other within the medical field. The first case study (presented in [20]) is developed within the context of a grade level subject where the aim is to implement an Intelligent System that allows the prediction of student performance. The second case study (presented in this work) is developed within a pediatric medical office where an Intelligent System is to be implemented to predict the number of normal and over-shift appointments for a particular date and time.

In both cases, the proposed process manages to successfully assist in the elicitation of the necessary requirements for the implementation of the Intelligent System that will be in charge of carrying out the corresponding predictions. The activities of the first phase of the process allow to identify the objectives that the Predictive Model will have together with the expectations and scope of the project. The second phase reveals the most significant business processes for the objectives whose information is used in the third phase to identify the data sources to be used in the project. These data sources are then evaluated in the fourth phase to identify the data set representative of the problem domain. Finally, in the fifth phase, the most appropriate architecture for building the Predictive Model is determined and an initial topology of the model is proposed.

As future lines of work, to complement the study carried out in this paper, the following are mentioned:

- To study the behavior of the proposed process model in other domains.
- To extend the technique of validation of the representativeness of the available data to be used in the construction of Intelligent Systems to other types of problems associated with Automatic Learning such as, for example, classification problems, segmentation (or clustering), detection of anomalies, among others.
- To extend the technique of selection of the type of architecture of the Predictive Model so that it can evaluate the suitability of other architectures, such as, for example, Induction algorithms, Regression algorithms or Deep Learning.

References

1. De Kohan, N.C.: Los Sesgos Cognitivos en la Toma de Decisiones. Int. J. Psychol. Res. 1(1), 68–73 (2008). ISSN 2011-7922
2. Robbins, S., Coulter, M.: Administración. Décima Edición. Prentice Hall, Upper Saddle River (2010). ISBN 978-607-442-388-4
3. Mair, C., Kadoda, G., Lefley, M., Phalp, K., Schofield, C., Shepperd, M., Webster, S.: An investigation of machine learning based prediction systems. J. Syst. Softw. 53(1), 23–29 (2000)
4. García, F.J.M., Martínez, M.A.P., García, J.S.: Gestión Estratégica del Conocimiento. Asociación Universitaria Iberoamericana de Postgrado (2003)
5. Nilsson, N.J.: Principles of Artificial Intelligence. Morgan Kaufmann, Los Altos (2014)

6. Russell, S.J., Norvig, P., Davis, E., Russell, S.J., Russell, S.J.: Artificial Intelligence: a Modern Approach, vol. 2. Prentice Hall, Englewood Cliffs (2010)
7. Shepperd, M., Kadoda, G.: Comparing software prediction techniques using simulation. IEEE Trans. Software Eng. **27**(11), 1014–1022 (2001)
8. Bontempi, G., Ben Taieb, S., Le Borgne, Y.-A.: Machine learning strategies for time series forecasting. In: Aufaure, M.-A., Zimányi, E. (eds.) eBISS 2012. LNBIP, vol. 138, pp. 62–77. Springer, Heidelberg (2013). https://doi.org/10.1007/978-3-642-36318-4_3
9. Wang, S.C.: Artificial neural network. In: Interdisciplinary Computing in Java Programming, pp. 81–100. Springer, Boston (2003). https://doi.org/10.1007/978-1-4615-0377-4_5
10. Wang, L., Fu, K.: Artificial neural networks. In: Wiley Encyclopedia of Computer Science and Engineering, pp. 181–188 (2009)
11. Barber, D.: Bayesian Reasoning and Machine Learning. The MIT Press, Cambridge (2012)
12. Premchaiswadi, W. (ed.): Bayesian Networks. In-Tech (2012)
13. Chatfield, C.: The Analysis of Time Series: An Introduction. CRC Press, Boca Raton (2016)
14. De Gooijer, J.G., Hyndman, R.J.: 25 years of time series forecasting. Int. J. Forecast. **22**(3), 443–473 (2006)
15. Zhang, G., Hu, M.Y.: Neural network forecasting of the British Pound/US Dollar exchange rate. Omega Int. J. Manage. Sci. **26**(4), 495–506 (1998)
16. Cohen, P.R., Feigenbaum, E.A.: The Handbook of Artificial Intelligence, vol. 3. Butterworth-Heinemann, Los Altos (2014)
17. Acquatela, H.: La Predicción del Futuro: desde el Oráculo de Delfos hasta la Medicina Actual. Gac. méd. Caracas **114**(2), 150–156 (2006). ISSN 0367-4762
18. Rodríguez, M., Márquez Alegría, M.: Manejo de Problemas y Toma de Decisiones, vol. 8. Editorial El Manual Moderno (2015). ISBN 9789684264670
19. Arsham, H.: Tools for Decision Analysis: Analysis of Risky Decisions (2006)
20. Vegega, C., Pytel P., Pollo-Cattaneo, M.F.: Elicitación de Requerimientos para la Construcción de Modelos Predictivos basados en Sistemas Inteligentes dentro del Ámbito Educativo. In: Workshop en Innovación en Sistemas de Software. Universidad Nacional de Río Cuarto, Facultad de Ciencias Exactas, Físico-Químicas y Naturales. Proceedings XXV Congreso Argentino de Ciencias de la Computación (CACIC 2019), pp. 980–989 (2019). ISBN 978-987-688-377-1
21. Vegega, C., Pytel, P., Pollo-Cattaneo, M.F.: Método basado en el Emparrillado para evaluar los Datos aplicables para entrenar Algoritmos de Aprendizaje Automático. Desarrollo e Innovación en Ingeniería - Segunda Edición, pp. 106–137. Editorial Instituto Antioqueño de Investigación (Licencia CCA, NonCommercial, ShareAlike 4.0 Unported License) (2017). ISBN 978-958-59127-5-5
22. Vegega, C., Pytel, P., Straccia, L., Pollo-Cattaneo, M.F.: Proceso de Selección de Arquitectura a fin de Implementar un Modelo Predictivo Inteligente. In: Memorias de 6to. Congreso Nacional de Ingeniería Informática y Sistemas de Información (CONAIISI 2018). Workshop de Aplicaciones Informáticas y de Sistemas de Información (2018). ISSN 2347-0372
23. Vegega, C., Pytel, P., Pollo-Cattaneo, M.F.: Resultados de la Aplicación del Procedimiento del Emparrillado Clusterizado sobre los Datos de Turnos Médicos en Consultorio Pediátrico. Reporte Técnico GEMIS-TD-2019-09-TR-2019-10-ResultadosTurnosMedicos (2019). https://bit.ly/39Mp8Cv
24. Vegega, C., Pytel, P., Pollo-Cattaneo, M.F.: Resultados de la Aplicación del Procedimiento para Evaluar la Arquitectura del Sistema Inteligente sobre los Datos de Turnos Médicos en Consultorio Pediátrico. Reporte Técnico GEMIS-TD-2019-09-TR-2019-10-MetodoEvaluadorArquitecturaTurnosMedicos (2019). https://bit.ly/323Apf5

25. NEAT4J: Java Framework – Home Page for users of NeuroEvolution for Augmenting Topologies. Sourceforge.net (2006). http://neat4j.sourceforge.net
26. Heidenreich, H.: NEAT: An Awesome Approach to NeuroEvolution. Towards Data Science (2019)
27. NeurophStudio: Home Page for Users of Java Neural Network Framework. Sourceforge.net (2011). http://neuroph.sourceforge.net

Signal Processing and Real-Time Systems

Localization System Using Artificial Landmarks for Indoor Low-Cost Mobile Robots

Rafael Ignacio Zurita[✉], Alejandro Mora, Candelaria Alvarez,
and Miriam Lechner

Facultad de Informática, Universidad Nacional del Comahue,
Buenos Aires 1400, 8300 Neuquén, Argentina
rafa@fi.uncoma.edu.ar

Abstract. Localization is a prerequisite for land navigation of mobile robots. It is usually implemented with multiple sensors and high performance computers, so it is not usually a low-cost mobile robot capability. In this paper we present the architecture and design of a prototype embedded system which reports its location using a minimum-performance hardware and artificial landmarks. In order to evaluate accuracy, experimental tests were performed in an indoor environment, obtaining repeated locations from the prototype system. Based on the results, it is concluded that the proposed system is able to localize itself, with $\pm 12\,\text{cm}$ of accuracy, at a frequency of $2\,\text{Hz}$. Conclusions raise the possibility, in future works, for the inclusion of land navigation using maps into low-cost robots, that until today do not usually present this characteristic.

Keywords: Mobile robot · Localization · Navigation · Embedded system · Locating system · AprilTag

1 Introduction

One of the requisites for land navigation in mobile robots is a localization system. Specifically, it is a system that can be used in a mobile robot to determine its exact orientation and location in the environment in which it is navigating. With this information and a virtual reference map which represents the real environment, the robot is able to plan a route and to travel to accomplish its objectives [10].

Currently, indoor mobile robots with the capability of navigation are designed and built for complex tasks; usually working in industrial environments for moving heavy loads inside large buildings. There is another type as well, working in public places, for example in hotels. Those robots navigate from reception to different rooms, delivering requested supplies to guests [3,12]. The cost and energy consumption are usually not an important restriction for this kind of robots, so these usually are made up of laser (LIDAR), visual (cameras) and orientation

© Springer Nature Switzerland AG 2020
P. Pesado and M. Arroyo (Eds.): CACIC 2019, CCIS 1184, pp. 321–331, 2020.
https://doi.org/10.1007/978-3-030-48325-8_21

and speed (inertial measurement units) sensors, for collecting data from the environment. These robots are also equipped with computers capable of processing large amounts of information in real time, which together with sensors, enable the robots to know their locations and navigate their work environments [4].

In contrast, low-cost indoor mobile robots have a low-performance microcontroller or microprocessor as a central control system. These robots perform simple tasks, like vacuuming dust in a living room (domestic), or performing simple movements (forward, left, etc.) when executing programs developed by students (educational robotics). In order to accomplish these tasks they use rudimentary sensors that allow a simple interaction with the environment, for example to avoid collision with obstacles or move within an invisible fence. The sensors in this class of robots can detect the object to avoid when it is at a very short distance, returning basic information that can be discretized to indicate only whether or not there is an object in front of the sensor. For this reason these simple robots only perform reactive navigation (without using maps) since they are not able to determine their locations [8].

In this article, which is an extension of [14], we present the architecture of a prototype embedded system, which reports its location using artificial landmarks and a low-performance microprocessor. It is designed to be easily integrated into low-cost mobile robots, so this category of robots can determine their locations in indoor environments. The system is based on the acquisition of signals using a video camera, and the detection of artificial marks through AprilTag software. The device has a low-consumption MIPS architecture computer that controls the capture sensor, processes the images with AprilTag, and calculates the location. In our previous work we studied the accuracy of the proposed device when it was static at fixed places. In this article we have extended that work with a second experiment, evaluating the measurements reported by the prototype device when it is moving in a real indoor environment. The main contributions of this work are two:

- The localization system: A portable application for embedded systems (developed in C with no external dependencies) that captures images from a camera and reports the location using AprilTag.
- The accuracy validation of the system proposed through its experimentation in a low-performance hardware, when it is mounted on a robot in motion.

The rest of the article is organized as follows. The next section introduces related works. Section 3 describes the architecture of the proposed system with emphasis on the location detection algorithm. Section 4 shows the results of the system evaluation, when experimenting with a low-cost robot to obtain location measurements. Finally, Sect. 5 reports the conclusions and future work.

2   Related Work

A solution to the location detection problem is through artificial landmarks, which must be placed in a way that they can be uniquely identified, in some easy and accurate way. This method makes it possible to avoid the sensors that are usually used for the location process, except for the camera, because computer vision is still required to recognise the orientation and location of the landmark. The detection of these landmarks is usually implemented and verified on computers with adequate resources to process a large number of images per second, using a wide range of libraries and applications simultaneously. For example, opencv for capturing and filtering images, and the matlab system for programming. This environment enables rapid prototyping and validation of vision algorithms on the same computer as well. In [11], the AprilTag design for robotics and augmented reality is presented. The validation was performed on a computer with an Intel Xeon E5-2640 2.5 GHz microprocessor. This article also mentions that it is possible to achieve good system performance on an iPhone device, without specifying which version of that phone. In [2], an autonomous landing of a drone to a moving station is implemented, using AprilTag, in a computer with an Nvidia Tegra K1 SoC, an ARM A-15 2.3 GHz microprocessor, and 8 GB of DDR3 RAM In [13], the design of a system for indoor location is presented, also using AprilTag. The experimentation was carried out using a Pioneer 3-DX mobile robot, which had a built-in notebook with a Intel Core 2 Duo 2.0 GHz microprocessor, and 2 GB of RAM.

An interesting use of location based systems on artificial landmarks is the one capable of estimating the relative position of two ships moored skin-to-skin using AprilTag, which is presented in [6]. A Lenovo W540 notebook with an Intel Quad-Core i7-4900MQ 2.80 GHz microprocessor and an NVIDIA Quadro K2100M for image rectification was used for processing the artificial landmarks. In [5] several landmarks detection systems are analyzed, and a mixed one is proposed. The experiments were performed using a computer with an i7-7600U 2.80 GHz microprocessor for image processing. In [7] an industrial manipulator arm is controlled using AprilTag marks on the objects to be manipulated. The execution of this control system in their experiments was performed in an embedded PC with a quad-core i7 microprocessor, and 8 GB of RAM.

Unlike the listed cases above, our work focuses on the implementation and validation of an embedded system that can report the location of a low-cost mobile robot, using a single modest processor (RISC only, neither multi-core nor superscalar) for running AprilTag 3 software for the detection of landmarks. To the best of our knowledge there are no other related works that evaluate the performance or accuracy of AprilTag 3 in low-cost and low-performance minimum systems.

3 Architecture

3.1 Hardware Architecture

The prototype hardware architecture comprises:

- The rotational camera device
- The embedded computer

The rotational camera device consists of a generic USB camera mounted on a servo motor, which allows the camera to be rotated from 0 to 360°, with a rotation resolution of one degree. The control signal to rotate the camera is an individual pulse width modulation (PWM) signal, with a standard frequency of 50 Hz for this device. The camera has a USB 2.0 interface and is a UVC class device. Both interfaces are connected to the embedded computer.

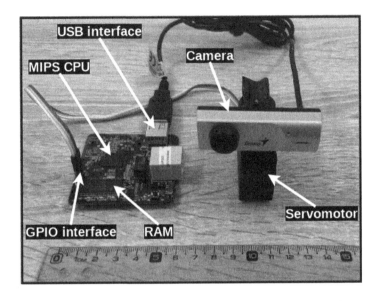

Fig. 1. Rotating camera device and embedded processing hardware.

The embedded computer runs the localization system software and the control system for the rotational camera device. It contains an Atheros AR9331 System On Chip (SOC) with a 400 MHz MIPS CPU. The main memory (RAM) is 32 MB. It also has several I/O ports (GPIO), a USB 2.0 port, a UART interface and a Wireless WiFi 802.11n/g/b interface. The module size, which is presented in Fig. 1, is 6 × 6 × 9 cm, and has a total weight of 120 g. The costs of the components is listed below:

- Embedded MIPS computer: USD 32.85
- Motor servo DS04-NFC: USD 4.5
- USB UVC Camera: USD 5

3.2   Software Architecture

The hardware is controlled by a Linux operating system built with buildroot[1], designed for embedded systems. The Linux drivers used in this device are the universal video class (UVC) for capturing images from the camera and the general

---

[1] https://buildroot.org/.

I/O port (GPIO). A pulse with modulation (PWM) driver was also integrated in user-space. This driver controls the servo motor used to rotate the camera in the rotational camera device. When a location is required, the application look for the landmark. For this purpose, the servo motor starts to slowly rotate the camera, while the camera is capturing a frame in each position. The frames are analyzed by the system until it detects a landmark inside an image. Then, the rotation of the camera is stopped and the system proceeds to perform the location process, which consists of three stages, presented in Fig. 2.

First, the embedded application captures an image from the camera, using the user-space interface of the UVC driver of the Linux system. The format of the digital image received is JPEG and the resolution is 320 × 240 pixels.

Fig. 2. Stages in the location process.

Next, the system uses the AprilTag 3.0 software to process the JPEG image. The AprilTag is a fiducial visual system, useful for a wide variety of tasks, including augmented reality, robotics and camera calibration [5]. It is capable of recognizing artificial reference marks called tags, which are similar to QR codes but with fewer bits, which allows faster detection than traditional QR systems. Another advantage, in contrast to typical QR codes, is that AprilTag has a low rate of false detections (false positives) even with changes in the lighting of the environment. This is a desirable feature in computer vision systems, which usually present problems with the light factor. AprilTag analyzes the image and reports the position and orientation of the identified landmarks. In our work we used only one reference mark in the environment, so the system obtains a single rotation matrix and a translation vector, which represent the position and orientation of the only mark that was detected. These results are in the camera's coordinate system with the focal lens center as origin.

Finally, the Location Algorithm determines the camera's position in the real-world coordinate system (which is the landmark coordinate system). This algorithm consists of three main operations:

1. The euler pitch angle is obtained from the rotation matrix returned by April-Tag. For its calculation, functions of the Eigen library are used, which were incorporated as part of the application code. In Fig. 3(a) it can be seen that the obtained Euler pitch angle α (alpha) is the angle formed by the axis X Cam of the camera coordinate system and the axis X tag of the tag coordinate system.
2. The point (X_c, Y_c) provided by AprilTag (Fig. 3(a)) is used to obtain the point X'_c and Y'_c in the real world coordinate system (Fig. 3(b) 2), where $X'_c = X_c$ and $Y'_c = Y_c$ (their algebraic values are equivalent).

3. Finally, a rotation of α degrees (obtained in step 1) from the point (X'_c, Y'_c) 1 is performed. For this a column vector is defined from Xc' and Yc', and it is multiplied by a matrix of rotation calculated from the angle α (formula 1).

$$\begin{bmatrix} X_t \\ Y_t \end{bmatrix} = \begin{bmatrix} \cos\alpha & -\sin\alpha \\ \sin\alpha & \cos\alpha \end{bmatrix} \begin{bmatrix} X'_c \\ Y'_c \end{bmatrix} \tag{1}$$

The point (X_t, Y_t) (Fig. 3(b)) is then calculated (formula 2 and 3).

$$Xt = \cos(\alpha).Xc' - \sin(\alpha).Yc' \tag{2}$$

$$Yt = \sin(\alpha).Xc' + \cos(\alpha).Yc' \tag{3}$$

The resulting point (X_t, Y_t) (Fig. 3(b) 3) indicates the position of the camera in the coordinate system of the reference mark; that is, the position of the portable device on the environment or real world.

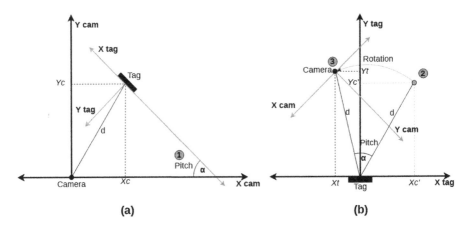

Fig. 3. (a) Position of the reference mark in the camera coordinate system. (b) Camera position in the real world coordinate system (the reference mark).

4   Results

In order to validate the prototype, the time, accuracy, and precision of the location measurements were evaluated and assessed.

4.1   Execution Time

This work focused on the low-cost mobile robots "Frankestitos", used by *Facultad de Informática* in educational robotics projects [9]. *Frankestito* robot moves at a maximum speed of 12 cm/s, so it was estimated that, for future navigation functionalities, this educational robot should obtain its location every 20 cm traveled. This requires that the location be calculated every 1.6 s in this robot, so a frequency of 1 Hz would be necessary, at least, if the location error is approximately ±12 cm.

Since our prototype comprises three software stages, when it calculates and reports a location, we use the gettimeofday() function from the Libc library to evaluate the elapsed time (I/O time and execution time) in every stage. The total time is then calculated for verifying if the time of the location process fulfills the requirements. Our experiment conducted of 415 location measurements using the prototype hardware. It had an average frequency of 2 Hz measurements and 1 Hz for the most unfavorable measurement (Table 1).

Table 1. Average I/O and CPU times on the prototype device at 415 locations.

Stage	Type	Time (A.M.) Max.	Time (worst case)
Capture	I/O time	74 (ms)	95 (ms)
AprilTag detection	CPU time	292 (ms)	750 (ms)
Location algorithm	CPU time	41 (ms)	46 (ms)
TOTAL	I/O + CPU time	407 (ms)	891 (ms)

4.2 Accuracy

We set for this experiment a global vision system, and we calibrated it as explained in [1]. On this system a camera is mounted over the robot navigating stage, and connected to a computer where the vision system is running. The system detects the position and orientation of the robot, and reports all this information to the system which controls the experiment. For this particular setting, both systems (global vision and experiment control) ran into the same computer. In order for the global vision system to identify the robot, we attached a few coloured patches on the upper part of the robot. The global vision system detects those patches, and uses them to identify and calculate the location of the robot within the environment. Since the global vision system, evaluated in [1], achieves an accuracy of better than 15 mm, its measurements were used in this experiment as the ground truth.

Then we placed a 10 cm × 10 cm tag (artificial landmark in AprilTag) on one wall of the environment perimeter and turned on the robot, which navigated reactively and randomly across the stage, automatically finding the tag with the rotating camera and reporting its location. A diagram of this environment can be seen in Fig. 4. When the prototype found the reference mark and was about to calculate its location, it triggered out the following four actions:

1. It sent a signal to the global vision system;
2. It captured a digital image and calculated its location;
3. The global vision system captured a digital image using its own camera, and calculated the location of the robot;
4. Both systems reported their calculated location measurements to the system which controls the experiment, for later analysis.

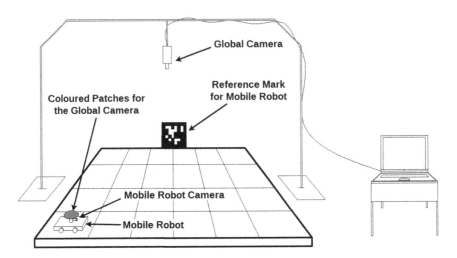

Fig. 4. Diagram of the real environment: measurements were made with the prototype device and the global vision system.

119 measurements were obtained from the prototype, and also from the global camera. The results obtained were graphically represented to estimate the accuracy of the measurements (Fig. 5). The graph represents the real-world coordinate system, and the circles and asterisks are the locations on the stage reported by the prototype system mounted on the robot. The reference mark (tag) was at X = 99 and Y = 0 of this representation (black rectangle at bottom). The filled circles indicate a small error of [0–5]cm from the ground truth. The empty circles indicate an error of [5–12] cm, and the asterisks an error of 13 cm or more.

It is observed that up to a distance in Y of 66 cm the robot reported accurate locations to the ground truth, in most cases, with up to 5 cm of error. When the prototype device was navigating at more than 66 cm of distance the accuracy decreased (it can be seen in the figure that there are several empty circles). At these distances, the maximum errors were 11 cm on the X axis, and 10 cm on the Y axis. Eventually, when the robot navigated reactively on the furthest place (more than 100 cm of distance from the tag), the measurements are no longer accurate to the ground truth, so these are labeled as unreliable measurements, and should be just used to know the approximate location area of the mobile robot.

In Fig. 6 and 7 two histograms (one for the X axis and one for Y) of the distances of the localizations with respect to the value of the ground truth are presented. The value $X = 0$ in both means a distance of 0 cm to the ground truth, and represents the most accurate measurements. It is observed that $\tilde{7}0$ measurements in both histograms had a small error ([0–5] cm), which represent the 56% of the total measurements; and also, that a high rate (91%) are in the range [0–12] cm of error. These results indicate that the prototype in motion is able to calculate its location without loss of accuracy, in comparison with our previous observations calculated in [14], when the device was static in its

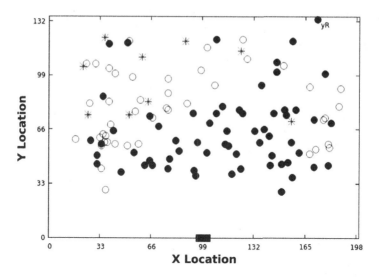

Fig. 5. Relationship between the locations reported by the prototype device and the ground truth (global vision system). Units of X and Y axes are in cm.

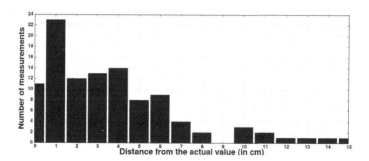

Fig. 6. Histogram of the distances in X of the locations with respect to the real value.

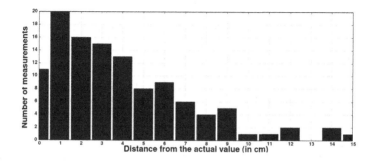

Fig. 7. Histogram of the distances in Y of the locations with respect to the real value.

measurements. It is important to take into consideration that the speed of the robot in motion was low (12 cm/s). For others settings further evaluations must be carried out, since low-cost cameras often capture blurred images if in motion.

5 Conclusion and Future Work

In this paper we presented the architecture of a prototype device for low-cost indoor mobile robots, which takes measurements and reports its current location. We also evaluated the frequency and accuracy, through experimental tests, using a low-performance hardware. In our preceding work we evaluated the accuracy when the proposed device was static at fixed places. In this article we have extended it evaluating the measurements reported by the prototype device when it is moving in a real indoor environment. More than 100 measurements were taken and later contrasted against the ones emitted by a previously calibrated global vision system. Based on the results, it is concluded that the proposed hardware and software are able to locate a low-cost robot at 2 Hz, with a resolution of centimeters, and ± 12 cm of maximum error in 90% of cases, if the robot navigates within the limits set by the size of the reference mark and the resolution of the camera used. Low-cost robots usually work in small environments (e.g. a room), and although the experiment was conducted with small reference marks we are confident (future validation is necessary, though) that a tag size of 40 cm x 40 cm would be a proper size in most of these cases (e.g. for a room up to 16 mt^2).

We plan, as future work, to continue with the implementation and validation of the remaining components to accomplish map navigation in low-cost mobile robots. Some of these components are: map representation, path planning, trajectory history, and estimation of location errors. It is also intended to increase the performance of the current localization module prototype, mainly making improvements to the software (for example, overlapping the I/O with the CPU time).

References

1. Ball, D., Wyeth, G., Nuske, S.: DA global vision system for a robot soccer team. In: Australasian Conference on Robotics and Automation, Canberra (2004)
2. Borowczyk, A., Nguyen, D.-T., Nguyen, A.P.-V., Nguyen, D.Q., Saussié, D., Ny, J.L.: Autonomous landing of a multirotor micro air vehicle on a high velocity ground vehicle. IFAC-PapersOnLine **50**(1), 10488–10494 (2017)
3. Chung, M.J.-Y., Huang, J., Takayama, L., Lau, T., Cakmak, M.: Iterative design of a system for programming socially interactive service robots. In: International Conference on Social Robotics (2016)
4. Jaulin, L.: Mobile Robotics. ENSTA-Bretagne, France. Elsevier (2015). ISBN 9781785480485
5. Krogius, M., Haggenmiller, A., Olson, E.: Flexible layouts for fiducial tags. In: Proceedings of the IEEE/RSJ International Conference on Intelligent Robots and Systems (2019)

6. Mangelson, J.G., Wolcott, R.W., Ozog, P., Eustice, R.M.: Robust visual fiducials for skin-to-skin relative ship pose estimation. In: OCEANS 2016 MTS/IEEE Monterey (2016)
7. Nissler, C., Büttner, S., Marton, Z.-C., Beckmann, L., Thomas, U.: Evaluation and improvement of global pose estimation with multiple AprilTags for industrial manipulators. In: IEEE 21st International Conference on ETFA (2016)
8. Corke, P.: Robotics, Vision and Control. Fundamental Algorithms in MATLAB. Springer, Heidelberg (2011). https://doi.org/10.1007/978-3-642-20144-8. ISBN 9783642201448
9. Rodriguez, J., Grosso, G., Zurita, R., Cecchi, L.: Intervención de la Facultad de Informática en la enseñanza de Ciencias de la Computación en la escuela media basada en robótica educativa. XI Congreso de TE&ET, pp. 221–231 (2016)
10. Siegwart, R., Nourbakhsh, I.R.: Introduction to Autonomous Mobile Robots. Massachusetss Institute of Technology, MIT Press, Cambridge (2011). ISBN 9780262195027
11. Wang, J., Olson, E.: AprilTag 2: efficient and robust fiducial detection. In: Proceedings of the International Conference on Intelligent Robots and Systems (2016)
12. Wise, M., Ferguson, M., King, D., Diehr, E., Dymesich, D.: Fetch & Freight: Standard Platforms for Service Robot Applications. Fetch Robotics Inc., Press, San Jose (2018)
13. Zhong, X., Zhou, Y., Liu, H.: Design and recognition of artificial landmarks for reliable indoor self-localization of mobile robots. Int. J. Adv. Rob. Syst. **14**, 1–13 (2017)
14. Zurita, R.I., Mora, A., Alvarez, C., Lechner, M.: Sistema de localización para robots móviles de bajo costo utilizando marcas de referencia artificiales en ambientes de interiores. XXV Congreso Argentino de Ciencias de la Computación, CACIC 2019, pp. 1081–1090 (2019). ISBN 978-987-688-377-1

Computer Security

Lightweight Cryptography in IIoT the Internet of Things in the Industrial Field

Jorge Eterovic, Marcelo Cipriano$^{(\boxtimes)}$, Edith Garcia, and Luis Torres

Instituto de Investigación en Ciencia y Tecnología, Facultad de Ingeniería,
Vice-Rectorado de Investigación y Desarrollo, Universidad del Salvador,
Lavalle 1854. C1051 AAB, Buenos Aires, Argentina
jorge.eterovic@gmail.com, ciprianol.618@gmail.com,
edithxgarcia@gmail.com, torreslu@ar.ibm.com

Abstract. Lightweight Cryptography is one of the current topics of Cryptology. A great variety of "lightweight" algorithms have been designed to guarantee Confidentiality, Authenticity and Integrity of data in devices of what it is known as the Internet of Things (IoT). Some of them arise from the academic field and are applied in the Industry, while some others are proprietary, developed by companies to achieve their security requirements. This paper presents the state of the art of some of these algorithms used in different IIoT devices. Their general cryptological features are briefly described, as well as the different attacks to which they were subjected. Finally, new trends for the design and implementation of lightweight algorithms are listed.

Keywords: Lightweight Cryptography · Internet of Things · IoT · Industrial Internet of Things · IIoT · Lightweight cryptosystems

1 Introduction

The concept known as *"Internet of Things"* or *IoT*[1] is one of the most used expressions in different fields. It is a very broad term that includes different devices and technologies. It is important to highlight that there is an overabundance of these devices nowadays; however, in the near future the number of interconnected devices will grow.

Some IoT devices run on battery and/or generate their own power using, for example, solar panels. To ensure the *Confidentiality, Authenticity and Integrity* of the data and information that travel through the communication channels between the sensors and their Control Centre (CC), cryptographic algorithms must be used. Some of these devices have large processors, so it is possible to use the conventional cryptographic algorithms used in PCs and Servers, cell phones, tablets and other similar objects. However, most of them need very low power processors, which means that only a small part can be devoted to security. They may also be limited in power consumption, memory capacity, or in their small size, due to the functionalities for which they were designed. These types of devices are characterized by their restricted or limited capabilities.

---

[1] Internet of Things: interconnection of sensors and everyday objects through the Internet.

© Springer Nature Switzerland AG 2020
P. Pesado and M. Arroyo (Eds.): CACIC 2019, CCIS 1184, pp. 335–353, 2020.
https://doi.org/10.1007/978-3-030-48325-8_22

Traditional algorithms could incur high resource consumption or cause delays in data transmission when they are made to run on these devices. Therefore, given the restricted capabilities and the fact that security is critical to their operation, the cryptographic algorithms used should be as "light" as possible.

While traditional cryptography methods, such as AES (encryption), SHA-256 (hash function), and RSA/Elliptic-curve (signature) are efficient on platforms with reasonable memory and processing capacity, they do not apply correctly, for example, in embedded system environments and sensor networks.

It is at this point, where Lightweight Cryptology has set out to meet the security needs in IoT. Their designs vary widely, but in all cases, they try to meet the limited resources of "things". Given the extent of the proposal, it is possible to establish a series of trends and criteria that the algorithms should pursue when implemented.

National (NIST)[2] and international organizations (ISO/IEC)[3] establish methods and criteria that can be applied in Lightweight Cryptology. To do this, they define the scope of cryptology as:

- Conventional cryptography: Servers and PCs; tablets, smartphones.
- Lightweight cryptography: Embedded systems; RFID, sensor networks.

In 2015, NIST initiated a call to evaluate and standardize lightweight cryptographic algorithms, recommended for restricted environments, where conventional standards are not acceptable. Currently, only 32 of the 56 algorithms presented have been selected to continue with the second round. It is expected that by 2021 lightweight standards be selected to ensure confidentiality, authenticity, and integrity in limited environments.

This work adds new schemes and lightweight design strategies to those presented in CACIC 2019 [1]. In 2, the stream cipher algorithm GRAIN 128 AEAD is presented in NIST Lightweight Cryptography. GRAIN v1 is a stream cipher submitted to eSTREAM competition in 2004 by Martin Hell, Thomas Johanson and Willi Meier. It has been selected for the final eSTREAM project. The stream cipher algorithm Shamash for authenticated encryption designed by Daniel Penazzi and Miguel Montes is also shown in this work. Finally, a new design based in sponge functions is introduced in Sect. 4.

A worldwide issue arises with respect to the security of the IIoT devices beyond the confidentiality of the communications, and it is of concern for manufacturers, enterprises, researchers and governmental organizations: the real possibility that IoT equipment (in particular, IIoT devices spread all around the world) can be infected by malware. This equipment is manipulated as "zombies" (bots) and receives orders from a Master. It is not about bitcoins mining or robbing, or about generation of spam mail. The malware attack could have mayor repercussions at the civil and military levels. Attacks of this nature could have a limitless reach. Malware attacks has gone beyond mere possibilities to become reality with multiple victims when executed.

---

[2] NIST: National Institute of Standards and Technology.

[3] ISO/IEC: International Organization for Standardization y International Electrotechnical Commission.

The authentication and encryption mechanisms are part of the solution as long as they can function in these devices (IIoT). Therefore, it is imperative to study Lightweight Cryptography in IIot.

2   Lightweight Algorithms Based on Stream Ciphers

A stream cipher is a symmetric encryption mode where the plaintext is combined with a pseudorandom sequence (keystream), which is output from an encryption algorithm (keystream generator). In a stream cipher, each plaintext array (bit, byte) is encrypted (e.g. Xored) one at time with the corresponding array of the keystream, to give an array of the ciphertext stream (see Fig. 1).

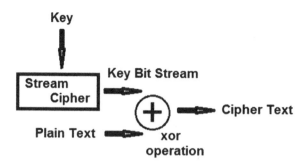

Fig. 1. Generic stream cipher scheme.

Below are some lightweight Stream Cipher algorithms used in the industrial field. Their general features as well as the cryptographic attacks to which they were subjected are described.

A5/x Family. The family of cipher algorithms A5 were implemented in the system of mobile communications GSM (groupe special mobile: Global System for Mobile communications) to provide confidentiality and authentication to those communications occurring between the mobile device and the receipting antenna. The basic authentication scheme (using ciphering mechanisms) can be observed in Fig. 2 below. The antenna covering the specific mobile phone device sends a challenge so that the device can appropriately respond. If both numbers coincide, then the mobile device is authenticated and starts the process sending encrypted data of the specific communication.

Even though some of these algorithms were created at the end of the XX Century, many are not yet being used or in operation.

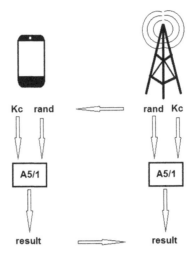

Fig. 2. GSM authentication.

A5/1. The exact design of the algorithm was not clear in its early days, a first approach to its inner workings was published in 1994 [2]. The algorithm generates a keystream from a 22-bit Initialization Vector (IV) and a 64-bit secret key, using three different Linear Feedback Shift Registers (LFSRs) whose lengths add up to 64 bits. Practical attacks have been implemented using Time-Memory Trade-Offs via Rainbow Tables (RTs), taking advantage of the fact that the Update Function of its internal state is not bijective [3]. Only 2^{24} steps are required after the setting up of the RTs. In addition, 10 bits of the key were always set to 0 in many deployments. The 2G GSM protocol still uses this algorithm.

A5/2. The algorithm is somewhat similar to A5/1 but still much weaker [4]. It was intended for use in some countries with U.S. export restrictions. It is vulnerable to ciphertext-only attacks with a complexity of 2^{16} steps, using the redundancy of error-correcting-detector codes. Possible attacks require a practical complexity pre-calculation [5]. Due to its weakness, the 3GPP standards organization strongly recommends not to use this algorithm from mid-2006.

The philosophy behind the design of the above-mentioned algorithm corresponds to non-linear operations therefore combining the exit of 4 LFSR clocked irregularly.

A5/3. The A5/3 algorithm, also known as Kasumi [6] is an algorithm created by SAGE (Security Algorithms Group of Experts). SAGE used the Misty algorithm as a base to create the A5/3 algorithm. For sometime, Kasumi was considered an improved version of Misti. However, in the year 2010, this assumption was demonstrated to be flawed as an attack against Kasumi was effective [7] and occurred five years before a successful attack against Misty1 [8].

Misty is a Block Cipher type algorithm, designed in 1995, and created by Mitsuru Matsui and other researchers as members of Mitsubishi Electric. It was chosen for the

NESSIE European Project. In 2013, Misty gained the Japanese Cryptrec Project's recommendation. In 2015, Yosuke Todo published a successful attack against Misty.

Kasumi, among its various functions, operates on Misty in an Accounting Mode, therefore achieving the bit-flow characteristic of Stream Cipher (Fig. 3).

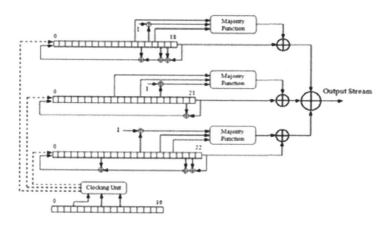

Fig. 3. A5/2 algorithm scheme

A5-GMR-x Group. These cryptographic algorithms were adopted by satellite telephony protocols. The **A5-GMR-1** and **A5-GMR-2** algorithms were reverse-engineered by Driessen et al. [9]. Although they are different, they can be easily violated.

A5-GMR-1. Is a variant of A5/2 with an internal state consisting of four LFSRs whose lengths add up to 81 bits. The records are irregularly clocked as in A5/2. It can be attacked using only known-cipher-text, reversing 2^{21} triangular arrays of size 532×532, having a complexity of approximately $2^{38.1}$ operations, making a significant pre-calculation.

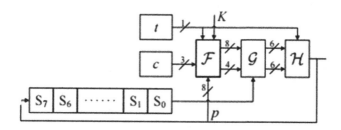

Fig. 4. General structure of the GMR-2 algorithm

A5-GMR-2. Is a bytes stream cipher, with a more sophisticated structure based on 3 components called F, G and H by Driessen et al. Structure H uses two S-boxes of the DES algorithm: boxes 2 and 6. A practical attack with little data and low complexity in time can be found in [10]. It is necessary to assume at most 32 bits using only a 15-byte frame with an average complexity of 2^{28} (see Fig. 4).

Atmel Ciphers. SecureMemory (SM), CryptoMemory (CM) and CryptoRF (CR) are a group of chips with extensive applications. They use similar stream ciphers called Atmel Ciphers. They are proprietary algorithms that were reverse-engineered and attacked by Garcia et al. [11]. Other much more efficient attacks were proposed by Biryukov et al. [12] breaking SM encryption with a time complexity of $2^{29.8}$ s, using 1 frame and CM encryption with 2^{50} s time complexity, using 30 frames and about 530 MB of memory. The algorithm consists of 3 NLFSRs[4] with a total size of 117 bits.

Crypto-1. It is a stream cipher used by the Mifare Classic smart cards line from NXP Semiconductors, formerly Philips Semiconductors. It was reverse-engineered by Nohl et al. [13]. It is based on a 48-bit LFSR combined with several nonlinear Boolean functions. It was subsequently attacked by several research groups [14, 15] with a time complexity of 2^{32}. These cards have been used since 1998 but the exact date of their design is not clear.

Content Scrambling System (CSS). This algorithm was applied in the encryption of DVDs to consider Digital Rights (DRMs Digital Rights Managements). It consists of two LFSRs of lengths of 17 and 25 bits that generate two bytes in parallel. Then module 2^8 were added to get 1 byte of keystream. Unlike most stream ciphers, this keystream is not simply XORed with clear text. The clear text is first modified by passing through an 8-bit bijective S-box whose result is added with the keystream to obtain the encrypted text. This operation is often called Mangling Step. A full description of the algorithm can be found in [16, 17]. Since the length of the secret key is 40 bits, it received several significant attacks. Encryption is only vulnerable to a brute force-attack with a time complexity of 2^{40}.

Common Scrambling Algorithm (CSA-SC). The CSA is used to protect digital television broadcast. It consists of two cascading ciphers. The first one is a block cipher called CSA-BC, the second one is a stream cipher called CSA-SC. The stream cipher is based on two Feedback Shift Registers (FSRs) of 20 4-bit content cells. The feedback function of the logs involves, among other things, several 5×2-bit S-boxes. They are combined using sum module 2^4 to extract 2 bits of the keystream from the internal state and the two registers, at each clock. This algorithm is very vulnerable [18]. Often the keystream has very short cycles. It is possible to retrieve the secret key by solving around 2^{28} systems of 60 linear equations with 40 unknowns which demands a complexity of at most $2^{45.7}$ operations.

Dsc. The Dect Standard Cipher (Dect: "Digital Enhanced Cordless Telecommunications") or Dsc is an algorithm used to encrypt communications from wireless phones. The first attacks focused on its protocol and its failures in implementation. It was gradually described by reverse engineering and attacks requiring only about 2^{15} key-stream samples and 2^{34} ciphers were found, therefore, it takes a couple of hours to retrieve the secret key. Authors [19, 20] describe it as "an asynchronous cipher with

---

[4] NonLinear-Feedback Shift Register.

low nonlinear complexity that uses a 64-bit secret key and a 35-bit IV". It resembles A5/1 algorithm because its structure is based on LFSRs that clock irregularly.

E0. The privacy of the Bluetooth protocol is currently based on the AES algorithm, which replaced the stream cipher called E0. Its 128-bit internal state is divided into 4 LFSRs and its filter function has its own design. A full description of E0 can be found in works showing attacks against the algorithm [21]. Lu et al. found an attack [22, 23] that allows to recover the secret key using the first 24 bits of $2^{23.8}$ frames, with a complexity of 2^{38} operations.

Espresso. It is an algorithm designed by Elena Dubrova and Martin Hell [24] intended to protect 5G (Wireless Communication Systems) communications. It consists of two fundamental parts: a 256-bit NLFSR in the Galois configuration and a 20-variable nonlinear Output Function. It uses a 128-bit secret key and a 96-bit IV. According to the authors, it is extremely light: it has 1497 GE. It processes 2.22 Gbits/sec and 232 ns latency. Since the structure of the Grain and Espresso algorithms are very similar, Wang and Lin [25] applied a Slide Attack using Grain analysis, they developed a chosen IV attack that allows them to retrieve the 128-bit secret key with only two pairs of related IVs, no more than 2^{42} IVs chosen and with a computational complexity of 2^{64}. Thus, the Espresso stream cipher is not safe for 128 key bits.

Hitag2 and Megamos. These stream ciphers are used in car immobilizers implemented by different companies that prevent the car's engine from starting unless the transponder is near the vehicle. Initially the algorithms were kept secret. Then Hitag2 was published by Wiener and detailed in [26], and Megamos was reverse-engineered by Verdult et al. [27, 28]. Both algorithms have a small internal state of 48 and 57 bits respectively (see Fig. 5). Key sizes, other weaknesses in ciphers and the protocol that uses them, allow practical attacks against devices whose security depends on these algorithms. For example, it is possible to attack a Hitag2 key using 1 min of communication between the key and the car with about 2^{35} encrypted messages. The Megamos secret key can be recovered with a time complexity of 2^{48}, although even more efficient attacks are considered when taking into account the method of handling the keys used on the device.

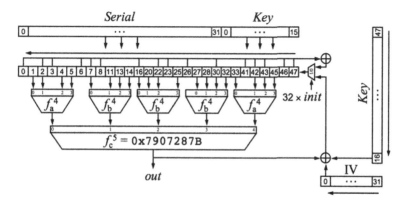

Fig. 5. HITAG2 algorithm diagram

Iclass. It is a group of smart cards marketed in 2002. The stream cipher used was reverse-engineered and attacked by García et al. [29]. It has an internal state of 40 bits, registering 2^{22} authentication attempts, the key can be retrieved with 2^{40} ciphers.

Kindle Cipher (PC1). This algorithm was first published on Usenet by Alexander Pukall in 1997. It was not technically designed in the industry or by academics. Amazon used it at least until 2012 for products with DRM digital rights, thus protecting their e-books using the MOBI file format. It uses a 128-bit secret key and a 24-bit internal state that is updated using different operations including modular multiplication. At each clock the algorithm generates 1 byte, resulting in a keybytestream. It has been broken by Biryukov et al. [30] using for example 2^{20} clear-texts-known and a time complexity of 2^{31}. Much more practical encrypted text attacks can be applied in certain contexts.

Oryx. While A5/1 secured GSM communications in Europe, the Oryx algorithm was chosen by Telecommunications Industry Association Standard (TIA) to protect telephone communications in the USA. A description of the algorithm can be found in [31] where practical attacks are presented. The algorithm uses a secret key of 96 bits, an internal state of also 96 bits distributed in 3 LFSRs of 32 bits each and an S-box of 8 bits variable. It is possible to attack it with a time complexity of 2^{16} using 25 bytes of known-clear-text.

Grain 128-AEAD. It is a stream cipher type algorithm for authenticated encryption (accepts associated data) designed by Hell, Johansson, and Meier [32]. It consists of a 128-bit key and a 96-bit IV (nonce). It is very similar to the widely studied Grain 128 algorithm, introduced in 2011. It is oriented to hardware environments where the number of gates, power and memory consumption are very limited. Essentially, it is based on two FSRs records and a nonlinear Boolean (filter) function. Its security and performance surpass other FSR-based stream ciphers such as the E0 and A5/1 (see Fig. 6).

The Grain group has been modified based on the crypto-analytic attacks that were applied, its latest version being a favourite in NIST's lightweight algorithm selection competition [33].

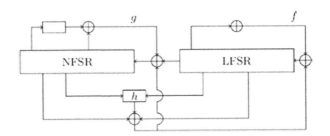

Fig. 6. General scheme of the GRAIN algorithm family.

Shamash 128-AEAD. Shamash is a stream cipher algorithm for authenticated encryption (accepts associated data) designed by Penazzi and Montes [34]. It is an authenticated cipher with 128 bit key and 128 bit nonce. The inputs to authenticated encryption are a plaintext, associated data, a public message number (nonce) and a key. Nonce and key are 128 bits each and the same nonce cannot be used with the same key for messages or associated data that are not equal. Reuse the nonce voids all security claims. Shamash is based on the *novel* sponge and duplex construction [35, 36], taking advantage of the improvements in security given by [37]. Last couple if years. this type authenticated ciphers have been widely studied and many proofs of security have been given on the structure itself, so the security is concentrated of the underlying permutation. Shamash was presented in NIST Lightweight Cryptography, but it was removed from round 2 without specifying its vulnerabilities.

3 Lightweight Algorithms Based on Block Ciphers

A Block Cipher is an algorithm that takes a block or finite quantity of bits from the plain text, and in conjunction with a secret key, transforms it into a block of cipher text (see Fig. 7). In order to achieve that, the Block Cipher uses a set of different techniques and mathematical tools that make each bit of the exit block dependable of the majority (or all) of the bits of the entry block. With not knowing the key, the process becomes irreversible, and that is where the security of the algorithm lies.

Many algorithms work with different lengths of keys and blocks. The most common ones are those of lengths of 128, 192, and 256 bits. The algorithm allows the "cut" of the plain text in blocks for messages with lengths grater those mentioned values.

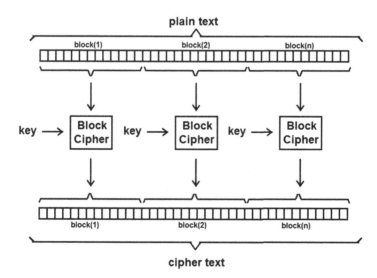

Fig. 7. Block cipher scheme.

Below are some lightweight Block Ciphers used in the industrial field. Their characteristics as well as the cryptographic attacks to which they were subjected are described.

BeepBeep. The BeepBeep (Embedded Real-Time Encryption) algorithm is an autokey block cipher. It works with 32-bit arrays and an IV (see Fig. 8) hat has different options according to the application in which it is being implemented. It was designed by Kevin Driscoll of Honeywell Laboratories [38] to cover security requirements that include wireless communications, remote management of control systems for chemical and power plants, for distributed network management, access and remote control. Except for the introduction of BeepBeep and the requirements of real-time cryptography FSE (Fast Software Encryption) in 2002, no information has been found about the analysis and attacks of this algorithm.

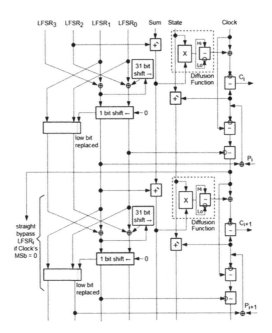

Fig. 8. BeepBeep algorithm encryption diagram.

CMEA. This algorithm was used by TIA to ensure the transmission of phone numbers over telephone lines. A good description of this algorithm can be found in [39], in which an attack against it is accidentally described. It encrypts a block of arbitrary length in bytes (usually in practice of 2 to 6 bytes) using a 64-bit key. It is vulnerable to clear-known-text attacks, needing between 40 and 80 blocks of data, considering 2^{24} and 2^{32} ciphers. Their S-boxes appear to contain a hidden structure according to [40].

Criptometría. It is known as "C2" for short. It shares the same structure as DES (Data Encryption Standard): it encrypts 64-bit blocks using a 56-bit secret key and uses a 32-bit Feistel function. It works by mixing a 32-bit sub-key through a modular sum, then using an 8-bit S-box followed by a 32-bit linear permutation. The S-box is secret, so a box recovery attack has been proposed in [41]. The same work features a complexity key recovery attack in time of 2^{48}. This algorithm was intended to be used in DVD players, in which case it could be a successor to the CSS algorithm, and also for some SD cards. In total, 10 rounds are used which means that only 10 calls to the box are needed to encrypt a 64-bit block, compared to the 160 calls to the box that are needed to encrypt a 128-bit block using AES-128.

Common Scrambling Algorithm (CSA-BC). The CSA algorithm uses a cipher stream (mentioned above) and a cipher block called CSA-BC. It encrypts 64-bit blocks using a key of the same length. Its structure resembles a Red Feistel of 56 rounds, using eight sub-blocks of 8 bits each. The functions are based on a single random 8-bit S-box (called B), composing a variant of it with a simple permutation of bits called sigma (σ), obtaining $\sigma° B$. A full specification of the algorithm can be found in [42]. At the moment, there is no knowledge of any kind of attack.

Dst40. This algorithm was reverse-engineered through partial information discovered in a patent and its physical implementation on a device [43]. It was used in RFID devices sold by Texas Instrument, for automotive immobilizers and electronic payment. The cipher works with a 40-bit block with a key of equal length, also using 200 rounds of an asymmetric Feistel Network. The Feistel function applies 38 bits of the internal state and 40 bits of a subkey and produces 2 output bits by composing several Boolean functions. Due to the size of its 40-bit key it is possible to perform a brute force attack.

Keelog. Also called "code-hopping encoder". Designed in 1985, it was granted the patent in 1996. It is used by many car companies such as Chrysler, Daewoo, Fiat, GM, Honda, Toyota, Volvo, Volkswagen, in remote door opening systems. It uses a 64-bit secret key, and 32-bit blocks (see Fig. 9). It is an iterative encryption, consisting of 528 rounds. In its early days the algorithm was secret but in 2006 its specifications were leaked. With this information several research groups presented attacks against the algorithm [43]. For example, the secret key can be recovered using 2^{16} known-clear-texts and $2^{44.5}$ encryptions. Much more efficient side-channel attacks have been proposed for commercial implementations of encryption. An interesting observation is that in some car brands it encrypts clear text 0 and increments the key by adding 1 to the integer represented by the bits of the secret key, so it would never use the same key. This is of course quite rare and Keeloq could be modelled by a dual algorithm where there is a clear 64-bit text and a key of only 32 bits, which would easily break the algorithm by brute force.

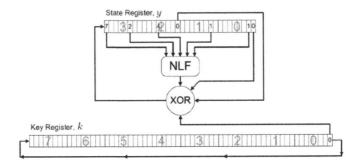

Fig. 9. Keeloq algorithm structure

4 Lightweight Algorithm Design Strategies

Lightness can be seen as a specific set of properties to take into account in the design of lightweight cryptographic algorithms (see Fig. 10). Considering the progress and current academic results, these aspects are adapted differently in each of them. Techniques, methods and operations that are used in conventional cryptosystems prevail despite new contributions.

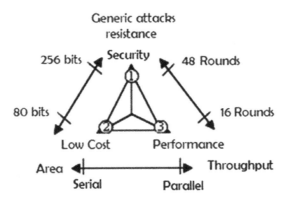

Fig. 10. Inspired by A. Poschmann, Lightweight Cryptography: Cryptographic engineering for a pervasive world.

When following a light design strategy, it is important to take into account a number of cryptographic characteristics that arise, such as: General Algorithm Structure, Sub-Key Generation Scheme and the Characteristics of Linear and Non-Linear Operations.

Algorithms designed from these properties must be safe, simple, fast and of high performance.

In cryptographic algorithm design, there is a tradeoff between the performance and the resources required for a given security level. Performance can be expressed as power and energy consumption, latency and throughput: gate area, gate equivalents or slices. Resources requirements are referred to as costs, as adding more gates or memory tends to increase the production cost of a device.

Last fifteen years, an important number of lightweight crypto primitives (including hash functions, message authentication codes) have been proposed to bring performance advantages over conventional cryptographic conventional standards. These primitives differ from conventional algorithms with the assumptions that lightweight primitives are not intended for a wide range of applications, and may impose limits on the capacity of the attacker. For example, the amount de data available to the attacker under a single key may be limited. However, it should be noted that this does not mean that the lightweight algorithms are weak, rather the idea is to use advancements that would result in designs with a better balance between security, simplicity, performance and resource requirements for specific constrained environments.

4.1 General Algorithm Structure

Depending on how the information is processed, one can opt for a Block Cipher, a Stream Cipher, or a "hybrid" mechanism between the two modes.

In the case of Block Ciphers one of the most commonly used set-ups is SP-Networks and Feistel-type networks within them.

For Stream Ciphers, the set-up is of Vernam type: the clear text is added XOR with the pseudorandom binary output stream of the algorithm.

4.2 Key Schedule

The KS is the most notable area of difference between lightweight and conventional algorithms. Algorithms with Conventional Subkey Generation implemented over PCs tend to be more complex so they require more processing time and memory, which is why the design of lightweight KS should not be neglected. A very common construction of lightweight KS merely "selects" different bits of a secret master key in each round of the algorithm. The purpose of this selection is that a very simple calculation is needed to produce a subkey for each round.

4.3 Linear and Non-linear Operations

Nonlinearity is an indispensable property for any cryptographic primitive. This can be provided by S-Boxes or through the use of nonlinear arithmetic operations. These must be well designed to prove resistant to known attacks. Likewise, they should be light, this means that they must use the least number of gates (GE) in their implementation. For nonlinear arithmetic operations, the sum with module 2^{16}, 2^{32} or 2^{64} and also modular multiplication is considered.

In ARX (Addition, Rotation, XOR) technology only these three simple operations are used in algorithm design. When it comes to building lightweight rounds, it is presented as the new paradigm. The use of NLFSRs and irregularly clocked LFSRs can be added to this concept of nonlinearity.

4.4   Linear Operations

In order to ensure an efficient broadcast of the key bits and the bits of the clear text throughout the encryption process, linear transformations must appear combined with the non-linear operations. This property can be achieved with different procedures: with linear transformations, with LFSRs and with MDS (Maximum Distance Separable) matrices known in error-detector-corrector codes, as can be seen in many of the algorithms presented.

4.5   Sponge Constructions

The sponge construction uses a function f (permutation or random function) which has a variable-length input and a fixed output length. It operates on a defined number of bits (b): the width. The sponge construction operates on a state of b = r + c bits, r is defined as the bitrate and c as the capacity (see Fig. 10). Initially an string input is padded and then segmented into blocks of r bits. Next, the b bits of the state are set to zero, and the sponge construction next defines (see Fig. 11):

- **Absorbing phase**: the r bits input blocks are Xored into the first r bits of the state, interleaved with applications of the function f. After all the input blocks have been processed, continue with the next phase.
- **Squeezing phase:** this is where the first r bits of the state are outputted as blocks and interleaved with the function f. The number of bits of the output is defined as part the process. The last c bits of a state are never changed by the input blocks and never output within the squeezing phase.

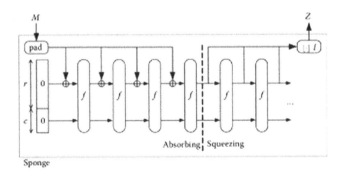

Fig. 11. Sponge function

5   Exploitation of Security Deficiencies in IoT Devices

5.1   DoS and DDoS Attacks

A Denial of Service (DoS) attack is an offensive action against a grid or system aimed at affecting or denying the service being offered to the legitimate users. This attack can be accomplished through one or various equipments. The most potent one is the attack called DDoS (Distributed Denial of Service). The key difference lies on the quantity of devices carrying on the offensive actions.

The attackers do not use their own equipment. They send malware that allows them to take control of the infected equipment without the knowledge or authorization of the owners. A grid named BotNet that follows only the attackers' commands is then formed. The infected equipment devices are named "zombies" or "bots", the name "master" is used to name the equipment that controls them (see Fig. 12). The more is the quantity of equipment devices in the grid; the most potent control is under master's direction.

In many cases, these grids are used to mine or rob bitcoins, spread virus or spam email.

5.2 DDoS in IoT Devices

In addition, various malware serve to recruit "bots" for their "master". Therefore, a proper equipment maintenance and installation of security mechanisms prevent the equipment from being infected. Unfortunately, this situation is uncommon in many IoT devices.

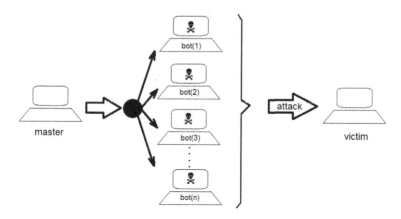

Fig. 12. BotNet scheme.

A malware can easily infect IoT devices since the majority of equipment devices lack encryption mechanisms and authentication of cryptographic quality.

Mirai is a malware that, by a systematic search of IP in IoT devices in the grid, intents to infect those devices as it find them.

On October 21, 2016, a series of DDoS attacks occurred throughout the internet. The most significant one created flow traffic of 1.2 Tbps. It is estimated that the attack required hundreds of thousands of coordinated equipment devices aiming at the victim. A vast majority of the devices were IoT devices (surveillance web cameras, printers), but not all of them.

The attack was aimed at the servers of Dyn, a company that manages the DNS (Domain Name System) infrastructure.

The attack was of such magnitude that prevented millions of users and clients from accessing sites such as Amazon, BBC, CNN, Fox News, GitHub, HBO, Netflix, PayPal, Starbucks, Spotify, The New York Times, Twitter y Visa [44].

It is believed that the attack was carried out by a group of hackers, and it was only a concept test, and not a direct attack to the central internet addresses.

6 Conclusions and Future Work

Lightweight Cryptography is the new paradigm of Cryptology by being able to respond to growing security needs on restricted devices. It is not possible to apply the most robust algorithms of Conventional Cryptography as they can use too many resources. It is possible for Lightweight Cryptography to replace Conventional Cryptography? The answer is an open problem and requires much more and more research.

In this paper, different lightweight algorithms that have been designed to meet the specific needs of the industry have been presented. Their cryptographic characteristics, resistance to different generic attacks and attacks in which some have been broken are also highlighted. New cryptanalysis techniques emerge as a result of new lightweight designs.

Some trends in the design of these primitives are listed, as they are observed through the principles and philosophies that gave rise to them. Design criteria based on sponge function require further research, more and more results. There are many symmetric primitives based in ARX (Addition-Rotation-Xored) constructions form the core of modern lightweight cryptography. ARX-ciphers security is an open problem.

Finally, the vulnerability of the internet infrastructure under attacks by DDoS generated by IoT devices worldwide was exposed. Therefore, it is reasonable to understand why governmental organizations such as NIST support the creation of standards for the use of IoT devices, and then eventually making communications more secure.

Beyond the economic loses on companies and users resulting from these attacks, it is more frightening to think of the possibility that someone decides to "turn off internet", by using our own IoT equipment devices commonplace in industries and residences against us.

Future research could carry forward investigations on the particular characteristics of the strategies presented here, as well as inquiring about new design philosophies that may appear in the upcoming years.

Acknowledgments. The research team thanks the authorities of the Facultad de Ingeniería de la Universidad del Salvador and the Vicerrectorado de Investigación y Desarrollo (VRID) through the Dirección de Investigación y del Instituto de Investigación en Ciencia y Tecnología, (in which this project is framed VRID Code 1935 - Academic Code 100091) for the support received to carry out this research and the Escuela de Lenguas Modernas that has carried out the translation of this document. Special thanks go to Marina Raffo for the translation of this paper, as part of the scheme of academic practices for the Scientific and Literary Translation course at the School of Modern Languages, under the supervision of Professor Edgardo España.

References

1. Eterovic, J., Cipriano, M., García, E., Torres, L.: XXV Congreso Argentino de Ciencias de la Computación (CACIC) Libro de actas. UniRío Editora, Córdoba, Páginas 1228–1240 (2019). ISBN 978-987-688-377-1

2. Anderson, R.: A5 (Was: HACKING DIGITAL PHONES). UK telecom (Usenet), June 1994. https://groups.google.com/forum/?msg/uk.telecom/TkdCaytoeU4/Mroy719hdroJ#!msg/uk.telecom/TkdCaytoeU4/Mroy719hdroJ

3. Golić, J.D.: Cryptanalysis of alleged A5 stream cipher. In: Fumy, W. (ed.) EUROCRYPT 1997. LNCS, vol. 1233, pp. 239–255. Springer, Heidelberg (1997). https://doi.org/10.1007/3-540-69053-0_17

4. Petrovic, S., Fúster-Sabater, A.: Cryptanalysis of the A5/2 Algorithm. https://eprint.iacr.org/2000/052.pdf

5. Barkan, E., Biham, E., Keller, E.: Instant ciphertext-only cryptanalysis of GSM encrypted communication. J. Cryptol. **21**(3), 392–429 (2008). https://doi.org/10.1007/s00145-007-9001-y

6. ETSI/SAGE. KASUMI Specification, Part of the Specification of the 3GPP Confidentiality and Integrity Algorithms (1999)

7. Dunkelman, O., Keller, N., Shamir, A.: A practical-time related-key attack on the KASUMI cryptosystem used in GSM and 3G telephony. In: Rabin, T. (ed.) CRYPTO 2010. LNCS, vol. 6223, pp. 393–410. Springer, Heidelberg (2010). https://doi.org/10.1007/978-3-642-14623-7_21

8. Bar-On, A.: A 2^{70} Attack on the Full MISTY1

9. Driessen, B., Hund, R., Willems, C., Paar, C., Holz, T.: Don't trust satellite phones: a security analysis of two satphone standards. In: 2012 IEEE Symposium on Security and Privacy, pp. 128–142, May 2012

10. Li, R., Li, H., Li, C., Sun, B.: A low data complexity attack on the GMR-2 cipher used in the satellite phones. In: Moriai, S. (ed.) FSE 2013. LNCS, vol. 8424, pp. 485–501. Springer, Heidelberg (2014). https://doi.org/10.1007/978-3-662-43933-3_25

11. Garcia, F., van Rossum, P., Verdult, R., Schreur, R.: Dismantling SecureMemory, CryptoMemory and CryptoRF. In: Proceedings of the 17th ACM Conference on Computer and Communications Security, CCS 2010, New York, NY, USA, pp. 250–259. ACM (2010)

12. Biryukov, A., Kizhvatov, I., Zhang, B.: Cryptanalysis of the Atmel cipher in SecureMemory, CryptoMemory and CryptoRF. In: Lopez, J., Tsudik, G. (eds.) ACNS 2011. LNCS, vol. 6715, pp. 91–109. Springer, Heidelberg (2011). https://doi.org/10.1007/978-3-642-21554-4_6

13. Nohl, K., Evans, D., Starbug, S., Plötz, H.: Reverse engineering a cryptographic RFID tag. In USENIX Security Symposium, vol. 28 (2008)

14. Courtois, N., Nohl, K., O'Neil, S.: Algebraic attacks on the crypto-1 stream cipher in mifare classic and oyster cards. Cryptology ePrint Archive, Report 2008/166 (2008). http://eprint.iacr.org/2008/166

15. Golić, J.D.: Cryptanalytic attacks on MIFARE classic protocol. In: Dawson, E. (ed.) CT-RSA 2013. LNCS, vol. 7779, pp. 239–258. Springer, Heidelberg (2013). https://doi.org/10.1007/978-3-642-36095-4_16

16. Becker, M., Desoky, A.: A study of the DVD content scrambling system (CSS) algorithm. In: Proceedings of the Fourth IEEE International Symposium on Signal Processing and Information Technology, pp. 353–356 (2004)

17. Pedersen, L., Munk, K., Andersen, L.: Cryptography – the rise and fall of DVD encryption (2007). http://citeseerx.ist.psu.edu/viewdoc/download;jsessionid=3672D97255B2446765D A47DA97960CDF?doi=10.1.1.118.6103&rep=rep1&type=pdf

18. Weinmann, R.-P., Wirt, K.: Analysis of the DVB common scrambling algorithm. In: Chadwick, D., Preneel, B. (eds.) CMS 2004. ITIFIP, vol. 175, pp. 195–207. Springer, Boston (2005). https://doi.org/10.1007/0-387-24486-7_15

19. Lucks, S., Schuler, A., Tews, E., Weinmann, R.-P., Wenzel, M.: Attacks on the DECT authentication mechanisms. In: Fischlin, M. (ed.) CT-RSA 2009. LNCS, vol. 5473, pp. 48–65. Springer, Heidelberg (2009). https://doi.org/10.1007/978-3-642-00862-7_4

20. Nohl, K., Tews, E., Weinmann, R.-P.: Cryptanalysis of the DECT standard cipher. In: Hong, S., Iwata, T. (eds.) FSE 2010. LNCS, vol. 6147, pp. 1–18. Springer, Heidelberg (2010). https://doi.org/10.1007/978-3-642-13858-4_1

21. Fluhrer, S., Lucks, S.: Analysis of the E_0 encryption system. In: Vaudenay, S., Youssef, Amr M. (eds.) SAC 2001. LNCS, vol. 2259, pp. 38–48. Springer, Heidelberg (2001). https://doi.org/10.1007/3-540-45537-X_3

22. Lu, Y., Vaudenay, S.: Faster correlation attack on Bluetooth keystream generator E0. In: Franklin, M. (ed.) CRYPTO 2004. LNCS, vol. 3152, pp. 407–425. Springer, Heidelberg (2004). https://doi.org/10.1007/978-3-540-28628-8_25

23. Lu, Y., Meier, W., Vaudenay, S.: The conditional correlation attack: a practical attack on bluetooth encryption. In: Shoup, V. (ed.) CRYPTO 2005. LNCS, vol. 3621, pp. 97–117. Springer, Heidelberg (2005). https://doi.org/10.1007/11535218_7

24. Dubrova, E., Hell, M.: Espresso: a stream cipher for 5G wireless communication systems. Cryptogr. Commun. **9**(2), 273–289 (2017). https://doi.org/10.1007/s12095-015-0173-2

25. Wang, M., Lin, D.: Related key chosen IV attack on stream cipher espresso variant. In: IEEE International Conference on Computational Science and Engineering (CSE) (2017)

26. Wiener, I.P.: NXP Hitag2 PCF 7936/46/47/52 stream cipher reference implementation. http://cryptolib.com/ciphers/hitag2/2007

27. Verdult, R., Garcia, F., Balasch, J.: Gone in 360 seconds: Hijacking with Hitag2. In: Proceedings of the 21st USENIX Conference on Security Symposium, Security 2012, p. 37. USENIX Association, Berkeley (2012)

28. Verdult, R., Garcia, F., Ege, B.: Dismantling Megamos crypto: wirelessly lockpicking a vehicle immobilizer. In Supplement to the 22nd USENIX Security Symposium (USENIX Security 13), pp. 703–718. USENIX Association, August 2013

29. Garcia, F., de Koning Gans, G., Verdult, R.: Wirelessly lockpicking a smart card reader. Int. J. Inf. Secur. **13**(5), 403–420 (2014). https://doi.org/10.1007/s10207-014-0234-0

30. Biryukov, A., Leurent, G., Roy, A.: Cryptanalysis of the "Kindle" cipher. In: Knudsen, L.R., Wu, H. (eds.) SAC 2012. LNCS, vol. 7707, pp. 86–103. Springer, Heidelberg (2013). https://doi.org/10.1007/978-3-642-35999-6_7

31. Wagner, D., Simpson, L., Dawson, E., Kelsey, J., Millan, W., Schneier, B.: Cryptanalysis of ORYX. In: Tavares, S., Meijer, H. (eds.) SAC 1998. LNCS, vol. 1556, pp. 296–305. Springer, Heidelberg (1999). https://doi.org/10.1007/3-540-48892-8_23

32. https://www.ecrypt.eu.org/stream/ciphers/grain/grain.pdf. Accessed 26 Feb 2020

33. https://csrc.nist.gov/CSRC/media/Projects/lightweight-cryptography/documents/round-2/ spec-doc-rnd2/grain-128aead-spec-round2.pdf. Accessed 26 Feb 2020

34. https://csrc.nist.gov/CSRC/media/Projects/Lightweight-Cryptography/documents/round-1/ spec-doc/ShamashAndShamashash-spec.pdf

35. Bertoni, G., Daemen, J., Peeters, M., Van Assche, G.: On the security of the keyed sponge construction. In: Symmetric Key Encryption Workshop (SKEW), February 2011 [34]

36. Bertoni, G., Daemen, J., Peeters, M., Van Assche, G.: Duplexing the sponge: single-pass authenticated encryption and other applications. Cryptology ePrint Archive, Report 2011/499 (2011)
37. Jovanovic, P., Luykx, A., Mennink, B.: Beyond $2^{c/2}$ security in sponge-based authenticated encryption modes. In: Sarkar, P., Iwata, T. (eds.) ASIACRYPT 2014. LNCS, vol. 8873, pp. 85–104. Springer, Heidelberg (2014). https://doi.org/10.1007/978-3-662-45611-8_5
38. Driscoll. BeepBeep embedded real-time encryption. In: International Workshop on Fast Software Encryption, FSE2002: Fast Software Encryption, pp. 164–178 (2002)
39. Wagner, D., Schneier, B., Kelsey, J.: Cryptanalysis of the cellular message encryption algorithm. In: Kaliski, B.S. (ed.) CRYPTO 1997. LNCS, vol. 1294, pp. 526–537. Springer, Heidelberg (1997). https://doi.org/10.1007/BFb0052260
40. Perrin, L.: More reverse-engineered S-boxes. Presentation at the Rump Session of ESC 2017 (2017). https://www.cryptolux.org/mediawiki-esc2017/images/2/2e/Rump.pdf
41. Borghoff, J., Knudsen, L.R., Leander, G., Matusiewicz, K.: Cryptanalysis of C2. In: Halevi, S. (ed.) CRYPTO 2009. LNCS, vol. 5677, pp. 250–266. Springer, Heidelberg (2009). https://doi.org/10.1007/978-3-642-03356-8_15
42. Bono, S., Green, M., Stubblefield, A., Juels, A., Rubin, A., Szydlo, M.: Security analysis of a cryptographically-enabled RFID device. In Proceedings of the 14th Conference on USENIX Security Symposium, SSYM 2005, USA, vol. 14, p. 1 (2005)
43. Indesteege, S., Keller, N., Dunkelman, O., Biham, E., Preneel, B.: A practical attack on KeeLoq. In: Smart, N. (ed.) EUROCRYPT 2008. LNCS, vol. 4965, pp. 1–18. Springer, Heidelberg (2008). https://doi.org/10.1007/978-3-540-78967-3_1
44. Graham, R.: Mirai and IoT Botnet analysis. In: RSA Conference 2017, San Francisco (2017)

A Better Infected Hosts Detection Combining Ensemble Learning and Threat Intelligence

Paula Venosa[1]([⊠]), Sebastian Garcia[2], and Francisco Javier Diaz[1]

[1] LINTI - Facultad de Informática, Universidad Nacional de La Plata,
La Plata, Argentina
{pvenosa, jdiaz}@info.unlp.edu.ar
[2] Stratosphere Laboratory, AIC, FEL, Czech Technical University,
Prague, Czechia
sebastian.garcia@agents.fel.cvut.cz

Abstract. Ensemble learning techniques have been successfully proposed and used to improve threats detection in cybersecurity. These techniques usually improve the detection results by combining algorithms that together have less errors. However there has not been any ensemble learning algorithm used to classify network flows when several methods are used to give individual detections for each of the flows. The state of the art in the use of ensemble learning techniques was analyzed to find an alternative for the current intrusion detection mechanisms. This research proposes to incorporate ensemble learning to the Stratosphere Linux IPS (SLIPS), a behavioral-based intrusion detection and prevention system that uses machine learning algorithms to detect malicious behaviors. Our ensembling method is used to obtain better results, taking advantage of the benefits of SLIPS's classifiers and modules. A contribution of our method is to extend the ensembling techniques by considering Threat Intelligence blacklists feeds as part of the detections. We present the results of the first stage of this project, i.e. ensemble learning algorithms to classify individual flows when they have multiple labels. on the other hand we also present the results corresponding to the second stage of our project, i.e. the detection of groups of flows going to the same destination IP.

Keywords: Ensemble learning · Cybersecurity · Malware · Intrusion detection

1 Introduction

Detecting malware and attacks by analyzing their network traffic remains a challenge. Although there are several detection mechanisms to accurately separate the malicious behavior from normal ones, it is still extremely difficult to have a detection system that can handle all the situations that arise in the network with low error rate. These techniques include machine learning algorithms, static signatures and experts-based rules. In particular, the most used method today is based on the contribution of rules by a large community of analysts, a method called *Threat Intelligence*. In a general sense, detecting malicious traffic in the network is fairly complex, with the main obstacles being: First, normal traffic is extremely complex, diverse and changing. Second, malicious actions change continuously, adapting, migrating and hiding as normal

© Springer Nature Switzerland AG 2020
P. Pesado and M. Arroyo (Eds.): CACIC 2019, CCIS 1184, pp. 354–365, 2020.
https://doi.org/10.1007/978-3-030-48325-8_23

traffic. Third, the amount of data to analyze is huge, forcing analysts to lose data in favor of speed. Fourth, detection must occur in near real time to be useful. Fifth, there is a large imbalance in the amount of normal traffic compared to the amount of malicious traffic, making it very difficult to have good detection results. Sixth, the cost of False Positives errors and False Negative errors is different, further complicating the decision process. To solve some of these problems, the security learning community proposed the use of ensemble algorithms. These algorithms implement techniques for using, adding and summarizing information about several different detectors in a final decision.

In this paper we present an extension for our previous work [1] that proposed an ensembling method to obtain better results, taking advantage of the benefits of SLIPS's [2] classifiers and modules.

Although there were some good proposals for ensemble learning techniques applied to the security of the network [3], there are two aspects of them that were not fully studied. First, the application of ensemble learning algorithms with Threat Intelligence data (e.g. VirusTotal [4]). Secondly, there are no ensemble learning algorithms that work as a function of time in the detection of the same source hosts. Meaning detecting an infected host in a specific time and then detecting it uninfected when it is cleaned later.

In the current cybersecurity state where it is extremely hard to stop all threats, the community effort should not only focus on protection and prevention, but be directed towards detection and response [5]. In this context, malware continues to represent the main threat, and its detection remains one of the main concerns [6].

Given the large amount and exponential growth of malware samples [7–9] an effective way to detect them is required. The tools that use signature-based methods require maintaining a database to store patterns based on the characteristics of the malware extracted by experts. They present their limitations since a small change in the malware produces a different signature.

Intrusion detection systems have the ability to detect threats in the network but sometimes they are not effective. It is of vital importance that the algorithm used is reliable and can provide high detection accuracy. There are many research works that address this problem using several methods [10].

In order to benefit from multiple different classifiers, and exploit their strengths, we propose the use of ensembling algorithms [11, 12], which combine the results of the individual classifiers into a final result to achieve greater precision and thus a better result. By combining a set of classifiers to decide, the ensemble learning methodology imitates the human nature of seeking various opinions before making a crucial decision, weighing individual opinions and combining them for a better final decision.

2   Ensemble Learning Techniques

Ensemble learning techniques allow combining multiple models, both homogeneous and heterogeneous, with the aim of better classifying new instances. In practice, after constructing a set of classifiers that use some parts of the original dataset, the predictions of the different classifiers are combined to make a final decision. Different schemes are commonly used, either the same algorithm can be trained using different datasets or different algorithms can be trained using the same dataset.

Ensemble learning models combine the decisions of multiple algorithms to improve the overall performance, minimize errors, bias, and variance. Among the main ensemble learning techniques are Majority Voting, Averaging and Weighted Averaging [13]. In **Majority voting** multiple models are used to make predictions for each tuple. The predictions of each model are considered as a separate vote. The prediction done by the majority of the models is used as the final prediction. The **Averaging technique** takes an average of predictions of all models (usually regression models) and this average is used to make the final prediction. In Weighted **Averaging** all models are first assigned weights that define the importance of each model for prediction and then the final prediction is made from the average prediction after weighting.

A group of more complex ensembling techniques is also commonly used, called bagging, boosting, random forest, and stacking [14]. In **Bagging** (also known as bootstrap aggregating) each classifier is trained with a random subset of the original training set (with replacement). With each sample a model is constructed. The results of these models are combined using average or majority voting. **Bootstrap or boosting** is an iterative technique that adjusts the weight of an observation based on the last classification and runs several models on the data. If an observation was incorrectly classified, it increases the weight of this observation. First, the algorithm is trained on the entire dataset and subsequent models are constructed by adjusting the residuals of the previous algorithm, thus giving greater weight to those observations that the previous model predicted incorrectly. It is based on the creation of a series of weak algorithms, each of which may not be good for the entire data set, but is good for a part of the data set. Therefore, each model actually increases the performance of the set. **Random forest** is a supervised machine learning algorithm used for regression and classification. The idea is to build multiple decision trees and add them to give a better result. Each tree is constructed with a different random subset of the data. Random forest is more accurate than a simple decision tree because it minimizes the overfitting. In classification problems majority voting is used to combine the predictions while in the regression, the predictions are made taking the average of the tree predictions.

Stacked generalization [14] is a method that uses a different way of combining multiple models introducing the meta learner concept. Stacking is the generalization of other ensemble learning methods. The process consists in the following steps: (i) split the training into a sample for training and a sample for testing, (ii) a set of base learners are trained with the training sample, (iii) the models are tested using the test sample, (iv) the predictions are used as input and the current response as output to train the highest level learner.

3   Ensemble Learning Applied to Network Security

Ensemble learning methods use multiple learning algorithms to obtain predictive performance that improves what could be obtained through any of the individual learning algorithms.

Current IDS have to deal with large volumes of data and with the difficulty of detecting new attacks. In this regard, there are several investigations that improve them using machine learning. The use of machine learning has the following advantages: (i) the ability of machine learning to generalize to detect new types of intrusions, (ii) attack signatures can be automatically extracted from tagged traffic data, (iii) ability to adapt to new attacks. At the same time, since in an attack they differ: intrinsic features (general information), traffic features (connection features) and content features (package info), there are proposals around implementing models with armed dataset samples from the different sets of features and different classifiers, which are then combined with ensemble learning techniques [15, 16]. Another advantage of the ensemble learning algorithms over the classic machine learning techniques is that they improve detection given the possibility of using parallel architectures.

The selection of characteristics is essential, so it is important to continue investigating in this regard It is also important to evaluate which base classifiers to use and how they should be combined in a way to design architectures that make multiple classifiers collaborate with each other instead of competing. This problem is addressed in a more specific way in [17], where ensemble learning is applied for intrusion detection to detect DoS, R2L, U2R and Probing attacks in FTP service traffic. The work performs the tests based on the UCI KDD and Neural Networks dataset with different feature sets: intrinsic features, content features and traffic features using MPLM and Majority, Bayesian Average, Belief, as ensemble learning algorithms. In this work the metrics to compare the results were: error percentage, average cost, false alarms percentage. And it was concluded that ensemble learning reduces the percentage of errors but also reduces the capabilities of generalization.

MPLM proposes to analyze the different phases or facets of a problem and build on this perspective of the problem. Perspectives are represented by a set of dataset features. Models are obtained from the different perspectives that are then combined with ensemble learning techniques. A problem to solve in this framework is the criteria and the implementation of the selection of features for each model to build the perspectives. MPLM can be applied to the detection of various attacks such as DoS, R2L, U2R and Probing [18] and for the detection of botnet activity [19], where the perspectives represent the different stages of their life cycle. In [19] a new model for applying learning in multifaceted problems is presented, focusing on the selection of features to be included in each perspective (network-based perspectives, host-based perspectives, DNS-based perspectives), one of the aspects that is raised as an aspect to be solved. In addition, the criteria of what features make sense to include in each model, taking into account that the inclusion of strongly correlated features may not contribute to the classification process.

There are also proposals as [20] based on modified Stacking to detect network intrusions (Probe, DoS, UR2 and R2L) where models are generated using samples from the random selection of dataset features, then select the best models according to a defined criteria (accuracy, information gain, recall mean and true positive rate) and combine them with stacking as the ensemble learning technique. And other more innovative works such as [21] that proposes to apply ensemble learning clustering to detect botnets. They generate partitions and use link based algorithms to combine them (in that step is where the ensemble learning takes place) and apply machine learning to perform the classification in each cluster of the final partition. No proposals described include Thread Intelligence in the classification process.

4 Ensemble Learning to Improve Detection of Infected Machines

Stratosphere Linux IPS (SLIPS) [2] is a behavioral-based intrusion detection and prevention system that uses machine learning algorithms to detect malicious behaviors. In addition to the different classifiers that this tool has today (MLDetection and Port Scan detector) other modules such as Thread Intelligence are in development to incorporate more information to the detection, and thus improve the accuracy of the tool from its use.

The proposal presented in this article and which is currently being worked on consists of the incorporation of ensemble learning algorithms that allow combining the information obtained from the different classifiers in order to improve the results in the detection of infected IPs, taking into account the anomalies that the classifiers are able to detect, in each of the stages, from the analysis of the flows that represent the connections of the hosts of the network on which SLIPS [2] operates.

The contribution consists in improving the detection process by implementing ensemble learning to take decisions based on different data provided by SLIPS [2], considering that to determine if a host is infected in a time window, it has: (i) different predictions for each flow, one for each classifier, (ii) a set of flows associated with the given IP (the source IP of those flows), with its corresponding prediction, (iii) a set of malicious behavior alerts associated with the given IP (that have this IP as source IP), (iv) information from different Threat Intelligence sources that indicate destinations of the analyzed flows that are malicious (with some confidence percentage).

Using the information described in the previous paragraph, we propose to apply ensemble learning to take differents decisions: first, if each flow is malware or normal, secondly, if the set of flows that go from an origin to a destination are part of an infection, in third place if a destination address is malicious or not, based in Threat Intelligence sources information and finally, if each source IP is infected or not.

5 Ensemble Learning Applied to Network Security to Classify Flows

As we mentioned in the previous section, within the framework of our proposal, a possible application of ensemble learning is to combine the results of multiple classifiers for a flow, where each one predicts whether it corresponds to malware or normal traffic. Then in SLIPS [2] we have n predictions for a flow, where n is the number of classifiers in operation. As described in Sect. 4 of this article, the advantages that can be obtained from applying ensemble learning to intrusion detection depends on the attack to be detected, the machine learning techniques to be combined and the features to be taken into account in the classification of the flows.

Thus, as a first stage of this project, performance tests of the teaching algorithms were performed to detect malware from flows evaluating its accuracy compared to a set of classic Machine Learning (ML) algorithms. To carry out the tests, the Stratosphere dataset [22] was used. It is a mixed dataset with tags corresponding to normal traffic and malware traffic, from a botnet known as Rbot. The following ML algorithms were tested: Logistic Regression (LR), Naive Bayes (NB), Random Forest (RF), Kneighbords (KN) and Decision Tree (DT). And the ensemble learning techniques used: voting hard (majority voting), voting soft (using the sum of the predicted probabilities), Weighted Voting, boosting and bagging [23]. Tests with the Scikit-learn library [24] were implemented and the accuracy obtained from applying the cross_val_score function to the model was used as a metric. Test results are shown in Table 1, Table 2, Table 3 and Table 4.

Table 1. Tests without applying ensemble learning

Algorithm	Accuracy
Logistic Regression	99,457% (±0.00641)
Random Forest	99,995% (±0.00004)
Naive Bayes	98,997% (±0.01246)
Kneighbords	99,975% (±0.00022)
Decision Tree	99,993% (±0.00006)

Table 2. Tests with Voting techniques including LR, Naive Bayes and RF

Algorithm	Accuracy
Ensemble [Majority Voting]	99,731% (±0.00286)
Ensemble [Voting with probabilities sum]	99,753% (±0.00295)
Weighted Voting (LR = 1, RF = 3 y NB = 1)	99,993% (±0.000041)
Weighted Voting (LR = 1, RF = 3 y NB = 2)	99,991% (±0.000075)
Weighted Voting (LR = 2, RF = 3 y NB = 1)	99,988% (±0.000092)

Table 3. Tests by changing random forest to Kneighbords

Algorithm	Accuracy
Weighted Voting (LR = 1, KN = 2 y NB = 1)	99,975% (±0.00025)
Weighted Voting (LR = 1, KN = 3 y NB = 1)	99,975% (±0.00025)
Weighted Voting (LR = 2, KN = 3 y NB = 1)	99,974% (±0.00025)

Table 4. Tests changing random forest to decision tree

Algorithm	Accuracy
Weighted Voting (LR = 1, DT = 3 y NB = 1)	99,993% (±0.00006)
Weighted Voting (LR = 1, DT = 3 y NB = 2)	99,991% (±0.00007)
Weighted Voting (LR = 2, DT = 3 y NB = 1)	99,993% (±0.00006)

The tests with both voting techniques give the same results. Both improve the LR and the NB but not the RF. This happens because when combining RF that gives good results with two other algorithms that are worse, and then the majority decides badly.

Weighted Voting does not present improvements for RF although it does show improvements compared to the other voting techniques tested. Those that best classify are those that give RF the greatest weight and the least weight to the other two algorithms.

Instead of using voting combining LR, RF and NB, it was tried to combine LR and NB with KN and with DT, and improvements could also be seen when applying ensemble learning regarding not applying it. Although the improvements were not significant there were for all the algorithms involved.

Table 5 shows that improvements are obtained in all tested algorithms.

Table 5. Bagging tests (using a seed value = 8)

Algorithm	Accuracy
Logistic Regression (con bagging)	99,419% (±0.01731)
Random Forest (con bagging)	99,997% (±0.00013)
Naive Bayes (con bagging)	99,165% (±0.02727)
Decision TÝree (con bagging)	99,997% (±0.00013)
Kneighbords (con bagging)	99,98% (±0.00033)

Adaboost improves for DT is the same for RF and does not improve either NB or LR, as shown in Table 6.

Table 6. Boosting tests (Adaboost)

Algorithm	Accuracy
Logistic regression (con boosting)	98,557% (±0.01707)
Random forest (con boosting)	99,995% (±0.00005)
Naive Bayes(con boosting)	77,884% (±0.29319)
Decision tree (con boosting)	99,993% (±0.00013)

6 Ensemble Learning Applied to Network Security to Classify All Flows Associated to a Source Address and Destination Address

As we mentioned in Sect. 4, after having a decision for each flow as a result of applying ensemble learning, we have a set of flows associated with the given IP (the source IP of those flows), with its corresponding prediction. In this instance, we make a decision for connections with each destination IP, from each source IP. For this purpose we apply. Ensemble learning involves multiple decisions for the different flows that go from an origin to the same destination address.

The criteria to establish if the set of flows between a source address and a destination address are part of an infected connection is to analyze the following features: percentage of malicious flows belonging to established TCP connections, percentage of malicious flows belonging to TCP not established, percentage of malicious flows belonging to UDP connections with data exchange and percentage of malicious flows belonging to UDP connections without data exchange. If any of these percentages exceeds a limit and the amount of flows is greater than a certain value, the flows belonging to that connection are considered part of an infection.

As we do not know a priori the limit values for the percentage and the amount that determine the best classification of a set of flows, the process was tested with a set of values for those limits and the algorithm created was trained.

To carry out these tests, three Stratosphere datasets [22] were used. These are mixed datasets with tags corresponding to normal traffic and malware traffic, from a botnet known as Rbot [22], a botnet known as NSIS.ay [22] and a botnet known as CoinMiner.XMRig [22].

Using these three datasets we repeated the first stage descripted in Sect. 5 obtaining as result a dataset to use as an incoming dataset for phase 2 tests. Testing using Weighted Voting (LR = 1, DT = 3 y NB = 1), the result shown in Table 7 was obtained.

Table 7. Test with Weighted Voting algorithm with the new database.

Algorithm	Accuracy
Weighted Voting (LR = 1, DT = 3 y NB = 1)	99,918% ($\pm$ 0.00012)

We used 80% of the dataset obtained as a result of the first stage for training and 20% for testing. aclarar que es el 80% de ips y el 20% de ips

After the training we obtained a labeled dataset, where the label, assigned to each set of flows between an origin and a destination, is the result of the process described below in that section. We built a confusion matrix [25] where the ground truth is related to the source address. From the confusion matrix we calculated the following metrics that we took into account when making decisions:

False positive rate.

- True positive rate.
- F1 Score.
- Accuracy.

Our goal was to minimize the false positive rate and maximize the rest of the selected metrics. With this criteria the best results we obtained in the training process were those shown in Table 8. To get these values we use the thresholds values shown in Table 9.

Table 8. Metric best values obtained in training

False positive rate	True positive rate	F1 Score	Accuracy
0	97,329%	98,647%	98,002%

Table 9. Thresholds values to obtain best metric values.

Threshold for percentage of malicious flows per destination address	Threshold for amount of malicious flows per destination address
75%	0
50%	0
25%	0
0%	0

Then we tested the method using the testing dataset portion and we use fixing the thresholds according to the following criteria:

- Percentage of malicious flows of some type of traffic (Established TCP, Not Established TCP, Established UDP, Not Established UDP) greater than 0.
- Amount of malicious flows of some type of traffic (Established TCP, Not Established TCP, Established UDP, Not Established UDP) greater than 0.

We calculated the confusion matrix in the test process too, and better results than those of the training process were obtained, as can be seen in Table 10.

Table 10. Metric values obtained in testing

False positive rate	True positive rate	F1 Score	Accuracy
0%	97,329%	98,647%	98,002%

We did a second test training with a dataset builded with the first stage result dataset with erroneous labels inserted in 10% of the records selected randomly. The same results as those with the original dataset were obtained using the same values for threshold.

Then we tested the method using the testing dataset portion of dataset with wrong labels and we used fixing the thresholds according to the following criteria:

- Percentage of malicious flows of some type of traffic (Established TCP, Not Established TCP, Established UDP, Not Established UDP) greater than 0.
- Amount of malicious flows of some type of traffic (Established TCP, Not Established TCP, Established UDP, Not Established UDP) greater than 0.

And the metric values for the test were those shown in Table 11.

Table 11. Metric values obtained in new testing process

False positive rate	True positive rate	F1 Score	Accuracy
0,015%	97,264%	98,585%	97,942%

As result of this second phase we had a decision for all flows going to a destination IP address.

To obtain the metrics the ground truth we had corresponds to the source IP, not to the destination IP. Even if a source IP is malicious not all flows going to all IPs destinations are malicious, but in this instance we didn't have a better way to do this.

7 Ensemble Learning Using Thread Intelligence Information, a Next Step

Threat intelligence solutions gather raw data about emerging or existing threat actors and threats from a number of sources. This data is then analyzed and filtered to produce threat intel feeds and management reports that contain information that can be used by automated security control solutions. The primary purpose of this type of security is to keep organizations informed of the risks of advanced persistent threats, zero-day threats and exploits, and how to protect against them [26].

While there are a lot of challenges related to threat intelligence [27], such as the definition of standards that allow information to be shared, there are numerous initiatives from different organizations, some of them widely used by the community.

SLIPS [2] has two threat intelligence modules called VirusTotal and Threat Intelligence. The first of them obtains the Virus Total [4] online information about an IP address and the Threat Intelligence Module (it is being developed) checks if an address is blacklisted from a given set of lists.

The next step will be to analyze the information provided by each module and implement ensemble learning of Threat Intelligence modules information (SLIPS's VirusTotal module and SLIPS's Threat Intelligence module) to make a decision about each destination address.

Finally, to determine if each source IP is infected or not, our proposal is to apply ensemble learning of all the data of the destination IPs to which that source IP was connected.

8 Conclusions and Future Work

Ensemble learning methods help to improve machine learning results by combining multiple models, even more so when the base algorithms are weak. In case of heavy voting, if any of the base algorithms has a high percentage of successes, giving greater weight to this algorithm, better results are obtained.

This technique is appropriate to make a prediction for a flow, given a set of predictions resulting from the different SLIPS [2] classifiers.

To infer that the set of the flows from an origin to a destination are part of an infection, the percentage of flows labeled as malicious of some type of traffic from a source address to a destination address, must be greater to zero. The types of traffic defined are: TCP Established, TCP Not Established, UDP "Established" or UDP "Not Established". In addition, the condition that there is at least one flow in that set is also necessary.

Of the works that describe the use of ensemble learning applied to cybersecurity, none incorporates the valuable information provided by Thread Intelligence sources, which is part of our proposal and it is the next phase we are going to implement and test.

On the other hand, to carry out the proposal described here, the most appropriate techniques to apply depend on the problem given, so in order to find the best options for the implementation of the proposal, specific tests must be carried out with the data that SLIPS [2] provides. These tests, the design of the solution and its implementation are the keys to the future work of this project.

References

1. Venosa, P., Garcia, S., Diaz, F.J.: Ensembling to improve infected hosts detection. In: XXV Congreso Argentino de Ciencias de la Computación, CACIC 2019, pp. 1251–1260, October 2019. ISBN 978-987-688-377-1
2. Technology in the Stratosphere IPS Project (s.f.). https://www.stratosphereips.org/technology
3. Vanerio, J., Casas, P.: Ensemble-learning approaches for network security and anomaly detection. In: Workshop on Big Data Analytics and Machine Learning for Data Communication Networks, pp. 1–6. ACM, August 2017
4. VirusTotal (s.f.). https://www.virustotal.com/
5. Panetta, K.: 5 Trends in Cybersecurity for 2017 and 2018 (2017). https://www.gartner.com/smarterwithgartner/5-trends-in-cybersecurity-for-2017-and-2018/
6. ENISA: ENISA Threat Landscape Report 2017 15 Top Cyber-Threats and Trends, December 2018. https://www.enisa.europa.eu/publications/enisa-threat-landscape-report-2017
7. PANDA: 2017 in Figures: the exponential growth of Malware, December 2018. https://www.pandasecurity.com/mediacenter/malware/2017-figures/
8. AV-Test (2018). https://www.av-test.org/en/statistics/malware/
9. McAfee Labs: McAfee Labs Threat Report, December 2018. https://www.mcafee.com/enterprise/en-us/assets/reports/rp-quarterly-threats-dec-2017.pdf

10. Mohd, R.Z.A., Zuhairi, M.F., Shadil A.Z.A., Dao H.: Anomaly-based NIDS: a review of machine learning methods on malware detection. In: International Conference on Information and Communication Technology, Kuala Lumpur, pp. 266–270 (2016)
11. Zhou, Z.H.: Ensemble Methods: Foundations and Algorithms (Chapman & Hall/Crc Machine Learning & Pattern Recognition), 1st edn. Chapman and Hall/CRC, New York (2012)
12. Zhang, C., Ma, Y.: Ensemble Machine Learning: Methods and Applications, 1st edn. Springer, New York (2012). https://doi.org/10.1007/978-1-4419-9326-7
13. Rokach, L.: Ensemble-based classifiers. Artif. Intell. Rev. **33**, 1–39 (2009). https://doi.org/10.1007/s10462-009-9124-7
14. Sewell, M.: Ensemble learning. United Kingdom: UCL Research Note (UCL Department of Computer Science) (2011)
15. Folino, G., Sabatino, P.: Review Ensemble based collaborative and distributed intrusion detection systems: A survey. J. Netw. Comput. Appl. **66**, 1–6 (2016)
16. Chih-Fong, T., Yu-Feng, H., Chia-Ying, L., Wei-Yang, L.: Intrusion detection by machine learning: a review. Expert Syst. Appl. **36**(2009), 11994–12000 (2009)
17. Didaci, L., Giacinto, G., Roli, F.: Ensemble Learning for Intrusion Detection in Computer Networks. ACM J. (2002)
18. Miller, S., Busby-Earle, C.: Multi-perspective machine learning (MPML) a machine learning model for multi-faceted learning problems (2018). https://doi.org/10.1109/csci.2017.60
19. Miller, S., Busby-Earle, C.: Multi-perspective machine learning a classifier ensemble method for intrusion detection (2018) https://doi.org/10.1145//CSCI.2017
20. Necati, D., Gökhan, D.: Modified stacking ensemble approach to detect network intrusionNecati DEMİR, Gökhan DALKILIÇ. Turkish J. Electr. Eng. Comput. Sci. **26**, 418–433 (2018)
21. Mai, L., Kun Noh, D.: Cluster Ensemble with Link-Based Approach for Botnet Detection. J. Netw. Syst. Manage. (2017). https://doi.org/10.1007/s10922-017-9436-x
22. Garcia, S., Grill, M., Stiborek, J., Zunino, A.: An empirical comparison of Botnet detection methods. Comput. Secur. J. **45**, 100–123 (2014). https://doi.org/10.1016/j.cose.2014.05.011
23. Aishwayra, S.: A Comprehensive Guide to Ensemble Learning (with Python codes). Analytics Vidhya, Haryana (2018)
24. Scikit-learn python library (s.f). https://scikit-learn.org/stable/
25. Confusion Matrix Online Calculator (s.f). http://onlineconfusionmatrix.com/
26. What is Threat Intelligence? (s.f). https://www.forcepoint.com/cyber-edu/threat-intelligence
27. Abu, M., Rahayu, S., Ariffin, D., Aswami, D., Robiah, Y.: Cyber threat intelligence – issue and challenges. Indonesian J. Electr. Eng. Comput. Sci. **10**, 371–379 (2018). https://doi.org/10.11591/ijeecs.v10.i1

Innovation in Computer Science
Education

Experiences in the Use of ICT and Digital Ramps for Students in Tertiary Education with Visual or Hearing Impairment

Adriana S. Fachal[1]([⊠]) [iD], María José Abásolo[2,3] [iD],
and Cecilia V. Sanz[2,3] [iD]

[1] Faculty of de Informatics, National University of La Plata, La Plata, Argentina
adrianafachal@gmail.com
[2] Institute of Research in Computer Science III-LIDI, School of Computer Science, National University of La Plata, La Plata, Argentina
{mjabasolo,csanz}@lidi.info.unlp.edu.ar
[3] Scientific Research Commission, CICPBA, La Plata, Argentina

Abstract. In the current context in which our society is highly impacted by the incorporation of ICTs, it is of fundamental importance to highlight the possibility of accessing to ICTs for people with disabilities. This article presents the use of M-Free, a didactic or mediation model, designed for inclusive education. Several educational experiences based on M-Free model were analyzed. Also two case studies are shown in order to use and improve the competencies of students from the tertiary level degree in Systems Analysis of the Metropolitan School of Higher Studies (EMAE), which present visual or hearing impairment. The purpose is to help them to achieve the implementation of software in the context of your personal, educational or work environment.

Keywords: Education · Inclusion · ICT · Technology · E-accessibility · Disability · Digital ramps · Didactic model · M-Free · Visual impairment · Hearing impairment

1 Introduction

The incorporation of ICT in the classroom does not in itself generate changes in educational practices, it implies a process of appropriation of tools and knowledge, and the construction of conceptions aimed at incorporating digital resources and materials as flexible, adaptable and transversal content. Contextualizing the strategies and didactic proposals for the incorporation of ICT in the classroom work within the concept of inclusive education implies the definition of objectives and the search for resources that promote significant contributions for each type of disability and introduce an improvement in the educational quality.

Accessibility consists in the requirement of reasonable adjustments or adaptation of the physical or social environment to the specific needs of persons with disabilities. This adaptation is considered reasonable when, without involving a disproportionate burden, it facilitates the access, use and participation of persons with disabilities on

P. Pesado and M. Arroyo (Eds.): CACIC 2019, CCIS 1184, pp. 369–388, 2020.
https://doi.org/10.1007/978-3-030-48325-8_24

equal terms to other citizens [9]. From the digital perspective, the concept of e-accessibility or Web accessibility is defined as the possibility of access with a successful interaction between people and computers at the Web interface level [7].

Theories of multiple intelligences provide a framework where users can learn to manage their difficulties. It is based on what is called the initial level of competence, that is, the strengths of people's learning style and didactic strategies are selected that can help stimulate their intelligences, thus achieving the most effective at even higher levels and drawing cognitive bridges in which the most developed are used to help improve those that present serious difficulties [13].

The concept of adaptation has a broad character and it is necessary to perform them to compensate for the restrictions to which the student is subjected as a result of their special needs. To carry them out, it is necessary to have specially trained personnel who design, if necessary, a plan for different needs such as, such as modifying physical spaces and eliminating architectural barriers to facilitate mobility in a wheelchair or a blind cane. Also it is necessary to take into account several issues: adapting the time to the student's rhythms, including pedagogical aids (complementary activities for learning Braille, language of signs and computer resources among others) and selecting a methodology that includes, modifies or excludes the contents that are considered convenient.

Regarding digital skills specifically when standard media are not accessible, Digital Ramps or Support Technology can be used (Assistive Technology), which are programs or utilities whose purpose is to facilitate the use of general-purpose computer applications to users with disabilities who would otherwise be forced to use only programs specifically designed for them. Sometimes in order to achieve the proper and complete implementation of certain digital ramps, some type of support product or technical aids is necessary so that the user can interact with the computer, tablet or cell phone.

Inclusive education in the higher level field assumes as a challenge teaching students with different characteristics in the same center and the same classroom. As proposed by [15], this challenge involves changing the way of teaching and organizing classroom activities and also favoring collaboration between students with different characteristics. It is important for universities to create spaces for inclusion for people with disabilities, eliminating accessibility barriers in order to guarantee the right to access to information for all users. Particularly [3] points out the importance that university libraries promote inclusion addressing the needs of users from the perspective of accessibility to information.

In order to carry out an adequate incorporation of ICTs into inclusive education work, enriching orientation processes for different types of disabilities, it is of fundamental importance to start by applying a didactic model. In Sect. 2 the teaching M-Free model and its complement B-Free model are presented. Our work revolves around studying selected cases that proposes the application of the M-Free model in order to enhance the creativity of teachers and how this circumstance can improve the performance of students with specific needs by strengthening existing competences in each of the students. This article is an extension on a previous publication by the same authors [6] where several educational experiences with students with disabilities based on M-Free model were analyzed. In the present analysis we focus on the digital ramps that were used and the evaluation of each of the experiences. Also in [6] we reported four educational experiences carried on by our team, based on M-Free model, with students with disabilities, from a career in the tertiary-level computing area, who intend to develop ICT-based projects. In Sect. 3 we describe in a more detailed way the M-Free phases in two of the study cases, one with visual impairment and the other with hearing impairment. Finally, Sect. 4 presents the conclusions and future work.

2   The Use of M-Free Didactic Model

2.1   M-Free Model

A didactic model is an instrument to address the teaching of different educational levels, while contributing to establish the links between theoretical analysis and teaching practice intervention [10]. In this case, the objective is to develop didactic strategies with a focus on multiple intelligences giving the opportunity to know clearly what are the strengths of the student and their motivations, and that, from that, they are formed in their individual skills detected [4].

The M-Free model [14, 18] is a didactic or intermediation model that aims to plan an educational activity aimed at students with specific needs, enhancing the creativity of teachers and how this circumstance can also improve school performance. It is of fundamental importance that the student is able to solve, produce or act on their reality. The teachers must begin thinking of people from their competences, that is, starting to work from their abilities and not from their disability. The original M-Free model consists of the following five phases (Fig. 1):

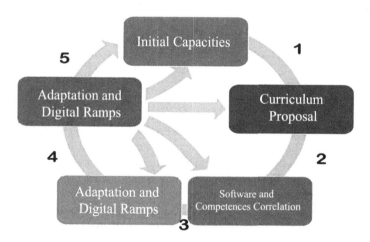

Fig. 1. M-Free didactic model

In the first phase the initial abilities of the student are ascertained. This initial assessment should not be satisfied only with determining the specific needs and deficits, but should indicate the best way to overcome them. FREE Iberoamerican Foundation for Cooperation defines the Wikinclusion Knowledge Base (WKB) [5] which offers a specific and classified list of competencies to evaluate. It is classified into six categories, namely: Autonomy, Sensomotor, Social Skills; Communication and language; Math, Natural and Social Environment; Digital Competition; Artistic Knowledge.

In the second phase the curricular proposal is organized under the theory called Multiple Intelligences. The development competencies detected in the first phase are used and there the selection of the objectives that can help the student to achieve the competences should be centered.

In the third phase, the objectives of the student's curriculum proposal are correlated with the available computer resources. In other words it is about weaving a group of objectives and software based on the proposals made by special education teachers. It is important to note that some questions that should be asked in this phase are: What does a student need ICT help for? Why use a technological aid and not another? How to integrate it into your tasks? How to redefine the objectives to adapt them to the needs of the student at any time according to the curriculum proposal? What criteria do you suggest changing one hardware or software for another?

In the fourth phase it must be observed if the student needs any adaptation or digital ramp.

In the fifth phase, the implementation and subsequent evaluation of the actions are carried out and the proposal for improvements that give continuity to the process may arise. What is relevant in this phase is to know if the actions carried out in the previous ones have been adequate and for this the analysis is usually divided into competences achieved, competencies in process and competencies not achieved.

To finalize the description of the model it is important to emphasize that its five phases do not occur in all occasions sequentially since as a result of the evaluation it is possible to distinguish that it is necessary to rectify the curriculum proposal, which needs some type of adaptation or different software because it does not meet the desired expectations or even arrive until new initial skills are discovered by the same educational process.

2.2 B-Free Simplified Model

The B-Free model [14, 18] completes the M-Free intermediation model, providing a visual structure that shows the different key elements involved in the intermediation with ICT from the point of view of the multiple interactions that characterize them. The B-Free model shows the links between the current multiple capabilities of the person, the competencies that are desired to be achieved or curricular proposal, the software and standard hardware that has been selected, and the digital ramps and adaptations that will allow him to interact with the computer and the disability that makes it difficult for him to participate in the activity. As shown in Fig. 2, the dynamic consists in the design of a ship-shaped template, designed with the Inspiration software.[1]

---

[1] Inspiration http://www.inspiration.com/.

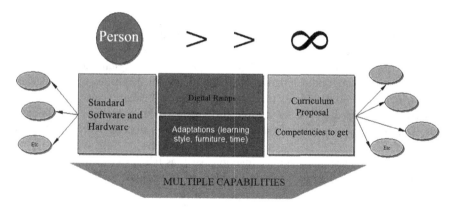

Fig. 2. B-Free model

2.3 M-Free Based Educational Experiences with ICT

The M-Free intermediation model has been applied in various educational experiences that try to give a new vision on how to address educational innovation with ICT in special education. Several recent educational experiences involving and in which M-Free has been applied were compiled. We found that the experiences correspond to the different levels of educations. They were developed in Spain and Latin-American countries were the FREE Iberoamerican Foundation for Cooperation imparted courses [2] in which M-Free model is taught. Table 1 shows the educational level and origin of the target population, the objective and the work area of each experience. Table 2 completes the information of each experience showing the disability of the target participants, the software and the digital ramps that has been used, and the performed evaluation.

2.4 Digital Ramps

Different ramps were used in [2] with visually impaired students. The software JAWS (Job Access With Speech)[3] which is a product of the company Freedom Scientific and it is a screen reader developed for PC users whose loss of vision prevents them from viewing the screen content or navigating with a mouse. This type of accessibility is called "read with the ears" since the screen reader software includes an integrated voice system that allows the student access to the PC with the possibility of interacting audibly with any installed software. This type of users does not have the possibility of using the mouse and through the use of this digital ramp they get access to both the software and the information of their PC through special keyboard shortcuts that would not be possible to access without it. Other possible options for free access are NVDA[4], free and open source screen reader for Microsoft Windows and Orca,

---

[2] FREE Iberoamerican Foundation for Cooperation. Course of Expert in ICT, inclusion and disability http://capacidad.es/.

[3] JAWS Freedom Scientific https://support.freedomscientific.com/JAWSHQ/JAWSHeadquarters01.

[4] NVDA https://www.nvaccess.org/.

screen reader for Linux. Braille Perkins typewriter[5] is used to obtain copies written in Braille code. It allows that visually impaired people can carry out activities such as reading and writing easily and effectively, reaching an ideal speed and without feeling excluded. Dragon Naturally Speaking[6] is used to transform digital audio into digital text. It is a voice recognition program available in several languages that particularly allows visually impaired students to write documents and emails.

Plaphoons[7] is used in [12] as a ramp for students with complex communication needs. This software is a communication board that allows a person to express ideas or actions.

Smartphones present accessibility functions such as talk back, increasing gestures, color settings, voice over, zoom, button and fonts adaptations, and also touch adaptations such as increasing assistive touch contrast [17].

Multisensory rooms area used for sensory stimulation [1] and cognitive stimulation [8] of children with disabilities in initial education.

In relation to students with hearing impairment the use of sign language is a very important tool. The main problem is that this language is dependent of every country and this fact limits the spread of resources available. In the two cases of students with this disability that are presented later in this work the teacher carry on the experience by means of Argentinian Sign Language (ASL) - or LSA in Spanish- as a mean of communication with the students, and also the production of educational material with videos in LSA and subtitles.

Table 1. Educational experiences that use M-Free intermediation model: educational level and origin of the target population, the objective and the working area

Ref.	Educational Level/Population/Place	Objective	Area/s
[1]	Special education/32 students between 6 and 13 years old from Beatriz Angélica Martínez Allio Special School/Córdoba, Argentina	Verify if the use of the technology installed in the multisensory room installed in the school favors the language, communication and learning of the students	Communication and language Autonomy, motor skills and social skills (subarea: stimulation)
[2]	University/National University of General Sarmiento/Buenos Aires, Argentina	Adapt study texts for students with disabilities who cannot access the texts in a traditional way. The adaptation of study materials with formats made available to this population of students serve as support for their inclusion in university life	Autonomy, motor skills and social skills Accessibility

(continued)

---

[5] Braille Perkins typewriter https://brailler.perkins.org/collections/perkins-braillers.

[6] Dragon Naturally Speaking Nuance Communications https://www.nuance.com/es-es/index.html.

[7] Plaphoons Projecte Fressa https://projectefressa.blogspot.com/2016/01/plaphoons-download.html.

Table 1. (*continued*)

Ref.	Educational Level/ Population/Place	Objective	Area/s
[8]	Initial education/Children from 1–4 years old./Cuenca, Ecuador	Propose a system of actions that promote sensory stimulation of children with neurodevelopmental disorders	Autonomy, motor skills and social skills Communication and language
[11]	Academic/Students of University of Sevilla/Spain	Improve acquisition of ICT educational skills with students from different socio-cultural and cognitive development levels	Autonomy, motor skills and social skills. Digital competences
[12]	Special Education (primary)/3 male and 2 female students of Víctor Mercante Normal School/Córdoba, Argentine	Develop the necessary skills to improve behavior problems, attention levels, social inclusion and self-esteem including ICT in a meaningful and gradual way. A workshop was given under the design of projects mainstreamed by various ICT resources where the activities proposed in the various spaces invited students to appropriately appropriate the content proposed in different areas	Communication and language Maths Natural and Social Environment Digital Competences
[13]	Special education/50 people between 16 and 55 years/Quito, Ecuador	Train people with multidisability who are part of the FINE organization incorporating ICT tools to achieve an effective labor and social insertion allowing this population to have a better quality of life both at personal and family level	Autonomy, sensomotor skills and social skills (subarea: work and study habits) Communication and language Transition to the world of work
[16]	Initial education/Boys and girls of the first grade of 8 schools/Panama	Create a portal of digital learning objects for the attention of a group of the population that becomes vulnerable due to their disability to enhance their school performance, favoring their integration into academic activities and daily life	Autonomy, motor skills and social skills Communication skills
[17]	Older Adults, Adults and Youth/Cultural Centers and at the El Vado Workshop School/Cuenca, Ecuador	Reduce digital gaps between sectors of society by achieving digital literacy in vulnerable sectors to potentiate skills and abilities in the productive use of ICTs and smart devices in order to improve the quality of life of people. Determine and compare accessibility functions that improve the skills of use and management of Smart Technologies	Digital Competition

Table 2. Educational experiences that use M-Free intermediation model: disability, software, digital ramp used and evaluation

Ref.	Disability	Software	Digital ramp	Evaluation
[1]	Psychomotor and intellectual disorders	Multisensory room complemented with touch screen and appropriate technology	No information	To evaluate each student was filmed performing the proposed activities and subsequently three observers per student quantitatively analyzed the information
[2]	Visual or other perceptual disabilities	Optical Character Recognition Software Text processors ABCD (Automation of Libraries and Documentation Centers)	Screen readers (JAWS, NVDA) Braille Perkins typewriter Dragon Naturally Speaking Windows accessibility	No information
[8]	Down syndrome | Sekeel syndrome | Autism | Child Cerebral Palsy (PCI)	Multisensory room and game system that respond to thematic axes that apply to daily life	No information	Qualitative and quantitative analysis with information collected both in the initial and final state
[11]	Cognitive - Specific Educational Support Needs (NEAE)	No information	No information	No information
[12]	Intellectual Disability West síndrome	Edilim, Aurasma, Robotics, Programming, Ludic environment, Microsoft Word, Microsoft Publisher, Image viewer, Webcam, Paint Scratch JR, Mat Ninja, Mat Duel	Plaphoons	The teacher individually completed an evaluation grid during the development of the various teaching sequences and at the end of them
[13]	Intellectual, physical and sensory disability Multi-disability	Active Presenter	No information	Executive functions were evaluated through a form
[16]	Cognitive - students with needs special education (NEE)	Portal of digital learning objects for the care of special educational needs	No information	Expected results are specified but not a result evaluation method

(continued)

Table 2. (*continued*)

Ref.	Disability	Software	Digital ramp	Evaluation
[17]	People with hearing, physical, intellectual, language, psychosocial (mental) and visual disabilities Older adults who may have a disability related to aging		Talk back Increase Gestures Color Settings Voice over Text options Button and Fonts adaptations Touch contrast	Competencies and accessibility functions were evaluated using Samsung and Apple phones, categorized in turn in Vision Settings and Interaction Buttons

2.5   Evaluation

In order to identify evaluation methods and instruments that are addressed at different educational experiences with students with disabilities, last column of Table 2 shows the evaluation carried out in each case.

In [1] the students were filmed performing the proposed activities and subsequently three observers per student quantitatively analyzed the information using nine variables and averaging the three tests.

In [8] the teacher individually completed an evaluation grid during and at the end of the development of the various teaching sequences. Various indicators were used such as motor area, volitional affective, autonomy, language and cognitive. Through a percentage calculation, the descriptive statistics have been presented in a bar graph, allowing the cognitive evolution in the children studied to be measured.

In [12] the evaluation was characterized as being a continuous process throughout the development of various teaching and learning sequences to make adjustments in, at the end of them the teacher completed the grids mentioned. The teacher individually completed an evaluation matrix designed specifically for each project, in which the contents addressed with the following assessment criteria are specified: sometimes, yes/no, in the process of being acquired, independent, with verbal and body help.

In [13] the participant worked with resources such as videos for the organization and daily work guidelines, counting with observations from Monday to Friday. At the end of the program, positive results have been evidenced since the participant has managed to meet objectives that have allowed her to stimulate competences in area 1, subarea of autonomy, motor skills and social skills included in the WKB [5]. The teachers uses a questionnaire of executive functions including working memory and monitoring, inhibition, initiative and planning, material organization, emotional self-control, flexibility. The results shows that the evaluated participant manages to comply with the appropriate processes, relate positively to her peers, show good spirits, express calm behavior and express tolerance in the face of frustration. With this, he obtains the qualifications required for a labor inclusion in addition to strengthening his personal development.

In [16] the achievements of the Digital Learning Objects Portal translate into the improvement of basic skills of children with Special Educational Needs such as: strengthening higher cognitive processes (thinking, language, memory, executive functions), motor skills and emotional activity; contribute to the improvement of communication skills, achieve independence in activities of daily life; initiate the use of ICT from early childhood and promote digital literacy for teachers. Although the achievements are detailed, no specification is made of the methods used in the program used to evaluate the expected results.

In [17] a comparative analysis of accessibility functions of Samsung and Apple brand phones was carried out in relation to ten competencies of accessibility functions classified with respect to vision, settings and buttons and interaction reflected in own elaboration tables. They correspond to the codes [9050, 9051, 9052, 9062, 9068, 9070, 9063, 9064, 9067, 9069] referenced in the WKB [5]. At the end, a table of the number of accessibility functions for each of the competencies was presented.

3 Study Cases

3.1 Methodology

Educational experiences with students with disability, from a technical career, have been carried out towards an inclusive education and the promotion of the students to working life [6]. The main purpose of the experiences is to glimpse and punctuate the development of an application that attempts to deepen the knowledge of computational thinking and the development of an integrating project in the classroom. In this section, two study cases are detailed; one corresponds to a student with visual impairment, and the other corresponds to a student with hearing impairment.

The experiences were carried out in the Metropolitan School of Higher Studies[8] from Argentina. This institution was the first tertiary education institute in Latin America to provide people with motor, visual and auditory disabilities a space to acquire the technical training required to be productive in a dynamic and competitive labor market. Disability is approached from the focus of equal opportunities, with special emphasis on universal design, free software and the elimination of technological and methodological obstacles that make insertion, integration, inclusion and standardization difficult.

In the subject "Professional Practice" dictated annually in the third year of the career "Analysis of Information Systems". Different proposals of computer projects are developed whose motivation passes through personal or work needs of the students. The planning of the curriculum based on educational projects allows students to reinforce existing skills or to develop new ones.

---

[8] Escuela Metropolitana de Altos Estudios (EMAE) http://alpi.org.ar/es/emae/.

The class is composed by ten students integrating visually impaired and hearing impaired students into the school routine. Also there is one teacher who teaches in both oral language and LSA, and one LSA professional interpreter. The teacher managed to facilitate the learning of all students, adapting his proposal for teaching and learning proposals to the needs and competences of each student.

The projects were carried out for 12 months, during the course and also overtime-curricular and orientation according to the need for implementation of each particular case. In addition, with the objective of carrying out a personalized reception and accompaniment of the student, a weekly individual extracurricular meeting of two hours was planned.

The proposed methodology incorporates three aspects for the planning of inclusive classroom activities: diagnosis of educational needs, accompaniment of the educational process and a continuous evaluation that allows establishing the progression of students, in order to adjust the strategies at the appropriate time. The M-Free was applied in order to present and carry out a didactic proposal that starts from the assessment of the abilities of each student. It is important to make the diagnosis, in order to determine the curricular adaptations, the teaching materials and the most appropriate technological aids for each situation. Considering that the profile of the students is informatics, it is necessary in the analysis of their initial abilities to focus on digital competencies.

In order to analyze the educational quality, the evaluation of three fundamental aspects is implemented. The first aspect of evaluation is about corroborating the level of conformity of the student regarding the achievements and integration in the classroom. The second aspect of evaluation is about the teaching practice allowing assessing the complexity of the activity carried out. Finally, the third aspect of evaluation is about the use of ad hoc didactic material prepared for the experience and assessment of digital ramps and pedagogical supports.

To obtain information, it is suggested to apply a mixed methodology based on both the use of qualitative and quantitative instruments. In this way it is possible to obtain information at the beginning, during and at the end of the project. According to this, a diagnostic evaluation (what the student knows before starting) is proposed as a starting point through an initial semi-structured survey. Secondly, a formative evaluation (what is he learning) through observation is done at each weekly meeting during the development of the project. The teacher registers an observation sheet of progress of the project, raises questions of concerns or difficulties that must be resolved, and identifies some new specific need regarding their visual impairment. Finally a summative evaluation (results at the end of the project) is done with the help of an interview.

3.2   Digital Skills

The M-Free model is based on the aspect of initial abilities beginning by defining the level of competence of each person, emphasizing the skills and abilities that can be developed always remembering that the model is based on the growth paradigm and not on the aspects relating to the incapacity of the person.

WKB [5] was used to define the competences. Since the original codes are in Spanish, Appendix A presents the English translation of the codes that were used. As part of this work, 29 new non-existent digital skills have been added to the Wikinclusion list in Appendix B, classified into the following categories: HTML, CSS, use of Local Servers, PHP Programming, Database Engine (MySql) and PHP programming to access database. This decision is justified in that the students are students of the systems analysis career and therefore the digital competences to be developed are of a higher level than the existing ones.

3.3   Case 1: Visually Impaired - Desktop Application with Database

This first case is about a visually impaired student with no perception of light at all. Table 3 presents the objective of the proposed work, the initial digital competences as well as the desired competencies related to the software and the activities to be developed. Figure 3 shows the B-Free diagram of this case.

In the first phase of M-Free, an initial evaluation carried out through an interview with the aim of identifying special educational needs according to their disability. It was pointed that the student has no possibility to read the screen or use the mouse. He used to record the classes as a method of taking notes at home into a word file which is possible to follow with the JAWS screen reader. The student handles minimum JAWS keyboard shortcuts, but he does not have great ability to use the tool. About the objective of the project, the student has raised his concern to the teacher to develop an information system that allows the registration of audio materials, the control of their inputs and outputs, as well as reports of all those historical movements.

In the second phase, the curricular proposal is organized in five modules. First module, called "Database", aims to know the working environment by means of keyboard shortcuts. The second module, called "Tables and Forms", aims to achieve skills in creating and manipulating the use of table functions and data entry through the generation of a form by using the wizard. The third module, called "Relations, Consultations and Forms", aims to deepen the concept of relationships, referential integration and connect these processes with the development of queries and forms with combo boxes for specific fields. The fourth module, called "Queries and Reports", aims to get into the learning of action queries and associate them with the generation of reports through the use of the wizard. The fifth module, called "Integration", aims to achieve the development of a menu, through the use of macros, with a series of organized options that allow the user to choose to perform certain tasks.

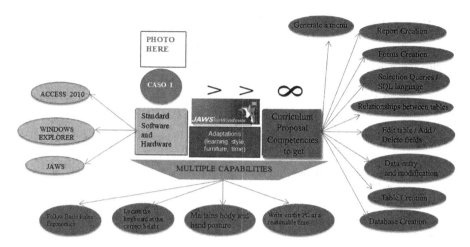

Fig. 3. B-Free corresponding to case 1

In the third phase, the objectives of the student's curriculum proposal are correlated with the available computer resources. A workstation (PC) with the Microsoft Office package, particularly its Access database engine, is used. On the other hand, for the accessibility JAWS screen reader is installed.

In the fourth phase, it must be observed if the student needs any adaptation or digital ramp. JAWS screen reader was used as a digital ramp. In order for the curricular adaptation to be fruitful, it is essential to deliver, in advance, mandatory reading texts of each of the topics that the student will study in PDF format accessible by the JAWS screen reader. A first type of material about the shortcuts of JAWS screen reader specific to the Access database engine has been research and elaborated by the teacher. A second type of material, about, the database engine, was an adaptation of existing material creating PDF format accessible by the JAWS screen reader.

In the fifth phase the implementation and continuous evaluation is done in the way described in methodology section. The achievement of the project has been in largely thanks to the possibility of accessibility offered by JAWS. The student put a very strong emphasis on the extra effort that he had to make to get all the specific keyboard shortcuts to access the access options. However he affirms that this has been part of what has allowed him to acquire all his new digital competences specifically referred to database management. At the end of the project, a personal interview was carried out inquiring the student about its conformity with respect to the results achieved, the accessibility to the didactic material and the work of the teacher. The student has stated that he has met his expectations regarding his initial concerns, thanked the teacher for his time, availability and dedication and has found the use of the material very useful during situations where he needed to either reinforce or go to specific information in order to continue advancing in the project with its own autonomy.

3.4   Case 2: Hearing Impaired - Website

This second case is about a hearing impaired student with totally hearing loss. Table 4 presents the objective of the proposed work, the initial digital competences as well as the desired competencies related to the software and the activities to be developed. Figure 4 shows the B-Free diagram of this case.

Table 3. M-Free corresponding to case 1

Personal information	
Gender: male | Age: 60 | Disability: Not sighted. Retiniti Picmentaria | Observations: it has no perception in the light Schooling: tertiary level | Work: does not work	
Objectives	
Development of a desktop application that allows the entry of personal data, audio materials data and audio materials loans made. You should also have the possibility of generating reports of historical loans and audio materials that are not available because they are currently provided **Motivation:** use of the application for your personal control of audio materials to avoid loss of them	
Initial Digital Competencies **6.1 Ergonomics and Device Recognition:** 9001 | 9002 | 9003 | 9052 |9058 | 9061 **6.2 Text processor:** 9100 | 9102 | 9104 | 9110 | 9111 | 9112 | 9113 | 9127 | 9129 | 9143	**Digital competences of the curriculum proposal** **6.3 Database** 9200 | 9202 | 9204 | 9209 | 9212 | 9214 | 9215 | 9218 | 9219 | 9221 | 9224
Software Windows Explorer | ACCESS **Adaptations and Digital Ramps** JAWS (Job Access With Speech), teaching material accessible with screen reader	**Activity to be performed** Build a desktop application that allows the entry of personal data, audio materials data and audio materials loans made | Generate reports of historical loans and audio materials provided at the time

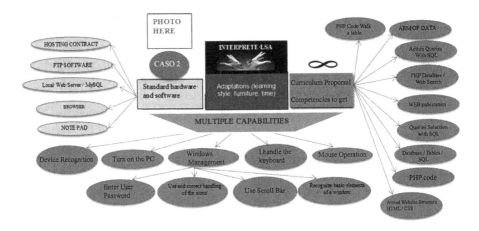

Fig. 4. B-Free diagram corresponding to case 2

In the first phase of M-Free, it was pointed that the student presents difficulty for both reading and understanding of technical texts. The student is very skilled in lip reading, but there exists always difficulty with terms with phonemes of equal vocalization. About the objective of the project the student proposed the development of a dynamic website for the real estate market. For this experience two external clients were involved as requestors. The system must allow simple and dynamic loading of properties for sale or rent with photos, technical characteristics and location of the property. The user must be able to easily find the desired property according to their needs by applying different filters.

Table 4. M-Free corresponding to case 2

Personal information	
Gender: male | Age: 22 | Disability: Bilateral sensor neural hearing loss Schooling: tertiary level | Work: does not work	
Objectives	
Development of a dynamic website for the real estate market that allows simple and dynamic loading of properties for sale or rent with photos, technical characteristics and location of the property. On the other hand, it has a search engine within the website in order that the user applying different filters can easily find the desired property according to their needs. Regarding the implementation, two potential clients are proposed **Motivation:** use of the application with real potential clients in addition to learning a new programming language including database management	
Initial Digital Competencies	**Digital competences of the curriculum proposal**
6.1 Ergonomics and Device Recognition 9001 | 9002| 9003 | 9052 | 9053 | 9055 | 9056 | 9057 |9058 | 9059 | 9060 | 9061 | 9063 | 9066 | 9067 **6.2 Text processor** 9100 | 9102 | 9104 | 9106 | 9108 | 9109 | 9110 | 9111 | 9112 | 9113 |9114 | 9115 | 9117 | 9120 | 9121 | 9122 | 9129 | 9131 | 9132 | 9134	**HTML:** A001 | A002 |A003 |A004 | A005 | A006 **CSS:** B001 |B002 | B003 **LOCAL SERVER:** C001 | C002 | C003 | C004 | C005 | C006 **PHP PROGRAMMING:** D001 |D002 |D003 | D004 | D005 | D006 | D007 | D008 | D009 | D010 **6.3 DATABASE:** 9200 |9202 |9213 | 9215 | 9216 |9219 | 9228 **PHP PROGRAMMING DATABASE:** E001 |E002 | E003 | E004 | E005 | E006
Software Notepad: HTML - CSS - PHP Code Web browser: use of local server, website test Easy PHP: Local Server PHPMyAdmin: Database **Adaptations and Digital Ramps** Sign language LSA Teaching material: videos with LSA and subtitles	**Activity to be performed** Develop a real estate ABM module. Build the structure of the web page | Add corporate client design | Enable the server and load the website | Build mail submission form | Implement database and tables necessary for the loading and consultation of real estate | Create property search with appropriate filters

In the second phase, the curricular proposal is organized in four modules. First module, called "Analysis", the users' requirements must be specifically known through information gathering techniques such as interviews, surveys and observation. Second module, called "Design", the student is asked to implement various models such as context diagrams, event table, Data Flow Diagram and Entity-Relationship Diagrams. Third module, called "Development", consists of a set of rules and practices included in two fundamental activities: coding and test plan. Fourth module, called "Implementation", was restricted to installing the product on the hosting server with the use of FTP and testing with the browser.

In the third phase, the objectives of the student's curriculum proposal are correlated with the available computer resources. A workstation (PC) is available that has a development environment enabled to interact with a local test server that includes a code editor, EasyPHP and phpMyAdmin, thus creating the necessary databases to carry out development of the project. For its implementation, a hosting service has been hired and the FileZilla software as an FTP solution.

In the fourth phase it must be observed if the student needs any adaptation or digital ramp. To overcome difficulty of the student for reading the teacher prepares the didactic material with videos that includes sign language LSA (LSA) combined with images and subtitles. In order to strongly incorporate the use of the LSA the teacher gives the master class explanations in LSA accompanied by a professional interpreter. Also the class is filmed to obtain videos that can be consulted by the student.

In the fifth phase the implementation and continuous evaluation is done in the way described in methodology section. The interviews were carried out in sign language (LSA) and the questionnaires were as consistent as possible with the assumed literacy level of the student. The student was able to achieve the implementation of their website by correctly implementing their database and properly controlling the necessary search filters. It is also important to highlight that another advantage in particular of this development is that the same user has the possibility to update their business information independently within the same application. In regards to design, the student points out that he has been able to adapt the design to the corporate image of another organization without having to modify the programming standards used. Obviously the student states that he has been able to participate actively in the development of his project thanks to the use of sign language, considering himself integrated in terms of accessibility to information and communication. At the end of the project, a personal interview was conducted in LSA that the student filmed. He was inquired about their compliance with the results achieved, the use of ICT as a resource to their bilingual education, the full access to curricular information through the material, and the teaching work. The student has stated that they have overcome their aspirations in the development of the project, which has provided him with tools to use within his work environment. The student also valued the work carried out by the teacher in bringing to their attention. About the material, the student stated that it was very complete and with friendly language that facilitates transmitting complex knowledge.

4 Conclusions and Future Work

This article presents the application of the M-Free and B-Free intermediation models to plan the development of an educational project that allows strengthening existing competences of students and applying cross-planning integrating knowledge of other subjects. Experiences found in the literature are reviewed pointing in aspects such as software and digital ramps used, and the evaluation carried on in each one.

Two educational experiences with tertiary level students in the area of computer science, one with hearing impairment and the other with visual impairment, are described. The results achieved show that the use of appropriate software and hardware together with a methodology based on the use of the person's multiple abilities and continuous monitoring, have enabled the achievement of the objectives proposed for the students on equal terms as its peers. Support technology as JAWS for people with visual impairment, and sign language for people with hearing impairment, allow students to access the digital environment, their promotion as a person to social life and inclusive education. Didactic material adaptation, such as readable text documents by JAWS and videos in LSA, became extremely necessary for the successful of the inclusive education experiences.

Future work includes the use of metrics for evaluation accessibility and usability. Traditional techniques such as surveys, observation and interviews are being modified to meet the needs of deaf communication through visual aids, subtitles and adaptation of question wording according to the level of literacy.

Acknowledgments. This work was funded by Subsidies for Innovation and Transfer Projects in Priority Areas of the Province of Buenos Aires (PIT-AP-BA) CICPBA "REFORTICCA Resources for the Empowerment of Trainers in ICT, Science and Environment".

Appendix A. Wikinclusion Knowledge Base

Existing codes can be found (in Spanish language) in the WKB [5]. This is an English translation of the codes that have been used in this work.

6.1 ERGONOMICS AND DEVICE RECOGNITION: 9001 Position the keyboard at the correct height | 9002 Maintain the correct posture of the body and hands | 9003 Turn on the PC | 9052 You can press two keys simultaneously | 9053 Place your hand on the mouse and press a button | 9055 Operation of the scroll keys (up, down, right and left) | 9056 Double click on a target | 9057 Performs mouse movements on the mousepad | 9058 Write to the computer in an acceptable time | 9059 Identify the elements that make up the desktop (icons, taskbar, start button) | 9060 Identify the shortcuts of the taskbar | 9061 Enter user password | 9063 Use and correct handling of desktop icons | 9066 Proper handling of the minimize, maximize and close buttons | 9067 Using the scroll bar.

6.2 TEXT PROCESSOR: 9100 Load the word processor | 9102 Upload a new document | 9104 Open an already created document | 9106 Recognize the work environment presented by a word processor (menus, bars, work area) | 9108 Insert and edit a document | 9109 Insert special characters and symbols | 9110 Cut a text | 9111 Copy a text | 9112 Paste a text | 9113 Undo a task | 9114 Search and Replace | 9115 Spelling and grammar check | 9117 Check synonyms | 9120 Format a document with different types of letters and size | 9121 Spacing, spacing and alignment of paragraphs | 9122 Configuration and design of pages | 9127 Save documents with different options | 9129 Print a document | 9131 Create and configure a table | 9132 Images and graphic elements | 9134 Header and footer | 9143 Advantages and disadvantages of different word processors.

6.3 DATABASE: 9200 Creating a database | 9202 Introduction and Modification of data | 9204 Edit an existing table | 9209 Add fields to a table in design view | 9212 Create a new table | 9213 Import and Export of Tables | 9214 Relations between tables | 9215 Simple selection queries | 9216 Selection queries with operations | 9218 Combined Table Queries | 9219 The SQL language (Structured Query Language) | 9221 Form Creation | 9224 Creating Simple Reports | 9228 Advantages and disadvantages of different database managers.

Appendix B. Added Digital Competency Codes

Listed below are the added competency codes that have been added to the existing WKB [5] as part of this work.

A - HTML: A001 Create a Web Page | A002 Structure of a page | A003 Use DIV tag | A004 Use image tag | A005 Use hyperlinks tag | A006 Create Web Forms.

B- CSS: B001 Font Properties | B002 Page Background Properties | B003 Style Sheet. C- LOCAL SERVER: C001 Load local server | C002 Download local server | C003 Start local server | C004 Stop local server | C005 Start PHP MyAdmin | C006 Stop PHP MyAdmin.

D- PHP PROGRAMMING: D001 Use of variables and data types | D002 Use of Constants | D003 Use of Arithmetic Operators | D004 Use of Comparison Operators | D005 Use of Logic Operators | D006 Conditional decision making | D007 Multiple decisions - switch | D008 Iterations - FOR loop | D009 Iterations - While Loop | D010 Handle PHP instructions for sending mail.

E- PHP PROGRAMMING DATABASE: E001 Tour a database | E002 Consult a database | E003 Create Web Report | E004 Register a record | E005 Modify a record | E006 Delete a record.

References

1. Ballarino, V., Rivarola, M., Beltramone, D.: Aplicación de Interfaces Naturales y Sala Multisensorial en Escuela Especial para Comunicación Aumentativa, Alternativa y Aprendizaje. Recuperado de (2018). https://revistas.unc.edu.ar/index.php/med/article/view/21275

2. Biset, D.H., Goyochea, G.L.: Tecnología y procesos aplicados a la inclusión de estudiantes universitarios con discapacidad (2015). http://bib.fcien.edu.uy/jbdu2015/wp-content/uploads/2015/05/Biset_Tecnolog%C3%ADa-y-procesos-aplicados-a-la-inclusi%C3%B3n-de-estudiantes.pdf

3. Chamorro, M.F.: Adaptive technology and access to information in university libraries. ACADEMO Revista de Investigación en Ciencias Sociales y Humanidades, vol 2, núm 2 (2015). https://revistacientifica.uamericana.edu.py/index.php/academo/article/view/25/23

4. Chrobak, R., Leiva Benegas, M.: Concept Maps: Theory, Methodology, Technology. San José, Costa Rica (2006)

5. Creatica Fundación FREE Iberoamericana para la Cooperación: Wikinclusion Knowledge Database. http://capacidad.es/Anexo.pdf (s/f)

6. Fachal, A.S., Abásolo, M.J., Sanz, C.V.: Experiencias en el uso de TIC y rampas digitales en la enseñanza de informática a alumnos de educación terciaria con discapacidad visual o auditiva. In: XXV Congreso Argentino de Ciencias de la Computación (CACIC), pp. 1110–1120 (2019). http://sedici.unlp.edu.ar/handle/10915/90556

7. Fernández-Aquino, L.C.: E-accesibilidad y usabilidad de contenidos digitales. Por una sociedad de la información y el conocimiento no excluyente (Tesis doctoral). Universitat Politècnica de València, Valencia (2009). https://riunet.upv.es/handle/10251/4330?show=full&locale-attribute=en

8. Figueroa Cruz, M., Milton, A., Molina, C., Calle Vintimilla, S.G.: Intervención Temprana en niños con alteraciones en el neurodesarrollo desde la Sala Multisensorial. Un reto en la Academia Ecuatoriana. Lat. Am. J. Comput. II(3), 55–62 (2015)

9. García Martín, J.M.: La discapacidad hoy. Psychosocial Intervention, vol. 14, núm. 3, pp. 245-253. Colegio Oficial de Psicólogos de Madrid. Madrid, España (2005). http://www.redalyc.org/articulo.oa?id=179817547001

10. Pérez, G.: Los modelos didácticos como instrumento de análisis y de intervención en la realidad educativa. Biblio 3 W. Revista Bibliográfica de Geografía y Cs. Sociales. Universidad de Barcelona, N° 207 (2000). ISSN 1138-9796

11. González Pérez, A.: El uso de las TIC a través del desarrollo de microproyectos con alumnos de Educación Especial. Universidad de Sevilla (2012)

12. Lamberti, E.M.: ¿Estudiantes aburridos o propuesta pedagógica poco motivadora? – Experiencia de inclusión significativa de las TIC en los procesos de enseñanza y aprendizaje. En: Gallegos Navas M. (eds.) La inclusión de las TIC en la educación de personas con discapacidad. Relatos de experiencias, p. 85 (2018)

13. Maldonado Garcés, V., Ortiz Carranco, N.Y.: TIC en inclusión y discapacidad. In: Robles, V., Sánchez, R., Ingavelez, P., Pesántez, F. (eds.) Inclusión, discapacidad y educación. Enfoque práctico desde las Tecnologías Emergentes, p. 419. Editorial Universitaria Abya-Yala, Ecuador (2017)

14. Sánchez-Montoya, R.: Tres claves para construir aulas inclusivas. In: Robles B., Sánchez-Montoya, R, Inclusión, discapacidad y educación. Enfoque práctico desde las tecnologías emergentes, pp. 621–626. Editorial Universitaria Abya-Yala, Ecuador (2017)

15. Suárez, B., Castillo, I.S.: Descripción de una experiencia educativa inclusiva con alumnado universitario: Trabajando habilidades para el empleo. Tendencias Pedagógicas **35**, 130–152 (2020). https://doi.org/10.15366/tp2020.35.11
16. Sugeys, I., Castillo, G., Montoya, R., Griffin, Y., Aguirre, L., Hernández, Z.: Portal de objetos digitales de aprendizaje para niños y niñas con necesidades educativas especiales (2013). http://www.ciditic.utp.ac.pa/sites/ciditic.utp.ac.pa/files/pdf/articulo_poda-4utp.pdf
17. Vizñay Durán, J., Molina, M.A.C., Ximena, P.J.D.: Funciones de accesibilidad que logran y mejoran las competencias de uso y manejo de los teléfonos inteligentes. In: Robles, V., Sánchez, R., Ingavelez, P. Pesántez, Y F. (eds.) Inclusión, discapacidad y educación. Enfoque práctico desde las Tecnologías Emergentes, p. 97. Editorial Universitaria Abya-Yala Ecuador (2017)
18. Wikinclusión (2018). http://wikinclusion.org/index.php

Primary Level Teachers Training in Computer Science: Experience in the Argentine Context

Ana Casali[1](), Natalia Monjelat[2], Patricia San Martín[2], and Dante Zanarini[1]

[1] Facultad de Ciencias Exactas, Ingeniería y Agrimensura FCEIA-UNR y Centro Internacional Franco-Argentino de Ciencias de la Información y de Sistemas (CIFASIS: CONICET-UNR), Rosario, Argentina
{acasali, dante}@fceia.unr.edu.ar
[2] Instituto Rosario de Investigaciones en Ciencias de la Educación (IRICE: CONICET-UNR), Rosario, Argentina
{monjelat, sanmartin}@irice-conicet.gov.ar

Abstract. This paper presents the design, development and preliminary results of the first specialization in Computer Science for the primary level, approved by the Ministry of Education of Santa Fe province. The "Higher Level Teaching Specialization in Didactics of Computing Science: Learning and Teaching Computational Thinking and Programming at the Primary Level" aims to empower teachers with this way of thinking and the potential of programming to include them in situated, interdisciplinary and non-exclusive teaching practices. The axes of the design of this training course are presented as well as the relevant characteristics of the students. In addition, results are provided that allow to account for the opinions of the participants regarding the dictation, the contents addressed and the inclusion in their practices. In this way, data is provided that makes it possible to review future training designs and implementations in an innovative field for primary level teachers.

Keywords: Teacher training · Primary education · Computer science · Programming · Computational thinking

1 Introduction

In the last decade, the introduction of Computer Science (CS) notions in the school curriculum, especially regarding the development of computational thinking (CT) and the appropriation of programming concepts and practices, has gained relevance in the international educational field [1–5]. Following Wing [6] the learning of CS benefits the whole society so, it is recommended to teach it at all educational levels. In 2013, Argentina launched the Program.ar project[1] that based on multiple initiatives, brings children and young people closer to learning computer science. Likewise, the Federal Education Council pointed that the learning of programming is of strategic importance for the National Educational System during compulsory schooling (Resolution CFE N° 263/15,

---

[1] www.program.ar.

P. Pesado and M. Arroyo (Eds.): CACIC 2019, CCIS 1184, pp. 389–404, 2020.
https://doi.org/10.1007/978-3-030-48325-8_25

2015). As an advance in this direction, in September 2018, the "Priority Learning Cores of Digital Education, Programming and Robotics" (NAP EDPR) for the different levels of compulsory education were approved (Resolución CFE N° 343/18, 2018). In this resolution (Annex II) is established a period of two years for curricular adaptation, where the contents set out in this core must be included. Also, the development of a continuous teacher training plan aimed at raising awareness, dissemination and integration of NPR EDPR must be attended. Moreover, the integration of these contents to the initial teacher training is essential. In this direction, there are two key and interrelated aspects that strongly condition the introduction of CS contents in the Argentine educational system. On the one hand, the need of changes in the curricula at the primary, secondary and teacher training levels, a task that is beginning to be carried out in different provinces, with different stages of development. On the other, it implies the immediate implementation of proposals for teacher training in the learning and teaching of computational thinking and programming, which could enable gradual transformations of both curricular and school educational practice. Particularly in the context of Santa Fe state, it is observed that almost all public schools and teacher training institutes were equipped with digital technology through national and provincial programs. In this scenario, teacher education and training has mainly focused on a first level of instrumental appropriation of applications, tools and digital resources of the current Information and Communication Technologies (ICT) applied to educational practice [7].

Considering these aspects and to bridge the gap in teacher education at the primary level at Santa Fe province, within the framework of an Academic Cooperation Agreement signed between the Sadosky Foundation[2], the National University of Rosario[3] and the Ministry of Education of the province of Santa Fe[4] we designed the "Higher Level Teaching Specialization in Didactics of Computer Science: Learning and Teaching Computational Thinking and Programming at the Primary Level" which was approved by the Educational Ministry (Resolution ME N° 1565/17). The first cohort of this specialization was carried out at the Higher Institute of Teacher Training (ISFD) N° 36 "Mariano Moreno" of Rosario city, Argentina. It was developed between August 2017 and July 2019 with a total of 400 h.

Notice that this is a pilot experience, unique as a teacher specialization at the primary level in computer science in the province and one of the three that are undergoing for this educational level in the country. Then, it is the aim of this article to share the most relevant points of its design and development and also, to analyze results from the data collected during the course. Preliminary results of this experience were previously published. In [8] we have presented the proposal for this specialization in CS, where the combination of unplugged and plugged approaches, together with a contextualized vision of education was highlighted. Then, in [9] partial results of this training were presented at the end of the third semester of dictation. In this paper, we have extended the analysis of all this experience, considering the results obtained of the

---

[2] www.fundacionsadosky.org.ar/.

[3] www.unr.edu.ar/.

[4] www.santafe.gov.ar/index.php/educacion.

students' opinions through a detailed evaluation process carried out at the end of this training (forth semester) and also different observations made by the teaching team were considered. This enriched analysis led us to take conclusions about the entire course process.

The structure of this paper is as follows, in Sect. 2 we present the principal insights of the curricular design, the teaching and learning adopted approach and the students' profiles. Then, in Sect. 3, we analyze some partial results obtained at the first year of the specialization that allowed some adjustments in the organization of the course. Besides, other results arising from the assessments of the students at the end of the course are discussed. Finally, preliminary conclusions are presented.

2 Development of the Specialization: Design, Context and Students' Profiles

2.1 Design: Objectives and Main Cornerstones

The design of this Specialization was in charge of an interdisciplinary team made up of professors and researchers in the fields of computer science and education, and professors of the institute of teacher training. A first challenge that had to be faced both in the design stage and during the development of this training course, was the construction of a good articulation within the team leading the curricular proposal. On the one hand, this project was challenged given there is a limited background in computer science training for primary level teachers in our region. On the other hand, we have an interdisciplinary team that has contributed with diverse perspectives but this implied an additional complexity linked to differences in the conceptual and terminological definitions, traditions, uses and customs frameworks, specific approaches and objectives of each disciplinary area. We had to establish dialogues and agreements between speakers of three dialects: "the pedagogical", "the computational" and "the teacher". From a spiral work of this interdisciplinary team, the *Specialization in Didactics of Computer Science* was developed, with the following design and principles.

The general aim of this course was to train teachers to be able to experience and reflect about computational thinking and programming development processes, in order to build the appropriate competences at the primary level that enable an innovative educational practice, with an emphasis on problem solving through collaborative and interdisciplinary production of Technologies for Social Inclusion (TIS) [10, 11]. In this frame, specific objectives were the following:

- To promote the study of the principles of computational thinking and programming for its didactic adaptation to the primary level of schooling.
- To activate a critical and ethical position on the use, impact and potential of CS in the current socio-cultural context.
- To provide theoretical, methodological and technical tools for the selection and application of concepts of computational thinking and programming based on the design and development of educational projects focused on the production of technologies for social inclusion (TIS).

- To develop the interest and responsible commitment towards participation in the collaborative production of simple programs integrated both to primary education topics and to institutional projects using various tools under interdisciplinary work methodologies.
- To promote, within the framework of the state education system, the development of institutional processes of curricular adaptation and transformation of primary level educational practices, providing theoretical-methodological and technical foundations on contents related to CS.

Considering the particularities of the context and in accordance with the guidelines of the Ministry of Education of Santa Fe, the specialization was framed pedagogically from a double articulation that considers both the processes and the products involved in the development of computational thinking and programming, as possible TIS, as mentioned before. This is intended that the processes involved in teaching practices that include contents related to CS, as well as the products generated (programs, videogames, interactive stories, etc.) can address socio-educational and regional issues from their complexity, promoting critical use of tools in project contexts, based on putting into practice active, critical and interdisciplinary pedagogical perspectives [12].

The Teacher Training was organized in four semesters, with three modules in each one (12 modules in total), as it is shown in Table 1.

Table 1. Specialization design: modules and load time.

Semester	Module	Load time
Sem 1	Introduction: CS in elementary level	20
	Computational thinking I	40
	Programming I	40
Sem 2	Integrating project I	20
	Computational thinking II	40
	Programming II	40
Sem 3	Integrating project II	20
	Introduction to computer organization	40
	Robotics	40
Sem 4	Data science, privacy and security of the information	35
	Mobile apps	40
	Final project	25
4 Sem.	**12 Modules**	**400**

It should be noted that the unplugged approach has been considered of great importance since it can be applied in any school without the need for computer equipment and in addition, many of the activities are familiar to teachers, being able to revisit and resignify acquired knowledge. Previous studies have shown that the development of teaching and learning processes through this approach is effective for the development of cognitive skills related to Computational Thinking (CT) [2, 5, 13].

Considering this, the design and development of the training proposed a distribution of hours that has a combination of unplugged, plugged and mixed modules along the two years. As Fig. 1 presents, in the first year unplugged activities had a greater load time, while in the second year the approaches are more balanced and mixed modules had a bigger load.

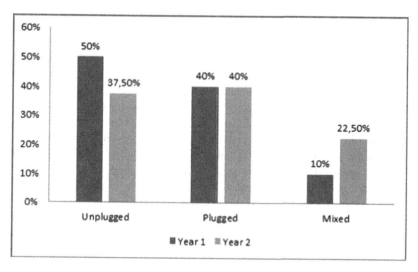

Fig. 1. Load time according to the predominant approach of the different modules.

Therefore, main cornerstones in the curriculum design were unplugged CT and Programming using different plugged tools and platforms. In this direction, five modules worked totally unplugged, while another four modules focused on the mentioned plugged approach. The curriculum design was completed with three Integrating Projects, including a Final Project. In these subjects, students gradually design a classroom and institutional project according to the context of their teaching work. In this individual project each student integrates the concepts learned, combining plugged and unplugged resources, activities and strategies.

On the other hand, learning programming concepts at the primary level of schooling also enables the development of CT, allowing participants to be active and creative protagonists of CS [14, 15]. The recursion of the processes of *learning to programming - programming to learn* permits not only different skills to be developed but new learning opportunities to be generated. Currently, the educational community has an important variety of tools suitable for teaching programming at the primary level such as Lightbot[5], Pilas Bloques[6] and Scratch[7], among others, which were used in the

---

[5] www.lightbot.com/.

[6] www.pilasbloques.program.ar.

[7] scratch.mit.edu/.

specialization programming workshops. In addition, and following recommended contents to be included in teacher training of CS [16] basic notions of organization of computers, operating systems, robotics and programming for mobile devices were provided during the course, in order to effectively use different tools and thus, develop different programming tasks. It was also relevant to include contents and training regarding privacy and information security, in order to encourage teachers to have a critical analysis of the use of technology.

The Training course followed a spiral approach to introduce different contents by the different modules, addressing the specific concepts of CS with increasing complexity and depth. For this, face-to-face classes were proposed (80% classroom classes and 20% virtual) with a workshop format. It is worth mentioning that the total time load as the percentage of classroom attendance was an initial requirement, set by Sadosky Foundation, sponsor of the project and respected the Ministry regulations for teacher Specializations. In the different modules, group activities were proposed to be solved within classroom activities, articulating with moments of reflection, dialogue and sharing, with the aim of revisiting the contents addressed from collaborative reviews.

Moreover, practical work assignments carried out within the modules were proposed as instances of connection with the daily practice of teachers, articulating primary level curricular contents with the situated and contextualized practice of each teacher. Qualitative criteria were used to evaluate the practical works, providing motivating reflections towards the revision of what was done from a constructivist perspective. Multiple tools, materials and didactical approaches were offered in the different modules, which allowed the participants to deploy a wide range of possibilities for action when developing their own practices and design their final projects.

Following the signing of a tripartite agreement between the Sadosky Foundation, the Ministry of Education of Santa Fe and the National University of Rosario, held in July 2017, the Specialization began to be issued in ISFD N° 36 of the Rosario city, in August of the same year, with 78 participants who attended the first meeting.

2.2   The Students Profiles

At the beginning of the training, a survey was administered to identify profiles and practices of the students, which allowed a better adaptation of the didactic proposals. The results of this first questionnaire (n = 78) showed that 46% are in the age range 41–50 and 41% between 31–40, 85% are women, 38% have between 10 and 20 years of teaching experience and most are regular teachers. Besides, 68% have completed training courses in education and ICTs although the experiences mentioned are diverse, where 45% are self-taught and 21% have some programming experience. On the other hand, 90% have a laboratory or digital classroom (although not always working) and 61% report bad internet connection in their school. We also highlight the heterogeneity of the group, given that teachers work at different levels and areas of primary education (Mathematics, Computer Science, Language, Social, Natural Sciences, Music, Special Education, etc.).

3   Results

3.1   Partial Results in the First Year of the Course

In reference to the permanence of the students in the curricular training, the main dropout rate was recorded during the first semester of the course, leaving 42 regular students at the beginning of the second period. From the queries made to people who did not continue, two main questions arose: a) they did not have a clear idea about what the training was about when starting the course, and b) the impossibility of being able to meet the requirements of assistance and delivery of practical work, given the usual intensification of teaching work towards the end of the school year.

Linked to the first item (a) in a survey where the students were asked how they were noticed about the specialization, 61% answered that it was through a journalistic note from a local newspaper, 28% through social networks and/or recommendation of a third party, 22% through the Ministry of Education of Santa Fe and 6% by informative note from the management staff of their institution. In addition, 41% had not attended any informative talk about the training. If the novelty of the subject is also considered at the regional level, the expressions of those who did not continue warn about the need to intensify communication regarding this particular training, especially from the official authorities and the institutional actors. Besides in relation with item (b), it is important to keep in mind that all the specializations offered for teacher training in ICT both at the provincial and national level have a distance or hybrid modality with very low in-person classes and thus, allow to work with more customized asynchronous times. It is worth mentioning that the total time load of 400 h as the face-to-face mode of classroom attendance was a national prerequisite for the design of this career.

For these reasons, students faced not only with innovative contents, but with a high demand course methodology. This was also frequently expressed to the teachers responsible for the modules during the first semester, which led to some adaptations in the curricular organization for the second one. In spite of these difficulties, both teachers and students agreed on the appropriateness of the face-to-face modality due to the active and participatory approach of the classes, where very suitable teaching and learning processes were experienced for future didactic transpositions. We can see in Fig. 2 pictures of unplugged activities during the different PC modules and in Fig. 3 the students are programming and sharing their programs with the group.

At the end of each semester, a survey to collect the students' opinions regarded the different modules were applied. An analysis of their opinions in relation to the organization of the training proposal in plugged and unplugged contents (n = 24), linked to the *didactics* of the modules more representative of these approaches in the first year of study (Unplugged: Computational Thinking (CT) 1 and 2; Plugged: Programming (Prog) 1 and 2). As Fig. 4 shows, favorable opinions are the majority and increased in the second semester. This may be due to modifications introduced in the dictation, since in the first semester the PC 1 and Programming 1 modules were worked in parallel. Given the difficulties presented by the students, it was decided to continue with a more sequential scheme, leaving in parallel the route through the integrating projects.

Fig. 2. Unplugged activities during PC workshops.

On the other hand, and also taking into account the plugged-unplugged binomial, the opinions of the students in relation to the *contents* addressed during the first year were analyzed. As we can see in Fig. 5, most of the valuations are positive and the negatives decreased in the second semester.

Fig. 3. Programming activities.

3.2 Relevant Results at the End of the Specialization

At the end of the course and prior to the implementation of the classroom experience, required to obtain the degree, an evaluation was carried out by an external consultant. Among the instruments used, an integrative survey was conducted on the perception of the students on specialization, in relation to different variables. In addition, a focus group was performed in order to gather relevant information regarding the training proposal in a more open format. Both activities were of voluntary participation following the modality of opinion consultations that were carried out along the way.

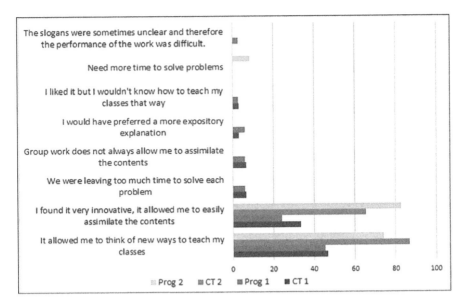

Fig. 4. Student opinions on applied didactics.

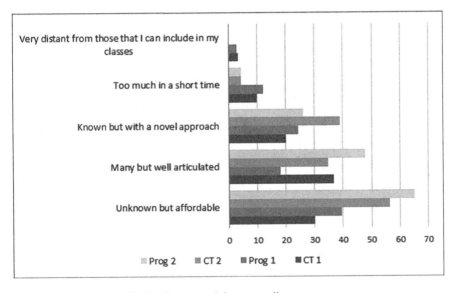

Fig. 5. Student opinions regarding contents

It is worth mentioning that 31 students began the last semester of the course and 21 finished it. Below we present some of the most relevant aspects that we have extracted from this process.

Incorporation of CS Content to Teaching Practice. Regarding this point of interest, it should be noted that all respondents (n = 18) stated that they feel prepared to include the contents learned during the specialization in the teaching space they are in charge of. Among its justifications, the possibility of having the necessary tools and being able to connect the contents with those of the primary level is highlighted, as can be seen in the following expressions received:

"The specialization provided me with tools to perform correctly", "A very complete training has been received developing the necessary competences", "Because they gave me the necessary tools so that I can relate the different contents of primary school with computational thinking and programmin", "I believe that the contents are fully adaptable to traditional curricular areas", among others.

They were also asked how they would apply the contents of the specialization in the classroom, if they did not have infrastructure restrictions. As Fig. 6 shows, the percentages of activities that could be implemented are high in all cases. The creation of digital learning objects (games, animations, etc.) to use in their classes, the performance of unplugged activities and the development together with the students of digital objects to present a curricular content, are the most relevant ones. These actions imply a change of perspective from user to creators of technology, which enables other types of practices in primary education. Likewise, it is observed that a large percentage of teachers point out the possibility of working on these novel contents and even taking on a specific subject (72%).

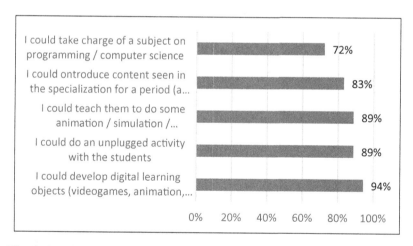

Fig. 6. Possible application of learned contents in the classroom: student opinions.

These data can be related to the fact that 89% said that during the course they carried out classroom experiences of the contents worked in the specialization, even before it was a requirement in the curriculum, since this instance was only requested at the end of the last semester, as a mandatory activity of the "Final Project" module.

When asked about what activities they had already implemented, it can be seen in Fig. 7 that the majority (56%) carried out both plugged and unplugged activities, while 38% implemented unplugged ones and only 6% done exclusively connected work. In this way, there is a tendency towards the development of activities that combine the two main approaches of the training course (i.e. plugged and unplugged).

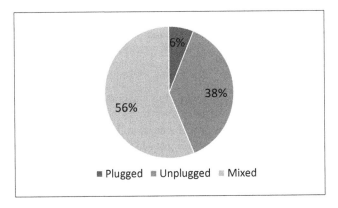

Fig. 7. Type of activity implemented by the participants during the course.

When asked about these experiences in the classroom, the teachers pointed out different issues that were significant, rating them from 1 to 10. Figure 8 shows that on average, the most prominent points at the time of carrying out the experiences were the usefulness of the educational materials made available during the specialization, and high motivation of the students to the proposal. However, the other aspects shown in the table, which highlight the teacher's confidence in carrying out his proposal, time management and the correspondence between implementation and prior planning, also scored high.

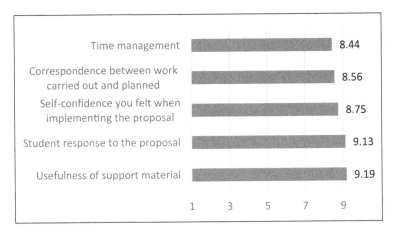

Fig. 8. Aspects valued with the implementation of the classroom experience: califications average.

It is worth clarifying that for the "Final Project" of the specialization, the students must plan and develop both connected and disconnected activities for their classroom practice. In this sense, the 20 teachers who completed this stage, managed not only to plan activities that combine both approaches but also, to relate them successfully to their contexts of school practice.

Highlights of the Training Course. Regarding the training experience, they were asked about their qualification in relation to different aspects. They point globally to issues of infrastructure, resources and materials, pedagogical aspects, among others. The students weighted these aspects on a positively increasing scale from 1 to 10 and in the following Fig. 9 an average of the score obtained is shown.

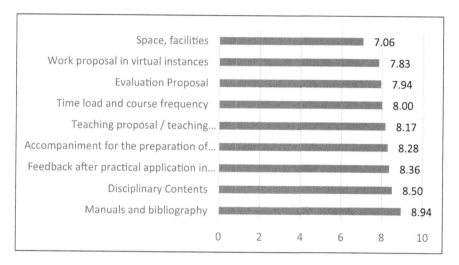

Fig. 9. Valued aspects of the course: califications average.

We can see that the ratings are overall very positive. Among the most valued aspects is the material offered, both in manual and bibliography format offered in the different modules, as well as the disciplinary contents addressed and the didactic proposal. The results of the focus group allowed to expand this information, pointing out among the main aspects assessed: the original nature of the offer, the thematic relevance and the quality of the materials, the proposal designed to be easily transferred to the classroom and possible to be contextualized in problems detected by the educational community, the work done by the teachers of the different modules, as well as the free nature of the proposal.

It should be noted that in the project modules the choice of the subject to be developed was always based on what was proposed by the students motivated from the theoretical-methodological framework of the specialization towards the development of a non-exclusive CS educational practice. Other aspects also highlighted by the students refer to:

- Tools provided by the specialization to think about teaching practices from another angle, for example, the development of practices and materials designed as Technologies for Social Inclusion.
- Unplugged activities, which provide the possibility of working "without the computer". There are restrictions on the availability of computers at school and they still perceive that they have to continue a process of creative appropriation of everything they have learned, in particular on programming skills.
- Training in the development and conceptualization of computational thinking.
- Software "Pilas Bloques" stands out as a suitable tool for students at an initial level of content approach.

4 Conclusions

In this article, we have presented some of the most significant aspects of the curriculum design and results of implementation of the first specialization for teachers of the primary level in Computer Science of Santa Fe province. This training experience results of great interest as a contribution to research in computer science didactics, since it is one of the first three in the country, as similar trainings are under way in Río Cuarto (Córdoba province) and in Tandil (Buenos Aires province).

The assessments expressed by the students are very encouraging, both from their appropriation of CS knowledge and from their perception of being able to implement the contents of CT and Programming in the classroom. Likewise, regarding the observations made by the professors responsible for the Final Project module in the institutions of the students (classroom activities), the opinions were also positive. It should be noted that in most cases the projects implemented, enabled in the schools involved the possibility of training the teaching group under the responsibility of the specialized teacher. In addition, through the classroom work, a novel and articulated practice of CS integration in primary school was made visible.

Beyond the evaluation monitoring instruments implemented, it is worth noting the fluid communication of the students and the good relationship that was built between the teaching team of this training and the future specialists. The open dialogue during the course was always present and allowed, as far as possible, more flexible adaptations to the diversity of problematic contexts presented by the students, bridging the gap of the cultural distance between the groups. This can be identified as a process of co-construction of knowledge, where a common theoretical framework was developed in two years. This process allowed a gradual understanding of the different discursive forms and conceptual frameworks that were initially presented as an obstacle to mutual understanding. Furthermore, this shared knowledge platform enables the discussion of the institutional tensions that arise in the problem of how to introduce the teaching and learning of Computer Science in primary school.

Another aspect of the curricular implementation to highlight is the consolidation of a team of professors-researchers that, under an interdisciplinary theoretical framework, systematically reflects on teacher training in CS for the primary level taking into account the regional context. These human resources can lead to new cohorts and the territorial expansion of the experience.

On the challenges to face for the improvement of this proposal, from all that has been collected, it will be necessary to study in depth how to achieve a better balance between the requirements of face-to-face time, the modules schedule, the amount of practical work requested, considering the working conditions and needs of primary teachers.

Finally, we expect that this specialization will be constituted as a reference proposal for the field of computer science education in Argentina, whose innovative and inclusive nature allows a transformation of current teaching curricula and practices.

Acknowledgements. We thank the support of Sadosky Foundation, the Ministry of Education of Santa Fe and the ISFD N° 36 "Mariano Moreno", that made it possible the development of this course. We recognize all the teaching team of this specialization for their commitment to this project and we highlight the effort of the students, primary teachers, who were the protagonists of this training. We also thank Martín Scasso and Quántitas Foundation for the preliminary results of the evaluation they conducted.

References

1. Balanskat, A., Engelhardt, K.: Computing our Future. Computer Programming and Coding. Priorities, School Curricula and Initiatives Across Europe. Brussels, Belgium (2015)
2. Brackmann, C., Román-González, M., Moreno-León, J., Robles, G., Casali, A., Barone, D.: Computational thinking unplugged: teaching and student evaluation in primary schools. In: Proceedings WIPSCE Nijmegen, The Netherlands, ACM, November 2017
3. Hubwieser, P., Armoni, M., Giannakis, M., Mittermeir, R.T.: Perspectives and visions of computer science education in primary and secondary (K-12) schools. Trans. Comput. Educ. **14**(7), 1–9 (2014)
4. Peyton Jones, S.: Computing at School: International Comparisons. Microsoft Research (2011)
5. Yadav, A., Hong, H., Stephenson, C.: Computational thinking for all: pedagogical approaches to embedding 21st century problem solving in K-12 classrooms. TechTrends **60**(6), 565–568 (2016)
6. Wing, J.M.: Computational Thinking Benefits Society. Social Issues in Computing (2014)
7. Tedesco, J.C., Steinberg, C., Tófalo, A.: La integración de TIC en la educación básica en Argentina. UNICEF, Buenos Aires (2015)
8. Casali, A., Zanarini, D., Monjelat, N., San Martín, P.: Teaching and learning computer science for primary school teachers: an Argentine experience. In: LACLO 2018, San Pablo, Brasil. IEEE Xplore (2018)
9. Casali, A., Zanarini, D., Monjelat, N., San Martín, P.: Formación docente en Ciencias de la Computación: experiencias de la primera Especialización para el nivelPrimario de la Provincia de Santa Fe, VIII Workshop Innovación en Educación en Informática (WIE) CACIC 2019, Río Cuarto, Argentina, RedUnci (2019)
10. Monjelat, N., San Martín, P.: Programar con Scratch en contextos educativos: ¿Asimilar directrices o co-construir Tecnologías para la Inclusión Social? Prax. Educ. **20**(1), 61–71 (2016)

11. Thomas, H., Juarez, P., Picabea, F.: ¿Qué son las tecnologías para la inclusión social? 1° Edición. Universidad de Quilmes, Bernal (2015)
12. Monjelat, N.: Programming technologies for social inclusion with scratch: computational practices in a teacher's professional development course. Educare **23**(3), 1–25 (2019)
13. Bell, T., Witten, I.H., Fellows, M.: CS Unplugged: An enrichment and extension programme for primary-aged students (2015)
14. Lye, S.Y., Koh, J.H.L.: Review on teaching and learning of computational thinking through programming: what is next for K-12? Comput. Human Behav. **41**, 51–61 (2014)
15. Grover, S., Pea, R.: Computational thinking in K–12: a review of the state of the field. Educ. Res. **42**(1), 38–43 (2013)
16. K-12 Computer Science Framework Steering Committee. K-12 Computer Science Framework. Technical Report. ACM, New York (2016)

Computational Thinking Skills in Primary Teachers: Evaluation Using Bebras

Francisco Bavera[1]([⊠]) [iD], Teresa Quintero[2] [iD], Marcela Daniele[1] [iD], and Flavia Buffarini[3] [iD]

[1] Departamento de Computación, Facultad de Ciencias Exactas, Físico-Químicas y Naturales, Universidad Nacional de Río Cuarto, Ruta 36 km 601, Río Cuarto, Argentina
`{pancho,marcela}@dc.exa.unrc.edu.ar`
[2] Departamento de Física, Facultad de Ciencias Exactas, Físico-Químicas y Naturales, Universidad Nacional de Río Cuarto, Ruta 36 km 601, Río Cuarto, Argentina
`tquintero@exa.unrc.edu.ar`
[3] Departamento de Matemática, Facultad de Ciencias Exactas, Físico-Químicas y Naturales, Universidad Nacional de Río Cuarto, Ruta 36 km 601, Río Cuarto, Argentina
`fbuffarini@exa.unrc.edu.ar`

Abstract. The results of a research on Computational Thinking skills in primary-level teachers, who completed a specialization in computer science didactics, are presented. The methodology was mixed – qualitative and quantitative. As data collection instruments, two tests based on the Bebras Problems were used. To analyze the texts written by the teachers on how they solve the problems, content analysis was used. It was found that a high percentage of teachers managed to solve problems of medium complexity that involve skills such as abstraction, pattern recognition, models and simulation, algorithms and decomposition. Moreover, it was observed that teachers manifest significant difficulties in describing and explaining when writing the process of solving the problems posed.

Keywords: Computational Thinking · Skills · Evaluation · Teachers' Continuing Training

1 Introduction

The construction of Computational Thinking (CT) manifests itself as an important challenge for current trainers of all educational levels. Nowadays, understanding and mastering information and communications technologies, is an important knowledge that helps solve different types of problems in the most diverse fields and contexts. It is a real challenge for teachers at different educational levels. Studies and trends worldwide warn about the importance of introducing and developing the CT in the compulsory education system. Introducing the CT at an early age is due to a social need of

© Springer Nature Switzerland AG 2020
P. Pesado and M. Arroyo (Eds.): CACIC 2019, CCIS 1184, pp. 405–415, 2020.
https://doi.org/10.1007/978-3-030-48325-8_26

this century, to develop capacities able to provide solutions to problems, using and taking advantage of the benefits of computing and technology.

Developing CT allows you to learn and understand technologies, including: decomposition strategies for problem solving, abstraction, generalization of the solutions, the application of processes that define rational and systematic steps towards the search for solutions and, achieving the definition and design of algorithms that allow finding the desired solutions or results [1–3]. The construction of CT allows the development of certain higher order skills that contribute and enrich the way of understanding and solving problems, and being able to create and automate these solutions, based on knowledge of fundamental principles and concepts of Science Computing, such as logic, abstraction, data representation and algorithm design [17].

Characterize the construction of Computational Thinking, in the context of the teachers' continuous training and the impact on their own practices is the main objective of the research and development project[1] that gives framework to this study. Between the aspects addressed, the analysis of the teaching practices of primary level teachers who participate in didactic training processes of Computer Science and CT development, are found. It is foreseen the need for deepen and consolidate research that addresses the study of the impact in the construction of the CT in the educators, for which it is necessary to evaluate, on the one hand, the proposed training activities, and on the other hand, the skills built by educators who undergo continuous training in Didactics of Computer Science. Depending on the complexity, inescapable use of different approaches, methods and techniques are needed to obtain evidence and indicators for analyzing and evaluating the impact of these formations.

The authors of this work are part of the team that coordinates and dictates a continuing education career aimed at primary school teachers, called Higher Level Teaching Specialization in Didactics of the Computational Science. This career emerges as a joint initiative between the Foundation Dr. Manuel Sadosky, the Higher Institute for Teacher Training Ramón Menéndez Pidal, and the Computing Department of the Faculty of Exact, Physical-Chemical and Natural Sciences, from the National University of Río Cuarto. In this framework, different studies are carried out in order to approach the inherent complexity of the CT construction process.

The evaluation of the CT is in development, educators find considerable limitations when assessing these skills that are considered primordial to the training of students in today's world [8]. In this context, it is shown that Bebras Problems [14] that are specially designed to assess computational thinking skills, constitutes an adequate instrument to measure these skills before and after training. Bebras is an international competition that aims to promote computational thinking among students of all ages with "disconnected" activities. There are studies that analyze the effectiveness of Bebras problems and also comparisons with other computational thinking tests [8–13]. However, there are no records of results obtained from the use of Bebras Problems in

---

[1] La construcción del pensamiento computacional: estudio del impacto desde la formación de formadores. Proyecto de Investigación y Desarrollo (PID) financiado por el Ministerio de Ciencia y Tecnología de la Provincia de Córdoba. 2019–2020.

the evaluation of teachers' continuous training in CT, so it is interesting to inquire about the scope of this evaluation alternative.

In this work, the results obtained from the analysis of an experience are presented, based on selected activities of Bebras problems, where the Computational Thinking (CT) skills of primary education teachers, who are studying the Specialty in Computing Science Didactics, are evaluated. Thus, providing another way of evaluating the CT skills.

This paper is an extension of the research presented by the authors at the XXV Argentine Congress of Computer Sciences (CACIC 2019) [16], in which is added a qualitative and quantitative analysis of the evaluation of CT skills performed to the group of teachers of the population in study. The main contributions given by this extension to the work [16] could be resumed in:

- The presentation of the results of a second test.
- Quantitative analysis of the results of both tests (previous and new tests).
- Qualitative analysis of the evaluation of the CT skills carried out at the teachers.
- Discussion of the results and presentation of related work.

This work is organized as follows: in Sect. 2 the evaluation experience carried out based on Bebras problems is exposed, the population of individuals that are evaluated and the test performed are described. In Sect. 3 an analysis of the results obtained is presented. In Sect. 4 related work is shown, and finally some conclusions and possible future works that give continuity to this research.

2   The Experience

2.1   Population

In this experience, an evaluation of the CT-related skills is carried out, which are presented by elementary school teachers who are studying for the Higher Level Teaching Specialization in Didactics of Computer Science.

The first cooperation began in March 2018 and has 47 teachers (44 female teachers and 3 male teachers) attending the second year. They are all primary level teachers, who teach classes to students between the ages of 6 and 12, 98% of grade teachers and only one teacher in the Information Technology area. The average age is 42 years, in a range from 23 to 54 years. We have a median and a mode of 43 and 44 years, respectively. The average deviation is 4.5. 50% are regular teachers and the rest are interim and substitutes, who work in different grades of primary school. In addition, currently two teachers are not related to any institution and one teacher performs activities ad-honorem. The teachers correspond to 28 schools, 80% are public institutions of state management and the remaining 20% are public institutions of private management. 75% of these schools are located in the city of Río Cuarto, and the other 25% in localities of its region of influence (within a radius of 30 to 150 km away from Río Cuarto).

The Specialization lasts 400 h, divided into 8 modules, over two years. The different modules introduce teachers to the concepts of computer science, digital citizenship, computational thinking, programming and robotics. The 8 modules are: (1) Communication and collaboration tools, (2) Introduction to Problem Solving, (3) Introduction to Programming Languages, (4) Software and Hardware Administration and Configuration, (5) Programming as an Educational Resource, (6) Introduction to Robotics, (7) Data Processing and (8) Integrative Project. The evaluation of each module was focused on class practice activities, generated and implemented in groups of teachers, as an integrative activity in each one of them. The first cohort ended in December 2019.

2.2   Methodology

The focus of the present study is mixed type, quantitative and qualitative, where the effects on learning that are to be observed and analyzed are studied once they have already occurred [7]. The study carried out uses a post-test without a control group, which limits the ability to analyze changes in teachers' abilities based on the training received, although it makes it possible to analyze the Computational Thinking skills of primary school teachers. The sampling is not probabilistic, the study is carried out with the group of elementary school teachers who attend the Specialty, in order to monitor the training received throughout their dictation.

As data collection instruments, two tests were used based on the Bebras Problems, specifically problems of the Bebras Australia Computational Thinking Challenge 2018 [15] were used. As mentioned earlier, Bebras is an international competition that aims to promote computational thinking, among students of all ages, with "disconnected" activities. The Bebras initiative is part of an international proposal open and based on collaboration between teachers. The project has an important popularity, since more than 50 countries are currently participating. Participants are usually supervised by teachers and the challenge is done in schools using computers or mobile devices. Problems or challenges do not require prior knowledge of programming or Computer Science [18], but all address these issues, for example patterns, coding, cryptography, trees, among others.

To build the assessment instrument, eleven problems of medium complexity of the Bebras Australia Computational Thinking Challenge 2018 were selected and translated into Spanish. The selected problems pose activities that include finding paths - a path and the best path -, recognizing patterns, identifying and applying algorithms, order sequences, cryptography and use logical reasoning. The problems were divided into two tests. You can check the complete tests in the following links http://drive.google.com/file/d/1uP66o5LCUdEnekITGFDDkcb-E0l5G7ad and https://drive.google.com/file/d/1M3mMSn24C3Vw19rwZ35PIW6qk5VN2mf2.

Table 1 lists the selected problems and the CT skills involved in them, which are:

- Decomposition: divide the problems into parts (sub-problems).
- Pattern recognition: analyze the data and look for patterns to make this data meaningful.
- Abstraction: eliminate unnecessary details and focus attention on important data.
- Modeling and simulation: create models or simulations to represent processes.
- Algorithms: create a series of ordered steps to solve a problem.

Table 1. Selected problems and associated CT skills according to Bebras

	Problem	CT skills				
		Decomposition	Pattern recognition	Abstraction	Modeling and simulation	Algorithms
Test 1	1 Way home	x	x	x		x
	2 Dancing man	x	x	x		x
	3 Beaver tournament	x		x		x
	4 Sticks and Shields	x		x	x	x
	5 Roundabout city	x		x	x	x
	6 Brackets	x	x	x		x
	7 Railroad	x		x	x	x
	8 Candy maze	x		x		x
Test 2	9 Order shelves	x	x			x
	10 Secret code		x			x
	11 Magic potions		x	x		

The activities in paper format were delivered to the teachers in the classroom, for their resolution a time of 40 min was assigned for the first test and 20 min for the second test. They were treated in this way, different compared to the Bebras contest that was realized in front of the computers.

The activities of the different modules of the specialization did not use Bebras Problems, but other types of activities involving skills included in the selected problems were developed. So it is important to highlight that the teachers when taking the test, faced for the first time a challenge with Bebras style problems.

As mentioned earlier the evaluation was divided into two instances. The first eight problems correspond to the first test and problems 9–11 to the second test.

In the first test, the results quantitatively analyzed around the associated skills were analyzed according to the identification carried out in Bebras. In the second test, in addition to the quantitative analysis, a qualitative analysis was approached based on the recognition of CT skills involved, as well as, the strategies used in the resolution of the problems by the teachers themselves were investigated.

3 Results

It was observed that teachers correctly answered 75.5% of the total test problems. With an average of 8 correct answers per individual. It should be noted that the median and the mode coincide with the average value. Approximately one third of teachers are above average and a similar amount below it. Table 2 shows the percentage of correct answers discriminated by problem. The results of both tests are similar. The percentage of correct answers does not present variations between the first and second tests in problems with the same characteristics and hardness levels.

Table 2. Percentage correct answers

	Problem	% Correct answers
Test 1	1 Way home	100,0%
	2 Dancing man	29,0%
	3 Beaver tournament	96,0%
	4 Sticks and Shields	58,0%
	5 Roundabout city	79,0%
	6 Brackets	66,5%
	7 Railroad	96,0%
	8 Candy maze	62,5%
Test 2	9 Order shelves	100,0%
	10 Secret code	77,0%
	11 Magic potions	68,0%

The best results were observed in the problems associated with finding a path and recognizing patterns in the order of elements. Although, there is a slight decrease in the effectiveness of resolution in the activities where they should found the best path. It is necessary to investigate the causes that motivate this difference, which can be numerous and diverse, but one of the possibilities is that most of the incorrect answers may be due to an erroneous interpretation of the slogans, not to identify a relevant fact in the statement, or difficulties related to abstraction skills.

The results obtained in solving problems 2 (Dancing man) and 4 (Sticks and Shields), are a consequence of the realization of the activity on paper. This generated an extra difficulty for teachers evaluated in the resolution of these types of interactive exercises (originally designed to be implemented as interactive), which was not seen in the multiple-choice challenges. Two cases were found that present a large number of incorrect answers. In the first case the factors that led to these results were the mis-interpretation of the statements and difficulty in understanding the slogans; in the second case it was directly the lack of interest in the activity.

The test results, shown in Table 3, showed that teachers, on average, correctly solved 7 of the 9 problems that involve skills related to decomposition and abstraction. In these skills, median and mode show the same value (7 correct answers of a possible maximum of 9). Taking the total responses associated with these two skills, teachers correctly solved 76% and 73%, respectively, of the problems. In the case of algorithms, they responded correctly 76% of the time, with an average of 8 correct answers per teacher (out of a total of 10 problems) with a median and mode equal to the average. As for pattern recognition, it can be seen that the average is 4 correct answers per teacher and that the median and mode yield 5 correct answers (of 6 possible maximum), with 73% of correct answers in total. In the case of modeling and simulation, it can be seen that the teachers answered on average 2 questions correctly (of 3 possible), but the average and the mode is 3 (of 3 at most); In this case, teachers responded correctly 78% of the time.

Table 3. Correct answers by CT skill

CT skills	Correct answers			
	Correct answers percentage	Mean (correct answers per teacher)	Median (correct answers per teacher)	Mode (correct answers per teacher)
Decomposition	76%	7	7	7
Pattern recognition	73%	4	5	5
Abstraction	73%	7	7	7
Modeling and simulation	78%	2	3	3
Algorithms	76%	8	8	8

In the second test, problems from 9 to 11 were approached (Table 2), the students selected and solved a problem of those assigned. In addition, they were asked to describe and explain how they proceeded to resolve it, as well as to identify the CT skills involved in the problem. Teachers selected problem 9 in 50% of cases, while 25% of them selected the remaining problems (10 and 11).

Teachers who selected problem 9 recognized that the problem is associated with Pattern Recognition (91%), Decomposition (41%) and Algorithms (16%). Only one of the teachers recognized the three skills (just this three). Almost half of them associated other skills not involved in this problem.

All teachers who selected problem 10 recognized that Pattern Recognition is a skill involved in solving this problem, but none could identify the use of Algorithms. In addition, 80% recognized skills that do not correspond to the problem, such as Data Representation and Verification.

On the other hand, those who selected problem 11 recognized that the problem is associated with Pattern Recognition and Abstraction (80%). As in the previous case, everyone associated other skills not involved in this problem.

In the descriptions made by the teachers about the procedure carried out to solve the problem, it was observed that most of them have difficulties expressing the procedure in a descriptive text. In general, they only name a list of procedures, for example, textually they express: "I observed and discarded", "I read, reasoned and recognized the pattern", "observation, replacing patterns, recognition", "by discarding", "I compared", among others.

In the case of problem 9, only two teachers wrote a descriptive and explanatory text about how they proceeded step by step to solve the activity. For problems 10 and 11, four teachers achieved to describe and explain the procedure followed.

It is important that teachers become aware of the procedures and skills used in problem solving. Therefore, it is necessary to continue studying this type of activities and the explicit explanation of the resolutions.

4 Related Work

To the best knowledge there is no work about assessing CT skills in primary school teachers.

The Bebras initiative [14] is closely related to this work. In [21] they state that research and applications involving computational thinking assessment are using Bebras with increasing frequency. As mentioned above, studies have been conducted that analyze the effectiveness of Bebras problems and also comparisons with other CT tests [8–13]. However, there are no records of results obtained from the use of Bebras Problems in the evaluation of teachers' continuous training in CT.

Lockwood and Mooney [8] uses Bebras' challenge problems to assess computational thinking in high school and undergraduate students. Our work shares many of the problems used by these researchers in their tests. We want to mention that the percentage of correct answers obtained by the primary level teachers (in our work) are very similar to those of the secondary level students shown by these authors.

Roman et al. [20] present the computational thinking test (CTt). CTt is a multiple-choice instrument assessment tool which has proven to be reliable and valid for secondary school students. CTt addresses programming concepts and problem-solving ability.

Boom et al. [18] address the relationship between CT and intelligence. They analyzed tasks based (partially) on the Bebras challenge of pre-service teacher students. Their goal is to measure problem-solving skills. An important conclusion reached by these authors is *"...the Bebras' tasks could be a promising way to evaluate CT without involving any programming or programming activities"*.

Souto et al. [19] presented a review of the instruments or artifacts used to measure CT abilities. But, they do not report at what educational level these instruments or devices are used to evaluate CT skills; nor do they analyze the relevance or effectiveness of each one.

The authors of this work, in an initial research, based their study in the productions of integration that were presented in poster format by students of the specialty, as the closing activity of their first year. Each production was analyzed using a Qualitative methodology, based on grounded theory; the data were triangulated with each other by at least two researchers considering the categories of the Bloom's taxonomy adequate by Churches [4]. This analysis allowed determining that all the productions and the proposals of class practices, reflected certain cognitive skills related to the digital world, showing different levels of development and deepness [5].

Subsequently, an analysis of CT skills was carried out, such as formulating problems where computers and other tools are used to solve them, organizing data in a logical way and analyzing them, representing data through abstractions, which are mostly addressed in the specific modules of Programming teaching. This analysis provided important evidence that the training received by these educators, has a positive impact on the transformation of their class practices [6].

5 Conclusion and Future Works

We It was detected that a high percentage of teachers (who are currently pursuing the *Especialización Docente de Nivel Superior en Didáctica de las Ciencias de la Computación*) were able to solve problems of medium complexity that involve the use of CT skills, such as abstraction, pattern recognition, models and simulation, algorithms and decomposition.

It was observed that teachers manifest significant difficulties in describing and explaining in writing the process of solving the problems posed. Only a small percentage could write the process in a detailed and understandable way. Most expressed it with short sentences and general terms.

On the other hand, a large number of teachers identified the CT skills involved in solving the problems, with pattern recognition being able to recognize with greater certainty.

The analysis of the explanation of the procedures for solving problems, made it possible through a more qualitative analysis, to know the procedures and skills that teachers recognize that they put into play. In line with continuing to deepen the analysis of the CT, interviews will be conducted and other instruments for data collection and analysis on CT will be applied. As well as, new evaluations will be carried out using more complex Bebras problems, complementing and deepening the monitoring of the CT skills of this group of teachers.

The results of these investigations try to contribute to the development of knowledge about the continuous training of primary school teachers in computer science. On the other hand, they represent an advance of the research that is being developed.

Likewise, this work provides data and knowledge for the debate that is currently taking place in our country. In particular in our province, regarding the adequacy of curricula for the inclusion of computer science and programming in the school.

It is intended to continue evaluating the Computational Thinking skills with other methodologies. Work is also being done on the evaluation of the inclusion of the CT in teaching practices and how the training on the subject impacts them.

On the other hand, it is planned to venture into the analysis of the perceptions of primary school teachers regarding Computer Science, programming and robotics. This analysis also aims to envision the contribution, in terms of the change of teachers' perceptions, of different formations in Computer Science, Computational Thinking, programming and robotics that are being developed in the region.

Acknowledgments. We want to thank all the primary school teachers who participated in the Higher Level Teaching Specialization in Didactics of Computational Science, Fundación Sadosky and Instituto Ramon Menendez Pidal. We thank our colleagues from Specialization who provided insight and expertise that greatly assisted the research.

A special thanks to Bruno and Augusto Ficco Daniele for their collaboration and contributions.

This work is supported in part by the Ministerio de Ciencia y Tecnología of the Province of Córdoba (Argentina) through Research and Development Project (PID 2019–2020) "The construction of computational thinking: study of the impact from teacher training". Funding from the UNRC is gratefully acknowledged for the project (PPI 2020–2022) "Computational thinking and teaching practices in science".

References

1. Aho, A.V.: Computation and computational thinking. Comput. J. **55**(7), 832–835 (2012). https://doi.org/10.1093/comjnl/bxs074
2. Denning, P.J.: Remaining trouble spots with computational thinking. Commun. ACM **60**(6), 33–39 (2017). https://doi.org/10.1145/2998438
3. Wing, J.M.: Computational thinking. Commun. ACM **49**(3), 33–35 (2006). https://doi.org/10.1145/1118178.1118215
4. Churches, A.: Taxonomía de Bloom para la era digital. Eduteka. Consultado 10/01/19 (2009). http://eduteka.icesi.edu.co/articulos/TaxonomiaBloomDigital
5. Daniele, M., Quintero, T., Bavera, F., Buffarini, F., Solivellas, D., De Dominici, C.: Análisis de producciones de docentes de educación primaria con formación en didáctica de las ciencias de la computación. In: Segundas Jornadas de Didáctica de la Programación (JADiPro), FAMAF, Universidad Nacional de Córdoba (2019)
6. Bavera, F., Quintero, T., Daniele, M., Buffarini, F.: Análisis de prácticas de docentes de educación primaria en el marco de una formación en pensamiento computacional. In: Proceedings of 48° Jornadas Argentinas de Informática, SAEI-JAIIO, Universidad Nacional de Salta (2019)
7. Bernado, J., Calderero, J.F.: Aprendo a investigar en educación. Ediciones Rialp, Madrid (2000)
8. Lockwood, J., Mooney, A.: Developing a computational thinking test using Bebras problems. In: Proceedings of the CC-TEL 2018 and TACKLE 2018 (2018)
9. Gouws, L., Bradshaw, K., Wentworth, P.: First year student performance in a test for computational thinking. In: Proceedings of the South African Institute for Computer Scientists and Information Technologists Conference. ACM (2013)
10. Dagiene, V., Stupuriene, G.: Bebras-a sustainable community building model for the concept based learning of informatics and computational thinking. Inform. Educ. **15**, 25–44 (2016)
11. Hubwieser, P., Mhling, A.: Playing PISA with bebras. In: 9th Workshop in Primary and Secondary Computing Education (WiPSCE) (2014)
12. Hubwieser, P., Mhling, A.: Investigating the psychometric structure of Bebras contest: towards measuring computational thinking skills. In: Learning and Teaching in Computing and Engineering (LATiCE) (2015)
13. Vaníček, J.: Bebras informatics contest: criteria for good tasks revised. In: Gülbahar, Y., Karataş, E. (eds.) ISSEP 2014. LNCS, vol. 8730, pp. 17–28. Springer, Cham (2014). https://doi.org/10.1007/978-3-319-09958-3_3
14. Iniciativa Bebras. https://www.bebras.org/

15. Bebras Australia Computational Thinking Challenge (2018). https://www.bebras.edu.au/wp-content/uploads/2019/02/Bebras-2018-Solution-Guide.pdf
16. Bavera, F., Quintero, T., Daniele, M., Buffarini, F.: Habilidades de Pensamiento Computacional en docentes de primaria: evaluación usando Bebras. In: Proceedings of XXV Congreso Argentino de Ciencias de la Computación (CACIC 2019), UNIRIO, Universidad Nacional de Río Cuarto (2019)
17. Wing, J.M.: Computational thinking and thinking about computing. Philos. Trans. Ser. A Math. Phys. Eng. Sci. **366**(1881), 3717–3725 (2008). http://dx.doi.org/10.1098/rsta.2008.0118
18. Boom, K.D., Bower, M., Arguel, A., Siemon, J., Scholkmann, A.: Relationship between computational thinking and a measure of intelligence as a general problem-solving ability. In: Proceedings of the 23rd Annual ACM Conference on Innovation and Technology in Computer Science Education, pp. 206–211. ACM (2018)
19. de Araujo, A.L.S.O., Andrade, W.L., Guerrero, D.D.S.: A systematic mapping study on assessing computational thinking abilities. In: IEEE Frontiers in Education Conference (FIE), Erie, PA, USA, pp. 1–9. IEEE (2016)
20. Román-Gonzalez, M.: Computational thinking test: design guidelines and content validation. In: 7th Annual International Conference on Education and New Learning Technologies (EDULEARN 2015), Barcelona, pp. 2436–2444 (2015)
21. Dagiene, V., Stupuriene, G., Vinikien, L.: Promoting inclusive informatics education through the bebras challenge to all K-12 students. In: Proceedings of the 17th International Conference on Computer Systems and Technologies 2016, pp. 407–414. ACM (2016)

.

Digital Governance and Smart Cities

Taxonomic Analysis of Mobile Applications for Government Services in Cities from Argentina

Rocío Muñoz$^{(\boxtimes)}$ ⓘ, Juan Santiago Preisegger ⓘ, Ariel Pasini ⓘ,
and Patricia Pesado ⓘ

Computer Science Research Institute LIDI (III-LIDI),
Partner Center of the Scientific Research Agency of the Province of Buenos
Aires (CIC), Facultad de Informática, Universidad Nacional de La Plata,
50 y 120, La Plata, Buenos Aires, Argentina
{rmunoz,jspreisegger,apasini,
ppesado}@lidi.info.unlp.edu.ar

Abstract. A taxonomy for the classification of mobile applications for government services in cities from Argentina is presented. Such taxonomy has a number of categories and subcategories that classify mobile applications according to the interaction between citizens and applications. For the development of such taxonomy, 53 cities from Argentina were selected and 89 mobile applications (offered and developed by such cities) were analyzed. Finally, all mobile applications were classified according to the defined taxonomy.

Keywords: Mobile applications · Taxonomy · City governments · Civic interaction

1 Introduction

During the last decades, a remarkable progress in technologies has been observed. Technology innovation has improved significantly, with substantial levels of sophistication, in particular, mobile technologies and communication. *Mobile technology* appearance has created ample opportunities to better the role of good governance. Historically, citizens have interacted with local governments in an off-line way, however, due to technological progress, several of these activities can be now carried out by the use of mobile devices.

A public service is an activity that governments provide to five receptors: *citizens, business, governments, visitors* and *employees*. When a government delivers a service through the use of mobile applications it is called a "Mobile public service".

A taxonomy is a group of similar objects under certain dimensions and characteristics. It enables us to define categories and subcategories to carry out a classification of objects. The developed taxonomy must fulfill certain attributes in order to be considered suitable: be concise, inclusive, comprehensive and extensible.

R. Muñoz and J. S. Preisegger—Fellow UNLP

P. Pesado and M. Arroyo (Eds.): CACIC 2019, CCIS 1184, pp. 419–431, 2020.
https://doi.org/10.1007/978-3-030-48325-8_27

Regarding such attributes, the necessity of analyzing different mobile applications in 53 selected cities in Argentina arose, with a view to classify them and create, thus, a taxonomy taking into account the interaction between citizens and these applications. Such taxonomy has four dimensions: *informative, interactive, contributive* and *recreative*, and each of them has a number of related characteristics.

In order to confirm that the taxonomy fulfills the attributes aforementioned, 89 retrieved applications were classified in each of the dimensions and characteristics that were proposed.

This article can be seen as an improved and extended version of our previous work [1]. In section two, the advantages of the use of mobile devices at present are described, and the definition of "Mobile public services" and some application cases in Latin America are presented. In the third section, definitions, characteristics and approaches are presented so as to create taxonomies. Then, a survey of the cities of Argentina and the official applications they offered is presented, followed by the creation of a taxonomy appropriate to the purpose that was laid out. Finally, conclusions are provided.

2   Mobile Devices for the Services Delivery

2.1   Use of Mobile Devices Today

During the last two decades, a remarkable progress in technologies has been observed. Technology innovation has improved significantly, with substantial levels of sophistication, in particular, **mobile technologies** and communication. Nowadays, smartphones have numerous functions with several ways of continuing communication. Also, they allow users to have access to applications in real time according to their concrete and specific needs, regarding their physical location, thus defining a new concept of *customizable device* [2].

The Smart City model has emerged strongly worldwide as a new way of reconsidering urban management. This concept deals with the idea of the integration of the use of TIC in the evolution of a city, thus improving greatly the service supply and cooperating with social and financial development. A *City with Intelligence* is characterized by the everyday use of technology to better efficiency as a response to daily requests [3].

The appearance of mobile technology has created considerable opportunities to better the role of good governance, specifically the rise of information, the interaction with the audience and the most effective and efficient means to carry out public transactions. Mobile applications are defined as the use of this technology used by a final user with a specific purpose [4].

2.2   Mobile Public Services Delivery

RAE dictionary [5] defines a "Public Service" as: "Activity carried out by the Administration or, under a certain control and regulation of such administration, by an organization, specialized or not, and with the purpose of fulfilling needs for the community".

Governments provide public services, firstly, to five receptors: *citizens, business, governments, visitors* and *employees*.

The "Delivery of services" is the part of the service business process where the interaction between the supplier and the service consumer is carried out. "Channels" is the name used to define the perception of the consumer or the administration regarding the way the service is delivered.

It's decision of each government agency to define how public services will be delivered to the citizens, being possible to define different delivery of services strategies, taking into account factors such as consumer needs, costs and capacities of channels, and common aspects between the elements, channels, processes and transactions.

The "Delivery of services Strategy" represents a group of decisions about how services will be delivered to the clients: "Multiple Channels" (the information known by a channel is not shared with other channels; to exchange data, each channel must be connected to the others) or "Multi-Channel" (the channels are integrated; data can be read from any of the channels and consumers can obtain such data from any location).

There are multiple channels for the delivery of services, some of them are: personally in the office, by phone, by web sites, by email, etc. When the delivery of a service is carried out by a mobile application it is called "*Mobile public service*".

Historically, citizens have interacted with local government agencies in an off-line way; however, due to technological progress, many of these activities can be now carried out by the use of mobile devices.

Government mobile applications are used as an additional channel for the government delivery of services and they enable citizens to have access to information at any time and place [6]. The different ways that citizens interact with city administrations are:

- Through *receptive interactions*: unidirectional transactions of information from the government agency to the citizen or vice versa. Generally, citizens search for governmental ordinance, citizen growth plans, etc. Additionally, governmental agencies seek to understand demographic characteristics of a determined part of census, dimensional characteristics of the area, etc.

- Through *interactive tools*: exchange between government agencies and citizens. "Off-line" interactive exchanges imply a bidirectional transaction of information, since citizens often want to share their thoughts about how things are done in the community and what plans can be discussed in the future. In the past, citizens had limited options: to assist to a public audience, to visit the planning office in person, to call the city administrators, etc. Mobile applications have provided additional options that make interactivity more accessible.

- Through *transactional tools*: exchange between governmental agencies and citizens. Many of these activities would have required, in the past, that a citizen visit local government offices, but nowadays the visits can be online. Some of them are: variation, appeals and application for licenses, fee payments for permissions and other request forms.

2.3   Application Cases in Latin America

Argentina. BA Movil is a mobile application developed and spread by the Buenos Aires City government, Argentina, in order to communicate car traffic flow and the location of the underground and the bike paths in real time at Buenos Aires City. This application combines information from many sources and can be sorted according to the means of transport that the user chooses. It gives accurate, constantly updated and real-time information so that users know what is happening on the street and the means of transport.

Brazil. With SIC.SP mobile application, the citizen can have access to public data and information produced or kept in custody by the organizations of the state government of San Pablo city. The application has been able to assist more than 37,000 request forms of information, news and notifications about administrative processing. The service is free of charge and it keeps information confidential and personal with limited access.

Colombia. The event tool "Government online", from Colombia government, allows citizens to get information and receive news of all the national and international events organized by the Online government office of the TIC secretary: calendar of events, public, guests, speakers, entries, activities, forum, awards, etc.

Costa Rica. "CR Public Security" application has been useful to inform and prevent citizenship through safety advice and government news in this area. Official information works for the location of policy offices in the country, security advice, crime prevention and general information about programs, recruitment requirements, community security and firearm carrying permission. Criminal incidents can be reported as well as wanted individuals or fugitives.

El Salvador. "El Trafico SV" application seeks to give information and tolerate car traffic supervision in this country in real time through live cameras (live streaming). Also, this development allows to incorporate a report with photographs of traffic in real time. This application has allowed a better evaluation of traffic in the city by users.

Mexico. SAT Movil is the official application of Tax Administration Service (SAT in Spanish). Some of the services available online are: online invoice, complaints, tax payment and refund procedure, payment and statement enquiry, tax signal, SAT store, appointment, board of directors and accountants, tax calendar and financial statistics.

Panama. The development of "Panama Mobile Migration" application, that belongs to the National Service of Migration of Panama, has been useful to carry out and follow migration administrative procedures such as edicts, naturalization processes and authorized visas from a mobile phone.

Venezuela. The "Online government" initiative in Venezuela has allowed for the use of mobile phones to offer information and orientation about public sector services to citizenship. With this mobile application, the user can have access to the board of directors, paperwork and available services in the government. The tool is still informative, but it is planned to transform it into a more interactive tool so as to go through procedures and services with a mobile phone.

3 Taxonomies

3.1 A Taxonomy Description

A taxonomy is a classification or aggrupation of objects that have characteristics in common. According to Nickerson [7], one of the main advantages that taxonomies offer is the reduction of complexity and the identification of similitudes and differences among such objects. Adequate taxonomies play an important role in investigation, since the classification of objects helps researchers and professionals to understand and analyze complex domains; thus theories can be formulated based on such relations.

There exists a difference between typology and taxonomy concepts [8]: typologies derive in a conceptual or deductive manner and taxonomies in an empirical manner. In the case of typologies, the researcher can propose a categorization based on an ideal or theoretical model. On the other hand, for taxonomies, the proposed classification is based on empirical data, starting with certain data and leading to a classification by analysing it. The goal is to find similitudes among data and classify similar objects in the categories.

For the taxonomy, dimensions and characteristics are defined. The dimensions offer a primary classification and the characteristics are grouped in the dimensions defining a secondary classification. A taxonomy will be useful if it contains the following ideal attributes [7]:

- Be *concise*: the taxonomy must contain a limited number of dimensions and characteristics easy to be understood and used.
- Be enough *inclusive*: the taxonomy must have enough dimensions and characteristics of interest.
- Be *comprehensive*: the taxonomy must provide the classification of all current objects within the domain in consideration.
- Be *extensible*: the taxonomy must allow for additional dimensions and new characteristics when new types of objects appear.

3.2 A Taxonomy Creation

The development of a taxonomy is a complex process. Before starting, the researcher must decide the most complete characteristics and metacharacteristics that are useful for the base of the classification. The election of the metacharacteristic must be based on the purpose of the taxonomy.

Bailey [9] describes the conceptual and empiric approaches of a model with two levels. Although researchers can tackle the classification through any of the levels, he suggests that by using a model with three levels that includes conceptual, empiric and indicator/operational levels can be a common approach and, often more useful. In this method, the researcher has two options: whether to start with the deductive approach and then examine the empiric cases (from deductive to empiric) to check how they fit into the conceptualization or to start with empiric data groups and then conceptualize deductively the nature of each group (form empiric to deductive).

In the field of information systems, Bailey's indicator model was found as the most attractive for the development of taxonomies. It doesn't have a unique approach but it is based in deduction as well as in empiricism: the researcher starts examining a subgroup of objects, willing to classify them and identifying general characteristics of such objects. The identification of these characteristics leads to the first effort in a taxonomy, being grouped in dimensions that create the *initial taxonomy*. Each dimension has characteristics that are mutually exclusive and collectively comprehensive. This process is based on empiric data (limited) that have been collected on the objects and the deductive conceptualization of the researcher. The researcher checks, then, the first taxonomy to seek additional conceptualizations that could not have been identified in the original empiric data. Hence, new characteristics, which can be adjusted to existent dimensions, can be deduced or conceptualized into new dimensions. The empiric cases are examined by using new characteristics and dimensions to determine their utility in the classification of objects. A *revised taxonomy* arises.

4   Mobile Applications in Cities from Argentina

4.1   Selected Cities

An analysis of several cities from Argentina was carried out. The aim was to include cities with different sizes and realities.

On the one hand, 50 cities which are members of RECIA (Smart Cities Network in Argentina) were taken into account. RECIA is a space for exchanging experiences and knowledge, whose goal is to promote smart cities and to better the government management. The network is set up by smart cities which are models in the entire country, and it works horizontally with local governments and other parts in topics such as politics design, tools and better practices [10].

Additionally, it was ideal to include in the analysis the 8 biggest cities from Argentina according to INDEC projections for 2018 [11]. Taking these cities, it was discovered that 3 of them didn't belong to RECIA, so they were added; this made a total number of 53 selected cities.

Finally, a wide variety of cities from the country with different sizes and characteristics was gathered: 5.66% of cities with more than 1 million residents, 9.43% between 500,000 and 1 million residents, 15.09% between 250,000 and 500,000 residents, 28.30% between 100,000 and 250,000 residents, 9.43% between 50,000 and 100,000 residents and 32.09% with less than 50,000 residents. Figure 1 shows the amount of cities for each size classification.

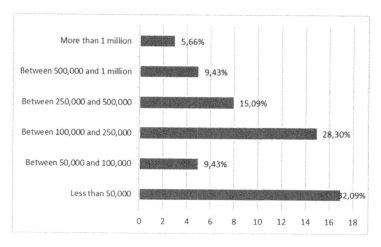

Fig. 1. Residents of the cities according to INDEC projections (2018)

The 53 selected cities for the analysis can be observed in Table 1.

Table 1. Selected cities

Buenos Aires	3 de Febrero	Mercedes
	Adolfo Alsina	Necochea
	Bahía Blanca	Pergamino
	Bolívar	Pilar
	Campana	Pinamar
	Castelli	Puan
	Chivilcoy	Ramallo
	Coronel Pringles	San Antonio de Areco
	Escobar	San Isidro
	Exaltación de la Cruz	San Nicolás
	General San Martín	San Pedro
	Junín	Suipacha
	La Plata	Tandil
	Lincoln	Tigre
	Luján	Vicente López
	Mar Chiquita	Villarino
	Mar del Plata	Zárate
Chubut	Esquel	Puerto Madryn
	Gaiman	Rawson
Córdoba	Córdoba	Villa María
Mendoza	Godoy Cruz	Luján de Cuyo
Neuquén	Neuquén	Villa La Angostura
Tucumán	San Miguel de Tucumán	
Salta	Salta	
San Luis	Juana Koslay	Tilisarao
Santa Fé	Rafaela	Rosario
	Reconquista	Santa Fé de la Vera Cruz
Ciudad Autónoma de Buenos Aires		

4.2   Search for Official Applications in the Selected Cities

Once the cities were selected, the search for mobile applications offered by each of them was carried out. Google Play store was used for such search.

In each city, the applications offered and developed by the corresponding government were collected. We will call them "official applications".

From the 53 cities studied, 26 of them (49%) didn't offer any official application (some of them didn't even offer applications of mediators related to the city administration), 9 of the cities (17%) only offered one official application (which, in some cases, included several areas of the city administration and worked as a general application), 11 cities (22%) gave two or three applications, 3 cities (5%) offered between four and seven applications, other 3 cities (5%) between eight and ten applications and only 1 city (2%) had a list of more than 10 mobile applications to offer their citizens. This can be observed in Fig. 2.

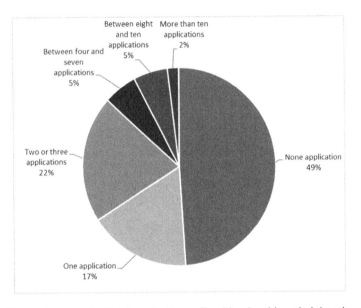

Fig. 2. Amount of official applications offered by the cities administration

Within the 89 mobile applications found for the different cities, applications of several types and with different purposes can be found. The can be classified in the following groups: Cultural calendars/tourism, City alerts, Public transport, Educational games, Radios, Payment services, Night shift pharmacies, Claims, Maps, Parking, Emergencies, etc.

5 Taxonomy for Mobile Applications

5.1 Creation of a Taxonomy by the Analysis of Mobile Applications

The purpose of the taxonomy presented is to classify mobile applications from a communicational point of view; therefore, it is defined as a metacharacteristic the interaction between citizens and applications.

To succeed in obtaining a taxonomy that fulfills the ideal attributes presented (be concise, inclusive comprehensive and extensible) the decision was to use the empiric approach: mobile applications that were offered by the city managements were analyzed, studied in 4.2, and similitudes in the way of interaction with the applications were found to create different categories. Therefore, four dimensions were identified:

- *Informative:* applications that give information to the citizen. Information is sent unidirectionally, from the application to the citizen.
- *Interactive:* applications that let the citizen exchange information with the application, sharing their opinion or participating in government managements. Information has a bidirectional flow between the citizen and the application.
- *Contributive:* applications that let the citizen give information of interest for the government. Information is sent undirectionally from the citizen to the application.
- *Recreative:* applications that let the citizen interact in a playful way. There is no exchange of information.

Once the four starting categories were defined, the decision was to include, besides, a deductive approach to establish subcategories/characteristics that give a better classification of the applications to achieve the purpose.

In the **Informative** category, four subcategories are defined: *Alert, Static, Dynamic* and *Based on location*. The *Alert* subcategory makes reference to applications that interact with the citizen in real time, sending information automatically, for instance, in emergencies. Applications categorized as *Static* are those which give information to citizens without interaction with them. On the other hand, when applications with *Dynamic* category are mentioned, this makes reference to those which wait for the citizen's initiative to give information. Lastly, the *Based on location* subcategory refers to applications that give citizens personalized information based on their geolocation.

For the **Interactive** category two subcategories are established: *Citizens assistance* and *Transport service*. Regarding *Citizens assistance*, it is a subcategory composed by those applications that let the citizen inform about several problems in the city or fill in request forms, with the chance of following them through the application. Furthermore, the *Transport service* subcategory refers to applications that let the citizen ask for a public transport and interact through different enquiries about it.

In the **Contributive** category, three subcategories are included: *Data collection, Request for help* and *Tax collection*. The *Data collection* subcategory makes reference to those applications that are nourished with information that citizens gives by filling in forms or interacting in another way. For their part, applications categorized as *Request for help*, are those that the citizen uses to generate an alert to ask for help by means of, for example, a panic button that sends the geolocation of the citizen to whom it may concern. *Tax collection* subcategory refers to those applications that let the citizen pay the taxes to the cities administration.

Finally, the **Recreative** category is defined by two subcategories: *Games* and *Virtual reality*. These subcategories do not need too much explanation; their names are enough self-explanatory. The applications of *Games* subcategory are those that let citizens know and/or learn, by means of some type of educational games, about the city or any other matters of interest, such as health, law, etc. Additionally, the *Virtual reality* category encompasses those applications that, by means of the use of technologies such as augmented reality, let citizens know more about the city in an innovative and enjoyable way.

The final taxonomy developed can be observed in Fig. 3.

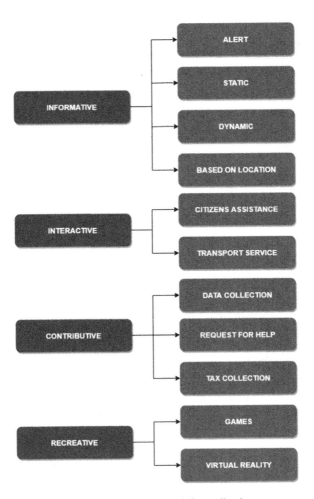

Fig. 3. Taxonomy for mobile applications

5.2   Classification of Applications According to the Taxonomy

To prove if the taxonomy developed is correct, that is to say, if it fulfills the required attributes, the decision was to classify each of the 89 mobile applications studied in the different categories and subcategories defined. Figure 4 shows the result of this classification.

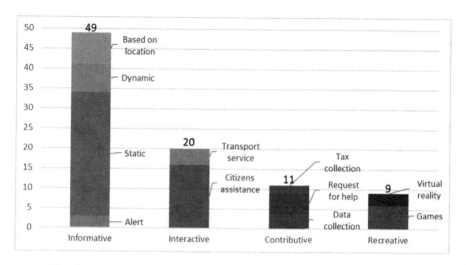

Fig. 4. Mobile applications classified according to the developed taxonomy

As it can be seen, a great part of the studied applications corresponds to the *Informative* category. There are 49 applications that belong to this category: 63% from *Static* subcategory, such as report applications, news, diaries, radios, etc.; 16% of *Based on location* subcategory, such as applications that show when the bus arrives, what activities the citizen can do in the surrounding areas; 14% of the *Dynamic* subcategory, for example, applications to check fines, debts, scan QR codes, etc.; and 7% of *Alert* subcategory, for example, applications that give advice about weather conditions, the swell of the river, etc.

From the studied applications that correspond to the *Interactive* category, it was discovered that from the 20 applications, 80% belong to the *Citizens assistance* subcategory, such as the case of the applications to make complaints to the city administration, whereas *Transport service* subcategory, there is only 20%, such as applications to call a taxi, which help to citizens' safety.

Regarding *Contributive* category, 11 of the studied applications were categorized as such: 45% belong to *Request for help* subcategory, for instance applications with panic buttons to alert the police, fire station or in case of gender violence; 37% belong to *Data collection* subcategory, with applications that let citizens notice about lost pets or applications to give data about traffic violation or the poor conditions of the roads; and 18% belong to the *Tax collection* subcategory, taking into account those applications related to metered parking or those which let pay services.

Finally, applications that belong to the *Recreative* category: from the 9 identified, it can be observed that 67% belong to the *Games* subcategory, educational games applications can be found in this group and 33% are part of *Virtual reality* subcategory, that include applications where the citizens interact with different parts of the city administration through the use of technologies, such as, augmented reality.

6 Conclusions

An analysis of the importance of the use of mobile devices and the way citizens use mobile technologies to communicate with city administrations was made. Additionally, there were analyzed different definitions, characteristics and types of approaches in order to create taxonomies.

For the present paper, 53 cities from Argentina were selected and a study of the mobile applications offered and developed by the corresponding administrations ("official applications") was carried out. It was discovered that almost half of the cities (49%) didn't offer any official application. Observing the remaining cities, 89 mobile applications were found. Each of these applications was analyzed from an interactional point of view: the interaction between applications and citizens. The aim was to create a taxonomy that allowed a classification of the applications.

In this article, a taxonomy for mobile applications of government services in cities from Argentina was developed, using an empiric approach as well as a deductive approach. As a result, a taxonomy that fulfills all the ideal attributes was obtained: it is concise (it has 4 dimensions and 11 characteristics, easy to understand and apply), it is inclusive (all necessary aspects for the categorization of mobile applications are covered), it is comprehensive (all studied mobile applications could be classified) and it is extensible (it is possible that the taxonomy enlarges in the future, if it is necessary).

Acknowledgments. This publication was made in the context of the CAP4CITY Project – "Strengthening Governance Capacity for Smart Sustainable Cities" (www.cap4city.eu) co-funded by the Erasmus+ Programme of the European Union. Grant no: 598273-EPP-1-2018-1-AT-EPPKA2-CBHE-JP.

References

1. Muñoz, R., Preisegger, J.S., Pasini, A., Pesado, P.: Taxonomía para aplicaciones móviles de servicios de gobierno en municipios de Argentina. In: Libro de actas XXV Congreso Argentino de Ciencias de la Computación, CACIC 2019, pp. 1374–1384 (2019). ISBN 978-987-688-377-1

2. Dutra, D., Soares, D.: Mobile applications in central government of Brazil and Portugal. In: ICEGOV 2019 (2019)
3. Jolías, L., Prince, A.: Definiendo un modelo de Smart Cities para el contexto argentino. In: Ciudades Inteligentes, el aporte de las TIC a la comunidad, pp. 15–30 (2016)
4. Riggs, W., Gordon, K.: How is mobile technology changing city planning? Developing a taxonomy for the future. Environ. Plan. B Urban Anal. City Sci. **44**, 100–119 (2017)
5. Real Academia Española (RAE) dictionary. https://www.rae.es/
6. Gobierno Móvil. Conceptos y características generales en Latinoamérica. uGOB. https://u-gob.com/gobierno-movil-conceptos-y-caracteristicas-generales-en-latinoamerica/. Accessed Feb 2020
7. Nickerson, R., Muntermann, J., Varshney, U., Isaac, H.: Taxonomy development in information systems: developing a taxonomy of mobile applications (2009)
8. Bailey, K.D.: Typologies and Taxonomies - An Introduction to Classification Techniques. Sage, Thousand Oaks (1994)
9. Bailey, K.D.: A three-level measurement model. Qual. Quant. **18**, 225–245 (1984). https://doi.org/10.1007/BF00156457
10. Municipios miembros de la Red de Ciudades Inteligentes de Argentina. RECIA. https://recia.com.ar/miembros/. Accessed July 2019
11. Proyecciones por departamento. INDEC. https://www.indec.gob.ar/indec/web/Nivel4-Tema-2-24-119. Accessed July 2019

Author Index